"[A] TOUR DE FORCE . . .

No one—soldier, sailor, airman, or Marine—wanted to be the last mother's son killed in Vietnam. This superb account of war ranks up there with Caputo's . . . *Rumor of War*."

—*Military*

"An inspiring story of moral and tactical courage; a journal of true leadership. Had there been more Hodginses in service during the era, perhaps the final results would have been different."

—JOHN DEL VECCHIO
New York Times bestselling
author of *The 13th Valley*

"*Reluctant Warrior* offers an absolutely authentic picture of the lieutenant's war in Vietnam. . . . Tough, informative, and worthwhile."

—RALPH PETERS
Bestselling author of *War in 2020*

"*Reluctant Warrior* is impossible to put down, and the prologue is the most accurate assessment that I have read on how many Vietnam veterans feel today about the war, those who went, and those who did not. A wonderful book."

—LT. COL. MICHAEL LEE LANNING
Author of *Inside the LRRPs*
and *Inside Force Recon*

RELUCTANT WARRIOR

A Marine's True Story of Duty and Heroism in Vietnam

Michael C. Hodgins

IVY BOOKS • NEW YORK

Ivy Books
Published by Ballantine Books
Copyright © 1996 by Michael C. Hodgins

http://www.randomhouse.com

Library of Congress Catalog Card Number: 97-93423

ISBN 0-8041-1120-0

Manufactured in the United States of America

First Hardcover Edition: January 1997

First Mass Market Edition: December 1997

10 9 8 7 6 5 4 3 2 1

WARRIORS

A class of men set apart from the general mass of the
community, trained to particular uses, formed to
peculiar notions, governed by peculiar laws,
marked by peculiar distinctions.

WILLIAM WINDHAM, 1750–1810

CONTENTS

PROLOGUE

Stranger, bear this message to the Spartans,
"That we lie here obedient to their laws."

Epitaph, Thermopylae, 430 B.C.

Twenty-six years have passed since I served in Vietnam. Many books have been written by and about the young men who served in that tragic endeavor. In the minds of the public, stereotypes have been created, lessons have been taught, wisdom instilled. Yet the angst of the entire episode is only vaguely familiar to most Americans now living, summarized in the media as "The Vietnam Experience." But, Vietnam was not an experience; it was a place. Many Americans, as young men, had formative experiences in that place sometime during the ten years that our servicemen fought there. Each was unique. *Reluctant Warrior* attempts to share with the reader the essence of one experience, mine, circa 1970. It is not a war story. It is not even about Vietnam, although the events recounted occurred there. Rather, this is a story about how things were when I was young and my Country was at war. It is a story about ordinary young men who did extraordinary things, together. It is a story about duty, about honor, about leadership. It is a story about moral courage, glory, and luck. It is a story about Marines.

As the title *Reluctant Warrior* suggests, I went to Vietnam with few illusions. Having served several years as an enlisted Marine, I well understood the undercurrents in the ranks. Upon reporting to OCS, I joined several hundred other young men seeking greater responsibility. We were volunteers, recruited from college campuses across the country, and from the enlisted ranks. The Marine Corps made each of us a promise: If you accept a commission in the United States Marines, we will shave your head and send you to Vietnam. Since one Marine in three was stationed in Vietnam at the time, it was a promise the Corps had no difficulty in fulfilling. Upon acceptance of the offer of a commission, each candidate took an oath to "preserve and protect" the United States of America from all enemies, "foreign and domestic." We then commenced an arduous training program designed first to test our resolve and then to instill the knowledge we would need to succeed. Each young man embarked on what became, for those who survived, the most formative experience of his life. And we were challenged, literally, by enemies "foreign and domestic." By 1970, a lieutenant of infantry stood an eighty percent chance of being wounded by enemy action before he finished his tour in "the bush," and the Corps, like the other armed services, was confronting a deterioration of discipline in the ranks. At the Basic School, my instructors, with few exceptions, wore Purple Hearts among their decorations. Many were outpatients from Bethesda Naval Hospital, recovering from wounds so horrible that we made jokes to ease the tension of their presence among us. The statistics for "friendly forces" were no more encouraging. In Vietnam, "Demeaning labor, boredom and bitterness led to drinking, drug abuse and fights in the rear, while in the bush arduous small unit activities were at once traumatizing and devoid of measurable success." In the words of one Marine general, "It [the bush] appeared to sap the souls and the spirit of the men."* "In some strife torn units, officers faced the daily threat of assassination. It was not enough simply to be vested with the authority

*U.S. Marines in Vietnam, 1970–71, pp 344–69.

of rank. The small unit leader had to earn the respect of his troops merely to survive."* And no one, officer or enlisted, wanted to be the last unfortunate son to die in Vietnam.

But the violence of the late sixties was not confined to the battlefields of Vietnam. It was rampant on the streets of our Republic as well. The period 1965–75 was one of the most tumultuous in our Nation's history. With the advent of television news, the war became a "media event." Everyone was involved, made to feel at risk, vulnerable to tragedy. People took to the streets all across the country demanding an end to compulsory military service. "Hell no! We won't go!" and "Ho, Ho, Ho Chi Minh!" became mantras of the era, "people's wars" the avante-garde movement of the time. Liberalism's heroes were such men as Che Guevarra, Fidel Castro, Mao Tse-tung and Ho Chi Minh, leaders of the enemy camp. Protests in the United States and around the world were led by student activists from the nations' universities, the same universities that spawned the young leaders of the Armed Forces upon whom the scorn of the nation was heaped. In fact, the most vexing moral question confronting the graduating college seniors of the day was, to serve or not to serve in the Armed Forces of the United States. The decision, once confronted, became the comprehensive final exam in moral courage for young men of the sixties. It was a question of core values, patriotism, and moral courage. The system was there, riddled with loopholes for any who took the time or had the intelligence to investigate. In many quarters, it was considered smart to avoid, evade, even cheat the system. Most simply let fate deal their hand, as the system intended.

The decision changed us, those who served and those who did not. After twenty years, the moral issue is blurred in the body politic, but there is still a dichotomy. Those who chose not to serve did no wrong, for the law of the land did not require them to go in harm's way. They had only to take their chance and do their duty if they were called. In fact, of the thirty-five million or so young men eligible for the draft during

*U.S. Marines in Vietnam, 1970–71, pp 344–69.

the war years, only about ten percent (3,500,000) actually endured the experience in any branch of service. But for each
principled young man who chose to avoid or evade his duty,
another, perhaps less privileged, went in his place. And while
the vast majority of the young people who were called, by patriotism, economic necessity, or the draft, to serve in the
Armed Forces during these years never saw an enemy or fired
a round in anger, some did. Some died. Many were maimed.
All returned to a Country devoid of empathy, changed forever
by their experience.

Today, it is common for men who stepped aside when faced
with the call to arms in the 1960s to set themselves out as the
"right choice" to lead America into the next century. They seek
the trappings and power of political office with the same self-
righteous conviction and deceit with which they sought to
avoid the hazards of military service in their youth. The self-
serving conviction that enabled them to shirk their responsibility and circumvent the law of the land in the sixties still
permeates their values today. The success of such men on the
contemporary political stage suggests that we, as a society,
have learned nothing from our sacrifice. I hope that this is not
so. I hope that America will choose its next generation of leaders from among those reluctant warriors of the sixties who in
the tradition of their nation's forefathers, went forward toward
the sound of the guns when they were called. They are men
who know the value of freedom, a value captured in a piece of
graffiti scraped in charcoal letters above the entrance to a
bunker I inhabited briefly in the Que Sons:

For those who have fought for it, freedom has a flavor the
protected never know.

Semper Fidelis!

INTRODUCTION
ICORPS Republic of South Vietnam*

CIRCA 1970
The Front is everywhere.
Maxim of Guerilla War

By the spring of 1970, the war in Vietnam had entered a new phase—withdrawal. President Nixon had declared a halt to bombing of the North, peace talks were underway in Paris, and U.S. Forces had commenced Operation KEYSTONE ROBIN, the staged withdrawal of combat forces from the theater. In the northernmost provinces of South Vietnam, known as the I Corps Tactical Zone (ICTZ), the III Marine Amphibious Force (III MAF) was under orders to reduce combat operations. The Third Marine Division (Rein) had been "redeployed" to Okinawa, and the First Marine Division (Rein) had been repositioned to defend the Da Nang Vital Sector. It was clear to everyone, private to general, that American involvement in the war was nearly at an end. It remained to conduct an orderly, disciplined, and politically palatable disengagement on the battlefield—one of the most difficult of military maneuvers.

In the ICTZ, the task fell to Marine Corps Maj. Gen. Edwin B. Wheeler, an able commander, who realized immediately that he must keep the North Vietnamese Army off balance, disrupt its effort to gain tactical advantage and give

---

*For a more detailed discussion please see Appendix One.

early warning of any attempt to embarrass the United States with a decisive military engagement in the waning months of the war. The nightmare scenario of the time was that the NVA would stage aggressive military operations in support of its diplomatic efforts in Paris, a tactic that was used, not coincidentally, by the Nixon Administration. General Wheeler's solution to the puzzle in ICTZ was to adopt what is known in military tactics as an "economy of force" game plan. Critical to his success would be to find a way to keep the NVA off balance and away from key installations, to isolate it from the population centers. General Wheeler decided to adopt an operational concept known as Stingray, utilizing his reconnaissance battalion. It was a concept developed and successfully implemented by Maj. Gen. Ray Davis in 3d Mar Div. The idea was simple: saturate the NVA base areas with small, heavily armed patrols, supported by artillery and close-air-support aircraft. The teams would engage and/or interdict NVA units in their base areas, far from the population centers. Because the teams were small, clandestine, numerous, and aggressive, the enemy would be required to defend its facilities and infrastructure, thereby reducing its capacity to put pressure on Allied installations. Wheeler wanted a highly skilled, aggressive force, willing and able to take the fight to the bush and he wanted a Commander to lead it. Wheeler decided to get the Commander and let him worry about the troops. He picked Lt. Col. William C. Drumright, known to his peers, friend and foe alike, as "Wild Bill."

Drumright was a warrior, known throughout the service for his aggressive leadership style, physical courage, and charisma. Wheeler summoned Drumright to Division headquarters shortly before Christmas, 1969, told him what he wanted, then waited for Drumright's response. After a day of mulling his options, Drumright went back to General Wheeler with a plan. It was the essence of simplicity. In Drumright's mind, the general was asking him to create a new kind of fighting force, a modern raider battalion of the sort that was so successful during World War II. Drumright envisioned a highly skilled, aggressive force, willing and able to find and fight the enemy in his own backyard. But, to create such a force would require months of training and indoctrination in new tactics. There was no time for that. He had to make do with what was available, people he could count on. Like his general, Drumright's solution was to pick his leaders, the most aggressive, best-trained people available to him—Marine lieutenants with at least six months of hard Grunt, i.e., Infantry, experience. With competent, aggressive leadership, Wild Bill was convinced that the handpicked Marines of First Recon Battalion could and would carry the fight to the enemy.

Although his leadership style was controversial, Drumright's tactical intuition was brilliant. The best-trained small-unit leaders available to him were Marine lieutenants. They were extensively trained in small unit tactics, scouting and patrolling, land navigation, the use of supporting arms. They were generally idealistic and likely to follow orders, i.e., go where they were told to go and do there what they were told to do. Those whom he could transfer from the Infantry would have endured their trials by fire, thereby instilling less seasoned troops with the confidence to go out and mix it up with the NVA. These young men, combined with the hand-picked Marines of the 1st Recon Bn (Rcin), would provide the Division with a highly skilled and mobile force. With proper coordination of the division's air and artillery support, the teams could and would raise hell in the NVA base areas. They would become, in fact, a screening force, disrupting the enemy's capability to operate in the ICTZ.

However, the young Recon Marines who were to fight the bitter daily engagements in ICTZ that year did not know much about the big picture, nor did they share Wild Bill Drumright's opinion of lieutenants. To them, there was no method to the madness, just day after day of mindless humping from place to place, punctuated by occasional terrifying but inconclusive engagements with a mythical enemy whose face was seldom seen. To them, there were only two zones, the Rear, and the Bush. The Rear was boring, populated with rear echelon motherfuckers (REMFs) and rife with "lifer bullshit" (military routines and discipline), which spoiled the creature comforts of the place. In the field, the troops had enemies, foreign, domestic and environmental. In addition to their North Vietnamese Army opponents, they had to deal with experienced politicians, "inexperienced officers," debilitating weather, inhospitable terrain, disease, wild animals (man-eating tigers and rock apes that could pitch in major league baseball), and each other. Many viewed the NVA as the least of their problems. In the vernacular of the time, the bush was a motherfucker.

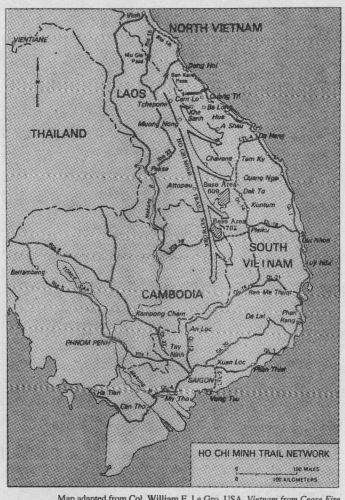

Map adapted from Col. William E. Le Gro, USA, *Vietnam from Cease Fire to Capitulation* (Washington: U.S. Army Center of Military History, 1981)

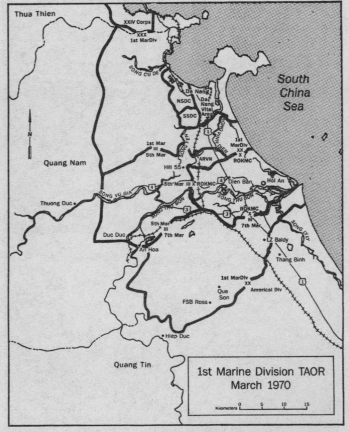

Map adapted from Graham A. Cosmos and Lt. Col. Terrance P. Murray, USMC, *U.S. Marines in Vietnam: Vietnamization and Redeployment 1970–1971* (Washington, D.C.: Headquarters, U. S. Marines Corps, 1986)

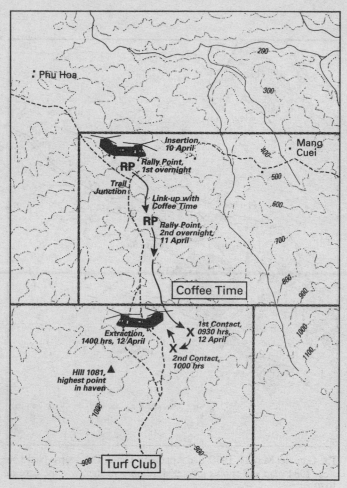

Charlie Ridge April 12, 1970. See Appendix Two.

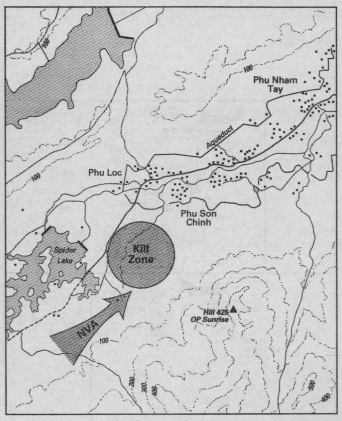

The Gauntlet May 11, 1970. See Appendix Three. This map is based on a ca. 1984 map and shows greater development than was the case in 1970.

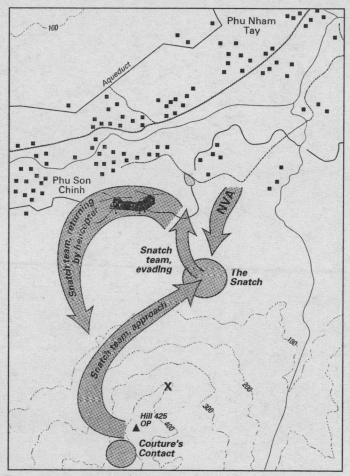

The Snatch May 23, 1970. The extraction CH-46 was flown by then-Captain now Lt. Gen. A. C. Blades. Note that the X marks the location of Sunrise-3 Charlie and its machine gun.

CHAPTER ONE
WELCOME ABOARD

3 MARCH 1970

*A small army consisting of chosen troops is far better than
a vast body, chiefly composed of rabble.*

The Hitopadesa, iii, c. 500 B.C.

My ears popped repeatedly while our Boeing 707 executed a
wide descending turn into the landing approach pattern for Da
Nang. Bile rose in my throat as the plane lurched into a steeper
descent. I swallowed hard, closed the dog-eared paperback I
had been reading, and shifted in my seat to peer into space
through a porthole. From my vantage point just forward of the
port wing, a panoply of colors flowed past, green hues of jungle,
yellow-browns of rice paddies, blue-green ribbons of water-
courses, the macadam strip of Highway 1, the stark green-black
mass of Ba Na ringed with clouds, buildings, and finally, the
airfield. Here and there, light flashed, reflections from the
windshields of vehicles on the roads below. Smoke from
countless small fires pillared and drifted in the clear blue morning sky. A pair of F-4 Phantom fighter-bombers streaked down
a runway and lifted into the morning sky, leaving telltale gray-
brown plumes behind. I looked at my Mickey Mouse watch (a
much coveted and hard to acquire matte-finish military issue
watch with a green nylon band and a black face). It was 0617
(6:17 A.M.). The war was starting early for somebody.

"Gentlemen, we are commencing our final approach into Da

1

Nang International Airport! The captain requests that you return your seats to their full upright position, return your tray tables to their upright and locked position, and insure that your seat belts are securely fastened. We will be landing in approximately five minutes. On behalf of Flying Tiger Airlines and your crew, we wish you the best of luck and hope to see you on a return flight!" The irony of her words was lost on the stewardess. I studied her as she clipped the microphone in its bracket on the aircraft bulkhead and set about collecting trash, impervious to the sea of anxious teenage faces staring at her from the cabin. She was old, past forty, and tired. It had been a long, no-frills ride, and she was clearly looking forward to her return flight. Hers was fourteen hours away. Ours was a lifetime. I followed her instructions, looking around as the cabin rustled with activity. The other stews were moving down the aisles collecting blankets, pillows, and trash from a sea of young, rumpled, big-eyed boys about to become men. Next to me, the army lieutenant colonel with whom I had shared bits and pieces of conversation on the long flight from Hawaii, leaned across me to stare out the porthole window. "What's all the smoke? They must have had a rocket attack this morning! Is it safe to land?"

As he spoke, he slumped back into his seat, embarrassed by his outburst. He had identified me back in Hawaii as a salt returning to the theater from R & R (rest and recuperation). My camouflage uniform and gauntness had given me away.

I smiled, remembering my own not too dissimilar thoughts months before. "Yes sir, it's safe. Those are outhouse fires, mostly. It's part of the daily routine in all the camps, sir. Troops have to pull the barrels out, pour kerosene in, and burn them every morning before it gets too hot. Prevents typhoid and stuff like that. The fires you see in the hills are charcoal fires—the farmers make the stuff all the time for cooking in the villages. Rockets and mortars don't make fires, Colonel, just messes." His face turned pale with the import of my remark.

The plane lurched suddenly toward the ground, leaving all

our stomachs at altitude. The colonel was startled again. "Tactical descent, sir. Just in case."

I leaned my head back against the seat, closing my eyes. Within moments, we were jolted as landing gear contacted the runway. It was a hard landing. The aircraft engines screamed into reverse thrust, braking us rapidly, then muted to taxi power as the aircraft turned and ran down an apron toward the huge Butler buildings which served as the terminal. As the big aircraft braked to a halt, the cabin doors were thrown open, and a rush of putrid air filled the cabin. The pervasive odor of kerosene and fecal matter tainted an ocean breeze that raised the cabin temperature to over one hundred degrees in seconds. We had, indeed, arrived in Southeast Asia.

"Gentlemen, please remain seated until the briefer has completed his briefing. Upon completion of his statement, you will be permitted to debark the aircraft. Once again, thank you for choosing Flying Tiger!"

An Air Force master sergeant in green fatigues appeared in the aisle behind the stewardess, a clipboard in one hand, a megaphone in the other. "Good morning, gentlemen! On behalf of the Joint Service Processing Center, welcome to Da Nang! I know you are all anxious to get off this aircraft, so listen up."

The aircraft engines continued to whine, drowning out his voice. All around me troops and troop leaders milled in the aisle, jostling one another as they recovered luggage and belongings from the overhead. No one gave the JTO a thought. I looked out the window, watching as the ground crew scurried about servicing the aircraft and unloading the cargo bays. In the shade of the Butler buildings was a bustling crowd of uniformed men, mostly in camouflaged utilities. Almost all carried small canvas or cloth bags. Some smoked. All laughed and joked as they watched the bustle of activity around the aircraft. They were going home.

The master sergeant finished his speech, having told us all how to get off the airplane and where to go once inside the terminal. No one had understood a word he said. I remained seated, outwardly patient, sweating profusely, while the field-grade officers (majors and above) debarked the aircraft. There weren't many, but as the cabin became insufferable, sweaty bodies continued to jostle one another in the aisle. Tempers flared and there were scuffles as teens of many races attempted to recover their carry-on bags from the overhead storage and scrambled to escape the stifling heat of the aircraft. I remained in my seat, skimming a few more pages of my Louis L'Amour, until the motley group began to dissipate. Finally, I stashed the novel in my kit and worked my way up the aisle, through the hatch, and into the harsh morning sun. Standing on the landing of the debarkation ramp, I squinted into the morning sun, taking in the sights and sounds of the terminal. In the shade, the vets were beginning to make catcalls and comments to the new arrivals, most frequent among them, "You'll be *sorrryyy*!!!"

I smiled at the thought and made my way down the ramp, into the terminal. Once inside, I cast my eyes about until I sighted the First Marine Division plaque, suspended from the overhead. Beneath the sign, there was a counter not unlike the airline service counters back in the States. In front of the counter, uniformed bodies struggled with seabags and other luggage, documents stuck under their arms. Farther back, there were benches littered with Marines and their gear, some sleeping, some engaged in card games or conversation. The uniforms were about evenly mixed between the green fatigues of Marines coming in country from Stateside and the camouflaged uniforms of those who had been in country. I moved to the counter under a sign reading OFFICERS, dropped my carry-on bag on the deck, and handed my orders to the corporal behind the counter. "Good morning, Corporal. My name is Hodgins. I have orders to report to First Recon Battalion. I need transportation."

The corporal took my orders, removed the staple, took a copy, stamped an endorsement on them, sorted the stack and handed them back to me. "Yes, sir! You're all set. You need to recover your gear from the baggage claim and wait out there under the 1st Mar Div sign. There'll be a six-by [6x6 truck] to pick you up in about forty mikes [minutes]."

He gestured toward the huge sliding doors on the opposite side of the Butler building. I gathered my gear and turned away in the direction of the growing crowd of green, sweaty bodies in front of the baggage claim area. I knew from experience that my B-4 duffel bag and valpack would not be in the pile just yet. Officers' luggage was first on, last off—revenge of the Snuffy (enlisted Marine). I slumped on a bench and lit a cigarette, content to wait for the crowd to dissipate, and mused about how things were. My thoughts were shaped, as in a hazy dream, by the comings and goings of the troops around me.

They were of many ranks and races. What they had in common was youth, bad luck, and the tradition of the Corps. Back in The World, the Marines were looking for "A Few Good Men." These were what they had found. Upon their arrival from CONUS (Continental United States) they became, in the vernacular of the time, fuckin' new guys (FNGs). No one wanted to be an FNG in Vietnam, circa 1969–70. And no one wanted to be led by one, followed by one, or flanked by one. Yet, the FNGs were everywhere, in every pay grade from private to general. In fact, with rare exceptions, even the senior officers being assigned to combat command and staff billets in 1970 had no combat experience in country, in grade, in billet. It was all on-the-job training, the typical high-profile stint being six months. By the time a man had learned or not learned how to do the job, he was transferred, replaced by a fuckin' new guy. It was bad for morale, and hard on the few good men the Marines had found. Yet, here we were—here I was, a fuckin' new guy again.

The lyrics of Country Joe and the Fish (of Woodstock fame) flitted through my mind. "One, two, three, what are we fightin' for . . ." Being an FNG was not new to me. I had been one in Battalion Landing Team (BLT) 2/26, a replacement, one of several, for a lieutenant who had stepped on a land mine during Operation HASTINGS. The fourth lieutenant the platoon had welcomed in six months, I outlasted all but a few of the good men I served with, and when word came that the BLT was to stand down, I resolved that I would find another place from which to fight. I had scores to settle. Rather than take a spot on the early rotation roster in one of the units being redeployed from northern I Corps in northern South Vietnam, I volunteered for duty with 1st Reconnaissance Battalion. I reasoned that I had experience better suited to the bush than to a desk. So, I had taken R & R in Hawaii, explained my thoughts to an unsympathetic spouse, and embarked on this latest adventure. I was a fuckin' new guy again, and determined to make the most of it.

Roused from my reverie by a scuffle in the baggage claim area, I pinched out the butt of my last cigarette, fieldstripped it, and scuffed the remains under my boot. Then I moved to reclaim my gear. My luck was holding, as both bags had arrived, although they weighed a lot more than I remembered. I struggled outside and dropped them on the ground under the 1st Mar Div sign as the corporal had instructed. Troops and vehicles bustled about, giving rise to a cacophony of multilingual shouts, horns, engines, bells, and whistles. Heat waves tainted with exhaust fumes shimmered off the ground. It was stifling hot! I sat on my duffel, sweating profusely and cursing under my breath. Just as I resolved that I had missed the scheduled truck, it appeared, literally, in a cloud of dust and the din of crashing gears. The driver skidded the vehicle to a halt, throwing gravel and dust in all directions. As the air brakes hissed off, he leaned out the passenger side window and shouted, "Yo! Lieutenant! Where you headed?"

I stood and shouted above the din, "First Recon Battalion!"

"Throw your shit in the back, sir! You can ride up here!" He threw the cab door open and slumped back behind the wheel. I muscled my duffel and valpack into the bed of the truck and leaped onto the cab, struggled inside, and slammed the door. As I did so, the driver jammed the truck into gear and jolted us into motion, the gears jumping unevenly. "Cold soda, Lieutenant?" As he spoke, a grin split his dust-grimed face and he gestured with his eyes to an ammo crate on the seat. I followed his gaze with my own and saw that, indeed, he did have cold sodas—Coca-Cola, chilled with dry ice in a burlap-lined ammo box. "Open me one, too, sir!"

"Fuckin'-A, Marine!" I grinned and reached into the box, recovered two cans, placing them on the seat between my legs. The chill from the can was almost a burn. I pulled the dog-tag chain from beneath my jacket and opened the John Wayne (C-ration can opener) I kept on it. As the truck bounced along the road, I struggled to open the first can then handed it to the driver. I rolled the other, unopened, across my face and the back of my neck. Refreshed, I opened the Coke, took a big swig, washing away the foul taste of bile with the dust of a dying country. I slumped back against the seat to take in the scenery.

"So, how long you been with Recon, Lieutenant?" My new friend was expertly navigating through a New York City–style traffic jam composed of trucks, jeeps, motorbikes, and an occasional automobile. The noise was mind numbing, and he had to shout to be heard over the din of the traffic. Diesel fumes from trucks and burning "shitters" clung to the humid air. The heat was oppressive. We finally passed through the gates of the airfield onto Highway 1, headed for Division Ridge, as the complex of headquarters compounds was known. As the truck picked up speed, we were rewarded with a cooler breeze off the ocean.

"I'm reporting for duty today. Just got back from R & R. I was in the Grunts, before." I took another pull on the Coke, the fluid foaming up my nose as the truck jounced down the macadam. I coughed and sputtered, wiping the Coke from my chin. The driver pretended not to notice.

"Well, sir. I don't envy you. I think if I went on R & R, I would have a hard time coming back! And I got a cushy job, driving this truck. No hassles, keep my own schedule, get to see what's happening. Say, you want to ride over to Force Service Group and get some fresh donuts? Or maybe we should stop at Freedom Hill—get a cheeseburger, some fries?"

"No, thanks. I'm broke, and I want to get checked in while I've still got the balls!" I smiled and rolled my eyes.

The driver laughed and turned his attention to the traffic. Within minutes, he was pulling the truck to the side of the road, air brakes squealing and gravel spraying as he ground to a halt. "This is it, Lieutenant!"

Looking out the window of the truck, across the driver's body, I saw a masonry work of art, a monument of quarried rock and concrete. It was a red, white, and blue rendition of the unit insignia of First Reconnaissance Battalion, a skull and crossed bones superimposed on a big red numeral 1 and the motto SWIFT, SILENT, DEADLY. It must have stood over eight feet high. Other words proclaimed the site to be CAMP REASONER. My new home away from home. There were power lines running into the camp, and paved roads. I was a long way from the Grunts!

The driver made a hard left turn into the compound, rolling down the hill past a number of Butler buildings, and pulled up in front of an olive drab wooden hut tucked under a banyan tree. The entrance was adorned with brass 105mm shell casings and more quarried rocks—painted white. Having painted my share of rocks as a private first class, I recognized the handiwork of an extra-punishment-duty detail. The truck ground to a halt. I opened the door on my side of the cab and climbed out on the step, then up into the bed of the truck. I muscled my gear over the side rail of the truck bed and let the bags drop, one at a time, to the ground, then jumped down myself. Turning toward the driver, I raised my arm and waved him on his way. "Thanks for the ride, Marine!"

He smiled, flipping me a salty salute, and put the truck in gear. Within seconds, I was standing alone, sweat soaked and dusty, in front of the sign. I felt like an orphan.

The camp was composed of hardback huts—prefabricated plywood structures with corrugated tin roofs and screened sides—set helter-skelter into the slope of the hill. I tucked my orders under my arm, bent to lift a bag in each hand, and trudged toward the building I had identified as the probable headquarters, looking for clues as to where to check in. Sure enough, each hut was identified with a little red and yellow plaque. The one I was looking for read S-1 (i.e., Personnel). I dropped my load outside the screen door, took a deep breath, and went inside.

It was slightly cooler. The tent was furnished with several field desks, footlocker-size sets of drawers with foldout tops, folding chairs, and makeshift file cabinets. A clerk, clad in jungle utility trousers and sweat-stained T-shirt, sat at each desk, using the traditional two-finger method to bang away on decrepit typewriters. Several portable fans whirred incessantly as they labored to move the heavy air. Flak jackets, helmets, and M-16s hung on the uprights of the screen walls behind each desk. As the screen door swung to behind me, one of the clerks looked up from his typewriter. "Be with you in a minute, sir. I just need to finish this morning report." As he spoke, he put the finishing touch on the document and ripped it from the typewriter with a flourish. He stood, motioning to one of the clerks, "Take this over to Major Turner, Johnson. Show him how I listed Captain McVey and Lieutenant Skibbe. He may want to change the captain to KIA also." He held the report out to his companion and turned to me. "Yes, sir! I'm Sergeant Smith, the admin chief." He smiled as he spoke.

"My name is Hodgins, Sergeant. I'm reporting for duty." I placed my orders, officer qualification record (OQR), and health records atop the service counter which separated us. My pulse throbbed in my throat. My mouth had turned to cotton. My bowels churned. I felt sick. Keep a tight asshole, Mikey, I thought to myself, You're back in the Nam.

Sergeant Smith opened the jacket on my OQR and removed the packet of orders. From under the counter, he produced an endorsement stamp and an ink pad. He stamped three copies of the document, removed them from the packet and handed the rest of the packet back to me. "You picked one helluva day to come aboard, sir! Can I get you some coffee, or a soda? I have to take your OQR over to the major. Colonel Drumright is airborne and the major is acting CO [Commanding Officer] right now, getting the rest of the teams out. He's busy as hell. We had a team whacked in the Que Sons last night, and they're trying to get another reaction force ready to go after the bodies." As he spoke, he was folding my life history into a packet of other documents and reaching for his cover (uniform hat), a neatly starched and blocked camouflaged version of the one I wore.

"A soda would be good. Where did you come by that cover?" My voice sounded loud and tight in my ears, but the sergeant didn't seem to notice.

"Sodas are in the fridge. Help yourself. If you have any MPC [military payment certificates], we'd appreciate a contribution to the can." He gestured in the direction of a miniature refrigerator behind the counter. I saw that there was a coffee can atop, stenciled with the phrase "Donations Accepted" on it.

"We get the hats from a mamma-san over at the laundry. They make 'em someplace out of stuff they steal from us. You might want to sit out back, Lieutenant. It's cooler. I'll come get you when the major's ready." He left, the screen door swinging to in his wake.

I stood motionless for what seemed an eternity, the noise of the fans and the clacking of the typewriters filling the void in my mind. Outside, a jeep motor stuttered to life. The vehicle sped away, gears clashing. For the first time I noticed voices, as Marines moving about in the compound engaged in the daily routine of war. The distinctive sound of CH-46 helicopters arriving at the helicopter landing zone (HLZ) broke in on my reverie. Overhead, I heard the clatter of AH-1G Cobra gunships circling the compound, then they also swooped onto the HLZ and were silent. I moved to the refrigerator, stooped, and pulled it open. As I did so, frigid air billowed out, carried by the fan atop a nearby desk. I shivered as a chill went through my body.

I could just sit right here for the rest of the war, I thought to myself. Instead, I selected a Wink and went outside, strolling in the direction of the helicopter noises. I found shade under a banyan tree at the head of a path that meandered downhill to the HLZ. Leaning up against the trunk of the tree, I performed the John Wayne ritual, letting the soda spray away from my body, took a swig. My taste buds rebelled against the sickly sweet fluid. Still, it was cold; and that made it better than it would have been in the Grunts. I relaxed and settled in to watch the activity on the HLZ. I had a panoramic view of the camp and the surrounding area. I counted forty-odd structures, including several Butler buildings, a motor pool, and a mess hall. The HLZ was paved with asphalt. Beyond the HLZ, rice paddies stretched into the distance. The compound was ringed with multiple strands of concertina wire, and there were bunkers at intervals along the perimeter. I noticed that the hardbacks were all sandbagged and that there were slit trenches alongside each building. The aircraft were parked in pairs, the CH-46s in one corner of the HLZ, the AH-1Gs in the other. There were a 6x6 truck, a jeep, and an ambulance parked side by side at the edge of the tarmac. Uniformed men were loitering near the vehicles, occasionally moving into or out of a shaded structure near the tarmac. As I watched, the aircrews suddenly appeared from under the roof of the structure and hustled to their aircraft. They were followed by a group of perhaps thirty men clad in camouflage uniforms and soft covers. They wore packs and were carrying weapons. These men milled around outside the building for a few minutes, as the aircraft engines came to life, then separated into two groups and jogged to the loading ramps of the CH-46s, where they were counted aboard by the crew chief of each aircraft. The AH-1G gunships lifted off, swooping out over the rice paddies then climbing rapidly to orbit over the HLZ. In moments they were followed by the lumbering CH-46s. As I watched, the aircraft joined up in a loose formation and disappeared into the western sky—"I launched an arrow into the air. It fell to earth, I know not where." The lines of the poem whispered across my consciousness, unbidden, a metaphor. Unknown warriors had gone to war. Soon, I would take my place among them.

I turned my gaze back to the HLZ. A solitary figure appeared from under the roof, exchanged hand salutes with the driver of the jeep and the other Marines standing on the tarmac, then climbed aboard the vehicle. I watched as the driver put the vehicle in gear and rolled toward the road leading from the HLZ up to the highway. With a sigh of resignation, I took my last swig of Wink, crushed the can between the palms of my hands, and turned to walk back to the S-1. I retraced my steps, went inside, and took a seat on a folding chair beside the counter. I heard the sound of the jeep gearing down on the roadway outside, accompanied by the crushing sound of its tires in the gravel. The fans whirred. The refrigerator hummed. Doors slammed, and conversation drifted about on the morning breeze. The clerks, oblivious to me, continued their incessant pecking at typewriter keys, talking sex, movies, and Stateside chow while they worked. Finally, the field phone atop the admin chief's desk clattered to life. He picked up the handset, listened briefly, then said, "Aye, aye, sir!" and replaced the handset. Turning to me, he said, "Major Turner will see you now, Lieutenant. I'll walk you over."

He was putting on his cover as he spoke, moving toward the screen door. I stood, taking my cover from atop the counter and went outside. The sun was high in the sky, bright and hot. We trudged down the gravel road to a hut marked XO. Sergeant Smith gestured that this was the place, snapped a salute, and said, "Good day, sir! I'm off to chow." He continued down the gravel road, while I turned to face my fate.

I mounted the steps leading to the door of the hut, took a deep breath, and banged three times on the frame of the hatch (as doorways are known in the naval service). From inside, a voice called out, "Come!" I opened the door and stepped inside, removing my cover as I did so. There was an anteroom partitioned off from the rest of the hut, makeshift furniture scattered about, including a field desk, several chairs, a hat rack, a map table, shell casings made into ashtrays, and other odds and ends. The major's jacket and cover hung on the hat rack along with a Model 1911A1, .45-caliber pistol in a shoulder holster. I positioned myself two paces in front of the desk at attention as Major Turner entered from the opposite doorway and sat down. From the corner of my eye, I noticed that the pistol had custom grips. "Sir, Second Lieutenant Hodgins reporting for duty, sir!"

I focused my eyes on a point above his head on the situation map (Hai Van Pass) pinned to the wall behind the desk. The map was overlaid with military symbols, notations, and little colored pins. My pulse throbbed in my throat. I saw that my officer qualification record lay open in the center of his desk.

"Stand at ease, Mike. So you're one of Lieutenant Colonel Drumright's peckerwoods! I was told to expect three of you. Skibbe is dead already. Where is the other guy?" As he spoke, he sat down behind the desk and shuffled my OQR in his hands. His face was grim.

"Sir, the lieutenant has no knowledge of other officers assigned, sir!" Better safe than sorry, I thought to myself, swallowing the bile that rose in my throat. I was comforted with the realization that the major had already familiarized himself with my OQR, at least enough to know my name and where I was coming from. I relaxed to parade rest, my hands clasped behind my back, and made eye contact with the major. He was about my height, powerfully built, with close-cropped sandy hair and a direct forceful gaze. I decided he was a competent officer. He was still evaluating me. "It says here that you are ex-enlisted. How did you get your commission?" His eyes bore into mine, challenging me to speak for myself.

"I came up through the Enlisted Commissioning Program, sir. I was in the air wing before OCS." I let my eyes meet his and waited for the next question.

"Oh? What grade were you when you went to OCS?" The major turned his attention back to my OQR, flipping through a few more pages.

"Sir, I was a buck sergeant, actually a staff sergeant selectee—I joined the Corps in July of '64, sir."

The major leaned back in his chair, smiled for the first time. "They lean on you at Quantico?" He held my gaze.

"Yes, sir. I was out of shape, had a hashmark [a longevity-in-service award]. I straggled on hikes and runs for a while. Almost got recycled, but they let me finish on time. Built some character in OCS, I did!"

"How did you do at Basic School?" Still staring.

"Better, sir. Ninth in my class." I stared back.

"Why didn't you go back to the air wing, then? You had your choice of MOS [military occupational specialty] didn't you?" His eyes were hard. He jolted forward in the chair, leaning toward me.

"Sir, I joined the Corps to be a Grunt. I ended up an 'aviation guarantee' because of my test scores. Taking a commission looked like a good way to get back to where I wanted to be in the first place, sir."

"It says here that you went to something called Recon Replacement School on your way over here. What was that all about?" He closed the OQR, maintaining his eye contact with me.

Rivulets of sweat were running down my back. I took a deep breath, shaping my answer in my mind. "Sir, they gave some of us a choice of schools after Basic School. My choices were Ranger School or Recon Replacement. Recon Replacement was in California. I figured I already knew enough about scouting and patrolling, and the Recon School was about using supporting arms, which I thought might come in handy over here, and it gave me time to get my wife settled. So, I picked that. We spent three weeks at LFTC* Coronado learning how to employ artillery, naval gunfire, and close air support, sir. It was a great school."

"And?" He continued to stare.

"And what, sir?"

"Has it come in handy?"

"Not yet, sir! All it's done is get me in trouble. People keep trying to assign me to COCs [combat operations cen-

*Landing Force Training Command.

ters]. All I did in the Grunts was use mortars and illumination once in a while—the only air support I've used since I got here has been to call for medevacs. That's why I asked to come here, sir. I want to stay in the bush."

The major seemed preoccupied for a moment, paging through my OQR again. Finally, he looked up at me. "That thought has crossed my mind, also. I need another lieutenant for the Three Shop [Operations]. Tell me about Two–Twenty-six—what did you do out there? How well does Drumright know you?" He barked the questions rapidly as he sat back in the chair again, twisting a pencil between his fingers.

"Well, sir, we did a lot of patrolling—mostly platoon size, mostly in the mountains north of Hai Van Pass and around Quang Tri. I ran some night acts ["night activities"—in this case ambushes] that worked out pretty well. We had a few firefights, nothing big—got mortared a couple of times. All my casualties were from heat, accidents, and booby traps, one guy with self-inflicted wounds. Just before I left for R & R, I lost most of one squad—eight guys—to a command-detonated mine. I think it was payback from the sapper outfit we had been working over. We caught them coming out of the villes at night a couple of times—shot them up pretty good." I took a deep breath. The major waited in silence.

"Sir, in six months of humping the bush, including Sparrow Hawk [reaction-force] missions, I've never seen a live NVA in daylight. When I heard that Two–Twenty-six was standing down, I put in an AA form [administration action—request for transfer] to come here. I thought, with my experience, I might do better in the second half. I didn't know that Lieutenant Colonel Drumright was going to take over this battalion at the time. They told me when I got my orders. I don't know the colonel at all, sir, except that he thought I did a pretty good job in Two–Twenty-six." I took another deep breath and waited for the major's response.

"Interesting! Mike, you picked an inauspicious time to join us. As it happens, we have two billets open in Charlie Company. The CO and a platoon leader were killed yesterday out in the Que Sons, and I need one of their lieutenants to help with our Vietnamese Rangers and ROK [Republic of Korea] Marines. We are supposed to train them to take over some of our patrolling responsibilities. There are a lot of new faces around here, including mine and the CO's. With your enlisted time and experience in the bush, you could help Charlie Company a lot. Your supporting arms training and patrolling experience would come in handy because we see a lot of live NVA in daylight. But, this is a volunteer outfit. You run the bush with a six-man team. We give you a map, a compass, a radio, and a ride. The rest is up to you."

He smiled, standing and offering his hand across the desk. "Why don't you sleep on it overnight and let me know your final decision in the morning." His eyes bore into mine in the silence that followed his pronouncement.

I stood to attention, then grasped his outstretched palm in my sweating one with what force I could muster. "Sir, with the major's permission, I'll stay, sir! I don't need to sleep on it."

I was light-headed, certain that he could smell the fear in me. He stared hard into my face for a moment, then smiled. "Welcome aboard, Lieutenant! See Sergeant Smith over in the S-One. He'll get you started checking in."

He released my grasp, and I did an about-face, went out through the screen door and down the steps to the gravel roadway. As the door swung to, I heard Major Turner ring up the field phone. "Smitty, Lieutenant Hodgins is going to Charlie Company. Have them send someone down here to show him the way."

I lurched into a space between the huts and puked the remains of my Stateside chow onto the ground. I was a Recon Marine at last. I kicked some gravel over the mess, took a deep breath, squared my shoulders, and approached the S-1 hootch, trying to project confidence I surely did not feel. The Basic School leadership indoctrination flashed in my mind, Bearing is nine points of command. Mind your bearing, Lieutenant!

I pulled the door open and stepped inside. Sergeant Smith was just replacing the handset of the field phone. "There'll be someone down from Charlie Company in a few minutes,

Lieutenant. Just let me get you a check-in sheet." He was reaching into a file cabinet as he spoke, and withdrew one of the routing checklists used to guide Marines from one administrative function to another. By the time I had collected all the required initials, I would know where everything was and would have all my gear and paperwork in the right places. I would also have money and a weapon. At least, I hoped I would. I took the sheet from his proffered hand.

Looking at the list, I tried to arrange the necessary stops in my mind to meet my most pressing needs. I decided I would need military payment certificates (scrip; U.S. currency was contraband in country) before I could do much of anything else. Then Supply—I would need new jungle fatigues for garrison time and another pair of boots. I had noticed that everyone at Camp Reasoner was squared away in their personal appearance—neatly pressed uniforms, boots shined, covers starched, and sporting high-and-tight haircuts. These were all things that had been next to impossible in the Grunts. I was wearing my only serviceable fatigue uniform, issued from ship's stores on the USS *New Orleans* months before. I had saved them for use on the ship, since the Navy had frowned upon both our appearance and our smell when we returned from our excursions to the bush. The bush had been hard on uniforms—and Marines. So had the Navy.

I looked up from the list, making eye contact with the sergeant. "Sergeant, what are my chances of getting to our disbursing clerk first? I need MPC for chow and the laundry. I also need some new utilities. This is the only set I have." As I spoke I looked down, gesturing openhanded at the uniform on my body. "We didn't have many creature comforts where I came from."

"Yes, sir! I've got your pay record right here. We can fix you up as soon as the adjutant comes back from chow. How much do you want to draw, sir?" He smiled as he spoke. "You have to see him anyway, sir, to join the officers' mess and the club." (Officers were required to contribute a monthly stipend for rations and entertainment, a tradition of the naval service not imposed upon enlisted Marines.)

"Two hundred dollars? What club?" I was dismayed at the thought of having to take an advance against my pay to meet these unforeseen expenses. I had just spent a queen's ransom in Hawaii, entertaining my wife on R & R. I was sure that she would need everything I could send home. An officers' club in a combat zone seemed a bit much. I realized, contemplating these mundane concerns, that the shock of my arrival was wearing off—yet more proof of the resilience of the human spirit. I was not in danger of anything at the moment, save making a fool of myself. I smiled at the thought and plunged ahead. To fit in, I had to get squared away!

"The O-club, sir—Valhalla, Warrior Heaven. It's just up the hill!" He gestured in the general direction of Division Hill. "It's the hootch to the left of the bridge, just before you cross over to Charlie Company's area. In fact, tonight you get steaks on the patio and a Korean country-western band courtesy of the USO! Saturday night in Vietnam!"

He laughed. I sighed.

"Okay, Sergeant Smith, let's make it three hundred dollars, and I'll put five in your soda fund . . . if, and only if, you can produce a *cold* root beer from that fridge! What can I do close by?" I wanted to get the check-in process behind me as quickly as possible.

"You can turn in your health record, sir, next door! And I'll have the root beer and your MPC when you get back. You know we got no root beer in this fridge!" He handed me the documents and sat down at his desk, my pay record and OQR in his grasp. He was still smiling as I turned and went out the door.

Outside, the midday sun beat down unmercifully. A few Marines were moving about the compound, none of whom had a choice about their activities. Traffic noise from vehicles passing on the road above the compound drifted on the heavy air, accompanied by smatterings of conversation and music from nearby huts. It seemed that everyone had a radio, stereo, or cassette player going. From behind me, I heard the singsong chatter of Vietnamese mamma-sans gossiping as they went about their housekeeping chores. Camp Reasoner had all the comforts of home! Hot chow, cold beer, a roof to sleep under, and maid service. Who would have thought? I looked around until I spotted the Battalion Aid Station, then moved off the porch in that direction.

The BAS was set up not unlike the S-1, with cots and medical paraphernalia taking the place of the field desks. As I stepped inside, a navy chief petty officer in Marine utilities (fatigues) stood from his seat at a field desk and moved to the counter.* "What can I do for you, Lieutenant?" I saw that he had been eating a C ration when I entered.

"Checking in, Chief." I offered up my health record and shot card as I spoke.

He took the documents from my hand, leafed through the shot card, then looked up with a questioning gaze. "Looks like your immunizations are up to date, Lieutenant. Where are you assigned?"

"Charlie Company."

As I answered, he made a note on the outside of the folder, initialed my check-in sheet, and handed it back to me. "Hope you do better than the last guy!"

"So do I, Chief. Where is Supply from here?" As I spoke, I was pushing the door open.

"Up the hill, on the right."

The chief was already back at lunch, crackers and cheese spraying from his mouth as he spoke. I went outside in search of clean clothes, flak gear, and a weapon.

Supply turned out to be in one of the large Butler buildings I had passed on my ride into the compound. The armory was colocated, the weapons secured in large conex boxes, heavy metal shipping containers, designed to be easily transported and secure. Both were "Closed for Lunch," so I went back to the S-1 to collect my pay and my personal effects. As I approached the hut, I overheard Sergeant Smith in conversation with another Marine, "I don't know, Andy. He seemed pretty squared away to me."

I mounted the steps firmly, pulled the screen door, and

*The Marine Corps is provided medical personnel by the Navy.

stepped inside. A young sergeant stood at the counter, engrossed in conversation with Sergeant Smith, who looked up and stopped talking as I entered. I noticed my OQR on the counter between them.

"The war gear will have to wait 'til after lunch," I spoke the words while making eye contact with the new sergeant.

His gaze was direct and speculative. "Sir, I'm glad you're back. This is Sergeant Anderson, the admin chief of Charlie Company. He came down to show you the way over." As he spoke, Sergeant Smith gestured in the direction of the man. I stuck out my hand to shake in greeting.

The young sergeant, his eyes locked on mine, came to a sullen semblance of attention. "Sir!" The word was tainted with disdain.

Well, fuck you, too, Sergeant! I thought to myself, letting my arm drop back to my side. I turned my attention to Sergeant Smith, who appeared embarrassed. "Well, how about the MPC, and I'll get out of your way for a while?"

Sergeant Smith was already shuffling the documents on the counter, offering me a pen as he did. "Sign here, sir."

He pointed to the appropriate spot. I signed, and he began counting hard-used miniature currency certificates into stacks on the counter. They reminded me of Monopoly money.

"Three hundred dollars in funny money, sir. Don't spend it all in one place." He gave a nervous laugh.

Sergeant Anderson stared sullenly as we completed the transaction. I shuffled the bills into a roll, put them in the leg pocket of my trousers, and turned toward my bags. "Thanks a lot, Sergeant Smith. Sergeant Smiley, if you'll get the door?" I gestured with my head, lifting a bag in each hand.

Sergeant Anderson moved grudgingly to the door, pulled it open, and went out, holding it ajar for me to pass. "The name is Anderson, sir. The Charlie Company officer's hootch is up there across the road, under that big tree."

I looked in the direction he pointed. There was a cluster of huts in the middle of the compound, one or two of which were shaded by banyan trees. It looked like an easy trip up the incline I had ridden down in the truck. I hefted the bags and stepped off the porch in the direction he had pointed. He fell in behind.

"Well, Sergeant Anderson, my name is Hodgins, Lieutenant Hodgins, or sir—without the slur—to you. And I made your grade in 1966. I was proud of my chevrons, because I earned them. I'm sure you did, too." I dropped the bags in the roadway and turned to confront him.

"How's that, sir?" He was still sullen.

"I know you didn't earn those chevrons by being salty and insubordinate. I know you must be a good Marine. So am I. I consider myself a Marine first, an officer second. And I don't like the attitude you displayed in there." I inclined my head in the direction of the building we had just left, keeping my eyes locked on his.

Doubt gradually replaced the surliness in his eyes. He broke eye contact. "I meant no disrespect, sir. It's just that it's been a tough night, and it seems like every time we get a new lieutenant, shit happens! It isn't personal, sir."

"Okay, Sergeant Anderson. I accept that." I said, "Why don't we start over with you telling me about Charlie Company?" I extended my hand. He looked at my hand, then into my eyes, let his shoulders drop, and accepted my grasp.

"Welcome aboard, sir!" He smiled, and stooped to shoulder my valpack. I took it from him.

"You talk, I'll hump the bags," I said, as we started off again.

"What do you want to know first, sir?"

We were already moving up a slight incline, and I was beginning to regret not having let him carry one of the bags. Still, the points on bearing and relationships might prove valuable. An FNG again, and I wanted to get in touch with the troops as soon as possible. If experience was any indicator, my very life might depend on it. "Tell me how the company is organized, who the players are, that kind of thing." I tried to keep the exertion I was feeling out of my voice. I was sweating like a pig.

"Charlie Company has had some hard luck with officers, Lieutenant, but right now we have Lieutenant Baker as the executive officer. Lieutenant Polster in Second Platoon—he's down in the Three Shop getting ready to go after the Skipper and Lieutenant Skibbe. Then we have Lieutenant Hodge with Third Platoon—he's ex-enlisted, like you. He's down at the Three Shop also. Then we have Lieutenant Duda and Lieutenant Pino. They're sort of designated hitters, patrol leaders—they're both in the bush right now. Then we have Lieutenant Curry in First Platoon—he is due back from OP Sunrise this afternoon with his platoon. Lieutenant Skibbe was new. He was going to take Third Platoon . . ."

I interrupted him, excited at the thought of finding a friend in these new surroundings. Curry and I were Basic School classmates. We had gone to Recon Replacement School together, come to Vietnam on the same plane. Our wives were keeping each other company in San Diego at that moment. It was the first good news of the day! "Is this guy Curry, first name Michael, from California?"

"Yes, sir. Must be. He came here from the Grunts back in January. Then Skibbe you know about already. He was only here a few days. First Sergeant Burke runs the company, and we have a staff sergeant, Staff Sergeant Ware, as the company gunny. We have a headquarters detachment. That's me and a couple of clerks. And three recon platoons with about twenty guys in each. Then, of course, we have some corpsmen attached to us, but they change all the time." As he finished speaking, he stopped in front of one of the huts. "This is the Charlie Company officers' hootch, sir. We'll get you set up in here, sir, until somebody tells us who is going to run the show."

As he spoke, he led the way up a wooden step and pulled open the door to the officers' hootch, making way for me as he did. My shoulders were burning from the effort of hauling the heavy bags up the road. My hands were cramped around the luggage handles. I lunged up the steps and through the screen door into the hut and dropped the tormenting load on the floor. At the sound, two Marines inside one of the cubicles turned to stare at me.

"Top, this is Lieutenant Hodgins. He's taking Lieutenant

Skibbe's place. Lieutenant, this is First Sergeant Burke." As he spoke, he moved aside, leaving me a space to climb over the bags and grasp the first sergeant's proffered hand.

"Welcome to Charlie Company, Lieutenant. We were just finishing our inventory of Lieutenant Skibbe's personal effects. His is the only empty rack in here right now, so why don't you just leave your stuff here and go on up to the company office? I'll finish this up, then come up to get you sorted out."

He shook my hand as he spoke and put his free hand on my shoulder, steering me back toward the door to the hootch. Before I realized it, we were all back outside.

"This is a tight outfit, Lieutenant. You'll be glad to be part of it."

With that, he turned and went back inside, leaving me in the company of Sergeant Anderson and my own thoughts. Sergeant Anderson started off in the direction of the company office. I called out after him.

"Hold up a minute, Sergeant!"

He stopped and turned in my direction. Moving to join him, I continued to speak. "I think I want to go on back up to Supply and the armory while I can. I'd like to get my war gear and some utilities before it gets too late in the day."

He nodded, then saluted smartly. "Good day, sir!"

We both smiled, and I returned his salute. I turned to walk back up the hill, my thoughts racing from one gloomy scenario to another. I decided that I needed to take things one step at a time. The first step had to be to get my imagination under control. The second had to be to get a weapon, flak gear, and some clean clothes. My stomach growled and I thought, And maybe some chow. I set off in the direction of the Butler building housing Supply.

I arrived at Supply, only to find a line! Eight or ten Marines were standing about counting items out of myriad piles of 782 gear (field equipment). I shouldered my way through the crowd and accosted a surly staff sergeant who appeared to be supervising the inventory.

"Sergeant, my name is Hodgins. I'm checking in." I tendered the check-in sheet as I spoke.

Without looking up from his clipboard, the staff sergeant said, "So are these guys, asshole. Get in line." As he finished his statement, he looked up from the clipboard, realized his mistake and stood up behind his field desk. "Oh, sorry, Lieutenant. I didn't realize you were an officer, sir!"

I laughed. "That's okay, Sergeant. Sometimes I don't either. But I was once a Staff NCO like yourself, and I remember that experience very well." I was stretching the point a little, having been selected for staff sergeant, but never wearing the stripes. "Can you fix me up with some serviceable war gear? I'm just reporting in from the Grunts, and I have shit. No clothes, no nothing."

Relieved that there was not going to be a confrontation over his unintended insubordination, the staff sergeant smiled and said, "Right this way, Lieutenant. For a former Grunt only the best of the best!"

He showed me into the depths of the building, where his treasures were kept. I emerged an hour later, burdened with two heavy rubberized equipment bags full of the paraphernalia of war. It was good stuff, all U.S. Army state of the art. I selected carefully, choosing the lightest, most durable, and wherever possible, brand-new equipment. No more blood-stained hand-me-downs for me! I muscled my burdens around the corner to the armory, where I worked my charms on the armorer, a crusty forty-year-old sergeant (E-5) and came away with a brand-new M-16A1 (The cosmoline was still on it!), fifteen brand-new magazines, a fairly tight (recently refurbished) .45-caliber M1911A1 Colt sidearm, and cleaning gear for it all. Outside the armory, I rigged a sling on the rifle, slung it over my shoulder, stuffed my remaining treasures in among the equipment in the WP bags. Then, grabbing a bag in each hand, I trudged down the hill, back to the officers' hootch. Music and conversation still drifted about the compound. I listened for sounds from inside the officers' hootch. There were none, so I went inside.

It was empty, but I saw that each of its usual occupants

had tried to make a corner of the hut home. The hut was divided into cubicles, six in all, one in each corner and two in the middle, with a walkway down the center. The partitions were made of plywood, about four feet high, painted olive green. Each cubicle had a cot with a mattress, a field desk, a footlocker, and assorted personal effects (mostly pictures of family and friends from happier times). From the photos, I deduced that the other lieutenants, like myself, were married. They had all hung helmets and flak gear on pegs above their cots, not unlike the arrangement I had seen in the other huts. I decided that this must be some unit SOP (standing operating procedure).

My valpack and seabag were in the middle cubicle on the left. I dragged the WP bags across the deck (floor in naval jargon) and into the cubicle, banging the M-16 against the upright as I did so. The rifle rebounded, and the barrel whacked me across the nose, bringing tears to my eyes. Cursing, I sat down on the cot, unslinging the weapon as I did so. I stood the rifle, muzzle up in a corner, then slumped back on the rack (bed in naval jargon), nursing my wound. Overhead, I heard the distinctive clatter of helicopter rotors again. From outside came animated voices, converging on the hut from several directions. Screen doors slammed. I heard the myriad sounds of heavily laden men as they scrambled down the steps leading to the HLZ, cursing as they jostled one another. Suddenly, there were heavy steps on the porch, the door burst open, and a camouflage-painted, bespectacled Marine surged into the hootch, cursing. He rushed into one of the cubicles, shrugging out of his web gear as he went.

"This is bullshit! Absolute insane bullshit!" he fumed, reaching for the flak jacket and helmet hanging on a nail over his rack.

I stood and moved into the space between the cubicles. "Hi! My name is Mike Hodgins. Can I help you get sorted out there?"

He was struggling to get the web gear on over the flak jacket. I picked up the back of the pack, relieving him of the dead weight so that he could buckle the belt at his waist. He was festooned with flares, hand grenades, canteens, and other paraphernalia. The pack must have weighed eighty pounds. He hunched over, taking the weight of the pack on his back, and buckled the cartridge belt.

Standing to face me, he said, "Larry Polster! Got no time to talk now, Mike, but welcome aboard! If I get back from this bullshit, I'll be pleased to meet you. I can't believe these bastards want us to wear flak gear to the bush! Fuckin' stupid idea to go back in there anyway." He was talking to himself, moving toward the door.

I moved to open the screen door ahead of him. Outside, a group of Marines was assembling near the tree where I had stood earlier in the day. They were also burdened with flak gear in addition to their standard load. All were grumbling and jostling one another. Polster joined the group, and they moved off down a wooden staircase leading to the HLZ. I was left alone again, in the void of their departure. Just like the Sparrow Hawk missions back in the SLF (special landing force), I thought to myself, as I turned to reenter the hootch. At least I know what's going on.

Alone with my gear and my thoughts, I began unpacking by dumping first one bag, then another, into a pile on the deck in front of my rack. Sorting through the mess, I assembled the parts to my new helmet (helmet, liner, headband, chin strap, and camouflage cover) and hung the finished product and the flak jacket on a nail in the bulkhead. Then I set about assembling my web gear (cartridge belt, belt suspender straps, magazine pouches, canteens, butt pack, poncho, poncho liner, and first-aid kit). Through trial and error, I got the whole kit to fit, then hung it alongside the flak jacket. The effort got me sweating again, and I noticed that I had sopped the deck with it. By some oversight, the first sergeant had left a portable fan in the cubicle. I turned it on, set it on HIGH, and fell back on the rack to let the artificial breeze cool me off. It didn't help, so I stripped off my cammy jacket and started cleaning my new M-16, the fan whirring incessantly for company. While I worked, I reviewed my situation in my mind.

Six months in the bush with the Grunts had toughened me, physically and emotionally, and had given me insights (life-saving insights) into how the troops would most likely be re-acting to the events that had just occurred. "It don't mean nothin'," would be the most common reaction. They would rationalize the events as yesterday's news, of no particular import to them. The loss of an officer so new to the unit would not be talked about for long, and the company com-mander was too far removed from their day-to-day survival to be missed. In the Grunts, I had seen even the most popu-lar leaders, cut down by booby traps, dismissed out of hand as soon as the medevac cleared the landing zone. It was na-ture's way of enabling young minds to cope with the horrors of war. Every mother's son was absolutely certain it wouldn't happen to him, until he got short. As the new guy, however, I would be an object of speculation and concern. They would be speculating about my competence in the field, about whether or not they could trust me to get them home in one piece. And I would definitely be needing them to get me home. I wondered if I had handled Sergeant Anderson prop-erly. He would be the source of the first word on me. I hoped it would be a thumbs-up. The thing to do was to get to the bush as soon as possible. Let the word get out that Little Mikey Hodgins could hack it. If I was going to get any pay-back out of the NVA, this was clearly the place to start, and I was going to need a lot of help. Skibbe was history. I would be, too, if I didn't put his fate behind me and focus on doing my job. In the Grunts, I had replaced a forgotten lieutenant, one blown apart on Go Noi Island. I had run the whole race as a platoon commander, even to medevacking my own re-placement. This was no different.

I closed the breech on the M-16, pushed the retaining pin home, and pulled the charger handle. The bolt slid smoothly home. I snapped the trigger and set the weapon aside, turn-ing my attention to the magazines. My mind continued to ramble as my hands worked automatically to disassemble, clean, and reassemble each magazine. I knew that I could manage my own fear. I knew that I could do the trigger time. I had done so already. What I wanted was to establish myself quickly as a reliable, trustworthy leader. I would need to be all ears and questions when I met the other lieutenants. I resolved that I would pick Curry's brain when he returned.

Finished with the magazines, I realized that I had no ammunition. Electricity or not, I thought we weren't so far in the rear as to not need a loaded weapon after dark. I stood up and looked about the hootch. I remembered Curry as a meticulous and careful guy. He would have ammo. I looked over the partition. Sure enough, he had an ammo crate on the deck under his rack. It was full of loose rounds and assorted pyrotechnics. I gathered up a handful of 5.56mm, armor piercing (AP) and tracers, and sat back down on my rack. Jacking the rounds into one of the new magazines, I realized that my hands were sore from working with all the metal surfaces. I loaded two magazines, a tracer first and every third round thereafter, banged the rounds back by tapping each magazine on the edge of the cot. I placed the loaded magazines on the partition near the rifle and stood to stretch, my labors complete.

I realized that I was hungry. Curry had a rat-fucked (rifled) case of C rations on the deck under his rack. I circled the wall and stooped to sort through the remaining boxes. He had taken all the B-3s (fruit), and the pound cakes out of the B-2s, but I selected "Beans and Franks," crackers and Tabasco (off the top of his field desk), and a pair of heat tabs. Back on the rack, I pulled my dog-tag chain and John Wayne can opener from under my jacket and set about making a stove out of the cracker can. With practiced skill, I cut the lid out of the can, sliced vents in the bottom, and cut the rim off the top, bending in the sides so that cans placed atop the stove would not slip off. I ripped the package from a heat tab, dropped it in the can, and set the whole thing on the floor. (Countless half circles had been scorched into the plywood by my predecessors.) I repeated the process with the beans and franks, poking a hole through the gunk to the bottom of the can so that the mess could heat without exploding all over me. That done, I opened an accessory pack, struck a match from the pack it contained, and dropped the match on the heat tab, placing the beans over the flame—the soup was on. Wishing for an onion, I poked and stirred the contents of the can for several minutes. The fumes from the heat tab gagged me, bringing tears to my eyes. Even after countless such endeavors, I still had not developed the knack for cooking without gassing myself. As the goo bubbled and spewed, I opened a can of cheese, dipped in a cracker, and sat back on the rack to munch my lunch. Before long, the contents of my B-2 had bubbled over onto the deck and were ready to eat. I choked the mess down, a spoonful at a time, then lay back on the rack to let jet lag overtake me. I was bone weary all of a sudden, and sleep came unbidden. It was hard to believe that, only hours before, I had savored mahimahi and slept in air-conditioned luxury between clean sheets in the arms of a beautiful woman. Times changed. I grinned at the thought of my stateside chow fertilizing the XO's gravel. Nerves! They'll keep you alive, Mikey!

CHAPTER TWO
THE LIEUTENANTS' PROTECTIVE ASSOCIATION

3–23 MARCH 1970

Fear has many eyes.

Cervantes, *Don Quixote*, 1605

I was awakened by voices and scuffling outside the hootch. The screen door crashed open. Polster was back, accompanied by another lieutenant. I stood up, awkwardly, to introduce myself. Before I could speak, Polster's associate lunged forward, his hand outstretched in greeting. "Stumpy Baker! Pleased ta meetcha!"

He grasped my hand in a firm shake, pulling me into the passageway. He was stocky, bullnecked, with dark close-cropped hair and freckles—full of energy. I liked him immediately.

"Mike, you picked a helluva day to come aboard. I guess I'm going to be your CO. 'Til Drumright fires me, anyhow." He laughed. "Polster here is the XO, as of now. I see the sleeve [first sergeant] has gotcha set up already." He took a silent inventory of my cubicle, noted the fact that I had already assembled my war gear.

"How about a cold beer?" Baker moved to a miniature refrigerator in the farthest cubicle. I noticed a guitar leaning in a corner. The wall was littered with thumbtacked newspaper clippings and photographs. He pulled three cans from the fridge, tossed one to Polster, one to me, and held one for himself.

"Church key?" He held up the utensil by a shoestring thumb-tacked to the wall beside the refrigerator. He opened his beer with a hiss, slurped the foam off the top, and sat down—dropped—on his cot. I moved to open my beer. Polster sat still, opening his with a John Wayne. There was an awkward silence.

"So, where you from, Mike?" Baker slumped back on his rack, taking a long pull from his beer and reaching for the guitar—all in one motion.

"California. You?" I took a pull on my beer.

"Midland, Maryland. Went to Frostberg State College. I was goin' to be a fuckin' school teacher. If Mom could see me now! And don't tell her I'm a Marine, motherfucker!" He glared at me over the top of the can. "She thinks I'm a pimp!"

I didn't know whether to laugh or not, so I kept silent. Polster just glared at me.

Baker took another long pull on his beer, strummed a lick on the guitar. "Well come on all you big strong men. Uncle Sam needs your help again. Got himself in a terrible jam, way down yonder in Vietnam. Put down your books and pick up a gun. We're goin' to have a whole lot of fun! And it's one, two, three what are we fightin' for? Don't ask me. I don't give a damn." He set the guitar aside, making eye contact. "Can you sing?"

"No."

"Neither can I. I been in this motherfucker since October of sixty-eight. I missed fuckin' Woodstock. That must have been some rainy day—four hundred thousand draft-dodgin' mother-fuckers in a pig farm! Good music, though. I'm short [due to rotate home]." He must have realized he was rambling, be-cause he fell silent abruptly, a morose look on his face.

Polster picked up the slack. "How long have you been in country, Mike?"

"Six months. I was in the Grunts, Two–Twenty-six, before this. Just got back from R & R."

"So you're one of Drumright's warriors, huh?"

Polster spoke from his cubicle. The challenge was openly hostile. I was taken aback.

"Lighten up, Larry! He's new. You got a hard-on for the CO, keep it to yourself! Don't mind him, Mike. Drumright's been all over his ass today, and everybody else's for that matter." Baker opened the fridge and came out with three more brews, underhanding one to each of us. "What we need to do is to take this party on the road. Here's a road pop—let's go up to the club and get a steak!"

We went, and over the course of the next few hours I learned about the LPA (the Lieutenants' Protective Association). Baker was a charter member, and he took seriously his hapless responsibility as commanding officer, Company C, 1st Recon Bn (Rein). As the night progressed, he plied me with beer and wisdom, shoptalk about how the battalion worked. He gave me a rundown on nearly everyone in the battalion, from Wild Bill to the battalion supply sergeant (whom I had already met). He told me who was squared away, who was a space cadet, who was "fuckin' gung ho"—and therefore dangerous. (The battalion commander was first on this list, followed by a tandem of "REMF Warriors" in the staff.) It was clear that Baker had no love for the operations officer (S-3), and great respect for the assistant, a lieutenant named Gregson. By midnight, I was pleasantly buzzed, full of false confidence, and convinced that everybody who was anybody in the battalion was a lieutenant. I made my way back to the hootch, my fear all but forgotten—Recon had it all over the Grunts. I had made a good decision. I slept.

The dawn brought a new reality. I was awakened by commotion within and without the hootch. Polster, cursing under his breath, was struggling into his war gear again. Outside, there was a bustle of activity as heavily laden troops assembled near the path to the helicopter landing zone (HLZ). I sat up, instantly alert. "Mornin', Larry. What's the buzz?"

"Your illustrious leader has decided we need to go get the fucking bodies. So Watash ["I," from the Japanese] is elected! That's the buzz! If I get back from this, I swear to God, I'm putting in an AA form for a transfer. I'm too short for this shit!" He plunged through the screen door, into the street.

In the silent aftermath of his outburst, I contemplated my own future, and resolved to keep a cool head. Luck and tactical diligence would keep me alive. In my mind, I wished Polster well, knowing he was going to need all the help he could get. I roused myself, gathered my shaving kit and a towel, and went out to the shower. The tepid water was as cool as I expected to be that day. Clean and dry, for the moment, I made my way to the mess hall. The troops, both teams (distinguishable by cammy paint in some cases, bush hats, and subdued attitudes) and REMFs were gaggled in line for fried eggs, one of Wild Bill's first innovations. As in 2/26, he was making sure that his warriors ate well. I took a place in line behind several lieutenants on the officer/SNCO side, patiently waiting for my cooked-to-order breakfast. Baker appeared, escaping from the CO's breakfast staff conference. He had a harassed look about him. "Say, Mike. Come up to the company office after chow. I've got something for you." Having ruined my breakfast, he hustled out the screen door without a backward glance. It was an order. I ate hurriedly and complied.

I found him in the company office, a sheaf of messages in one hand, a grease pencil in the other. He was annotating the situation map on the wall when I announced my presence. "Say, Stump. What's going on?"

He looked up at the sound of my voice, startled. "Mike, it's time for you to break your cherry as a Recon Marine." Baker handed me the frag order for the patrol, pointing to the RAO (Recon Area of Operation) he had sketched on the situation map on the wall of the office. My gaze followed his to the map. I saw that he had similar boxes delineating the RAOs for several other Charlie Company patrols, including Polster in the Que Sons. The thought of Polster's developing saga chilled me. The facts were bad, the rumors worse. It was getting to be a very spooky situation, and we were all on edge.

"They want us to put a team in the east end of Happy Valley. I think that is a good place for you to start, Mike, so I'm giving this one to you—with Sergeant Domnoske." He turned to make eye contact with me. I said nothing. "Your haven is in an area that has been pretty quiet for the past couple of months."

"Haven?" I was puzzled by the word.

"Yeah. Your RAO is a 'haven'—you're supposed to be safe in there. Nobody but gooks can shoot at you without your permission [clearance]." Baker laughed at the irony, then continued, "Let Ski call the plays, so you get to know the ropes. He's real squared away."

I broke eye contact with him but held my silence, focusing on the frag order. I saw that I held copy 14 of 15. Last guy to know, first guy to go. Some things don't change. Call sign Patty Shell. Paperwork. Should I read all the references? My ruminations were interrupted by banging on the bulkhead. We turned in unison toward the sound.

"Sir, Sergeant Domnoske reporting as ordered, sir!"

"Hey, Ski. Come on in." Baker took a seat on a corner of his field desk, in front of the situation map. "Ski, meet Lieutenant Hodgins."

Domnoske had stepped off the cover of a *Post* magazine, the epitome of a Norman Rockwell midwestern farm boy. He was a big, ruddy, freckle-faced kid with a shock of red hair and an easy smile. His eyes, locked with mine, were older than his years, and not smiling at all.

"Sir!" Domnoske faced us, coming to the position of attention.

I moved into the center of the room, extending my hand in greeting. "Lieutenant Baker has told me great things about you, Sergeant. Relax and let us get acquainted. Mr. Baker, here, was just telling me that you have the honor of indoctrinating me in the ways of Recon patrolling."

Domnoske grasped my handshake, firmly, his expression skeptical.

Baker had been silent throughout the exchange. Now he spoke. "I was just telling Mike, er—Lieutenant Hodgins, that we have to put a team into the east end of Happy Valley,

Ski, at the foot of Ba Na. You've been up there recently, so I thought it would be good for Lieutenant Hodgins to take that walk with you. Yours is the only team we have available right now, anyway."

He paused for a moment, gathering his thoughts, then rushed on. "You will have an ARVN Ranger with you on this one, Lieutenant Lan. He just finished RIP [Recon Indoctrination Program]. He's going to live up here with us for a few weeks. Here is the frag order. Why don't you and Lieutenant Hodgins do your map recon now, and get acquainted. I'm going to hit the pool." He laughed and went out, leaving the door ajar.

Domnoske and I exchanged speculative stares across the room. Domnoske's expression suggested that he was coming to terms with bad news—me and/or the ARVN. Finally, Domnoske shifted his feet and moved toward the map. "So, how long you been in country, Lieutenant?" The question was cast over his shoulder as he studied the map.

"Six months." I moved to the map, standing beside him. I saw that the area we were slated to patrol was in a valley, the west end of which was steep, almost a gorge, bisected by a stream. The easterly portion was more open, and included what appeared to be some major trail junctions. The stream at the bottom of the valley was year-round, denoted by a dark blue line. The terrain on the south side of the stream was dark green on the map—canopy—and so steep as to be impassable. (I deduced this by the density of the contour lines on the map; each one denoted twenty meters of elevation—it was a fucking cliff.) The map showed an abandoned structure and a major trail running east/west, generally parallel to the river. The haven outlined an area of six klicks (six thousand meters square) oriented parallel to the stream. It was a very logical place to put a team, and a very logical route for the NVA to use in and out of the mountains.

"The last two Grunt lieutenants we got in Charlie Company got killed on their first patrol . . ." Domnoske was engrossed in the map, making notes with a grease pencil on a makeshift map case. He turned to face me to finish his thought, ". . . humping on trails. They were both gung ho motherfuckers."

I felt cotton mouthed again. My stomach did a backflip. I thought to myself, in good Basic School subconscious, What now, Lieutenant? Aloud, I said, "What's the game plan, Ski?" I kept my eyes and my voice steady, using my best barracks poker face. This was no time to let a troop inside my head, even a good troop. Domnoske stared at me for another moment, realized that I wasn't going to take the bait.

"Well, sir. First we give my guys the heads-up on what we're doing. Then we go down to the Two Shop [S-2, Intelligence], get our maps and find out who else has been in there lately, what they found. Then we go to the Three Shop [S-3, Operations] and see if we can get a VR [visual reconnaissance] this afternoon or tomorrow. Then we go to chow." He turned to face me, smiling. His eyes said, You may have the bars, but I've got the time in country. You're nothin' to me but a pain in the ass. "And what has the lieutenant been doing here in Heaven these past six months?" It was an FNG challenge.

"Patrolling, Sergeant Domnoske, patrolling." I returned his stare, my stomach churning.

"Did you know Lieutenant Skibbe?" He was direct, watching for a reaction.

"No. Did you?" I kept my eyes cold, staring him down. My pulse throbbed in my throat. Could he sense my fear?

"No, sir. He was here and gone while I was in the bush. But shit like that works on people's minds, you know. Makes 'em skittish. Captain McVey was a good man. He was a mustang [former enlisted man], like you, a real hard ass. But he took care of the troops. We all miss him." He paused for a moment, then continued, "I'm a careful guy, Lieutenant. I do my homework."

"So what does the map tell you, Sergeant?" I decided to take the conversation into more productive ground. It was clear that the NCO telegraph was working—Anderson had already passed the word on the "boot lieutenant."

"Well, every patrol area is different. Some you hump,

some you peep. This one looks like a hump. Maybe we can find some places to hole up and monitor that trail. We'll know more if we get a VR."

He looked at his Mickey Mouse watch. "I need to get the guys a warning order, sir. Meet you at the Two Shop in twenty mikes?"

He strode to the door, firmly in control of our budding relationship. Experience gave him the moral authority to lead, for the time being. I resolved to follow, and reserve judgment. "Sure."

I turned to study the map as he went out. Domnoske was an impressive guy, but attitude did not equal aptitude in my mind. I thought myself better safe than sorry. I would do my own plan, make up my own order, and let Domnoske run. If things didn't shape up, I would be ready. After six months in the Grunts, I knew that being bush smart did not necessarily translate into tactical proficiency. I did not want my life depending on a twenty-year-old sergeant's tactical expertise. I reasoned that Recon patrolling couldn't be a lot different from my PPB (platoon patrol base) actions farther north. Well, maybe the NVA would not booby-trap their own back yard. Or maybe they would. Maybe . . .

"The terrain dictates the tactics, Lieutenant." The Basic School instructor's assertion had been true at Quantico. It had been true in the Grunts. It was true now. I picked out a key terrain feature in the haven, Hill 142, in the upper left quadrant of the haven, then another in the lower right, Hill 502. I looked for a possible HLZ in the east end, on the low ground, picked a spot on a finger above a major trail junction, north of the stream. From the map, I deduced that there would not be HLZs in the west end of the haven, except for the stream bed. Hump up hill, run down . . . The thought came unbidden into my mind as I traced a horseshoe patrol route, open at the east end, around the perimeter of the haven. I looked at my watch. It was time to meet Domnoske. I folded the frag order, tucked it into my shirt pocket, picked up my cover, and went out.

When I arrived at the Two Shop, Domnoske was nowhere

to be seen, but several officers and NCOs were perched on
ammo boxes or chairs or leaning up against the bulkheads,
studying maps and other papers. A gunnery sergeant sat behind a field desk, typing in two-fingered hunt-and-peck. I
stood in front of him, waiting for him to notice me. Finally,
he looked up from his decrepit Underwood. "Can I help you,
Lieutenant?"

"Gunny, my name is Hodgins. I'm with Charlie Company, and I'm here to pick up the maps and briefing sheet for
Patty Shell." As I spoke, I pulled the frag order from the
pocket of my jacket, extending it toward him.

"Domnoske picked up that stuff, already. He went out
back."

The gunny gestured with his head in the direction of a side
door to the hut, and returned his attention to the laborious
task in the typewriter. I was dismissed. I felt my face flush.
The room hummed with fans turning fetid, sweat-soaked air,
and muted conversations between team members studying
the documents they had been provided. I turned to the door
and went out, determined not to let my sudden surge of inse-
curity and anger displace my determination. Bearing is nine
points of command, Lieutenant! I moved onto the porch and
found Domnoske ensconced in a homemade chaise lounge,
reading patrol reports.

"Say, Lieutenant. I got here a little sooner than I thought.
There's a set of maps for you." He pointed to a pile of documents on an ammo box next to his chair. I picked them up
and took a seat on the ammo box, my temper in check. It was
not a test, just a circumstance. Or maybe it was a test. His
eyes gave nothing away. "I turned in the patrol roster already, but you need to give the gunny your zap number [ser-
vice number]. We're in luck. Delivery Boy was in this area a
couple weeks ago. They ran an air strike on a base camp right
here, grid eight-one-six-six-eight-one."

He leaned toward me, extending his map in one hand and
pointing to the spot with the other. I unfolded my map and
located the grid. My heart was in my throat. The base camp
was outside our haven, but only just. According to the map,

there was a major trail running approximately northwest to southeast in the draw, and parallel to a year-round stream. The camp was on a finger, less than three hundred meters south of the trail. The location struck me as odd. "Isn't that a weird place for a base camp?"

I looked at Domnoske as I spoke. He shrugged his shoulders. "It was only a couple of hootches and a bunker. Like a lineman's shack back home. The Gooners use them to get out of the weather when they're workin' on trails and such. My bet is there was nobody home."

He continued his inspection of the map as he spoke. So did I. "So why an air strike?" I posed the question in my mind, not realizing that I had spoken aloud. Running an air strike on three huts and a foxhole did not make sense to me. Domnoske's answer, like divine intervention, did.

"Because the dudes in Echo Company are gung ho and they couldn't hit it with artillery." As he spoke he was making notes in a notebook similar to the one I carried.

"Oh?" I posed the question, my thoughts racing.

"Yeah—I mean, yes—sir. They tried to use the one-oh-fives at An Hoa, but it was in defilade behind this hill here, Five-Twelve."

He pointed to the spot on my map with his grease pencil, taking a long pull on a Coca-Cola as he did.

"Where did you come by the soda, Ski?" I saw that it was ice cold, condensation on the can. My jaws ached at the thought of tasting one.

"Fridge in the corner, sir. Help yourself. The Six keeps it stocked for us—the teams, I mean. Five-Twelve used to be a fire support base [FSB]. Buckskin, or something like that. The Grunts ran a big operation west of there last year about this time. I wasn't a team leader then, but we had to screen for the Grunts farther west. This is all gook base area in here. You can look at it on the wall inside. Anyway, they had to put tubes [cannons] on the hilltops so they could shoot into these valleys." He finished off his soda, and stood up. "I'm goin' for another soda, Lieutenant. Want one?"

I nodded my head in silent assent, lost in thought. Domnoske did not seem to attach much significance to the information he had just passed to me. To him, it was the way things were. To me, it was not the way things ought to be. It meant that we were going to be patrolling in an area where we could not count on artillery for fire support in the event of contact. My Basic School training, reinforced by the Supporting Arms Employment Course I had taken on my way overseas, told me that this was a serious issue, something to consider carefully. I studied the map more closely.

"Here we go, Lieutenant." Domnoske handed me an ice-cold Coca-Cola, already open, and slumped back in his chair. "The way I see it, sir, we insert in the northeast corner, maybe on that finger above the trail junction, then hump west to Hill One-Forty-two, maybe two days to do that. Then south to the stream junction, harbor on the south side of that on the third day. Doesn't look like any HLZs in there, but it's only for one night. I like to harbor up near an HLZ every night, but sometimes you can't. Day four, we hump east, parallel to this big trail and hope for the best. Harbor up close to our extract HLZ for the last night. It's a bitch to try to hump into an LZ on extract day. We should be able to get out easy close to the river."

He slurped the Coke, waiting for my response. I had followed his monologue on the map. It was a good plan, not a lot different from my own. "Does it bother you that we will spend most of our time in defilade from our artillery?" I spoke in a low key, studious voice.

"No, sir!" He laughed. "Fuckers can't shoot at us—we'll just have to use the Broncos [OV-10 ground-attack aircraft] for fire support. I kind of like that better. You never know where them cannon cockers [artillerymen] are going to drop their shit, anyway." Domnoske stood up abruptly, tossing off the dregs of his soda.

I followed suit, my thoughts still swirling around a fire-support plan for the patrol. It was becoming clear to me that Domnoske was not going to submit any kind of preplanned fires or other arrangements, as I would have done. In fact, he seemed to be more afraid of our own artillery than he was of the NVA. I decided to ask one more stupid question. "Ski! Tell me this. What do we normally do in the way of fire-support planning for this patrol?"

I held his gaze, compelling an answer. He folded his maps, putting them in the leg pocket of his trousers. His answer was the essence of simplicity. "Sir, we don't do nothin'. The Three Shop coordinates everything with the air wing. They put up an OV-ten, and coordinate any artillery that way. The rotorheads [helicopter pilots] don't like us calling fire missions when they're in the area. So, I guess the whole thing is centralized. I know the S-three prepares a fire-support plan for inserts and extracts, but I have never done one for a patrol. I guess we could, though . . ." The quizzical look was back.

"What about a patrol route, checkpoints, rally points?" He was moving toward the door, and I followed him with my stupid questions.

"Naw—I mean, no—sir. We usually hump 'til we drop, then call it in. It works. The Broncos can see more than we can anyway, and they have super navigation aids . . ." He paused, thoughtful, then continued. "Lieutenant, I got to get the team ready. We'll have a team meeting in the hootch tomorrow morning, say oh-eight-thirty. Then we have to have an inspection and practice some immediate-action [IA] drills. The colonel is hot on that kind of stuff right now. So why don't you catch up with us then, sir?"

He was moving through the hatch, onto the gravel road. He put on his cover and executed a hand salute. I found myself mimicking his actions, mulling the significance of what he had said. That was not at all what I had expected in the way of planning. Even in the Grunts, I had done more, with less time and no support. It felt bizarre, and scary. My thoughts churning, I watched Domnoske disappear up the gravel road toward the Charlie Company area. Clearly, a conflict was developing between what I had been trained to do and what was being done. Like the Grunts, these troops did what worked, not necessarily what was doctrine. As in the Grunts, I decided to march to the beat of my own drummer.

While my thoughts had rambled, so had my feet. I found myself back at the hootch with time to kill. So much for the "troop leading steps." Having no troops to lead, save myself, I decided to spend the time getting my troop self ready for war. The map was my most important tool. With that, a compass, and a radio, I was God in the wilderness. Preserving the map from the weather, I had learned from bitter experience, was a lifesaving effort, and it gave me something to do with my mind. I began by drawing the outline of our haven on the map. Then I cut the map sheet down to a ten-klick square, with the haven in the center. Along the right side, I wrote the grids for key terrain features. Then I cut the declination diagram from the margins of the piece to be discarded and taped it in the lower right-hand corner. Finally, I covered the map sheet with contact paper (I had purchased a stash of the stuff in Honolulu on R & R). It would fit in the leg pocket of my trousers and, wet or dry, I could use it easily.

The map took an hour. When it was done, I had the general terrain features of the patrol area absorbed in my subconscious. I plotted two potential insert HLZs and several checkpoints within the haven. Using a protractor, I plotted compass headings from point to point, planning on moving a klick (one thousand meters) a day—an ambitious concept for a recon patrol, but consistent with what Domnoske had said. Then I made an overlay of my proposed patrol route, using a grease pencil on a piece of acetate. I was jerking off. In my heart, I knew that no amount of planning would shape the results. Once we were in, terrain, weather, and enemy action (or lack of it) would determine our experience.

Mental masturbation carried me to chow time. Rumor had it that there were steaks and baked potatoes at the club, so I went. By the time I got inside, a line had formed behind the grill. Beer and conversation were flowing freely. As an FNG, I waited silently for my turn at the steaks, listening to clips of conversation between the lieutenants and SNCOs already gathered. The hot topic was Polster. Someone from the Three Shop was filling everyone in on Larry's adventure as a pathfinder for a Special Forces/CIDG* operation to recover the bodies of Captain McVey and Lieutenant-Skibbe-the-New-Guy. At least one helicopter had already been shot down, the CIDGs were taking casualties, their perimeter had been mortared, and Polster was moving around in the general area trying not to get shot up. The consensus was that the whole operation was a cluster fuck and Polster would be lucky to get out alive. By the time I reached the head of the line, I had lost my appetite for steak, or anything else.

I accepted the next steak off the grill, recovered a baked potato wrapped in aluminum foil, some salad, and a fresh-baked dinner roll, thinking as I did that Recon Marines ate better than the sailors on the last ship I had endured (the USS *New Orleans*, which had air-conditioning and great chow). As I turned to look for a place to sit, Baker slapped me on the back, then steered me by the elbow to a table already occupied by two of his peers—Chip Gregson and Charlie Kershaw. "Gents, meet Mike Hodgins. He's just joined us from the Grunts."

Baker took a seat at the table as he spoke. I felt compelled to do the same. The introductions were exchanged, and I listened as my companions talked shop. As had been the case in the chow line, the topic of immediate interest was Polster's escapade in the Que Sons. I deduced from the conversation that Gregson worked in the operations section. He and Kershaw had been platoon commanders together in Alpha Company, which Kershaw now commanded. Gregson had been shot while evading an NVA counterreconnaissance unit and had been medevacked to Guam. He had rejoined the battalion in mid-January and was not yet fully recovered from his injury. A Naval Academy grad, he was an energetic, personable man clearly well versed in the Recon operation. He chain-smoked.

---

*Civilian Irregular Defense Group: military units composed of men from Vietnam's ethnic minorities, Khmers, or Nung Chinese. These were under the command of Vietnamese Special Forces officers but paid by the U.S. Army's Special Forces.

Kershaw was tall, laconic, and sincere. He asked cogent questions of his friend regarding the colonel's attitude and goals for the operation. It was clear to me that he was concerned should he have to deal with a similar situation. No one wanted to be in Polster's shoes. Nor in Gregson's. It became clear that Chip was the guy in the know, someone who could help when the field-grade shit got too thick. He was the go-between for the company commanders (his peers), the patrol leaders, and the field-grade trinity running the battalion.

As the meal progressed, Baker reasserted himself, encouraging me to participate in the conversation. By the time we had finished our meal, I felt I had found a new home. Patty Shell was doable. Thinking of Gregson, I wondered if I'd have had the fortitude to get back in the groove after being wounded. I wondered if I had the fortitude to stay "tactical" in such circumstances. The thought of being wounded so far from friendly forces, of being ambushed and captured, made my stomach turn over. These and other thoughts plagued me on the walk back to the hootch and for the rest of the night.

With daylight came a new reality. When I arrived at the company office, word from Baker was that Polster was still in a "shit sandwich." They had been mortared during the night; his CIDGs had run off; the NVA was giving the ARVNs* a lesson in squad tactics. A helicopter had been shot down, and there were "beaucoup" casualties, including the gunner and crew chief of the bird. There was to be no visual reconnaissance for my patrol. My friend Mike Curry, out on Hill 425, was acting as radio relay for Polster and the reaction force. From the notes on the sitmap, I deduced that the whole show was going down within five klicks (five thousand meters) of the OP. Food for thought.

With these sobering thoughts filling my head, I made my way over to the team hootch where Domnoske intended to give his patrol order. I stood unobtrusively, just inside the door, while Domnoske gave his order. They were a diverse

*Soldiers of the Army of the Republic of Viet Nam, i.e., our allies.

group, with only the Corps and the war in common. They viewed me as a stand-in, if they thought about me at all. I kept my own counsel while Domnoske went through his patrol order in an abbreviated fashion. While he talked, I took in the sights around the hootch, assessing the men, their equipment, what sort of preparations they had made for the upcoming patrol. It was most clear that they had prepared to eat well. There were rifled C-ration cartons all over the place. My ruminations were interrupted by Domnoske. "Sir, do you want to introduce yourself? Say anything?"

I stood up from my relaxed position leaning against the upright in the center of their hootch when I realized that he was talking to me. "Sure. Gents, my name is Mike Hodgins." I tried to smile while I spoke. "As you can see by this butter bar on my collar, I am a second lieutenant. What you cannot see is that I have been a Marine for nearly six years. I enlisted in 1964. I am an Infantry officer by choice. Before I came here, I spent six months in the bush as a platoon commander in Hotel Two–Twenty-six, farther north. Since this is my first recon patrol, I intend to let Sergeant Domnoske show me the ropes. Any ropes you gents want to show me will also be appreciated, so long as they are not around my neck. Any questions?"

There were none, although there were a couple of smiles. Domnoske picked up in the awkward silence, ushering us all outside to practice IA drills on a short stretch of trail below the hootch. After twenty minutes of our half-hearted effort at fire and maneuver in response to his shouted warnings of "Contact Right!"; "Contact Front!"; "Contact Left!"; "Contact Rear!"; he secured the group with a last warning about staying sober and getting into the rack early. Reveille was to be at 0430. The team was to assemble by 0500 for chow. As if I would be able to eat any.

I spent the balance of the afternoon and early evening alone with my thoughts. I wrote a letter home to Joyce, another to my parents (saying nothing of my circumstances or the prospects for the next few days). I checked and rechecked my personal

equipment, test-fired my M-16 on the thousand-inch range below the HLZ, made another pass through the S-2 to pick up
last-minute tidbits. Finally, it was time for the evening meal
and movie at the SNCO and officers' club—*Sands of Iwo Jima*
and a skin flick. I felt very alone. In the midst of one of the in-
evitable broken-film-spool beer breaks, I became aware of a
dichotomy among the officers and staff NCOs gathered. Those
who were facing the prospect of combat were somehow remote from the rest. You could pick them out by their subdued
demeanor. Those who knew with certainty where they would
wake up were relaxed and gregarious—REMF Warriors knew
how to party!

Back in the hootch, I made myself rest, but sleep would not
come. My stomach churned. My mouth was cotton and alum
. . . my thirst unquenchable. The revelry of the REMF Warriors
drifted down the hill on a humid breeze. My fan hummed back
and forth, stirring putrid air. The occasional pop and flash of an
illumination round cast shadows on the walls. Over and over
again I dozed, then startled alert to look at the Day-Glo dial of
my Mickey Mouse watch. The hands never changed position.
Suddenly, the Duty NCO was shaking me awake. It was
0430—time to go back to war.

I roused myself, hustled through my morning routine,
shrugged into my war gear, and went out into the predawn
light. Others had done the same, and we converged on the
stairs leading down to the HLZ. I felt like a stranger among
them. Domnoske and the rest of the team had taken the Charlie Company shortcut, the same path we had used for our IA
drills. They had their gear staged in a corner of the Ready Shed
when I arrived. Lieutenant Lan stood a little apart from the others. I dropped my gear beside theirs on the deck and followed
them back up the stairs to chow, thinking that troops always
knew the easiest route to anywhere—and that I had more in
common with Lieutenant Lan than I did with the Marines tram-
pling up the stairs in front of us. This escapade was taking on
ominous characteristics. We were too many to hide, too few to
fight. We were going into an area known to be used by the

NVA and poorly covered by supporting arms. What else could be wrong?

While we were at chow, the helicopters arrived, almost with the sun. We moved back to the HLZ to await the aircrew briefing, which was conducted by Chip Gregson. He and the pilots huddled to decide the order of inserts and extracts. After an interminable time, the pilots broke from their huddle and headed back to their aircraft. Gregson shouted side numbers for the teams, and we saddled up to board the aircraft. Patty Shell was to be shunted off at An Hoa, to await the second round of inserts. It was a wrinkle I had not anticipated. The import of it was not lost, however. It meant that we would be inserted later in the day than originally planned. It meant that we would not be able to move as far from our insert HLZ. It meant that we would be in relative safety for a few more hours. That was the thought I fastened upon as we rode the grumbling CH-46 west.

An Hoa Combat Base turned out to be a sprawling complex of bunkers and barbed wire set on a low hill overlooking the Vu Gia River. Our experience of the place was confined to the shade of a communications bunker on the HLZ, where we staged our gear to await the return of our transportation. The troops spent the time grab-assing and joking with one another. Lieutenant Lan and I found spaces apart from them and took stress naps. As the morning wore on, the troops did the same. Morning turned into midafternoon with no sign of our helicopters. We sat in the sparse shade of the bunker, broiling in the midday Asian sun. Our radio operators had monitored the inserts and assured me that there had been no problems. Finally, we called back to Stone Pit (1st Recon) for a status report. The word was that our ride, the Jesters, had secured for chow. They would pick us up at 1400. Expecting the helicopters to appear any minute, we had used a day's ration of water already, and gone hungry ourselves.

When they finally did arrive (at 1400, 2:00 P.M.), I was so angry I didn't even notice the ride. From the time we boarded the aircraft to the gut-wrenching drop into our HLZ, less than fifteen minutes elapsed—and we were in the wrong place. The fact of our erroneous insert became apparent as we settled to earth. Over the objections of our insert officer, the pilot, a major, chose a nice barren spot on low ground some four hundred meters from where Domnoske had planned. The major selected a major trail junction, devoid of vegetation or cover—a great place to land a helicopter. When the crew chief let down the tailgate, we ran off, taking prone positions in a fan aft of the helicopter. Hannon got a positive comm check, and the bird lifted off. We had two hours until dark.

My first thought was to get to higher ground and cover. Domnoske had the same inspiration. With Burnsworth on point, we peeled back from our hasty defense, formed an Indian file, and jogged off the HLZ toward high ground to the southwest, i.e., our original plan. Once into the elephant grass, we sat down to listen. Domnoske got himself oriented, as did I. After ten minutes of silence, we moved off at a more measured pace, breaking brush as we moved up a finger toward the site we had selected as our first OP. We moved quietly, stepping laboriously through high grass and wait-a-minute vines, with frequent stops to listen. Within minutes, we were all soaked with sweat and breathing hard. The air beneath the undergrowth was stifling. It was grueling work. Each man became focused on his own next step; the world outside our little universe had ceased to exist. We moved in this stop-and-go manner for the better part of two hours, perhaps six hundred meters, up the finger in a generally northwesterly direction, until we came upon a jumble of rocks overlooking what the map told us was a major trail which ran parallel to a year-round stream. Domnoske called a halt and indicated with hand signals that this would be our harbor site for the night.

The idea suited me. It was tactically sound. We knew where we were. It was getting dark. We had a defensible position deep in brush where the NVA was not likely to look for us. If we had to flee, we had a natural landmark (the stream) to follow back to an area where a helicopter could pick us up—even one flown by the dummy who had put us in. And I was tired—out of bush shape after R & R and two weeks in the rear.

Domnoske and his troops flopped on the ground in a loose circle around the radios, leaving Lieutenant Lan and me to fend for ourselves. I motioned for him to take a spot nearby, our backs against a small boulder. Domnoske set the watch with hand signals, detailing Burnsworth and Corporal McBride to the first watch. Hannon called in a spot report, giving our position and intention to harbor for the night. I waited to see what other measures Domnoske might take. According to the map, we were within a hundred meters of a major trail leading down from Ba Na. I thought we should have more than organic weapons in our defense.

When the sergeant settled back against a rock to open his first can of Cs, I decided to assert myself, if only a little. I stood, weapon in hand, and moved quietly to his position. He looked up as I arrived, and I took a seat on the ground beside him. "Ski, who knows where we are besides you, me, and Hannon?" I whispered. Exasperation surfaced in his eyes. "Write our grid location and azimuth to the nearest HLZ on a message pad and give it to each man. And while you're at it, have them set out our claymores, one on our back trail, and one over there." I pointed to a tree about twenty meters away in the direction of the stream. Domnoske glared at me, slowly chewing cold beans and franks. I held his gaze. Finally, he set the can aside and followed my bidding. I went back to my rock.

Domnoske set the claymores himself, after stuffing a page from his message pad in each man's shirt pocket. The rest of us busied ourselves with our rations. I relaxed, somewhat more secure with the idea that we could now blow the ears off anyone on our trail and clear an escape route should the need arise. I watched Domnoske for a few minutes, trying to determine from his body language whether or not he had accepted the merit of my intrusion. In the fading light and shadows, he was unreadable.

Lieutenant Lan, on the other hand, was anxious to make a friend in the wilderness. What better way than to share meager provisions. He had freeze-dried rice, shrimp flakes, and *nuoc mam*. I had "Beef with Spiced Sauce," crackers, and peaches. We shared. The rice was a find, filling and tasty. I mixed it with the beef, and we ate from the rice bag. With hand signals and facial gestures, we carried on a conversation about the meal.

He was clearly pleased to have meat and fruit. They were not part of his usual fare. I was happy to have the rice, and the dried shrimp was okay—like eating fish food. The *nuoc mam*, a fermented fish sauce the Vietnamese use as a condiment, was more than I could take. Our meal consumed, we repacked our trash, sorted our gear for a quick start, and settled down for the night.

Fatigued though I was, sleep would not come. In the dark, every sound seemed amplified. The rustle of Marines and critters on the damp ground, the muffled squelch of the PRC-25, a metallic click now and again as one of the team moved a piece of equipment. They were sounds that would not carry far in heavy brush, but to my ears they were instant alarms. Too many to hide, too few to fight. The thought, like a childhood ditty, oscillated in my mind. As in the hootch the night before, the Day-Glo hands of my watch never moved. Finally, someone kicked my foot. I rolled onto one side and shook Lan awake. It was our turn on watch.

Dawn crept through the undergrowth, bringing with it new senses—sight and smell. With daylight came a different awareness, more energy. The team came to life around me, each man still wrapped in a cocoon of personal habits that were only slightly modified by his surroundings. Within minutes, we had consumed another light meal, reassembled our gear, recovered the claymores, and policed the harbor site. Domnoske took a compass heading, and we moved off in a generally northwesterly direction. In the best traditions of the Corps, we were moving to high ground. Our progress was slow as the undergrowth thickened, seemingly with each meter of elevation. The going was tough. Try as we might to avoid it, we were making noise and a trail. I hated both. In addition, all we could see was the back of the man in front of us. The enemy could be fifteen feet in any direction, and we were none the wiser. It was miserable work and poor tactics—dangerous even.

"Ski!" I whispered to get his attention. We were on a break, sweat soaked and filthy from fighting our way through the brush. "Let's hook a left, see if we intersect that trail and stream." Domnoske's original plan had been to walk a horseshoe up the finger we were on, crossing the stream/trail at its head, then move downhill for the last leg. At the rate we were traveling, we would spend another two days in the brush before we could determine whether or not the trail was being used. By dead reckoning, I believed we were far enough up the draw to take the risk of crossing the trail in daylight. We might even find a vantage point from which to observe a section of it. The prospect of humping blind for another two days did not appeal to me.

Domnoske must have had similar thoughts, because he acquiesced immediately. After the break, he pointed Burnsworth on the new heading, and we quickly found ourselves on the edge of a forty-foot cliff. At the bottom of the drop, the trail and the stream bed were clearly visible through the trees. In the vernacular of the Basic School, we were confronted at once with an obstacle and a danger area. We sat in a hasty ambush while Domnoske and I pondered the problem. Someone had to descend to the bottom of the drop and determine whether it was safe to cross. What now, Lieutenant?

Domnoske was looking at me speculatively. With an inward sigh, I rose to my feet, tapped Burnsworth on the shoulder, and moved to the edge. I signaled Domnoske to cover us, then began a careful descent, working my way down hand over hand. The rocks were slick with moss. It was treacherous going. Burnsworth followed with the M-79 grenade launcher. I imagined myself doing a "slide for life" right into an NVA patrol. But the God of Fools was looking out for us.

At the bottom, I moved upstream, weapon at the ready, for about twenty meters. The trail was hard packed, but showed no signs of recent use. The stream ran clear and cold, no mud, fishnets, or laundry to indicate recent use by humans. I did an about-face and nearly knocked Burnsworth off his feet. He had followed. We grinned foolishly at one another as we moved back to where the rest of the team waited. Once abreast of their position, I stared skyward, looking for Domnoske. He peered over the edge, and we made eye contact. I signaled for two men to join us. He waved his understanding. Burnsworth and I took cover facing in opposite directions, he downstream, I upstream. Within seconds, Hannon and Lieutenant Lan joined us. I motioned for Lan to take my place and for Hannon to follow me with the radio. His eyes said he thought I was crazy, but he followed as I made to cross the stream. We waded across without incident, fighting the urge to dash for cover on the other side. The coast was clear. I signaled the fact to Burnsworth, who passed the word to Domnoske on the cliff above. Within minutes, the whole team had crossed and reassembled on my side. We moved quickly up a steep slope, perhaps a hundred meters, before setting in to a hasty ambush in another jumble of rocks. Domnoske and Burnsworth set claymores on our back trail without a word. The composition of the team had changed— Lieutenant Lan and I were now part of it.

We spent an uneventful night on the finger, then moved laboriously to higher ground the following day. "Higher ground" turned out to be an old, company-size observation post atop an inconspicuous Hill 142. We approached the position with great caution, aware of the possibility of leftovers—booby traps set by friendly troops when they abandoned the position. We found none. We deduced that the position had been occupied by ARVNs, well-provisioned ARVNs at that. They had expended no fewer than fifty 60mm mortar illumination rounds and consumed several cases of *Ba Muoi Ba* ("33," a brand of Vietnamese beer). Using binoculars, we scanned the surrounding terrain for the better part of the day, taking turns on watch. Delivery Boy's base camp was abandoned, which delighted me. We called in a spot report to that effect. Against my better judgment, we decided to spend the night on the position. My decision was based upon a trade-off between the advantage of occupying a fortified HLZ with good observation in all directions and the possibility of having been compromised by moving around in the open. In the end, we flipped a coin.

On the morning of the fourth day, we were out of water. I

cursed the air-wing mentality, pilots in general, and ours in particular for leaving us to roast at An Hoa. That and three days of serious humping in heavy brush had defeated our attempts to ration our water. We were now faced with the unpleasant prospect of replenishing our water from the stream at the foot of the hill. It was unpleasant for two reasons: first, it was dangerous; second, halazone tasted like shit. Going without was worse, so we resolved to move as cautiously as possible down the finger in a generally southeasterly direction until we intersected the stream and trail again. It took the morning, five hours, to move the klick (one thousand meters) to the stream. Once there, we set flank security while Lieutenant Lan filled our canteens. He was a clever lad, stringing several canteens on his belt, the lids off, and dunking the whole string in a pool. He stayed in cover the whole time.

I watched as each man dropped halazone tablets, two each, into his canteen. The temptation to guzzle water was powerful. I splashed some over my face and soaked a towel as we crossed the stream—if I couldn't drink it, at least I could cool off. We set a hasty ambush on the south side of the stream, above the trail. Having given our halazone time to work, we tanked up and moved east, above and parallel to the stream and trail recorded on our map. The brush was more sparse, and movement down a slight incline was easy. We made another fifteen hundred meters before dark and found a harbor site in a draw. We were three hundred meters from our extract HLZ and far enough off the trail not to attract unwarranted attention. Hannon called in our spot report and the shackled (coded) coordinates of our proposed extract HLZ. The claymores were set again, this time to cover the mouth of the draw in which we had found shelter. Domnoske had led us into the brush in a fishhook, leaving no trail to point directly at us. Without preamble, we settled in for the night.

I slept fitfully through the night, waking at the slightest sound that was out of context in the jungle. When Hannon finally shook me awake for my shift on watch, I was sweat-soaked and feverish. Whether from bad water or nerves, I was sick—and getting sicker by the moment. I felt my strength ebb with the darkness. The radio came alive, too loud for my ears.

"Patty Shell, Patty Shell, this is Stone Pit. Over!"

"Stone Pit, this is Patty Shell. Over." I whispered, shielding the handset with a cupped hand. Around me, the team was coming alert.

"Patty Shell, this is Stone Pit. You are number four in the lineup. ETA I set Alpha Tango, I shackle Zulu, Tango, Sierra, Oscar, how copy? Over."

I confirmed the transmission, jotting the letters on my map with a grease pencil, then handed the map to Hannon, indicating with hand signals that he should decode it. I slumped back against a rock, feeling nauseous and dizzy. Hannon showed me the decoded letters—0930. We had three hours to wait. I began to shake.

"Patty Shell, this is Scarface Three-Six, inbound. How about a brief? Over." The clatter of the Cobra gunships' rotors reverberated overhead as they cleared the crest of the ridge behind us and began to orbit. Behind them, and at higher altitude, the trucks (CH-46s) circled in the sun. I looked at my watch with difficulty. Everything was blurry. My arms weighed ten thousand pounds. It was 1115. They were late. I struggled into my war gear. Lan gave my pack a shove to get me upright. I was too weak to help myself. Domnoske made eye contact across the intervening space. He realized that something was wrong.

Domnoske gave the brief while the rest of the team struggled into their gear. Burnsworth and McBride recovered the claymores, then remained in position at the mouth of the draw as security while the rest of us filed past. I found myself stumbling over the uneven ground in trace of Domnoske and Hannon. Hicks, Lan, O'Farrell, and the others brought up the rear. We moved cautiously into the open area, Domnoske in constant radio contact with Scarface. The last thing we wanted to do was get hosed down by our own gunships. Finally, we stopped in elephant grass, clear sky overhead. At Domnoske's signal, Burnsworth flipped a smoke grenade into the clearing. Weapons at the ready, we all crouched as it burst and billowed into the air.

"Patty Shell, this is Scarface Three Six. Tallyho, yellow smoke! Over."

"Scarface, this is Patty Shell. Confirm yellow smoke. Out."

One of the CH-46s suddenly dropped out of its orbit and plunged earthward in a tight spiral. The aircraft flared over our heads, the downdraft of its rotors blowing brush and debris in all directions. As the tailgate came down, we rose from the ground in unison and dashed for the bird. I could not, and fell behind the others, on the verge of delirium. Domnoske, watching from a position at the rear of the aircraft, came back to help. So did Lan. Together, they lifted me between them and dashed aboard. The last friendly face I saw was Stumpy Baker's, reaching out to help lift me to a seat. It was Friday, the thirteenth of March.

I came to my senses between clean sheets. A corpsman was taking my pulse. When I looked at him, he spoke. "Welcome back, Lieutenant. We thought we had lost you for a day or two." He smiled.

"Where am I? What day is this?" I tried to sit up, but fell back against the pillow.

"Well, sir. You are in Charlie Med. This is Tuesday, March 17. You have had a bout with FUO [fever of unknown origin]. When they brought you in, you had a temperature of one-hundred-six. Another hour or two of that would have made you a vegetable. We've been giving you ice baths for three days. Hungry?"

I nodded my head, too weak to speak. He went off and returned with soup and juice, which he fed to me with a spoon. I slept.

I graduated from soup and juice to Jell-O over the course of the next twenty-four hours. My fever abated, but I was weak and skinny. I had lost more than twenty pounds in a few days and weighed only 129 pounds in shower shoes. I learned this on my first walk down the aisle of the ward. There was a scale at one end, near the duty station. In Hawaii,

I had weighed just over 160—only a month before. It was a depressing thought upon which I dwelled for several hours.

My reverie was interrupted by the arrival of the irrepressible Stump, with my friend Mike Curry in tow. Curry was skinny, too. They brought my mail, some smokes, and sodas. It was a short visit, full of news. Polster was back, unscathed. His escapade had ended in disaster, a failure in the sense that the remains of Captain McVey and Lieutenant Skibbe had not been recovered. Several Marines (aircrew) had been killed, and a slew of CIDGs had been wounded. All this had taken place within a few klicks of our observation post, so there was now a push to beef up our defenses. The rumors had been true. We had a full plate operationally. Second Platoon was on the OP. Curry was fragged for the Que Sons, the rest of his platoon to other patrols, and Tom Hodge had the Third Platoon in training for a week. Wild Bill was driving people crazy in the rear, firing lieutenants left and right. The tempo of patrol operations was increasing, with an emphasis on Stingray patrols. Drumright wanted the teams to get out and "mix it up" with the NVA in their own backyard. Curry thought he was crazy. So did Baker. They left after twenty minutes or so.

After seeing Curry and Baker, I felt guilty and depressed. I resolved to get myself back in the bush as quickly as possible. Curry had said he would be out for six days, from the eighteenth to the twenty-second. I wanted to be back in the company and fit for duty when he got back. I read my mail, ate some soup and Jell-O, and mulled my situation. I needed to get moving to get fit. That night, I started pacing the aisle between the racks, doing push-ups (one at a time) and deep knee bends on the deck beside my bed. I had to be careful with these activities, sneaking them in between the corpsman's rounds. By the twenty-first, I was strong enough to con the duty physician into approving my release. Then I got on the field phones and called Stumpy to come get me. He showed up that afternoon in the company jeep with clean utilities, boots, a side arm, and a cold beer for me. While I changed from hospital garb to the clean uniform, Baker brought me up to date on the war. It had been raining off and on for the past week. The weather was causing problems for the teams in the mountains. Jim Duda was socked in on 425, Tom Hodge was in training with the 3d Platoon, Curry and Chet Pino (whom I had not yet met) were due back in the afternoon, weather permitting. Polster was doing his XO thing.

It was a short ride back to the battalion area. On the way, Baker plied me with stories about Wild Bill and the REMFs. He and the other company commanders had become charter members of Wild Bill's Breakfast Club. Within minutes, Baker had me teary-eyed with laughter, having regaled me with anecdotes from the daily meetings. According to the Stump, there was no shortage of "very red asses" in the battalion area. Drumright had made a rogue's gallery of service photographs of all his officers and staff NCOs on a wall in his hootch. He marked each with an *X* across the face when he "fell from grace." There had been lots of *X*s in the past few weeks. Baker conceded that he was glad to have me back, but said he was concerned that I might not be fit for the bush. I assured him that I was. Our ride lasted only a few minutes. As we made the turn in front of the concrete pagoda that marked the entrance to our compound, I resolved to make the most of this fresh start.

The Stump had to turn in the jeep, so I jumped out and tried my land legs on the slope back to the company area. I broke a sweat, but decided I was feeling stronger. I took an unobtrusive stroll through the Charlie Company compound, taking in the sights and sounds. Shitbird-the-Dog was asleep on the porch of the company office. He lifted his head and wagged a curly tail as I climbed the steps. He looked fatter than I remembered. The troops were in the pool. Janis Joplin blared from a tape deck in their rec hootch ". . . Take another little piece of my heart now, Baby . . ." It was Sunday, holiday routine. I suddenly felt tired and homesick. It was a song Joyce often sang. The thought of her came in stark contrast to my surroundings. I had not written since before the patrol.

I stood for a moment, lost in thoughts of home, emotion clutching at my throat. There was nothing to do here. I was an orphan, abandoned like the scruffy dog on the step. With a physical effort, I collected myself and teased the dog into following me back to the officers' hootch. The walk had me breathing hard by the time we arrived. Inside, nothing had changed. Someone, Baker probably, had recovered my war gear. It was all cleaned up and hung on its nail over my rack. My rifle had also been cleaned and hung on its pegs. I smiled at his thoughtfulness and was about to stretch out on the rack when I heard the distinctive clatter of CH-46s approaching overhead. Teams were coming in. I decided to take the nap anyway. I was awakened by a commotion on the steps of the hootch as Curry and another lieutenant scrambled through the door. Shitbird dashed to meet them, his tail awag. They stank; six days in the bush had ripened them. I stood up to introduce myself while they struggled out of soggy war gear.

Curry was first to speak. "Hey, Mike! Welcome back. Are you back to full duty? This is Chester Pino. He runs Second Platoon. Say 'How!' Chief."

Pino stepped over his pile of equipment, extending a hand, a broad grin on his face. "Welcome aboard, Mike. My name is Chet Pino, but most guys call me Chief."

Curry and Pino wasted no time getting out of their filthy uniforms, soggy boots, and paraphernalia. They dumped the lot on the deck and made for the showers. I went back to my nap. There would be time to catch up and get acquainted when everyone was clean and rested. The odor of their rancid uniforms radiated about the hootch. My last conscious thought, as sleep overtook me, was to hope that they would make a trip to the laundry before they secured for the day. Curry and Pino returned from the shower in a boisterous mood, hollering for mamma-san as they reentered the hootch. An elderly Vietnamese woman appeared like a wraith, her face lit in a toothless grin, scooped up the filthy clothing, boots, and web gear, and departed as she had come. The mystery of my pristine equipment and living space was solved.

Curry and Pino were carrying on a lively conversation about their experiences of the past few days. They were energized by their flirtation with danger. Pino had the trump suite in war stories, for his team had had a chance encounter with three NVA soldiers who were fishing with hand grenades at the bend of a river. They had killed them all and captured a pistol and some documents. Curry had a close call when an NVA soldier walked through their harbor site in the dark. I listened as they bantered back and forth. The idea half formed in my mind that all these Charlie Company contacts had something in common. It was an unfinished thought, left in my subconscious when Curry banged on the partition between us.

"Come on, Mike! Let's go to chow."

We went to chow at the battalion staff and officers' club, where we were joined by Polster and Baker. I ate lightly, listening without comment as my peers discussed matters of import over beer and Scotch. Pino was the center of attention for a period of time as word of his escapade made its way through the club. Bush lore became the topic of conversation, with lieutenants from other companies stopping at the table to participate in the debate. The conversation was grist for my tactical mill. I assessed the participants and their contributions with a professional detachment. There were clearly schools of thought among the officers gathered. Some, the college jocks, were outwardly gung ho and contemptuous of their adversary. Convinced of their personal invincibility, they seemed to view patrolling as an opportunity for self-aggrandizement. Others, Tom Hodge and Charlie Kershaw among them, were more deliberative. They seemed to feel a responsibility to preserve the lives of their fellow Marines. I put myself in that camp. War was no football game.

With the consumption of two-bit beers and thirty-cent shooters, the debate became more animated. Baker, a charismatic man, a prankster, and a musician, took it upon himself to "lighten up" the gathering. He seized a tired guitar from under the bar, leapt upon the stage, and broke into song, "You ain't nothin' but a hound dog . . ." Before long, he had assembled "Stumpy Baker's Magic Show and Jug Band" on-stage and an ad hoc committee of critics at the tables below. It was a group with a reputation, I soon deduced. They were infamous for singing bad songs out of tune. In the midst of this revelry, Wild Bill crashed through the door.

There was a long pause, as if time had stopped. Baker was in mid-chorus. Drumright surged into the room, straight to the bar. All eyes followed his progress. "Bartender, gimme Scotch! You! Peckerwood! Keep singin'!"

Drumright, a shot glass in one hand, a bottle of Cutty Sark in the other, shouldered his way through the crowd to a table in the center, where he kicked back a chair and estab-lished court. Within minutes, a bevy of REMF Warriors sur-rounded him. The debate on mission tactics, equipment, and results resumed with greater enthusiasm. "Oorahs!" and other traditional Marine barnyard sounds reverberated from the walls. Tales of glory and Valhalla were shouted into the night. Chief Pino was toasted under the table. The party was still lively when I left. Fever of Unknown Origin was not likely to get me the kind of attention among my peers that a gunshot wound would, but it was no less debilitating. I made my way back to the hootch and collapsed on my rack, exhausted.

I awoke feeling stronger. Curry and Pino were dead to the world, and Baker had already departed to the Breakfast Club. Polster and I hit the shower and the shaving rack about the same time. He was sullen, and I decided he was not a morning person. I made my way to breakfast alone. Inside the mess hall I watched the Breakfast Club while I waited in line for eggs and toast. The colonel was working over his staff and commanders with strong words about the need to insure that their Marines were properly cared for. By the time I finished my breakfast, his meeting had adjourned. I caught up with Baker, and we walked up the hill to the Char-lie Company together. He was morose.

"So, Stump, what's the buzz? You guys look like you were having nothing but grins with the colonel."

"Mike, you are so right! We have a new SOP—wherever

possible, patrols will be led by an officer. All the enlisted patrol leaders are being reviewed and recertified before they can lead patrols again. And, we got a new training schedule. Polster is going to love that. And, we got a memorial service for Skibbe and McVey, all available hands, on the twenty-sixth. And, we are going to have our company area inspected by the XO. And—" he held up a sheaf of papers "—we got fragged for three patrols. So you and Curry and Pino are going back out on the twenty-ninth. When those guys get up to the company area, you can pick out of my hat. I ain't playing God no more."

He strode off toward the company office, leaving me standing on the bridge. I was stunned by his outburst. It was suddenly clear to me that the Stump was feeling incredible stress from his newly acquired responsibilities as company commander. My stint in the hospital had put me out of touch with developments within the battalion. I was still, in relative terms, a new guy. Baker was an old hand. He had close, personal ties to the other lieutenants and to some of the enlisted Marines in the company. He was troubled by the increased operational tempo and the dangers inherent in it. For the first time in his young life, he was required to make decisions that had a direct, and perhaps fatal, effect on his friends. I resolved to do my part to ease his stress. If that meant acquiescing to games of chance to determine my next mission, so be it. It was probably as fair as any other procedure we might have devised. With that thought in mind, I made my way up the hill to the company office.

Outside the office, I decided to take a smoke, giving Baker a chance to collect his thoughts. Curry and Pino had trailed us from the mess hall by only a few minutes. When they arrived, we went inside together. Baker and Polster were arguing as we forged into the office. Red-faced, the Stump stood in front of the situation map. Polster was at his desk. When we came in, he fell silent, his head down, while Baker turned to confront us. He was as good as his word.

Tom Hodge and the Third Platoon were scheduled to complete training, then flip with Jim Duda's Second Platoon on 425. Third Herd would be brought back from Monkey Mountain to be our contingent for the memorial service. That left Curry's First Platoon, augmented by the lieutenants and our ARVN or ROK (Korean) Marines to carry out the patrol commitment. Baker wrote the call signs for the three patrols on paper from his notebook, folded them up and put them in his cover, then offered the upturned hat to each of us in turn. Curry drew first, "Offspring." I was second, "Defend." Pino was last, "Thin Man." We moved to the situation map, where Baker briefed each mission. Curry was going to the Que Sons. Pino was going to Nong Song. I was going to Elephant Valley, at the northernmost edge of the division TAOR.

CHAPTER THREE
WARRIOR AT LARGE

23 MARCH–3 APRIL 1970

*In doing what we ought, we deserve no praise, because
it is our duty.*

St. Augustine, A.D. 354–430

Since we were all to be provisional, Curry made the team assignments based upon what he knew about his men. The ARVNs were going to be potluck, the two living with us and four coming out of the RIP (Recon Indoctrination Program). The lineup for Defend turned out to be a Corporal Brasington, assistant patrol leader (APL); Lance Corporal Jaqua, radiotelephone operator (RTO); Lance Corporal Vaughn; Lieutenant Chi; Lance Corporal Cortez, point man, and Warrant Officer Thanh, both ARVN Rangers; and Watash ("me," from the Japanese). Our haven was a six-klick area bisected by a river, the Bac, with high ground all around. It encompassed a pass, through which an all-weather road ran generally east to west. According to the map, the terrain cover was sparse in the low ground, probably elephant grass, and steep on the rim, with high canopy. To hump or to peep? That was the question. Considering my physical condition, I thought peeping would be a good idea, but I didn't see how. A visual reconnaissance (VR) was in order. Our meeting was breaking up, and my ruminations were interrupted.

"Okay, Mike. I'll have Corporal Brasington report to you

here, after I give them their warning order . . . say sixteen-hundred?" Curry was talking to me, while making notes in his pocket notebook.

"Sure. I'm going down to the Three Shop [Operations] to see about a VR. I'll plan to be back here by then." I stood, settled my cover on my head, and made to leave. The others, save Baker, followed my lead. Curry went up to his platoon's area. Pino and I made our way across the bridge and down the road to the S-3 in silence. I was turning over various aspects of the upcoming patrol in my mind, lessons learned from my first patrol, and bush lore that I had picked up while listening to the other lieutenants talk about their patrols in the mess and in the club. I was beginning to form my own SOP, incorporating my own convictions and experience into the system. I still had no troops of my own, but I was clearly going to have the responsibility. With that thought in mind, I followed Pino into the S-2/3 complex.

Pino and I parted company on the gravel landing in front of the COC bunker, he to the S-2 for background information on his new patrol area and I to the S-3 in search of our air liaison officer (ALO). I found my man, Lt. Rick Rasmussen, hard at work plotting inserts and extracts on the situation map in the combat operations center. It was a transportation problem of some complexity, as he had to determine what order would be most time and fuel efficient for his aircraft. I watched silently for a few minutes while he wrote date/time groups and call signs on a roster. Finally aware of my presence, he looked at me and spoke.

"Say, Mike. What brings you down here this time of day—not to complain about my singing, I hope."

I laughed. "No, although you guys did set the dogs to howling last night. I just want to hitch a ride on the insert tomorrow—get a VR on my next patrol."

"No sweat. Where are you going?" As he spoke, he turned back to the map. I joined him.

"Elephant Valley, out here on the west end." I pointed to the haven.

"How many packs [people] do you want to take?" He was making notes on a clipboard.

"Three—Me, my APL, and my point man." He made a note.

"Okay. Be down at the HLZ for the pilot brief at oh-six-thirty. I'll need your zap numbers before you board the air-craft. You may be gone a while because we have four teams to flip up there. Okay?"

"Thanks, Rick."

Rasmussen's body language said he had things to do, so I made tracks—to the S-2. Now familiar with the routine, I drew my maps, pulled recent reports from teams in the area, got a Coke from the fridge, and went out the back to do my homework. Pino and several others were already ensconced in the available seats, so I found a spot on the ground, my back against the wall of the hootch. Paging through the op-erational summaries, I deduced that there had not been a team in the vicinity of my assigned haven for nearly a year. There was no recent information to help me formulate a game plan. I decided to concentrate on the map and what I knew about NVA habits. I looked at my watch, 1545. It was time to meet my troops.

I returned the intel excerpts and made my way back to the Charlie Company office. True to his word, Curry had as-sembled his team leaders outside. As I approached, he sepa-rated himself from the group, a tall, wide-shouldered corporal in tow.

"Lieutenant Hodgins, this is Corporal Brasington. He is the new team leader of my second team." As he spoke, Curry turned to invite Brasington to step forward. Brasington gave me a less than crisp salute, his eyes guarded. "Sir," was all he said, but his body language spoke volumes. New lieu-tenants were about as popular with troops as prickly heat.

I returned his salute, and spoke to Curry. "Thanks Mike. Pino is still at the Two Shop. He should be up here pretty soon." I turned to face the NCO. "Corporal Brasington, let's go find some shade and get better acquainted."

I moved off in the direction of the rec hootch and training tank (the pool). We found seats under the awning. I handed him a set of maps, the frag order, and some MPC. "See if they've got a spare soda or two in there. I buy, you fly?" I held his gaze for a second. He was still guarded.

"Aye, aye, sir." He went inside, came back out with a pair of Cokes and a church key. We commenced our get-acquainted chat.

"So, Corporal Brasington, how long have you been here?" I kept my voice low key, friendly.

"Since the beginning of November, sir." He was giving nothing away.

"And when did you make corporal?"

"March first, sir. And that is when I took over Second Team."

His attitude became a little defensive. I wanted him to feel at ease. "So, you made rank with time in grade?"

"Yes, sir."

"What's your MOS [Military Occupational Specialty]?"

"Oh three forty-one, sir—mortarman." He took a swig from his Coke, his eyes on me.

"You're a long way from any mortar platoon I know of . . ." I let the question rest, unspoken.

"Yes, sir. Back at Camp Pendleton I got acquainted with some Recon guys doing land-navigation training. It seemed like they got to call more of their own shots instead of having to sit around waiting for things to happen. So, when they asked for volunteers at the processing center, I raised my hand."

"And?"

"And it beats humping a fuckin' baseplate up and down these mountains." He took a long pull on his Coke, relaxing somewhat.

"How many patrols have you been on, Corporal?"

"This will be my fourth, sir—my second since I made rank—not counting the OP. Lieutenant Curry and I were up there for a long time on account of the weather and getting the platoon back in shape after the old lieutenant got killed. Charlie Company has gone through a lot of lieutenants in the last six months . . ." He let the words hang in the air between us, watching for my reaction.

"So I've heard, Corporal. And there'll be more before this war is over, I'm sure." I kept my eyes steady, but he had struck a nerve. "Tell me about our team."

"Well, sir, Lieutenant Curry split up *my* team for this trip. We got Lance Corporal Jaqua for RTO. He's real squared away, but getting short. Then we got Lance Corporal Vaughn for aidman and Lance Corporal Cortez for point man. They are both new, like December. Lieutenant Curry said we would have two ARVNs, so we don't have room for a corpsman—I have to tell you, sir, the guys are not keen about that. And neither am I." He paused for effect.

"Okay." I ignored his challenge. We were going to go with the ARVNs. There was no point in debating the order. "Here is a map and a copy of the frag order. I made arrangements for a VR tomorrow morning. You, me, and the point man. When can I give the warning order?" I took a pull on my Coke.

"I did that already, sir. Everybody in the team has a job."

"Oh?"

"Yes, sir. For this patrol, Jaqua is RTO, so he is responsible for drawing all our comm gear, checking it out, signing for shackle sheets, whiz wheels, and shit. Cortez and Vaughn will draw our chow and ammo. Vaughn gets to hump the Unit One [medical supply bag], on account of the ARVNs. He'll draw our Thorazine, saline solution, itch pills, and stuff. I'm humping the blooper [M-79 grenade launcher]—it's the closest thing to a mortar that we can take to the bush!" He laughed, but his eyes were serious. "The ARVNs are on their own, although I do think they should do the immediate-action drills with us . . ." His voice trailed off, waiting for my response.

"You do good work, Corporal Brasington. Take a look at the map and our haven. Tell me how you see us working that area." As I spoke, I smoothed my map on the table. I intended to do my field-expedient waterproofing job later in the day. For the time being, I had to deal with the cumbersome map sheet as issued. With difficulty, I folded the map sheet so that the area of interest was in the center. Brasington followed suit. We studied the map in silence for several minutes, he to familiarize himself with the area, I to confirm my prior impressions.

"I see why you wanted the VR, Lieutenant. This does not look like an area where we will have many HLZs, especially in the west end. We should work the ridge in the middle. Maybe we could OP up there, watch the road. The river could be a bitch to cross . . ." His voice trailed off. He was still thinking.

"I was thinking we would go in at the east end, near the river, then hump up to this ridge, see what we can see. We should cut that trail at least once, to see if it is being used. I am not a big fan of walking on trails, Corporal Brasington. You can tell that to the team. We will try to use the terrain to our advantage."

He nodded his head in agreement. I stood up, folding the map as I did. "Okay. See you at oh-six-thirty. After the VR, we'll know more. Meet me at the HLZ, and bring the patrol roster with you. Okay?"

"Aye, aye, sir."

We split up. Brasington went to brief his people on "the new lieutenant," while I went to arrange for fire support. I knew that the battalion would have something going for the insert. What I wanted was a list of targets along my proposed route of march. Thinking about this, and other things, I made my way back to my hootch. Once inside, I settled down to work on my map. Thus engrossed, I passed the balance of the afternoon. Curry and Pino came and went, doing similar things. Polster appeared, grousing about training schedules and other "chickenshit," then left for chow. I continued my mental preparations, committing key terrain features to memory, as well as probable compass headings from point to point. I wanted to be able to use my time in the air over the haven to maximum advantage. I drew up an equipment list, a target list, and made notes about immediate-action drills and other things, drawing upon my Basic School training and practical experience from the Grunts. Six months running combat patrols in the mountains of Quang Tri had imposed a certain tactical discipline upon me. I knew what worked, what didn't.

My plans complete, I wrote a letter to Joyce, made myself a mocha and read Louis L'Amour until my eyelids were heavy.

The night passed uneventfully. I awoke to the voice of the Duty NCO. It was time to go to war. The VR was also uneventful, unless one counted fighting airsickness. Our pilot only knew how to fly in circles, lifting and falling hundreds of feet in altitude with each turn. By the time we arrived over what the insert officer identified as my haven, I was thoroughly disoriented and ready to puke. Brasington and Cortez were no better off. The pilot, after dropping a team farther east, had followed the Yellow Brick Road up the valley, changing direction and altitude at random intervals. He was either drunk or tactically paranoid. I was just sick to my stomach.

Peering out the door gunner's hatch, I identified the dogbone-shaped hill that marked the southeast corner of our haven. It was covered with elephant grass and heavy brush, as was the "meadow" into which we expected to be inserted. The terrain to the immediate north of the meadow was so steep and thickly vegetated as to be impassable, although the map indicated several trails leading down from high ground to the valley floor. The river was wide and slow moving in this area. The road was overgrown, showing no signs of use, at least by vehicles. The whole area was pockmarked by bomb craters and shell holes—H & I fires,* most likely. Many were fresh. I made a mental note to be careful of unexploded rounds.

The pilot made a high orbit over the area, then headed for Da Nang—in a straight line. I decided it must be time for

---

*"Harassment and Interdiction," artillery rounds fired into likely areas of enemy concentration or infiltration.

lunch. Sure enough, my Mickey Mouse watch said 1145. Back at HLZ 401, Brasington and I made plans to talk after chow. It was now clear that we had a "hump" to contend with. We agreed to meet at the team hootch after chow. My intention was to brief the team on what we could expect to do in the field, now that I had eyeballed the playground, and to establish my own SOPs for movement, equipment, and assorted other ideas that had come to me in the hospital. Water discipline was high on the list.

Thus distracted, I found myself in line at the mess—confronted with the choice of "cold cock" or peanut butter, with Kool-Aid or milk. I chose peanut butter and milk, made quick work of it, and went back to my hootch. Time to make some field-expedient training aids and take a nap. Inside, I turned on my fan, finished my notes, and located a sleeve from one of our C-rat cases—my chalkboard. Thus prepared, I slept for the better part of an hour. At 1400 (2:00 P.M.), I gathered up my training aids and made my way back to the company area.

"Garza's Guerrilla's" (as Second Platoon was called) were billeted in two hootches in the center of the company area. I found Brasington and the team, including the ARVNs, gathered in the shade of one of the billets. They had weapons on hand, but no gear. They came to their feet as I approached.

"Good afternoon, sir." Brasington rendered a hand salute, which I returned. Behind him, legs dangling off the roof of the bunker, the team slouched in waiting.

"It's customary to call your detail to attention before you do that, Corporal, even for second lieutenants."

"Yes sir." His freckled face flushed with anger. He turned to face the team. "Team, atten*hut*!"

They stared in disbelief, then grudgingly slipped off the sandbags to the ground and came to the position, weapons alongside their legs. Brasington turned about and rendered another salute. "At ease, gents. Let's move down to the rec hootch."

Sullen eyes stared at me. It was bad enough that they had to go out with a "boot" lieutenant, worse that he was a lifer—a chickenshit lifer at that. I led the way. When I had them gathered in the shade, I started my spiel.

"Gents, I understand that you may have some reservations about me, about the mission, about the composition of the team. This is the time to set those things aside." I made eye contact with each man.

"Tomorrow morning we are going to Elephant Valley for a six-day patrol. According to the Two Shop, no team has been that far west for over a year. The area we are going to walk is heavy vegetation, mostly elephant grass, bounded by a river and bisected by several streams. According to the map, there are several major trails in the area, as well as a road. We are going to avoid those things, to the extent possible. That means we will break brush most of the time. I have some strongly held views on actions in movement, in the harbor sites, immediate action on contact, and equipment. Let's take them one at a time."

I moved my gaze from man to man. They were paying attention, but only just. Jaqua and Brasington were resolute. The ARVNs were having trouble with the language. Vaughn and Cortez were morose. I continued.

"Okay. First, equipment. For this patrol, regardless of what you may have done in the past or may do in the future, each of you will carry the standard load itemized on this list." I gave the list to Brasington.

"There will be an informal equipment inspection at eighteen-thirty. I expect you to have the items on that list in your possession at that time, except for ammo. After I look at your gear, we will practice IA drills—actions at danger areas and actions in the harbor site." I paused for effect, then continued, "From this point until the patrol is over, we will operate in pairs. Cortez, you and Warrant Officer Thanh are a pair. Vaughn, you and Jaqua are a pair. Corporal Brasington, you and Lieutenant Chi are a pair. You also get to look out for me." I looked again, from man to man. There were quizzical looks.

"When we are in movement, we will move in pairs, with at least fifteen feet between us. We will use a staggered column where we can—no Indian files. No more than two men will move at a time, leapfrogging one another in the line of movement. The others will cover their movement and watch for signs of the enemy. Any thoughts on why I want you to do this?"

I stared at Vaughn until he answered.

"No fuckin' idea . . . , sir."

"Best of all possible reasons, Vaughn—it's safer. Four guns cover two in movement. Four pairs of eyes watch the terrain while two watch the trail. It's quiet. Any questions about that?"

They shook their heads.

"Okay. Actions on contact. Corporal Brasington, in your experience, what is the most common occurrence of contact with the enemy?"

Brasington's eyes were level, his voice soft as he answered, "Depends on the terrain, sir."

"Very true, Corporal. And the enemy probably knows the terrain better than we do, since they live there. So, what is the best way to respond to a contact, or an ambush? Assault, defend, or withdraw?" I looked from man to man, searching for a response. They were silent.

"The answer is to break contact and withdraw to a defensible position of our own choosing. The maneuver which we will use to accomplish this in most circumstances is called the Australian Peel. Raise your hand if you are familiar with this maneuver." No hands were raised. "Okay, what have you been doing?"

"Well, sir, we have been taught to assault through the ambush, sir. Like, if the fire is from the left you assault left, to get out of the killing zone. If it's right, you go right. For point-to-point, we just shoot and move back the way we came."

Vaughn was talking, asserting himself. I picked up my C-ration sleeve and my grease pencil and drew a big arrow down the middle of the box.

"Gents, this arrow represents our line of march." I drew circles representing the staggered column formation of the seven men in our patrol. "The circles represent each of us. This is just like football. We draw up the plays, we practice the plays, we run the plays in the game if the situation arises. You with me so far?" I looked at each man to insure I had his undivided attention. Then I continued, "Okay, the first situation is the point-to-point contact. In that situation, point man and the deuce point lay down suppressing fire to the front and withdraw down the middle of the column, all the way past tail-end Charlie, and take covering positions on the back trail. The other members of the patrol do the same, firing only as necessary to cover the withdrawal of their partner. Notice that we are moving inside our defensive fires and back in the direction in which we came, which is the safest ground in the area. We move in this manner until the patrol leader determines that it is safe to take some other evasive action."

As I spoke I drew arrows on each man showing the team what they were supposed to do.

"Any questions about point-to-point contact?"

There were none. Even the Vietnamese were all eyes. I turned my cardboard easel over, quickly sketched my arrow and player symbols on the clean side.

"Okay, the most unpleasant contact is contact from the flanks because contact from the flanks usually means an ambush, or just as bad, that we have walked into a prepared position, such as a bunker. The squad doctrine that you gents have been taught is based on the idea or principle of shock and fire superiority, and the idea that the squad is operating as a part of a larger unit. Recon teams, as a matter of principle, should not assault their way out of ambushes. Rather, we should attempt to gain fire superiority, then maneuver out of the kill zone by withdrawing in the safest direction possible. In most cases that will be back down the line of march upon which you traveled prior to the contact." I focused their attention back on the cardboard easel. "Look at this diagram." Six pairs of eyes focused on the cardboard box.

"Is it not true that this formation provides maximum firepower to both flanks? Is it not true that this formation provides maneuver lanes for men on either side of the column to withdraw from contact without masking the fire of the other team members?" I looked at each man to assure myself that the point was being made.

"Is it not also true that, if you maintain your dispersion in this formation, it is hard as hell for more than one or two guys to get caught in a field of fire at one time?" I looked again from man to man to ascertain whether or not they concurred with my assessment. There were quizzical looks on their faces. They were willing to be convinced.

"It is true. And this is what we do."

As I spoke, I made notes with my grease pencil on the cardboard easel, drawing arrows showing the movement of pairs in response to the situation I was about to describe.

"Ambush left. Everybody takes cover, returns fire, patrol leader calls for withdrawal by individual rushes. Each man covers his partner; men closest to the source of fire withdraw behind supporting fire and take new positions along the line of march to cover withdrawal of the rest of the team. We continue in this manner, leapfrogging one another until the team leader determines it is safe to resume the mission." I looked from man to man; I still had their attention.

"Okay, that leaves contact rear. Different situation."

I set my cardboard easel aside.

"Contact from the rear happens for one of two reasons. We are being followed, or we have stopped and the enemy walks up on us by accident. In either case, the appropriate response is to set a hasty ambush. Take the enemy under fire, if necessary, and wait to see what happens next. Why wouldn't we want to run off in a new direction in this circumstance, Cortez?"

"Because we don't know what else is happening, sir. We might run right into more bad guys."

"Exactly right. Which brings me to my last point before we walk through these IA drills. Whenever we break from movement we will assume a defensive posture, a hasty ambush. Each man in the team has the same responsibility for maintaining visual security when we are on breaks as when we are in movement. When we are going to break for an OP and when we go into harbor sites, the point man and tail-end

Charlie, assisted by their partners, will set out claymores. That will be the very first thing we do when we set into a position. Tail-end Charlie's claymores will be set to cover our back trail. Point man's claymores will most likely cover the avenue of approach into our harbor site or such other danger area as I might direct. The third claymore will be held in reserve. Any questions so far?" There were none.

"Okay, last two chickenshit items. Eating, drinking, movement, etcetera, is done port and starboard. One guy watches, the other guy eats, drinks, sleeps, or whatever. On radio watches, two men will be awake at all times. Okay, Corporal Brasington, take a soda break and have the team down to the HLZ at sixteen-thirty, that's fifteen minutes from now. We will work on these IA drills for a half hour before chow." I stood up.

Corporal Brasington called the team to attention and rendered a hand salute. I returned his salute and made my way from out and under the awning and headed back to my hootch. It had been a terse and, I hoped, effective chalk talk. It was clear from their skeptical response that I had made changes in their SOP. If my experience in the Grunts was any guide, there would be a heated discussion among the team members about my ideas, at least among the Marines. I thought that I had won Jaqua and Brasington. I wasn't sure about Vaughn. Time would tell.

Inside my hootch, I took a few minutes to smoke a cigarette and collect my thoughts. Now that I was actively engaged in preparation for the patrol and asserting some influence over the possible course of events, I felt more comfortable with myself. Putting my training to use gave me a sense of confidence and helped me overcome my personal fear. That I was going to go back to the bush and do my best was never in doubt. That my best would be good enough remained a question in my mind and, I was convinced, in the minds of my fellow Marines. I plucked my weapon from its resting place, stubbed out the cigarette, and went out to resume the troop-leading steps.

I found Brasington and the others gathered in the shade of

the ready hut on the HLZ. Upon my approach, Brasington called the team to attention and rendered a salute.

That's a good sign, I thought to myself, returning the courtesy as I approached. "Okay, Corporal Brasington, let's start with actions upon helicopter debarkation and get this done as quickly as we can."

We spent the next thirty minutes walking through the immediate-action drills that I had outlined during my chalk talk. It was a cursory effort by all hands, done primarily to reinforce the principles of immediate action in their minds, and mine, so that we would be more likely to react in an appropriate way to the shock of contact. No one was happier to secure for chow than I. It had been a long and arduous day for me. I realized that I had a long way to go to recover to the level of fitness that I had enjoyed before my bout with FUO. I departed the HLZ with the understanding that we would all meet after chow for an informal equipment check. Brasington took the team back to the company area, practicing his own IA drill along the way. I labored up the stairs from the HLZ and made my way back to my hootch. Inside I stripped off my utility jacket and soggy T-shirt, toweled myself dry, and flopped on my cot to recuperate. I was exhausted to the point of quaking. I felt weak and nauseous—from fear or fever, I could not say.

At 1815, I struggled out of my rack, made myself "presentable" again, and made my way back to the company area for the gear check. Brasington had made certain that each man had the specified equipment, making my effort perfunctory. We were as ready as we could get. I left them to their personal preparations, relieved to know that Corporal Brasington was backing my play. A loyal NCO was a rare and vital asset. It was a good omen.

Back in my hootch, I wrote letters home and busied myself with meaningless tasks while AFVN radio played songs from home. Sounds from the club, a movie, boisterous laughter, curses, and oorahs floated on the evening breeze, reminding me of my mortality. Finally, I cut off the lights and made ready to deal with the demons of uncertainty until dawn. I slept fitfully, tormented by what-ifs, until exhaustion overcame anxiety. When the duty NCO shook me awake at 0430, it was from a deep sleep. I performed my perfunctory morning routine in the dark. Curry and Pino, roused about the same time, did likewise. Each of us was confined to our individual thoughts. Like football players before the big game, we wordlessly assembled our gear, checking each piece of equipment, making last-minute adjustments. Finally, we gathered our gear, plunged through the screen door into the predawn. We proceeded in single file down the steps to the HLZ, where we joined the other members of our teams, enlisted Marines and ARVNs.

The predawn air was damp and cold. A soggy, foul smelling mist hung close to the ground above the rice paddies that bordered the HLZ. Here and there the ash of a cigarette glowed, briefly illuminating teen faces. There was subdued grumbling as troops jostled one another in the staging area. Gradually they sorted themselves out, staged their equipment, and made their way in twos and threes up the stairs to the mess hall. From the crowd I deduced there were eight or ten teams to be inserted this day. I staged my gear alongside Lieutenant Lan and made way without comment back to the mess hall. The conventional wisdom called for me to eat hearty, but I felt no appetite. Instead, I took coffee, canned juice, toast, and canned fruit, and found my way to a table. Pino and Curry joined me, unbidden. We ate in silence, comrades-in-arms.

Our spartan meal consumed, we made our way outside just as the sun broke on the horizon. The helicopter package arrived overhead as we made our way back down to the ready shed. Brasington and I exchanged cursory greetings on the way inside. He was vigorously applying camouflage paint to his face and neck. Over his shoulder, I saw that the team members were doing the same. I decided that I should follow his example. Outside the troops smoked and groused about life in the Nam while they awaited developments.

The pilot's brief was tedious and uneventful. I applied my cammy, using "bug juice" to soften it, while the briefer droned on about weather and other issues unrelated to our patrol. My ears perked up at the mention of our call sign. We were assigned to aircraft side number sixteen. Luck put us in the second flight for the day, which meant we would lay about on the HLZ for another two hours. But, unlike my first patrol, there was to be no layover. The briefing broke up, and we went outside to rejoin our teams. Brasington carried the word to our group while I finished my cammy job and found a smoke. After a flurry of activity, the teams sorted themselves out and boarded the helicopters. Those of us left on the HLZ availed ourselves of the opportunity to cop a few more zees. The helicopters had no sooner lifted themselves off the HLZ than we were all horizontal, using our packs for pillows.

Whether from stress or fatigue, sleep came easily for me. I was awakened by the sound of the helicopters returning. It was time to go to war. As the CH-46 trucks settled onto the tarmac, we struggled into our gear, assembled in a file, and jogged out to our assigned aircraft. I led the way, followed by Lieutenant Chi and the rest of the team. Brasington brought up the rear. At the ramp, I stepped aside and counted the team aboard. When all were accounted for, I gave the crew chief a thumbs-up and found a seat inside for myself. Within seconds, we lifted off.

It was a short flight. Within minutes, the aircraft was orbiting the area of our pending insert. The insert officer, a tall lieutenant whom I did not know, motioned for me to join him at the gunner's door. He wore a helmet/headset identical to that of the aircrew, and was obviously talking to the pilot as I struggled over knees and weapons to get near him. I found a handhold and leaned forward to hear him. He was pointing to his map, then out the door. I couldn't hear a word he said. Finally, with sign language and shouts into the wind, he conveyed to me that the pilot wanted to set down on the road, instead of in the elephant-grass-covered area I had selected. It meant no concealment for the team, and worse— we would have to ford the river to get into our haven. With gestures and shouts I argued my case for the original plan.

The lieutenant talked and talked, arguing our case with the pilot while I watched in consternation. Finally, he gave me a thumbs-up. The pilot had agreed.

Almost coincident with the decision, the aircraft dropped from under us, plunging earthward in a sickening spiral. Off balance, I caromed down the center aisle to my position at the tailgate opposite the crew chief. I signaled the team to "lock and load." There was a bustle of activity as we jammed magazines into rifles, shot the bolts home, and safed our weapons. Disoriented by the aircraft's maneuvers, I peered over the ramp and through the nearest porthole window as the aircraft came to a hover several feet above the ground. The crew chief let down the hydraulic ramp, motioned us forward to debark. We were at least fifteen feet above the grass, debris whirling everywhere. I screamed in his ear, clutching his shoulder for emphasis.

"Tell the pilot to get us down, down!"

The crew chief spoke into the headset, his eyes big in his head. The aircraft lurched and yawed, throwing the team off balance. I kept my feet with difficulty. Finally, I could see mud through the stalks of elephant grass. Still clutching the crew chief's shoulder, I gave him a thumbs-up and motioned for Cortez and the others to move. Weapon at the ready, I lunged off the ramp, taking the five foot jump with knees flexed; I rolled to one side to make room for the others. We had been hovering for interminable minutes. If we were a surprise to anyone in the area, the effect had worn off. I clutched my cover atop my head with one hand, gripping my M-16 with the other, as debris from the rotor wash pelted me mercilessly. Behind me, I felt rather than heard the others come to ground. The cacophony of the helicopter numbed me. I could see nothing but stalks of elephant grass in every direction. The stuff must have been twelve feet high, and thick. The rotor wash only beat it down to waist height. Finally, the helicopter moved away, then lunged into the air. I stood up and turned about to see where the rest of the team had assembled. My ears were ringing, my hearing shot. I saw no one.

I felt a momentary clutch of panic—just my luck to get shot by my own team, or become an MIA. It was a nightmare with which I had wrestled for months. I held my position, looking slowly from side to side while I waited for my hearing to come back.

"Joker One Six, Joker One Six, this is Defend. Comm check. Over." Lance Corporal Jaqua thought he was whispering into the handset of his PRC-25. Fortunately for me, his ears were as blown out as mine had been. He was prone in the grass, less than ten feet from where I crouched. I moved cautiously to his position, listening for the response. If we had comm, we would continue the mission. If not, we were to pop smoke for an extract. I touched the smoke grenade taped to my harness—wishful thinking.

"Defend, this is Joker One Six. Gotcha five-by. How me? Over." The radio crackled and hissed, the squelch too high. We had comm and no good reason not to continue. I cast my gaze about the underbrush, locating the other members of the team. They were arranged in a loose half-moon formation around my position—an accident, not a tactical maneuver. Brasington was twenty feet away, whispering into the handset of the secondary radio. He must have felt me staring at him, because he gave me a thumbs-up as he handed the handset back to our ARVN Warrant Officer. I returned his signal with an "okay" of my own, then pulled the compass from my jacket pocket by its lanyard. I took a sighting on the only high ground I could see—due west. From my map recon, the visual reconnaissance, and what I had seen from the helicopter as we made our approach, I knew that the ridge due west of our insert offered good potential for observation and defense. I resolved to move in that direction.

It seemed like hours since I had leaped off the tailgate of the now distant CH-46. In reality, it had been only a minute or two. I moved past the other team members, who were getting to their feet, tapped Cortez on the shoulder, and pointed him in the direction of march. Within seconds, we had formed our staggered column and were moving in a generally westerly direction through the elephant grass toward high ground. We could see barely a few feet in any direction. It was stiflingly hot—and only 0900. We moved cautiously, a few paces at a time toward high ground, making an effort to move as quietly as possible. The grass was sharp and abrasive, cutting at exposed skin and clothing and impeding our progress. We expended two hours' time and a day's worth of energy moving five hundred meters. Suddenly Cortez held up his hand for a stop. He signaled to me to join him, then resumed an alert position, scanning the brush to either flank. I moved to his position, leapfrogging Lieutenant Chi, and discovered that we had intersected a trail. The trail appeared to lead up the back of the ridge, generally in our direction of march. It was overgrown, showing no signs of recent use. It was at once a temptation to expediency and disaster. By using the trail we could move with greater comfort; we risked the possibility of contact with the enemy, even being ambushed. On the other hand, we would determine very little about enemy activity in the area breaking brush. I decided to compromise. I withdrew from my vantage point, moved back down the line of march, directing the team with hand signals into a hasty ambush. Cortez became right flank security, Lieutenant Chi left flank, Brasington and Vaughn in the middle; Jaqua and I took positions somewhat to the rear and just off our back trail. I placed a claymore on our back trail and another in front of a rock, facing uphill and covering the exposed section of the trail above us. We settled in to wait.

An hour passed. We heard nothing but the muted scuffles of jungle creatures. We saw nothing but leeches and bugs. We felt nothing but the stifling heat and the beginning pangs of hunger and thirst. It was time to move. I decided to test our luck. With practiced skill, I moved carefully to Lieutenant Chi, whose face slid into a wide grin at my approach. We held a brief discussion using extemporaneous sign language from which I deduced that he had reached the same conclusion as I—the trail was not being used. I moved from man to man, Lieutenant Chi in tow, conveying my intention to move and retracting the ambush. The team members recovered the claymores and were soon prepared to resume the march. With sign language and eye contact I indicated to WO Thanh, whom I believed to be our most bush-wise associate, that I wanted him to take the point and proceed up the finger along the trail. Lieutenant Chi was to be deuce point, followed by myself, Corporal Jaqua, Lance Corporal Vaughn. Corporal Brasington and Lance Corporal Cortez brought up the rear. If we made contact, our Vietnamese allies would be first to fight.

WO Thanh was less than enthusiastic about his new role and protested in an urgent singsong whisper to his lieutenant who, his eyes locked with mine, quelled the sergeant's objections with a gentle shove in the direction of march. We moved west and uphill, falling automatically into the staggered column formation on either side of what turned out to be an old, as in ancient, trail. It was hard packed but overgrown. Here and there along the ridge there were shell holes, remnants of bombardments past. We moved cautiously, wary of booby traps and other unspeakable hazards. The Vietnamese was a master of bushcraft. He moved with a stealth and agility that I had not observed in any Marine. I tried to imitate his movements as we progressed up the hill. Suddenly he halted and turned to motion me forward. Payback. If he was going to occupy a hazardous position, he was going to require me to back him up. I moved to his position carefully, but without hesitation. He pointed to an alien object half-buried in the mud some fifteen to twenty feet in front of us. It was an eight-inch, high-explosive artillery round, olive drab with a yellow band of paint clearly visible in the shadows.

It was evidence of two things: quality control in U.S. defense industry was not all that it could be, and the enemy had not been in this area recently. I reached both these conclusions upon sighting the round, knowing that any NVA or VC worth his salt would have found a way to salvage this mother lode of high explosives for use against us foreign devils. I motioned for the ARVN to continue the march, followed by Lieutenant Chi, and passed the word by hand signal and eye contact to Jaqua. We moved in turns past the hazard and assembled some thirty meters farther up the hill. We were near the crest, and I was near exhaustion. It was one of those rare occasions in the bush when I knew with a high degree of certainty where we were. We had two to three hours of daylight left and no better place to be. I resolved to locate a good, defensible position near the summit, and harbor up for the night.

The site we selected, after making a "fishhook" around the summit of the hill, was a jumble of rocks overgrown by brambles. With difficulty, we found a way to crawl between the rocks and under the thorns into a sheltered and concealed harbor site beneath the undergrowth. It was a perfect hiding place. We could neither see nor be seen. We had good cover from the rocks and the likelihood of anything, man or beast, stumbling through our thicket was remote. We set a claymore on the back trail and another to clear a way out, called in our spot report, and like a covey of quail, settled in.

The night passed uneventfully. I awakened to the sound of the squelch on the radio on innumerable occasions, only to find the assigned team members alert to their responsibilities. Putting two men on watch at a time solved the security and communications problem. The battalion would not be popping artillery rounds over our heads (wake-up call for teams who did not respond to security checks at night). We roused with the dawn, rested and hungry. The team members went about their morning routine with subdued movements, careful not to rattle equipment or make other unnecessary sounds. We ate, renewed our camouflage paint, packed up our equipment and trash, and made ready for the day's hump. By the time the sun had reached above the horizon, we were ready to move. It remained to select a direction.

Brasington and I put our heads together over the map and decided to work our way down into the valley in a northerly direction, hoping to cut another trail. It was clear that we would find no evidence of enemy activity in the brush or on the high ground. They would be near water. I set a course by dead reckoning for the next likely stream or trail, and we crawled out from under our thicket, formed up in our staggered column, and stumbled into the undergrowth. We moved with difficulty in ten-minute spurts (move ten, listen five) for the better part of three hours before encountering the stream. We nearly fell into it, breaking brush to the bitter edge of the stream bed; we found ourselves on a precipice, sixty feet above a picturesque mountain brook straight out of *Field & Stream*, only we were in Southeast Asia, not Montana, and we were looking for NVA, not trout.

Crossing precipice danger areas was becoming my forte. I had an eerie déjà vu feeling. The terrain and circumstances were very similar to those I had encountered during Patty Shell. I shifted my eyes and mind from assessing the danger area to assessing the team. Lieutenant Chi was waiting expectantly at the edge of the drop. He had already located what appeared to be a safe descent. With hand signals and eye contact, I conveyed my intention to cross at the stream, set security, and followed Lieutenant Chi, hand over hand over rocks and roots to the stream bed, where we collected ourselves to look and listen. All was quiet, save for the babble of the water over the rocks. We moved across under the protection of the remaining team members, Lieutenant Chi in the lead. I had no sooner stepped from cover into knee-deep water than Lieutenant Chi stopped abruptly and scooped something from the water into the palm of his hand. He turned toward me, his palm outstretched; I moved the fifteen feet to join him and stared at his open hand—fish scales.

I looked about in the water, scanning the rocks more closely. The scales were swirling here and there, reflecting beneath the water the speckles of sunlight that filtered through the trees overhead. Peering into the shadows of the far bank, I saw further evidence of a successful fishing party. There were scales and entrails stuck to the rocks that protruded into a pool of deeper water. A chill grasped my psyche. I suddenly felt exposed, naked, and helpless. By the look in his eyes, it was an emotion I shared with my Vietnamese companion. I motioned for him to continue across the stream, then turned to give the danger signal to Brasington. He acknowledged my hand signal, then passed the sign to the others. I made my way to join the ARVN. Together we scanned the embankment for evidence and clues as to the whereabouts of the fishermen. There were none. Nor was there any trail. In fact, the vegetation on our side of the stream was so tangled as to be impenetrable. From the vantage point of our position behind the entrail-stained rock, I saw that the stream pooled into deeper water downstream. The fishermen could not have gone that way, nor could we. I scanned the embankment and streambed from which we had come. There was concealment in the undergrowth on that side of the stream, and it appeared shallow enough for the team to be able to move with relative ease. We would go upstream and try to locate the fishermen. Pino's escapade crept unbidden into my mind. His fishermen had been NVA.

The decision made, I tapped Chi on the shoulder and led the way back across the stream to join the team. When we regained the east bank, I directed Lieutenant Chi to take a position upstream where he could provide security for the other team members as they made their descent into the streambed. That accomplished, I motioned the others to join me, and waited vigilantly while they effected the maneuver. Brasington joined me, last man. He showed me his message pad, indicating that he had called in a position report (posrep). I showed him a handful of fish scales and pointed across the stream to the entrail-stained rocks. He nodded his head to indicate his understanding. The word was passed from man to man as we set out single file to find the enemy, or an HLZ. We moved north in the streambed, under the overhang, as if in a tunnel, for what seemed an eternity. We moved a step or two at a time, every splash and misstep sending a chill of fear through us. We peered with anxious eyes through the brush, scanning the far side of the stream as far ahead as possible for signs of the enemy. That there was a base camp somewhere nearby was a high probability. That we could or should locate the base camp was an issue open to conjecture. The thought had no sooner flitted through my mind than our

Vietnamese Warrant Officer turned abruptly from his point position, making a hand signal for danger.

I moved forward to join him under a carapace draped with vines. He gestured with his weapon toward the opposite bank. I stared uncomprehending into the shadows for indeterminable seconds. Finally, I discerned the unnatural straight lines of man-made objects amongst the rocks and trees. It was a repair/storage yard. Fishnets were draped across rickety bamboo frames. They were barely discernible in the shadows. The Vietnamese gripped my shoulder and turned my attention back in our direction of march. We had reached a stream junction. In front of us, across a shallow flow of water, there was a sandbar. The larger tributary continued north. The ground opened up, then flattened out under the canopy. To our right, a lesser tributary led more or less east. The overhang offered us concealment in that direction for about another one hundred meters, if we went on hands and knees. It was the lesser of evils. We still had no HLZ, and the idea of walking into an NVA base camp did not appeal to me. We changed direction.

We had reached the limit of concealment offered by the berm of the stream. Before us was a glade. The tributary was shallow and wide, with low grass and hip-high brush stretching out in the low ground. Upon closer inspection, it appeared that the open area was man-made and had been used for some agrarian purpose. That it was now fallow and somewhat overgrown was no comfort to me. It was another classic danger area, which we could cross only at great peril. It was also a beautiful HLZ. I took a moment to determine our position on the map and wrote the grid of the clearing in my message pad. If we needed an extract, the information would come in handy.

Crossing the clearing in daylight was foolish. I elected to stay in the tree line instead. I grasped the ARVN by the shoulder, my lensatic compass in hand, and showed him the new compass heading. He shook his head in assent, intuitively understanding the tactical decision I had made. We spoke the common language of the bush, though not a word had passed between us.

Warrant Officer Thanh hoisted himself over the berm and moved with great stealth and agility for several meters in our new direction of march. I covered him as he advanced, watching and listening for any clue as to the whereabouts of the fishermen. My vigilance was rewarded when the sound of ax on wood drifted to us on the evening breeze. There were enemy soldiers upstream. With eye contact and hand-and-eye signals, I conveyed my intention to change direction to the RTO, then hoisted myself over the berm in trace of the ARVN. Like a centipede, the patrol progressed through the brush and trees toward what I hoped would be relative safety. I wanted to find a secure harbor site quickly, as darkness would soon be upon us. We moved for perhaps twenty minutes before Thanh signaled me to join him at the point again. He was reading my mind.

We had been moving in a generally easterly direction, away from the stream, and the slope underfoot had become steeper as we progressed. Upon joining the Vietnamese Ranger at his vantage point, I saw that he had identified another ideal harbor site. It was a bamboo thicket. I signaled my understanding and agreement, in response to his hand signal, that this might be a good place to stop. He had indicated his recommendation by pointing to the thicket and placing his hands beside his head with his eyes closed to indicate a place to sleep. The ARVN moved off to circumnavigate the thicket in search of both a way in and a way out, while I gestured for the other team members to leapfrog past me. They did so one by one—except for Corporal Brasington, who was nowhere to be seen. Lieutenant Chi was the last man. When we left the stream, our order of march had made Corporal Brasington tail-end Charlie. Something had gone drastically wrong. I made my way to Lance Corporal Jaqua's position.

"Jaqua," I whispered, "Brasington missed the turn. I'm going back for him. You are acting team leader until we get back. We are going to harbor up in there." I gestured with my rifle toward the thicket.

The RTO stared at me in silence for a moment, then muttered softly, "Aye, aye, sir," and rose to his feet. It was clear from the expression on his face that he was apprehensive about the latest developments, and rightly so. We were less than five hundred meters from a suspected enemy base camp which we knew to be occupied—whether by fishermen or woodcutters—and we had a man missing. From Jaqua's point of view, one missing and one about to be missing. It was an unwritten rule that no one was to be separated from the group in the bush, even lieutenants. His thoughts and mine could not have been dissimilar. It was a bad situation which would get a lot worse if not resolved before dark.

I set off down our back trail in search of Corporal Brasington. I moved cautiously, imitating Thanh's technique to the best of my ability. As I moved a step at a time, I wondered if the ARVN had as sensitive a bowel as I did at the moment. The origin of the vernacular phrase, "scared shitless" was now known to me. Infantry combat had been an entirely different emotional ballgame. There was the group, there was the mission, there was responsibility, and a myriad of details to occupy one's mind. Contact with the enemy had been infrequent and unexpected. One reacted, applying training to situations as they developed. Fear was an afterthought. *This* was a long walk, alone, toward the enemy. The fear was a living thing. It lived in my gut. With each step toward the stream, I felt certain that I would void my bowel. Once again, the Basic School instructor's litany, "What now, Lieutenant?" rang in my ears.

Brasington was having an even less enjoyable experience. He was alone, in close proximity to the enemy, and for all he knew, abandoned by his friends. Considering my own fear, and touchy trigger finger, I paused in midstride to reconsider my options. Would Brasington be moving? Would he be tracking us or would he sit and wait for us to come back for him? Had he continued along our original route? Just where the fuck was he, anyway? My frustration saved us both, for as I crouched against a rock on our back trail, Brasington's image materialized out of the shadows. He was, in fact, tracking us in the failing light. No mean feat, even for a seasoned deer hunter from South Carolina. Either that or we had left a trail a blind man could follow.

I gave a low whistle, careful to conceal my body behind the rock. (Getting shot by my APL was not on my troop leader's list of good ideas.) Brasington dropped to the ground and rolled into a firing position, looking for the source of the noise. I whistled again, focusing his attention in my direction, then raised one gloved hand slowly above the rock. Brasington gave a low whistle of recognition, and we stood to confront one another—angry and relieved. He because we had "left him," I because he had "got lost." The anger and relief passed quickly into new-found anxiety. We now had to rejoin the team—in the dark if we didn't hustle. I motioned him to follow me, and we set out cautiously to retrace my route to the bamboo thicket. It took another ten minutes. Ten harrowing minutes.

Lance Corporal Jaqua had set Thanh for rear security. He was watching for us, and gave an alerting whistle when we approached the harbor site. We worked our way circuitously through the thickening undergrowth, finally locating the animal trail the other team members had used to crawl beneath the bamboo. They had cleared a space among the stalks just large enough for the group to lay prone, more or less in a circle. It was home, safety after our trek alone in the trees.

Brasington was clasped back into the fold with subdued backslaps and a proffered canteen. He and Lieutenant Chi exchanged a poignant look. There was tension, but no trouble. I followed Brasington's example by shrugging out of my web gear and making myself comfortable for the night. Warrant Officer Thanh, unbidden, bellied his way back to our entry point with a claymore—doorbell courtesy of Cadillac-Gage (manufacturer of the mine). Vaughn had the whip antenna up and was busy grounding the PRC-25s. I decided he was a better troop than first impressions had suggested. I wrote out a spot report on my message pad—our position, observations, and the time—and handed it to him in silence. He sent the message without comment while the rest of us settled in for the night.

Rain came, sometime after midnight, first a sprinkle, then a shower, then a torrent. We went from hot and miserable, to wet and miserable, to wet, cold, and miserable within the space of a few hours. The only good thing about it was that it kept the bugs away and converted prickly heat into chills in a matter of minutes. In the Grunts, I had sat out nights like this on my helmet, burning heat tabs between my legs under my poncho for warmth. Here, we just sat and shivered, waiting for daylight. The storm had a tactical content upon which I dwelled to pass the time—there would be no back trail for migratory NVA to find, come morning. I slept on the thought, in spite of the rain.

Dawn was a gradual thing, a lightening of the darkness while the storm beat down through the jungle. There was thunder and lightning, followed by torrential crescendos of rain. The radios did not work. We sat, like stray animals, while the storm worked its fury. There was no point in moving, so we ate and dozed, bludgeoned into acceptance of the force of nature, our war on hold. As the morning wore on, the force of the storm dissipated, replaced by an overcast sky that hugged the surrounding mountains in clouds. The rain abated. Vaughn and Jaqua changed the batteries in the radios and did their best to dry out the handsets. We tried to reestablish communications with the battalion, to no avail. Our comm in the valley had been intermittent in good weather, and I deduced that our radio relay had fared no better in the storm than we had. The idea of moving from our last known position without establishing communications did not appeal to me. So we sat, wet, cold, hungry, and bored for the balance of the day, reconnoitering our bamboo thicket for Corps and Country.

We shivered through the night, inundated periodically by thundershowers. By morning, we were literally waterlogged. Our skin, especially our hands and feet, was wrinkled and cracked from immersion. I had real concern when looking at the sunken eyes, pale complexions, and bluish lips of my associates that we would succumb to the effects of exposure and hypothermia if we did not take immediate action to forestall the attack of Mother Nature. We had to move. At the instant I reached this conclusion, the god of war smiled upon us and gave us comm.

"Defend, Defend. This is X ray. Sitrep,* please. Over."

Vaughn answered immediately, confirming that we were, in fact, alive and wet. By the grin on his face, I deduced that we were about to be flown home. As if by telepathic communication, our change of tactical circumstance galvanized the team to individual action. They checked their weapons, sorted out and repacked their equipment, policed up the trash from the harbor site, applied fresh camouflage to one another's faces, and made ready to move. I decided that the clearing we had passed on our way into the harbor site was as good as we were likely to do for an extract HLZ. It remained to select a route back to it, to make the movement, and be in position when the helicopters arrived. I decided to walk an L back to the clearing. We would walk a hundred meters due north, then make a left turn and walk back to the clearing, approaching from the north side. This would put high ground between us and the suspected enemy base camp. I drew our proposed route on the map with a grease pencil, showed it to Brasington and Jaqua, who conveyed the information to the other members of the team. The helicopter ETA (estimated time of arrival) was 0900. We had a little over two hours to make the trek.

With Warrant Officer Thanh on the point, we set out on hands and knees to crawl from the shelter of the bamboo thicket. Once clear of the bamboo, we stood upright, one by one, and moved off in a bedraggled single file, on the first leg of my L route back to the clearing. It was tough going. We slogged through mud and heavy brush, on a compass heading due north for thirty minutes, a 150 meters by dead reckoning. The pace was both punishing and dangerous,

*Situation report.

punishing because the brush and vines tore at our immersion-damaged flesh; dangerous because we were making too much noise. I called a halt and had Vaughn get an ETA on the helicopters. They were late. So were we. I gave the ARVN a new compass heading due west, and we set off at a slower pace, letting the terrain push us downhill in the general direction of the HLZ.

We arrived at the edge of the clearing with time to spare because the vegetation thinned as we descended. The team set up in a hasty ambush, Brasington and Lan covering our back trail, and the rest of the team in a loose arc facing the clearing. I hoisted myself into the crotch of a tree, a painful endeavor because of the condition of my skin, and observed the clearing as best I could through my binoculars. There was no evidence of recent human incursion, booby traps, or obstacles. The brush and tree lines surrounding the clearing were silent and gave no indication of human presence. If the area was under observation by the enemy, I could not determine it. We waited.

I felt a Pavlovian surge of energy at the sound of approaching helicopters. No sooner had the clatter of rotors invaded our subconscious, than the gunbirds were on the phone.

"Defend, Defend, this is Scarface Oscar. Over!"

The lead Cobra swooped over the ridge south of our position and commenced an orbit over the clearing. I reached for the handset held in my direction by Vaughn's outstretched hand. The other team members were adjusting equipment and preparing to move—packing it in.

"Scarface Oscar, this is Defend Actual. Stand by for Zippo Brief. Over." I gave the pilot a description of the clearing, an estimate of the wind conditions, and an alert to possible enemy activity in the streambed opposite the clearing. After acknowledging my transmission, the gunships swooped low over the area, challenging the forest and anyone in it to offer resistance to their incursion. There was none.

"Defend, this is Scarface. Your HLZ appears secure. Pop smoke! Over."

The gunships had seen no signs of enemy activity around us. In their judgment, it was safe to proceed with the extract.

I gestured to Brasington, who stood in a crouched position just inside the tree line, a smoke grenade in his hand. At my signal, he pulled the pin and hurled the pyrotechnic into the middle of the clearing, where it plopped in the mud and began to fizzle. Green smoke spewed along the ground, clinging to the vines and brush, then slowly wafted skyward in wispy plumes. It wasn't much of a marker.

"Defend, this is Scarface. Tallyho green smoke, over." The pilot knew his safety procedures.

"Scarface, this is Defend. Confirm green smoke, over."

The troops were restless, gaggling near where Brasington stood. I held my fist clenched toward them—the signal to stand fast. Overhead, one of the CH-46s fluttered toward the clearing in a gradual turn. One would have thought he was on a Sunday excursion. He was taking entirely too long to get down. A fuckin' new guy. "Defend, this is Scarface. Roger that. Joker Four Six is inbound. Over."

"Roger Scarface. Break, break. Joker Four Six, this is Defend Actual. Over." I wanted to talk to the "truck driver." The last thing we wanted was to break cover and have his door gunners hose us down with a .50-caliber. The CH-46 was still at five hundred feet, approaching our fizzled smoke at a lumbering pace and only gradually losing altitude. On his present glide slope, he would land on the opposite side of the clearing, two hundred meters from our position in the tree line. I wanted him to come to us—a sound tactical requirement, given the nature of our mission—and radioed that request to him.

The pilot had set down. The CH-46 sat like a giant grasshopper, its rotors whipping debris in every direction, square in the middle of the open area. There was no answer from the pilot. I cursed, then shouted to Brasington to lead the way. We dashed from the shelter of the trees, crouched at the waist, and zigzagged our way across the clearing to the helicopter. It was a long way to go, and we arrived winded. Brasington counted the team aboard, handing each man over the tailgate while the crew chief stood by complacently. I was the last man, and on my last legs. I stumbled aboard and found a handhold near the ramp as the aircraft surged air-borne. Inside the aircraft, the team members slumped against the aircraft bulkheads, exhausted. The tension seemed to drain from our bodies as the helicopter gained altitude and set a course for home. HLZ 401, cold beer, hot chow, mail, smokes, hot shower, dry clothes, and movies . . . the opportunity to talk out loud after six days of silence. I fell asleep.

My nap was terminated by a sudden change of altitude. We had arrived. It was time to reassert myself as a troop leader. The crew chief motioned us off the aircraft as the tailgate let down. I stood and led my team off the bird and across the HLZ to the debriefing hootch. We stopped outside to clear our weapons at the safety pit, then went inside to deliver our "raw intelligence." The debriefing was cursory. A gunnery sergeant quizzed us from a form, collected our message pads, and served cold sodas. We were the last team in before chow, and chow was on his mind. The debriefing complete, I caught Brasington's attention once more. "Hold the team outside for a minute, Corporal Brasington. I want to talk to them before you secure."

"Aye, aye, sir!"

They went out, while Lieutenant Chi and I gathered up our equipment. Outside the debriefing hootch, Brasington had gathered his team for my last-minute instructions. They were grumbling as I approached. Filthy, hungry, and bone weary, they were in no mood for a pep talk, or any other "lifer shit." Lieutenant Lan trailed my approach.

"Okay, gents! I just wanted to tell you that, in my opinion, you did a good job out there. Your teamwork in movement and in the harbor site was excellent. I also want to remind you to clean up your weapons and equipment. Corporal Brasington, I will be over to your team hootch at sixteen-hundred to look at weapons, web gear, and feet. Any questions?"

"No sir!"

Brasington kept his facial expression bland. Behind him, four pairs of militant eyeballs glared at me from grimy faces. I maintained eye contact with Brasington for interminable seconds after dropping my bomb. Finally, he came to attention and rendered a hand salute. I returned it and strode off, followed by Lieutenant Chi. Behind me, the team broke silence.

"Squirrelly motherfucker! I wonder if his gear is going to be clean by then?"

"Shut the fuck up, Vaughn! Let's get on up to the company area."

I smiled to myself as the words reached my ears. Being a pick-up patrol leader was going to provide its share of leadership challenges. If I was to survive, it would be necessary to leave a reputation behind with each team I led on a patrol: "Hodgins knows his shit and is nobody to fuck with." And, I would need NCOs upon whom I could call when things got tough. Brasington had potential—moral courage to go with the physical courage and tactical aptitude I had observed during our stroll in Elephant Valley. Brasington was mature beyond his years, and he seemed to have an aptitude for the bush. He had uttered not a single complaint during the entire ordeal of Defend. Now, faced with carrying out what was clearly an unpopular order, garrison chickenshit, he was equally stoic. In my mind, he became a marked man.

Lieutenant Chi and I struggled up the stairs from the HLZ. Actually, I struggled; Chi seemed none the worse for wear. At the top, we split up—the ARVN went to report to his *dai uy* (captain) and I went looking for mamma-san. She and her associates were back of the hootch, washing and chattering in their singsong fashion. When I approached, she gave me a huge, black-toothed grin. "Mamma-san! You washy war gear, clean boot—ricky tick?" She gave an enthusiastic nod of her head and made as if to strip the equipment from my weary body. I fended her off, making clear with sign language and pidgin English that I wanted her to do the chore while I was in the shower. That accomplished, I went around front and entered the hootch. There was a stack of mail on my rack— the Stump at work. Everything else was as I had left it. I shrugged out of my web gear, dropping the whole rig on the deck beside my rack, set my M-16 against the wall, and began to disassemble my load. I pulled all the magazines from their pouches, recovered the strobe light, compass, K-bar, pen flares, and other pilferable items, then tossed the whole paraphernalia into the aisle between the cubicles. Then, I stripped off my filthy uniform, boots, socks, and utilities and added them to the pile. I wrapped myself in a towel and set about cleaning the rifle with practiced skill, my stomach growling. Hot shower, hot chow, cold beer were my goals. But first, my job.

Twenty minutes finished the rifle. The mamma-san had taken my web gear. I took a long shower, scrubbing cammy paint and grit from my hair and face, and shaved. It was a chore. Refreshed, I put on clean utilities, my "garrison boots" (shined by the mamma-san), a starched cover, and went for a haircut. The camp's Viet Cong barber (we had long ago decided that all barbers were VC) made short work of the two-week fuzz on my head, gave me a good shoulder massage, a straight-razor trim, and a slap on the back. I was a new man—a lifer. It was 1530. I went back to the hootch. The mamma-san had scrubbed my web gear and left it on my rack. It was wet but clean. I slung the now empty harness over my shoulder, plucked my M-16 from its pegs, and set off to make a believer out of Lance Corporal Vaughn.

Troop sounds, grumbling, equipment clatter, etc., emanated from the team hootch as I approached. Brasington was ram-rodding his team into some semblance of order. I banged on the hatch to announce my arrival and pulled the screen door open. Four pairs of unfriendly eyeballs confronted me out of youthful faces still wet from the shower. Some showed razor nicks and shaving cream behind the ears. They were dressed, but only just. Their web gear and weapons were disassembled and laid out for display on their racks, as if for a junk-on-the-bunk inspection. They had been in the process of sweeping up the deck. There was trash in one corner, C-rat boxes, and assorted garments. The place was a mess, but they were trying. I smiled to myself.

"Atten*hut*!" Brasington had a great "parade voice." They all rose from their last-minute preparations and assumed a sullen upright position which resembled "attention."

"Relax, gents. I'm here to make a point, not to fuck with you. Corporal Brasington, have your men reassemble their weapons. Lance Corporal Vaughn, why don't you inspect mine?" As I spoke, I faced him and tossed my rifle in his direction. Startled, he caught the weapon and stood staring at me, his jaw slack.

"You're right, Vaughn. I am a squirrelly motherfucker. But I want to go home with all my body parts and live to fuck my life away. You gents are going to help me do that. When I take you out, I am going to be as ready as I can be. I expect you to be the same. When we get back, the first thing I have to do is get ready to go again. So do you. After that, we can all fuck off. Understand?"

Vaughn's demeanor had relaxed. He said nothing. I held his gaze for another few seconds, then started my inspection. I made it quick, but thorough.

"Okay, Corporal Brasington. When they've got everything reassembled, secure for chow. There will be a case of beer for you in the rec hootch when you get back. Sergeant Anderson will be the man to see."

I recovered my M-16 from Vaughn, shouldered my soggy web gear, and went out to find Anderson. Behind me there was silence.

I found Sergeant Anderson in the company office, engrossed in his decrepit Underwood (typewriter). He had the "hood" up, muttering under his breath. He looked up as I banged through the screen door.

"Say, Lieutenant. Congratulations. We got a message says you and Mister Curry are officially first lieutenants in the USMCR. Lieutenant Baker is looking for you. He's up in his hootch." He went back to his repairs.

"Okay, I'll go on up there right now." I grinned, pleased with the news. "How about getting a cold case of brew for Brasington's team? They'll be in the club in about ten minutes. In fact, the beer is on me tonight—tradition of the Corps!" As I spoke, I offered him a handful of MPC.

He took the scrip with a smile. "Sure thing, Lieutenant."

I reversed my course and went out to find Baker. In my

absence, he had moved into the company commander's hootch behind the company office. No more fraternizing with the troops. From inside came strumming sounds of yet another Stumpy Baker country hit. I climbed the steps, banged on the door, and went in.

"Sir, Wanna-Be-a-First-Lieutenant Hodgins reporting as ordered, sir!" I stood at attention, just inside the hatch, mocking him.

Baker laughed and rose from his rack, set the ever present guitar aside, and underhanded a cold beer in my direction. "Have a seat, asshole. I may be the man for the moment, but at least I ain't no lifer like you."

He took a pull on his own beer, while I struggled to open mine with a John Wayne. It fizzed all over the place. Baker laughed.

"You are going to be a warrior at large for a while longer, Mike. Until Tom Hodge comes down from Four-twenty-five [the observation post]. You will take over Third Herd [3d Platoon] from Tom when they come down. I'm not exactly sure when that will be, but in the meantime, you get to go to Charlie Ridge. Your call sign is Turf Club."

CHAPTER FOUR
TURF CLUB

3–12 APRIL 1970

Adversity introduces a man to himself.

Anonymous

Turf Club. It had a ring to it. Call signs were a security measure intended to deceive eavesdroppers as to the identity of military units in radio and message traffic. In practice, call signs became noms de guerre for personalities, pilots, commanders, recon teams. Some were considered good-luck talismans, others were cursed. Turf Club was among the latter, a hard-luck call sign assigned to a hard-luck unit, Charlie Company, 1st Recon Bn. Bad things happened to Turf Club, no matter the team composition. Polster's Turf Club fiasco, searching for the bodies of Skibbe and McVey, had become a formative experience for all of us. Larry had been unnerved by it. Baker, too, in a way. The Stump turned morose for a moment. He shook himself like a soggy dog, as if to shed his forebodings. Then he laughed, took a pull on his beer, and regained his composure. "You get your team from First Platoon this time. Sergeant Couture, an ARVN, and some other guys. He'll need a warning order." The Stump handed me a crumpled frag order from atop his field desk, then slouched back on his cot. "Wished I was goin' with you guys . . ."

He took another long pull on his beer, then continued, "Tom [Hodge] is going to train ROK Marines for this shit. Lucky bastard. He's out of the bush for good, except maybe for a Mission Impossible dance now and then. The Six [CO] says we are going to start running joint ops [patrols] with the ROKs pretty soon. They moved a whole company in here while you were gone. First thing they did was get in a big hassle with the ARVNs. So now, all the ARVNs are going to be billeted in the company areas. You get to bunk with Lieutenant Lan. That ought to be fun."

He paused for a moment, as if contemplating the potential problems, then continued, "You and Curry are officially first lieutenants. We got the message yesterday. Wild Bill has scheduled a wetting down for all you dudes on the fourth. In the meantime, I've got an extra set of bars. Why don't you take one for your cover, and I'll give the other to Curry. You guys will have to take the jeep up to Freedom Hill to get your own tomorrow."

He tossed me the little silver insignia as he spoke. I was touched by his thoughtfulness. Nobody wanted to be a second lieutenant a day longer than absolutely necessary. I had been counting the days to promotion almost from the moment I put on the butter bars. The promotion meant I was finally an adult. "So, what's Couture like?"

My thoughts had turned to the upcoming patrol. I scanned the cryptic operations order, looking for clues while I waited for Baker's answer. There were none, but I had been around long enough to know from shoptalk that Charlie Ridge was serious business. I took a pull on my beer, making eye contact with Baker.

"I don't know him that well, Mike. He's salty. On extension. In fact, I think he's pretty short. He and Domnoske have been here about the same time. You'll have to ask Polster." He paused for a moment, then went on, "Have you met Jim Duda? He was on the OP when you were in here last time. He's had his platoon in training this past week. Funny guy. You'll like him. Curry found a base camp—nobody home. He should be in pretty soon."

As if summoned, the clatter of helicopter rotors broke in on our conversation. Baker was distracted by the arrival of the helicopters. Curry and the others were back. The Stump made a habit of greeting the teams at the HLZ after every mission. He claimed it was part of his duty as a commanding officer to see his troops in from the bush. Watching him, I suspected that it was his way of showing that he cared about our safe return. Now, he stood, as if to leave, focused on the teams returning from the field. I was on my own.

I decided to go find salty Sergeant Couture and get started. Asking Polster anything about anything would probably be a waste of time, given the mood he had been in since his Turf Club escapade. Baker and I went out together and parted company on the path. Baker strode in his bearlike fashion across the bridge toward the HLZ, while I went in search of new adventures. I found Couture in the First Platoon hootch. He was alone, crashed on a cot, a magazine on the floor near his hand—skin mag. He was clad in a pair of cutoff fatigues, a big man with a heavy beard and lots of body hair. He looked to be my own age, perhaps a year or two older. He outweighed me by at least forty pounds.

Neanderthal motherfucker, I thought to myself as I approached. This is going to be a contest. Aloud, I called out, "Sergeant Couture?"

Couture's deportment was as rough as his looks. He was sullen and aggressive, clearly perturbed by my encroachment on his turf. He roused himself to one elbow as I approached his rack, glaring at me. "What can I do for you, sir?" There was an insolent pause before the "sir," an assessment and a challenge.

I took up the challenge. "For starters, Sergeant, you can stand up. Maybe even pretend to assume the position of attention, being an NCO and all. Or maybe your stripes don't mean that much to you?" I stared him down, a contest of wills. His face was an open book. Anger flashed in his expression, followed by caution. I waited, a few feet away, while he made up his mind. He would have made a lousy poker player. With a sigh of exasperation, he stood up, scratching, and assumed an indolent position of attention. We were off to a bad start.

"Thank you, Sergeant. At ease."

Couture made an imperceptible adjustment to his stance, his eyes on me.

"My name is Hodgins. You and I are going to take a walk on Charlie Ridge together. We will be going in on the tenth. I'm told that we can put a team together from your platoon. We will have one ARVN Ranger with us." I paused, inviting his response.

"Why me, Lieutenant? I'm short. I've done my twenty [patrols]." He stared at me.

I paused for thought, shaping a response to his challenge. Maybe his aggressive attitude was a front. Short-timer's nerves was certainly a malady that struck everyone, sooner or later. Twenty patrols was the magic number, at least by scuttlebutt. You were supposed to get a REMF job after twenty patrols, and a medal. Couture had paid his dues. I decided to try a softer approach.

"Bad luck, Sergeant. There aren't enough bodies to go around. The good news is that we have a week to get ready."

"No shit!" Couture muttered the phrase, then seemed to realize that he had limited choices. He decided to participate. "Well, Lieutenant, if it's you, me, and a gook, I guess we need three more guys and a corpsman. We got no corpsman, and I sure don't want to hump Charlie Ridge without one. They got five-hundred-pound bombs hanging from the trees up there!"

He was still looking for a way out, but more constructively. I went for dialogue. "Good point. We'll get one from BAS [battalion aid station, a centralized pool of medical personnel]. We need two RTOs and two riflemen. One has to hump the M-79 [grenade launcher]. Why don't you scare them up, while I get the corpsman? Plan to meet me down at the club at sixteen hundred [4:00 P.M.]?" I made it a question, soliciting cooperation, but it was an order just the same. Couture sat down on his rack, thinking. I waited.

"Sir, all I got left is fuckin' new guys. We're not supposed to take too many rookies on one team. People have been getting whacked left and right around here, especially First Platoon. That's why we're in training now. We're supposed to be getting a rest!"

"We don't have a lot of choice, here, Sergeant. Or time to screw around. I'm going. You're going. And so are the people you pick, so pick the best you can. See you at sixteen hundred!" I turned on my heel and walked out. I felt his eyes bore into my back as I went through the screen door into midday sun. My stomach growled, reminding me that even warriors had to eat. Couture was going to do his duty. He would pick troops we could both live with. The wild cards were the ARVN and the corpsman—my responsibility. Still, we had a week to get ready. I decided to take things one step at a time. Step one was to go to chow.

I ate a hearty lunch, then worked my way back to the company area, making arrangements as I went, first to the S-2 to draw intel reports and maps, then to the combat operations center to arrange an overflight for the following day. There were several other lieutenants gathered in the COC when I entered. Chip (Gregson) and the others were gaggled around the situation map. There had been no red light (indicating that a team was in contact) above the COC entrance when I entered, so I concluded that the discussion was tactical. The air liaison officer, whom I had come to see, was part of the group. I moved unobtrusively into earshot and discovered that Gregson was talking about proposed activities on Charlie Ridge, including the Charlie Company patrols, which he had briefed to the Stump earlier in the day. I recognized the tall form of Jim House, a TBS classmate. I did not know the others.

According to Gregson, we were to create a reconnaissance screen of four teams across the ridge, supported by a radio relay, in order to interdict a suspected movement of a "large enemy force" from Laos into base camps on the ridge. My friend Jim House was going to be the radio relay for all the teams. He was to be located on Ba Na. His call sign was Take Out. The others were Delivery Boy, Coffee Time, Thin Man, and Turf Club. At the mention of my call sign, my ears perked up. I looked closely at the map and saw that the four teams had neatly symmetrical havens. On paper, the deployment appeared to place us on the ground in position to observe and/or direct fires upon the most likely avenues of approach onto the ridge. The fact that we would be under two-hundred-foot canopy in terrain so steep that the contour lines on the map looked like ink blots must have been lost on the tactical genius who had dreamed up the idea. We would be lucky to see daylight through the trees, let alone NVA— unless we walked right up on them. The thought sent a chill through my body. I tapped Rasmussen on the shoulder, gesturing for him to join me away from the group.

"John, I'm Turf Club. I need an overflight tomorrow. What do you say?"

Rasmussen grimaced when I told him where I wanted to go, a concession to the probable difficulties that I would encounter. He booked us, like a good travel agent, for three "packs" (people) and told me to be at the HLZ at dawn. I thanked him and left the COC as quietly as I had come. My next stop was the battalion aid station. I strode across the gravel street, up the steps and through the screen door. Inside, the chief petty officer who ran the place sat on a rickety chair stamping entries in service record books. He looked up from his work when I entered.

"Say, Chief, my name is Hodgins—Charlie Company. I'm told that you are the man to see about picking up a corpsman for one of my teams."

"Could be, Lieutenant, but we are a little shorthanded right now." He looked at a personnel status board which hung on a nail behind his field desk. "We got five kids in RIP,* a couple of short-timers—what did you have in mind?"

"Charlie Ridge . . ." The name, with all its connotations, hung in the air like an omen.

"So you want a volunteer, someone with experience." He pulled on his face, then scratched his crotch, deep in thought. "When?"

"Now would be good. He needs to be at the Charlie Com-

*Reconnaissance Indoctrination Program.

pany EM Club at sixteen hundred tomorrow for briefing. This mission could be a bitch, Chief. Don't send me a shit-bird." I made harsh eye contact with him, remembering our last encounter.

"No sweat, Lieutenant. We'll take care of you." He meant it.

"Roger that!" I turned on my heel and went out, mentally checking off another item on my list.

It was time to catch up with Couture, give him his maps and discover what he had come up with for troops. With a week to get ready, I was beginning to feel optimistic. A little training would help us all feel better about going to the bush together, or maybe not. At least I would have a chance to evaluate the group and make adjustments where necessary. Couture was going to be a tough nut. It might be best to try him out separately. With these and other thoughts occupying my mind, I found that I had arrived back at the Charlie Company area. I crossed the bridge and went in search of Sergeant Couture.

Couture was as I had found him last, supine on his rack, clad only in cammy trousers and boots. The incessant whir of a fan mixed in with Jimi Hendrix from a Pioneer stereo. I had not noticed the stereo during our previous encounter. Couture stood up when I called out his name, turned the stereo off. I noticed that he clutched a sheaf of notepaper in his hands.

"Say, Lieutenant. Didn't hear you knock." He was still salty, but not as mean about it. I decided to make the most of it.

"Not surprised. Nice stereo."

"Yeah. Got it in Hong Kong. Should be packing it up to ship home about now . . ." His voice trailed off, as if he were think-ing of happier times.

"Well, this should be your last mission, Sergeant." I meant it as encouragement, but the irony was apparent.

"Any mission can be your last mission, Lieutenant. But, what the fuck . . ." He shrugged into a utility jacket. "Let's go get a beer and do business." He stuffed the notes into a pocket of his jacket, picked up his soft cover, and moved to join me in the passageway. Couture had accepted the inevitability of the upcoming patrol, but he was not about to be led. I followed him outside, struggling subconsciously with the force of his personality. This was a man who would not concede to authority. He had a lot of experience, which might or might not be a good thing. I stared speculatively at his broad back as he led the way down the hill to the EM Club/briefing hootch. We ducked under the awning and made our way inside. There were troops in the pool, but the hootch was empty. Couture helped himself to a pair of Pabst from a cooler behind the bar. We took seats at one of the cable-spool tables. He opened both beers with a John Wayne, scooting one across the table to me.

"Semper fi, Lieutenant!" He raised the can in toast, took a long pull while holding my eyes with his own. I returned his stare for a moment, then reasserted myself.

"Trade you maps for troops?" I grinned, offering one of the map sheets from my trouser pocket. "We have an overflight tomorrow morning—you, me, and our illustrious point man. We need to be on the HLZ at dawn." I was practicing Troop Leading 101—presume consent and press on. "Who have you picked for point man?"

Couture pulled his notes from his pocket and spread them on the table. I saw that he had been in the process of writing a warning order when I interrupted him.

"Well, Lieutenant, I haven't decided that yet. We got four guys, plus a gook and a squid.* Maybe the thing to do is take Corporal Kelly on the overflight. He's boot [an FNG], but he's pretty squared away—knows how to read a map and call for fire—came from Second Force at Camp Lejeune. This will be his second patrol. After that, we got two boot RTOs and a blooperman. Maybe the gook should walk point. I talked to Staff Sergeant Keane. Our gook is named Sergeant Thi. He's an old fucker, fought with the Viet Minh."

He took another pull on his beer, waiting for my reply. His gaze was direct, speculative. "Is this asshole coachable?" was the thought I read in his mind. He made sense. I decided to go with it.

*Sailor.

"Sounds right to me, Sergeant. Post your warning order for a team meeting here at sixteen hundred [4:00 P.M.] tomorrow. I'll meet you and Kelly at the HLZ at oh-five-thirty. The chief at BAS is supposed to get us a doc [corpsman]. Why don't you check with him a little later this evening and see who that is? Make sure our ARVN and the doc get the word on the team meeting. Anything else?" I finished my beer, awaiting his response.

"No sir. All we can do between now and the overflight is jerk off." He stood, smiling. "No disrespect intended, sir."

"How many times have you been a sergeant, Couture?" I smiled, my eyes hard.

He laughed aloud, "Ain't nothin' but a pay grade, Lieutenant. See you in the mornin'."

Couture was strong and more professional than I had concluded during our first encounter. When we parted company outside the hootch, he to join the troops at the pool and I to stroll back to my billet, I came away with the feeling that things were going to work out. He knew his job. He was, in effect, setting a standard for me. It wasn't a contest, exactly— more like a trial. All of our lives were on the line. I decided to give him the benefit of the doubt, as he was giving me. It was all a game of pickup ball. If the chemistry turned out right, we would win—survive. If it was bad, or if we were just unlucky . . . I found myself at the door to my hootch. Curry was back.

I could tell by the smell, and the sight of his filthy uniform and equipment on the deck between our cubicles. The man himself was nowhere in sight. Taking a two-hour shower, no doubt. I was just coming to the conclusion that I should remove his gear with a stick, when the mamma-san appeared and did just that, leaving me to engage in what had now become almost a rote preparation for the upcoming patrol. The threat was still distant, days away. I had time to prepare, in relative safety, for the foreseeable events, one after the other. There was no point in spending time on things I could do nothing about. I made up my map, familiarizing myself with the topography of the area as I went. There was little to be gained from a map reconnaissance at this point, other than to conclude that we were going to hump some very steep terrain. Parts of Charlie Ridge had been defoliated, all of it targeted for Arc Light (B-52) strikes. Yet, the mountains absorbed these insults with minimal long-term effect. Having observed the general area from the air on prior patrols, I knew that the vegetation (triple canopy) atop the ridge would be very similar to the Hai Van and Quang Tri areas where I had patrolled in the Grunts. Navigation was going to be a real problem. I would need to depend on dead reckoning and spotting rounds from the artillery. I studied the terrain of my haven, searching for possible HLZs. There were none. I decided to pick some hilltops and hope for the best. If we could get in on high ground, a known terrain feature, the rest of the hump would be simple—dangerous, but simple. Thinking . . .

Curry bounded up the steps and into the hootch, letting the screen door bang in his wake. He was full of energy, elated to be back in camp, clean and alive. His energy filled the space. Shitbird stood up on my rack, his tail awag. Like the dog, I rose to greet the returning warrior. He spoke before I could. "Say, Mike! What a hump! We found a base camp—no gooks, but lots of gear. Fuckin' rained on us for three days. Boy, am I glad to be back. How about a steak? I'm goin' up to division [officers' club]. They've got a band up there tonight—round-eyed women!"

A man of boundless energy, Mike was already recovered from what must have been an arduous adventure in the Que Sons. His game was over. He had hit the shower and was now prepared to celebrate victory. I, on the other hand, was about to enter the arena. My outcome was in doubt. I put a face on it, hiding my personal travail behind a veil of comradery. "Steak and round-eyed women—in one place? How can I refuse? Welcome back, leatherneck." I grasped his outstretched hand. "Maybe you should put some clothes on first. We don't want to give California Marines a bad name."

Curry laughed and continued down the passageway to his own cubicle. Still ruminating over unknowns, I sat down to finish my map while he dressed. I folded the map, stuck it in my web gear. Shitbird wiggled expectantly from the door. I fed him a can of beef with spiced sauce. Curry was ready. We went out, checked out at the gate, and made our way up Division Hill to the club.

The club turned out to be a field-grade officers' heaven, but there were no round-eyed women. We had our steak and a couple of beers, enjoying the air-conditioning and a chance to reminisce about home. Outranked at the bar, and weary from our toils, we decided to make an early night of it after all. We were back in camp by 2200 (10:00 P.M.). Curry went straight to bed, while I sat down to compose a letter home to Joyce. My mind strayed from home to the bush and back—leaving nothing on the paper. Finally, I set the tablet aside and resolved to get some sleep. It was getting late. Troop things would have to wait for troops, so I settled for checking my web gear one last time then went out to find the Duty NCO. It was none other than Sergeant Anderson, ensconced in a makeshift chaise longue in the company office. I signed my name to the roster for a wake-up call at 0430, noting that Couture and Kelly had their names on the list as well, then turned in for the night. I slept the sleep of the damned, plagued by visions and voices—the shattered body of Sam Hutton, "Don't get squirrelly on me, Lieutenant—Just get me my medevac . . ." Joyce nude and sobbing in our Fort De Russy hotel room, "Why are you doing this, Michael?"— The Basic School staff shouting, "What now, Lieutenant?" I awoke in a cold sweat. Sergeant Anderson was calling my name. It was 0415.

I sat up on my rack to let Anderson know that I was awake. He went on about his rounds, while I shook off the dream, smoked a cigarette to compose myself, and set about my morning routine. It was a physical effort to wash my face, brush my teeth, swallow my daily ration of pills, don my war gear. I set out across the bridge, morosely, to join yet another predawn gathering of disembodied warriors. There was a chill to the air. Like wraiths to a graveyard, troops and their leaders emerged from the shadows as individuals, pairs, an occasional trio, and gravitated slowly toward the mess hall. The faint odors of the place testified once again to Drumright's excellent chow. I ate, alone with my thoughts. When the group in the mess hall began to disperse toward the HLZ, I tagged along at the back and mustered my game face upon arrival at the HLZ. It was time to recommit to my role as a troop leader—Little Mikey's doubts and fears would have to wait for another night.

"Mornin', Lieutenant. What's your zap number?"

Couture had obviously preceded me to the HLZ. He spotted me in the crowd at the staging area and positioned himself so that I could identify him in the dark. He was still in charge. My stomach turned. My earlier decision to feast before battle plagued me. Fried eggs, hash browns, toast, coffee, and a helicopter ride might not fit well together after all. Couture was cheerful and to the point. The ALO collected the casualty identification numbers of all "passengers" prior to their boarding the aircraft. He recorded the information on a manifest for each aircraft side number that was kept until the mission was complete; if the aircraft went missing, higher-ups would know who had bought the farm. The zap number was the first initial of the last name and the last four digits of the service number. I was an "Oscar type," an officer in the lingo of communicators. Real Marines were "Echo types," enlisted personnel.

"Hotel niner, eight, eight, seven. Good mornin' to you, Sergeant." I answered with a confidence I did not feel. Couture made note of the information on a page from his message book and elbowed his way through the crowd to turn it in. In his wake, he left a tall, well-built Marine looking a little bewildered.

"You must be Corporal Kelly." I spoke to him as I moved closer. "My name is Hodgins. I'll be your patrol leader on this mission."

Kelly came to attention without thinking and rendered a hand salute. "Sir!"

"Relax, Corporal. Hasn't Couture taught you not to do that yet?" I laughed, returning his courtesy smartly. "Too much military courtesy around here will get you a bad reputation."

Kelly was nervous, preflight jitters in all probability. He seemed an earnest young man, and I wanted to win him over with dispatch. There were going to be lots of leadership challenges in the days ahead. I didn't need to create another one by behaving like a martinet for no particular reason.

Couture rejoined us, muttering under his breath. "Sir, we got to wait for the next flight. They are briefing for two hops, south first, then north. We could have slept 'til noon. Fuck!"

" 'Hurry up and wait' is the name of a course at Command and Staff College, Sergeant. Let's find a spot to cop some zees [sleep] while this thing gets sorted out."

We couldn't leave until we knew for sure what the order of the day's missions would be. I found a spot on the tarmac, dumped my web gear for a pillow, and assumed the supine position, tipping my bush hat over my eyes. It was leadership by example. Couture and Kelly stared at me for a moment, then followed suit. I knew that Rasmussen or some other lieutenant would emerge with the game plan sooner or later. There was no point in being pushy about getting our turn. Some twenty minutes passed before the aircrews emerged and made for their aircraft. They were followed by four recon teams and an assortment of support personnel, the insert officer, a PIO photography crew, and some straphangers. The teams broke off and jogged toward their assigned aircraft as the engines began to whine. Within seconds, the birds had lifted off into the morning sun, leaving a void of silence in their wake. I roused myself and went inside.

There were four more teams in the hootch, in varied states of relaxation. Chip Gregson was collecting his notes from the briefing when I approached.

"Say, Mister Gregson, what's our ETD [estimated time of departure] for our overflight? I'm supposed to take Turf Club to Charlie Ridge." I smiled at Gregson, but my stomach turned over. Somehow, when I uttered the destination aloud, the threat became more real. I might as well have said I was going to downtown Hanoi. There were just as many NVA in either place.

Gregson shrugged and spoke. "Got a smoke?"

"Sure." I handed over my plastic box of Countrys (Marlboros). "Need a light?"

"Yup." I offered my trusty Zippo. "How 'bout a kick in the chest to get it started?"

"Naw, I can do that part myself." He laughed, blowing smoke through his nostrils. "You may as well crash for a couple hours, Mike. Plan to be back here around ten thirty, or when you hear the birds coming back. We'll get you up then. Okay?"

"Thanks, Chip. But this flying standby sucks!" I turned to leave, yawning.

"Hey, at least you're not going on R & R!"

Gregson laughed. We went out together, he to return to his tomb in the combat operations center and I to my troops. I rousted Couture and Kelly from their naps and told them what the plan was. We agreed to reassemble at the HLZ when the birds came back. They were stoic, and returned to the company area via a shortcut through a draw that separated Charlie Company area from the rest of the complex. Leave it to troops to find the easiest way from point to point. Left with time to kill, I went back to my hootch, wrote a superficial letter home to Joyce, and took another snooze. The cacophony of the helicopter package arriving overhead brought me back to life, groggy but determined. I dragged myself back to the HLZ to await developments, only to discover that the aircrews were briefing again. There had been yet another change of plans. Couture and Kelly had gone directly to their previous spots and resumed the supine position upon their return to the HLZ. Twenty minutes of discussion produced a new insert order, and we were assigned to one of the aircraft, along with one team and the insert officer (IO), a lieutenant whom I did not know. By the time we had all hustled aboard the CH-46, I was convinced that nothing good would come of the exercise. We could not communicate with one another, let alone with the pilot.

The insert officer was preoccupied with getting his teams in, so I waited my turn as patiently as possible. The team aboard our aircraft was inserted at the west end of Elephant Valley. When our ride lifted clear of their HLZ, the IO motioned for me to join him at the door gunner's hatch. He had a map in his hand. I struggled forward from handhold to handhold until we could peer shoulder to shoulder out the hatch. I pointed out the area we were interested in on his map, and he briefed the pilot through the aircraft intercom. The CH-46 changed course, and we were soon orbiting over Hill 1081, the dominant terrain feature in my Turf Club haven. The terrain was heavily forested and rugged. We could see only trees and rocks, with an occasional sheer cliff below us. It was difficult to pick out terrain features from the air. On the ground we would be blind. The pilot orbited lower and wider, searching for clearings, a streambed, a bomb crater, anyplace where a helicopter could safely approach the ground. There were none. In the end, we settled for a clearing atop a finger on the north slope of the ridge, more than a klick (one thousand meters) outside the haven and two hundred meters lower than I had hoped for. I had no extract HLZ or secondary HLZs in the entire haven. Couture and Kelly, who had taken turns peering over my shoulder, slouched in the nylon webbing of the troop compartment seats, clearly disappointed at our prospects.

I dozed throughout the ride back, numbed by the reverberations of the helicopter. We had wasted an entire day, or not. Sometimes what you didn't see was more important than what you did [see]. We now had a clear idea of the terrain, and the absence of HLZs, while chilling, had become a key factor in my planning. If things went wrong, we were going to have to run, downhill, to get into terrain open enough for helicopter extraction. We would need to be sneaky, move slow, leave no back trail, harbor up in inaccessible terrain to insure that the NVA couldn't walk in on us. The map indicated several major trails on the ridges in the haven, but our overflight revealed only canopy. If the trails existed, they were concealed from aerial observation by the canopy—another bad omen. We arrived back at HLZ 401 without fanfare, the last flight of the day. We disembarked from the helicopter, straggling away from the rotor wash while it lifted off. In the silence following its retreat, I waved Couture and Kelly off to the company area. "See you guys back at the ranch after chow, say eighteen hundred [6:00 P.M.]?"

"Sir, there's a USO show tonight . . ." Couture let his thought hang in the space between us.

"Very well. How about tomorrow morning, the EM Club, oh-eight-hundred. Bring the rest of the team." It was a snap decision, but the correct one if their body language was any indication. There was plenty of time for war, but round-eyed women were rare in Southeast Asia. They went off in good spirits, while I made the trek up the hill to my hootch, alone with my thoughts and responsibility. I spent the balance of the day in limbo. There was little I could do to influence events in the near term. Since I had no team and no "collateral duties" (extra jobs assigned by the battalion commander), I passed the time reading, writing letters home, and, ultimately, sleeping. I discovered that the one thing I was becoming good at since my arrival in Vietnam was taking naps—maybe it was stress. In any event, I awoke from such a nap to the sounds of troops gathering in our "amphitheater" for the much anticipated USO show. By the catcalls and rabble-rousing that ensued, I deduced that the troops were disappointed—there was only a Korean country western band. I went back to sleep to the tune of "Home, home on the range . . ." with no *L*s and no *R*s. It was bizarre.

Dawn brought a new reality, and the ever anticipated helicopter "package," two Cobras, two CH-46s. I took my time with chow, hanging back to let those who carried the fight for the day precede me. I noticed that my food tasted better without the prospect of a helicopter flight. By the time I left the mess hall, the birds and their reluctant warriors were gone. I strolled back to the Charlie Company area just in time to walk in on our 0800 team meeting. We had four days to prepare.

"Team, atten*hut*!" Corporal Kelly still had not acquired

his quota of salt. The men gathered around the table reacted without thinking, coming to the position with their backs to me. All except Couture.

"That works for you, too, Sergeant." I said it softly, but my expression was hard. It was time to have our fight. Instinct told me that there could only be one leader in the group. I was determined that it be me. I watched Couture, holding his stare, while he went through the mental process of deciding how far he could go. Finally, he stood up.

"At ease, gents. Take seats and let's get acquainted." I moved quickly to face them, the wall at my back. "My name is Hodgins. I am the patrol leader for this mission. Sergeant Couture, why don't we have each man introduce himself—name, rank, MOS [military occupational specialty], time in country, and number of patrols."

It was a place to start, significant only as a way to establish the pecking order. If I was correct in my assessment, Couture didn't know these men any better than I did. I had the bars, but he had the image, the aura of credibility troops tended to vest in peers who had survived the rigors of the bush for a period of time. We would have to change that if the group was to work as a team. There could be only one leader. It was going to be me.

They went through the routine one at a time. Corporal Kelly, a Ranger School graduate, product of Second Force Recon Company, Camp Lejeune, a rookie, but the best-trained man in the group. Lance Corporal Finchum, 2511 (RTO), second patrol, three months in country. Lance Corporal Nichols, 2511 (RTO), third patrol, three months in country. Private First Class Ward, 0311 (rifleman), blooperman (M-79 grenade launcher), third patrol, five months in country. Hospitalman Second Class Pearston, corpsman, fifteen months in country, transfer from the CAPs (Combined Action Platoons—something like a well-armed Marine Peace Corps unit)—spoke Vietnamese, "enough to get laid." Sergeant Thi, ARVN Ranger, forty years in country, spoke no English—my old friend from Lunchmeat. We grinned at one another, brothers in arms. Now that I knew something about the group, I found the presence of the Vietnamese strangely comforting. He was the only man with whom I had formed the bond of trust necessary to success in the field. We had suffered together, weeks before, and taken the measure of one another. The rest of my team were wild cards. I had no idea what they were good for, nor had they of me. I decided to get all the cards on the table. I made eye contact with Couture. "And what about you, Sergeant Couture?"

"Well, sir, I've been here since Tet, sixty-eight. My first firefight was Hue City. This will be my twenty-first patrol, and with a little luck, my last. I'm so short I can dangle my legs off the edge of a razor blade. What about you, Lieutenant?"

It was a legitimate challenge. "This will be my third patrol. Sergeant Thi and I were out in Elephant Valley together a couple of weeks ago. I'm an oh-three-oh-two [Infantry officer]. I've been in country about seven months. Before I came here, I was a Grunt platoon leader in Hotel Company, Two–Twenty-six [Second Battalion, 26th Marines]." I said it all matter-of-factly, then changed the subject, "Have any of you worked together before?" I addressed my remarks and my question to the group, ignoring the challenge in Couture's deportment. It was time to focus on the mission.

"No, sir." Corporal Kelly answered for the group.

"Okay. Sergeant Couture, this is a standard load for the team. I want each man to carry the items of equipment, ammunition, food, and water specified on the list, no more, no less." I handed the list to Couture, then turned to address the group. Couture stared at the paper as if it were contaminated.

"Gents, this patrol is going to be a bitch for three reasons. First, the terrain is steep and covered with triple canopy. There are no HLZs. Second, the NVA are known to be in the area in large numbers. Third, we have to hump the whole damn thing. So, the first thing that has to happen is that we get our act together on immediate action and movement."

I focused on Couture. "Sergeant Couture, I want you and Corporal Kelly to work out an order of march and immediate-action drills this morning. Walk through them this afternoon and get your equipment assembled. Use the trail to HLZ Four-oh-one for your training area. I will meet you down there at sixteen hundred [4:00 P.M.] to evaluate our progress. Any questions, so far?"

I made eye contact with each man. They were going to follow. Even Couture. By reinstating him as the man to establish the tactical standards for the team, I had won the first round. It now remained to determine whether or not they were tactically proficient. It was time to withdraw, to let the NCO show his stuff. I wanted it to be good "stuff." My life depended on it.

I left them as I found them, head-to-head around the table. They now had structure to their discussions, my equipment list, and requirements for IA drills, among other things. I went back to my hootch intent upon finalizing a patrol route and a fire-support plan for the mission. Now that we had a known point of origin, it was a matter of map reconnaissance—evaluating the terrain as depicted by the map to determine a likely route. It was in my mind that we could probably be extracted from atop the ridge. So, I plotted a route from the HLZ along the ridgebacks to the top of Hill 1081, noting the grids of key terrain features to be used as targets for land navigation if necessary. I fiddled with the map for what seemed like hours, engraving the terrain in my mind. Once we were on the ground, we would see little but trees and rocks. I resolved to have a chat with my friend Jim House at chow. Take Out would become our communications lifeline once we were on the ground. His team would be the key to my land navigation, and whatever else, if things got confused. I had noticed on the situation map that the fire support base at An Hoa was east/southeast of our haven. I wanted to know the back azimuth to it—a trip to the company office with my protractor was in order. These and other tactical ruminations occupied me past noon. A nap took me to 1500 (3:00 P.M.).

The deck of the swimming pool in the company area provided a good platform for observing the team in their IA drills. I went there to see what I could see. It was sneaky, spying on my own troops, but necessary. I wanted to know how seriously they were taking their work. I was pleasantly surprised. Just as I occupied my perch, I heard Couture call out, "Ambush right!" from the gully. At the shouted command, Kelly and the others pivoted off their route of march and moved lethargically into the brush along the right side of the trail. By the sweat-stained uniforms, I deduced that they had been so engaged for some time. Couture was a taskmaster. He was also standing in relative comfort in the shade. I moved to join them.

"Say gents! Hot, ain't it."

They were drenched in sweat. At my arrival tension rose in them. They were suffering at my command, and keenly aware of it. "Sergeant Couture, what say we go up and get some cold soda, talk some tactics?"

I made it a question, but it was an order. We went, Couture in the lead. I pulled drag (walked at the back), watching them as they traversed the slope back to the club. We were city boys to the bone, accustomed to walking on concrete, not uneven ground, all but Sergeant Thi. He moved like a wraith over the ground, all economy of motion—and quiet. It was a skill I had admired on our previous patrol. I decided to use him. These and other musings occupied my mind on the short hike back to the hootch. Having refined my presentation with the last team briefing, I went straight to the salient points with this one when we arrived back at the hootch. "Doc, how about slipping behind the bar over there and getting us all a cold soda?" I handed him a wad of MPC, and he moved to obey without comment. The rest of the team stood uncertainly just inside the hatch. I moved past them to one of the tables and sat down. "Take seats, gentlemen."

There was a shuffling of feet, sweaty bodies, and equipment. Sodas were passed around, one for each man—except Sergeant Thi. I slid my ice-cold Coke across the rough-hewn surface of the table to a point between his hands, made brief eye contact, and stood up. Sergeant Thi grinned and took a long pull on his Coke, while I commenced my spiel on movement and actions on contact. It was a short presentation, including my pitch on the virtues of the staggered column and the Australian Peel. When I concluded, I made eye contact around the group once more. "Gents, we are going to Charlie Ridge as a team, seven sorry motherfuckers . . ." I stared at each man in turn, emphasizing my point with eye contact. "Once we get on the ground, there is no difference between us. Each of us has something to contribute for the good of the group, including Sergeant Thi." I looked each man in the eye once more, then continued, "I have been to the bush with him. He can teach us things about moving in the bush, about the NVA, about comfort in the field."

I focused on the corpsman, my interpreter, as fortune would have it. "Doc, when we finish here, I want you to explain to Sergeant Thi that he is to instruct the team on his techniques for moving through brush and on trails." I looked again from man to man. "I want you all to practice his moves. Sergeant Couture, work on that 'til chow. We'll get together here tomorrow morning, oh-eight-hundred, for the patrol order and an equipment inspection. I expect each man to have all the gear on the list I gave you, including ammo. Any questions?" I made eye contact with each man. There were no questions. I made to leave, plucking my cover from atop the table.

"Team, atten*hut*!" Corporal Kelly again. He was either a great troop, or an Eddie-Haskell two-face. Time would tell.

"Thank you, gents." I went out, feeling their eyes drill into my back. It was party time—Drumright's Last Rites for those of us who had the misfortune to be promoted while a member of his illustrious command. It meant that I had to get cleaned up before presenting myself, along with a half-dozen others, at the Staff & Officers' Club to imbibe warrior spirits and be indoctrinated on the finer points of bush lore and leadership. The REMF Warriors, as I had come to think of them, would be in full chase, fueled by the wallets of those of us who had been promoted. It would be a wetting down for which I felt only aversion. Ruminating, I found myself back at the hootch going though the motions of shit, shower, and shave. My mind on autopilot, I wandered up to the club alone. The crowd was gathering. By the look of it, some had been there for a couple of hours. Preoccupied as I was with my own fate, I took little interest in the revelry of the REMFs. I donated a hard-earned twenty dollars MPC to the hat on the bar, snagged a beer, and found a seat in an unobtrusive corner. Drumright was not on the scene. Besides Curry and myself, there were several of our classmates in attendance—Jim House, Mike Hoke, Gene Fitzsimmons, Ray Walters, all Grunts and recently assigned to the battalion, and Marty Zeagler, the motor transport officer. It was getting dark.

Drumright arrived, the sergeant major in tow, and put the party in high gear. He had a presence, an aura of menace and high energy which compelled younger men to seek his approval. The group quickly separated, like oil from water, as the courtiers gravitated toward the king. Cheap shots and beer began to flow in earnest. Raucous laughter and bawdy jokes soon rocked the plywood walls and drifted about the camp on the evening breeze. The leadership was in full chase, like a pack of hounds after a fox—or in the vernacular of Tennessee (Drumright's home state), a "coon." And like the coon, I felt treed, cornered with no place to hide.

"Hey, you peckerwoods!" Drumright was banging on the bar with a K-bar gavel to get the attention of the crowd, mostly lieutenants, that had gathered. "Now we got to pin the bars on these peckerwoods! Sergeant Major!"

Sergeant Major Skinner emerged from the crowd, a paper bag in his hand. At the bar, he emptied the contents onto the mahogany surface—ten sets of brand new silver bars. A stillness settled over the room.

"All right, you peckerwoods. Front and center!"

Drumright was grinning, malice in his face, as he turned his back to the bar and faced the room. Sergeant Major Skinner took a position on Drumright's left shoulder. We, the promotees, materialized from the crowd to form a ragged line in front of our commander. The sergeant major pulled a tattered sheet of paper from his trouser pocket, smoothed it on the bar, then turned to the crowd, the document in hand.

"Attention to Orders!"

Sergeant Major Skinner read the terse document aloud, then put the paper in his pocket, gathered up the packets of silver bars, and took his place beside Drumright. Drumright and the sergeant major moved down the line performing the ritual of placing insignia of rank on the collar of each man, "pinning" them with a slap of his hand, then moving to the next. The task complete, Drumright resumed his place at the bar while the promotees endured the pinning and congratulations of all senior to them—which was nearly everyone in the bar. By the time the group tired of the ritual, my shoulders felt as if I had been shot. Bruised and beguiled, I found a seat in a corner from which to observe the shenanigans for another hour. When I was certain that the attention had focused on other pursuits (tossing shooters), I left.

Sunrise brought the birds (helicopters) and the realization that I had another two days to get my team ready to play. Based upon what I had observed the day before, I wanted to make some changes in Sergeant Couture's SOPs. The time to do it was after our preliminary inspection and patrol order. Ruminating on this and other things, I got through my morning ritual, including a good breakfast, donned my own war gear, and made my way to the company area. Crossing the bridge, I sighted Couture and the team arrayed in the shade of the team hootch.

"Good mornin', gents." I made myself sound cheerful. "Sergeant Couture, let's make this a little less formal. Bring the team on down to the club." I went in that direction, leading the way. Behind me, there was a bustle of equipment and a shuffling of boots on gravel. They followed, grudgingly. I was moving to neutral ground. It was a subconscious decision, a way of taking control of the group without making it a military ritual—them against me. I wanted to make it an "us" (Marines) against "them" (NVA) game. Inside the hootch, I shed my web gear and waited for the team to gather. They gaggled, just inside the hatch, uncertain of what came next.

"Drop your gear, stack your weapons, and take seats, gents. We're going to go through our patrol order, take a look at our gear, and practice some more IA drills." Eyeballs rolled at that statement. They dropped web gear at their feet, propped their weapons against the bulkheads, and took seats around the table in front of me. It was time for my show—SMEAC in the attack (Situation, Mission, Execution, Administration & Logistics, Communications). I ran through the whole presentation by the book, suffering glazed eyeballs and skeptical facial expressions each step of the way. There were no questions. I had the distinct impression that everything worth saying, from their point of view, had been said before I arrived. So be it.

"Okay gents. Bring your rifles and two magazines apiece and follow me."

There was a scuffle of feet, and grousing behind me as I left the hootch. Outside, I lit up a Country, collected my temper, and waited for Turf Club to reassemble. Troops liked to fire weapons and blow up things. I wanted to see if they could shoot, if they still had "battle sights" on their weapons. I would make it a contest.

"Okay, Sergeant Couture. Let's truck [walk] on down to the thousand-inch range [a training range set up to scale for zeroing weapons]. Run the whole team through the course."

He obeyed without comment. The team preceded me down the trail to the HLZ and around to the base of the hill where the range was located. I let Couture run the drill. He was informal but professional. He set the targets up himself, demonstrated the proper technique for zeroing his weapon, then a quick-fire/quick-kill drill. After clearing his weapon, he had each man come to the firing line and go through the drill, even Sergeant Thi. Sergeant Thi was a good shot.

"Okay, Lieutenant. It's your turn."

Another legitimate challenge, the one I had been hoping for. Six years of USMC marksmanship instruction, endured with varying degrees of pain and aggravation, were about to pay off. When asked about why I had sought a commission, I often joked with my peers that I had done it to get off Range Detail. From boot camp to Basic School, I had developed a love/hate relationship with that tradition of the Corps. I liked shooting, hated everything else that went with it—especially "police call," i.e., picking up brass, trash, and cigarette butts at the end of the day. I had become an Expert Marksman in the process, with rifle, pistol, and machine gun.

I moved to the line under the watchful gaze of six pairs of skeptical eyeballs, took a prone position at one of the firing points, loaded a magazine, and fired a quick three rounds—a one-inch group at the *X*. I switched to sitting position, did the same thing, then to offhand to empty the magazine. I changed magazines quickly and emptied the new one into one of the silhouette targets using the quick-fire, point-and-shoot technique. The rounds were neatly grouped in the chest. As a lieutenant, I might not be worth much to these guys, but at least I could shoot. That was the demonstration, a place to start. "Okay, Sergeant Couture. Let's break for chow. Have the team back at HLZ Four-oh-one at fifteen hundred [3:00 P.M.] to rehearse IA drills."

There were smiles. In effect, I had just given them the afternoon off. We had quickly reached the point of diminishing returns. If I worked them too much more, it would be harassment, "lifer shit." I still wanted to practice getting on and off the bird, and some IA drills for breaking contact. But there was no point in doing it in the heat of the day. I left them on a positive note and went in search of a nap. Shitbird-the-Dog kept me company while I cleaned my rifle, reloaded magazines, and wrote a letter to Joyce. Those tasks complete, I set my alarm for 1400, and went to sleep to the sound of my fan buzzing and garrison noise drifting on a humid breeze. The alarm was a brutal awakening.

Feeling drugged, I struggled to my feet, shrugged into my web gear, and staggered to the hatch, willing myself into a more alert state of mind. It was time to become a troop leader again.

By the time I got to the HLZ, I had my act together. Turf Club did, too. We went through the embarkation and debarkation drills flawlessly, then spent a few minutes on breaking contact. They had it down.

"Okay, Sergeant Couture. Let's secure this shit. We're about as ready as we can get. I want to look at equipment and ammo loads tomorrow afternoon, say sixteen hundred [4:00 P.M.]. Have them lay out their standard load on their racks, so we can count the beans, bullets, and bandages. In the meantime, you're on your own." I made to leave.

"Aye, aye, sir." Couture saluted crisply, a courtesy I returned with a sense of relief. I felt a little safer, at least with my own troops. The NVA were another matter, and still thirty-six hours away. At loose ends, I occupied the balance of the evening with chow and a bad movie at the club. Brooding as I was about the upcoming patrol, I found the revelry of our REMF Warriors particularly irritating and made an early, antisocial evening of it. After a fitful night's sleep and another day at loose ends, I became convinced of another truth—it was much better to be in and out of the company area in one or two days, than to spend a week getting ready for one of these treks. By the time we got to D day, my nerves were frayed. Turf Club had all the gear I had specified, and some I had not. I gave them my pitch about loading their magazines with a tracer every third round, and another caution about packing enough water. There was nothing else to do, save follow my own example and try to rest up.

Dawn on the tenth of April 1970 found me wide awake when the Duty NCO banged on the hatch for my early call. I had spent the night in torment, nauseous with fear, rethinking every possible scenario for the patrol in my mind. I had slept only fitfully, awakened by the slightest sound and tormented by recurring nightmares of the Grunts—Hutton, Clough, McLean, and the others—"Don't get squirrelly on me, Lieutenant. Just get me my medevac." I was ready to go, to get on with it. "It" was not to be.

The teams—there were twelve to be inserted—assembled at the HLZ in the predawn gloom. There was a drizzle. The troops huddled together, smoking and stamping their feet in the morning chill, while team leaders assembled in the briefing hootch. Before long, it was apparent that weather was going to be a problem—Charlie Ridge was socked in. After much discussion and debate amongst the pilots and our operations people (Chip Gregson), it was decided that we would be staged at An Hoa, a fire-support base in the Arizona, located at the foot of Charlie Ridge. The southern inserts and extracts would be flown first, at lower altitudes. The birds would put us in when the weather cleared later in the day, before they returned to Da Nang to refuel. We loaded the aircraft for the short flight to An Hoa, feeling let down. The best thing that could happen was a quick insert; once committed, everyone felt better. Instead, we were offloaded at An Hoa, where we spent the morning smoking and sleeping on the HLZ. It was midafternoon when the birds finally returned. The plan had changed. It was a different aircraft, a different pilot, and a different insert officer—Hank Rathmell, one of the Operations Alphas.

I discovered all this when Rathmell debarked to brief me on the change. There had been a snafu on the morning mission; the aircraft had malfunctioned and returned to Marble Mountain for repairs. We were the last insert for the day. It was already 1300 (1:00 P.M.). We sorted out the grid for my insert, and Rathmell went back aboard the CH-46 to brief the pilot. Turf Club saddled up laboriously, and trudged across the steel decking to board the aircraft—resolute if not enthusiastic. I scrambled up the ramp, last man, and gave the crew chief a thumbs-up. We were off to war. Strangely, I felt better. Until I got a dose of field-grade airmanship.

We approached Charlie Ridge, more or less in a straight line at an altitude of several thousand feet. It was cold. The pilot flew us over the crest, clearing the ridge by several thousand feet, then began a sinking orbit over the area where we had conducted our VR. I recognized the dogleg of a stream in Happy Valley, an abandoned fire-support base (Hill 444). We were two klicks north of my haven. I had selected a clearing on a finger below Hill 1081. My plan had been to hump up to the crest of the ridge, then work our way east and lower until we found a place to get out. Our pilot was not cooperating. I stumbled over knees and boots to a position at the gunner's hatch, next to Rathmell. He knew what the problem was.

"He won't go in there. The guns [Cobras] thought they saw movement in the zone. He wants to put you in behind Coffee Time! They're talking about it now—major to major!" Rathmell shouted above the din of the helicopter's engines. The whole aircraft shivered with vibrations as we gyrated all over the sky—evasive measures, no doubt. I was ready to puke, from exasperation or airsickness. The pilot was a major. He was revising our insert plan over the radio by talking to our operations officer, another major—a "fallen angel" (failed aviator) who was not known for making good tactical decisions. I felt a sinking feeling in my stomach, when Rathmell gestured for me to take the headset.

"Turf Club, this is Stone Pit Three [operations officer, the major]. You are going to be inserted at Zulu Charlie one-seven-nine-six-four-eight. You will link up with Coffee Time and stay with them until you clear their RAO. How copy? Over?"

"Stone Pit, this is Turf Club Actual. Roger. Out." It was an order, not open to debate. I handed the headset back to Rathmell. We exchanged a look, unspoken communication. He felt bad about what was about to transpire. I struggled back to Couture, took a knee, and tried to explain the change of plans using the map and sign language. I shouted into his ear, "We are going to link up with Coffee Time. Pass the word!" He stared in disbelief, then turned to carry out my instruction.

We flew around and around, swooping here and there toward hilltops and vales—none sufficed. I became convinced that our command pilot would only land on asphalt—

therefore, we had to go back to Da Nang, there being no asphalt on Charlie Ridge. I was wrong. The IO motioned me to the gunner's hatch, map clutched in his fist. I could see that he was as angry as I was. He pointed to a grease-penciled note on his map—the grid of our new insert LZ. It was five hundred meters from where Haillston had started. It was 1600 (4:00 P.M.). Quitting time. I nodded my understanding and turned to signal to the team. Six pairs of airsick eyeballs followed my every move. I pulled my ready magazine from the leg pocket of my trousers, slammed the magazine in my M-16, and jacked a round into the chamber, weapon on safe. It was time to lock and load. They followed suit and turned expectantly toward the rear of the aircraft as the bird began another swooping turn toward the ground. Below us, our escort of Cobra gunships was busy shooting up the countryside with guns and rockets. So much for stealth.

I lurched aft to a position beside the crew chief, struggling to keep my balance. The helicopter flared some fifty feet above the ground, then wallowed onto the elephant grass—hot pilot. We dashed off the bird into twelve-foot elephant grass. No sooner had the last man cleared the tailgate, than the aircraft swooped away, out of sight in a matter of seconds. I made a mental note on survival—whenever possible, avoid flying with majors. The guy had nerves of jelly. But then, so did I. With these thoughts in my subconscious, I scanned the immediate area, waiting for my hearing to return to normal.

Turf Club was arrayed in a half-moon, just as we had rehearsed on HLZ 401. Under the grass, the air was foul and stifling. I began to sweat. I heard nothing but the occasional rustle of equipment as one of the team members shifted position. Nichols and Finchum were busy with comm checks. We had comm with the birds and with Take Out, but not with Coffee Time. The grid I had been given for Coffee Time's insert HLZ was a half-day hump east of us. We had three hours 'til dark . . . What now, Lieutenant? Take a break. With hand signals, I directed the team into a hasty defensive perimeter, then sat down to develop a new plan. It was late in the day. Coffee Time had been moving since early morning. We were out of position, out of our haven, and nearly out of daylight. There had been helicopters flying around our position off and on for hours. Every gook on Charlie Ridge knew that we had been dropped on this position. If they wanted to do something about it, they were on their way. Fire support was the first order of business. Then a new patrol route. "When in doubt, wait it out." The tactical ditty came unbidden to my mind. The thing to do was to find a defendable position on a known piece of terrain, set up some supporting arms, and await developments. The idea of hustling off in search of Coffee Time did not appeal to me. The best-known piece of terrain I could think of was the one we were on. I set about determining where that was, exactly.

It didn't take long—grid Zulu Charlie 175649, only four hundred meters of elephant grass between us and where we were supposed to cut Haillston's back trail. He was supposed to have headed south, uphill, from his insert. Therefore, if we humped east-southeast, we should intersect his route of march before dark. Fuck the major, and all other field-grade officers! This link-up idea is shaping up as an intramural firefight. What we should be doing is humping up this fuckin' mountain on our own. My thoughts and doubts aside, we had orders. I was confident that Haillston would obey his—to halt and wait for Turf Club. Turf Club, therefore, had to hump and hope for a little luck. I decided to try raising them again. They needed to know that we were in their yard, lest they take us for the enemy. Coffee Time was in control of the space. No supporting arms would be fired in Haillston's haven without his clearance. That meant that there would be delays, perhaps terminal delays, in obtaining clearance for us. I turned to Finchum, gesturing for the handset to the radio. He passed it over. I couldn't raise Coffee Time, but Take Out was in radio communication with Coffee Time, and we were in communication with Take Out. There was a God. We could not move safely until we knew where Coffee Time had harbored up. Once that piece of information was conveyed to me, our situation became an orienteering exercise, something that I had been really good at in Basic School. Only instead of a yellow box, we were looking for seven heavily armed, scared-spitless Marines. Not the same game. I asked Take Out to relay a position report from Coffee Time.

I waited, impatiently, for a response. We were making progress. Once we had a fix on where Coffee Time had harbored up, we could move with relative safety. I occupied my time awaiting the next transmission from Take Out by shackling (encoding) the grid for our present position. When Take Out came back on the air, we would trade position information, in code. I would then be able to determine a route from our position to a likely point of intersection with Coffee Time's route of march from its insert HLZ. The idea was that it would be safer to link up with them by following their trail through the elephant grass, coming upon them from an expected direction, than it would be to walk in on them from out of the bush. I wasn't so sure.

When the report came, I copied the encrypted grid into my message book, confirmed it with Take Out, sent my own, and signed off. After a minute or two with the whiz wheel (encryption device), I had a location for Coffee Time, and a new problem. Haillston had hustled. They were more than a klick from our position, and uphill. I deduced from the map that Haillston had elected to monitor one of the trails on the map. He was sitting on the nub of a finger, just off a trail—due south of us. There was no way we could close on them before dark. I made eye contact with Couture, motioned him to join me.

"Well, Sergeant, we have a little humping to do. Coffee Time is up there." I pointed toward the crest of the ridge. "About a klick. We are here." I pointed to the position I had determined. "I want you to prove that to yourself before we do anything else, then pass the word to saddle up. I want Ward on point, you walk drag. Our heading is one hundred seventy-five degrees, magnetic (south-southeast), unless you have a better idea." I handed him my map, watched while he went through the drill of taking his sightings on key terrain features. He picked the same ones I had, Hill 1081 and Hill 1163.

"I make us to be about where you did, Lieutenant. What about these trails?" Couture whispered his concern as he handed the map back to me. Trails were danger areas, or opportunities, depending upon one's disposition. Gooks used trails, therefore . . .

The terrain dictated the tactics once again. If we broke brush, we were relatively safe until we came into the vicinity of the first trail junction. The NVA knew the terrain better than we did, and they knew where we were as well as we did. If they wanted to do something about us, it would be done by outmaneuvering us—using the trails above us to position a unit in ambush and/or by following our back trail into our harbor site, and/or by watching us until they could find a spot to bring us under mortar or small-arms fire—like the spot we were in. It was time to move. I motioned to Couture, who set the order of march. We moved off in a staggered column, Ward in the lead, then me and my compass, then Finchum with his radio, then the doc, then Marvin the ARVN, then Nichols with the other radio, then Kelly, then Couture. If the shit hit the fan, Couture would lead the retreat. We humped, laboriously, up the hill, battling our way through razor-sharp stalks of elephant grass, wait-a-minute vines clawing at our bodies. It was arduous work, and noisy, even with my squirrelly move-and-watch technique. After thirty minutes, I decided to slow down. There was no way we could close on Coffee Time before dark.

With this realization came another. We did not want to walk into the trail junction either. With each meter we climbed, the brush got thicker. Coffee Time was in the canopy. There were no HLZs in the canopy. Down where we were we could still be extracted—if only by ladder. The thing to do was to harbor up in the elephant grass and get a fresh start in the morning. The decision came to me on instinct, a product of a continuing evaluation of our tactical situation. As in the Grunts, the troops had become engrossed in the labor at hand, climbing the "motherfucker" of a mountain. My job was to climb and think at the same time. I thought it was time to set in for the night. I whistled softly to Ward, stopping him in his tracks. When he turned to look in my direction, I gave him a hand signal for a left turn—we would circle onto our back trail in the elephant grass and set into a harbor site. He nodded his head in comprehension, then veered slightly to the left. I turned to signal my intention to the next man in line, then moved off after Ward. After ten minutes or so of lateral movement, we cut abruptly downhill and found a flat spot, a small swail on the hillside upon which to harbor. There was no cover, i.e., physical protection; we settled for concealment and fire superiority—I had them set out the claymores, one on our back trail, the other in the general direction of our recent line of march. I estimated that we were less than twenty meters from our trail through the elephant grass, and a hundred meters lower than our highest point of advance—close enough to hear pursuit and prepare for it. We lay under the giant stalks in dirt and decay for twenty minutes, listening for telltale sounds of pursuit. There were none.

With hand signals, I directed the team to prepare for the night. The radios were staged in the center of our circle. Each man cut a space for himself under the grass with his K-bar combat knife, trimming the stalks just below ground and leaving them standing in the tangle overhead—like burrowing in the brush. No one could come upon us without making a racket that would wake the dead. While the team was thus engrossed, I made a final determination of our position and composed a spot report stating our intention to harbor for the night, then passed it to Finchum for transmission through Take Out. We still had no comm with Coffee Time. It was time for grits (food) and zees (sleep). We set the watch and settled in for a quiet night in the woods.

"Turf Club, this is Take Out. The time is oh-four-thirty. Break. If you are all secure, key your handset two distinct times, over."

Take Out was atop Ba Na (mountain), secure in the remnants of an old French resort. They could talk. I keyed the handset, peering in the gloom at the luminous dial of my Mickey Mouse. It was, indeed, 0430. The night had passed uneventfully, punctuated by identical radio communications every hour. I stared askance at Sergeant Thi, my watchmate. He stood nearby, a darker blackness. And another tactical lesson—it was hard to sleep standing up, no matter how weary you might be. I followed his example, rising carefully to my feet. It wouldn't do to wake the team by tripping in the brush—great way to get shot. It was not yet time to muster the troops, but a plan of the day's march had formed in my mind. If Coffee Time held their present position, we could link up with them in a matter of hours. It was the safest option for traversing their haven. It was time to raise Coffee Time myself.

"Coffee Time, Coffee Time, this is Turf Club. Comm check. Over."

"Turf Club, this is Coffee Time. I hear you five-by. How me? Over."

"Coffee Time, this is Turf Club Actual, I hear you same, same. Break. Get your Actual on the hook. Over." I wanted to talk to Haillston myself. No chance of a garbled message. Walking in on his team unannounced could lead to a firefight—disaster. Haillston was probably asleep. I waited while the first light of dawn turned the night sky gray. Standing the last watch was a habit I had formed in the Grunts. It served me well here, but it was not SOP with every patrol leader. Like everything else in the bush, each man had to find what worked for him.

"Turf Club, this is Coffee Time Actual. Send your traffic. Over." He was alert, calm, no nonsense.

"Coffee Time, this is Turf Club Actual. Our ETA your pos is two hours. We can move at first light. Will you sit tight? Over?"

"Turf Club Actual, this is Coffee Time Actual. Roger that. Confirm posreps by shackled message before you move. Over."

Good thinking. Haillston would stay put, but he wanted to know exactly where we were coming from before we started to move. It was still too dark to work the shackle sheets without a flashlight. Around me, the other members of Turf Club began to stir, aroused from fitful sleep by the subtle change in activity I had wrought with my radio chat. It had been only a whisper, and brief, but it was enough to have everyone alert within seconds. Small sounds emanated from the group, men shifting position on damp ground, rustling through their packs for food, moving weapons and equipment in preparation for the day's march. Nature's calls were strong: before long, the odor of urine and canned peaches permeated the harbor site. Gradually, there was light. I could pick out the features of the other team members where they sat.

I worked out our shackled posrep, double-checked my work, then raised Coffee Time once more. We exchanged terse messages, then sat down to determine one another's positions. After fumbling with the whiz wheel for a few minutes in the predawn gloom, I deciphered Haillston's posrep—we were like-minded. He had spent the night in the grass, below the timber line, half a klick (five hundred meters) east of us. By dead reckoning, Coffee Time was on the opposite side of the finger we now occupied, and about two hundred meters higher. Turf Club had buried their trash, cammied up, and saddled up, while I was occupied with whiz wheel, map, and radio. I followed their example, quickly, then motioned for Couture to join me at the map. "Coffee Time is on the other side of this finger, up there." I pointed in the general direction we had to travel. "Let's cut across down here, then move up the draw. We should cut their back trail, follow it in." It was a whisper, both of us looking at the map. "Same line up [order of march] as yesterday." I looked at Couture. "We don't want to walk in on these guys by surprise." He agreed.

We set off in a generally easterly direction, and uphill, moving carefully through heavy brush. I kept one eye on Ward, the other on my compass, counting paces (yards) on a mental register in my mind. Ward developed downhill syndrome (a tendency to drift off course with the slope of the ground underfoot), and I had to tap him on the shoulder repeatedly to keep him on course. Behind us, the rest of the team labored in trace and silence. It was grueling work. Should have had Coffee Time come to us. With the thought, we stumbled upon their back trail, or someone's back trail in the brush. It was a wide swatch of broken stalks, bent uphill—Marines for sure. It was the right thing, going the right way, at about the right place. I decided to go with it. I turned to take the handset from Finchum, gesturing with a hand signal for the team to sit down. "Coffee Time, Coffee Time, this is Turf Club, over."

I waited, blotting sweat from my brow. We were close, therefore in danger. I broke out my whiz wheel and message pad, worked out a posrep, and encoded it awkwardly (gloves were a hindrance) then traded coordinates with Coffee Time, which was another hundred meters uphill, with a claymore covering their path. We wanted to set their minds at ease. I sent the message, authenticated, then turned to reorganize the team. With hand signals, I changed the order of march— I would take point, then Finchum, then Sergeant Thi, then the others in their same order. Ward would become drag (last man). The order passed from man to man. I watched to ensure that everyone had the word. No more wrong turns or lost troops if I could help it. We set out in staggered column again, well dispersed. Coffee Time had broken the trail for us, so the going was relatively easy—steeper, but with less tugging, tearing and pulling. Twenty minutes passed. With each step, I felt dread. Suddenly, there was movement ahead. I had seen a shadow, a flicker of movement in the brush. I froze, then knelt slowly on one knee, beckoning to Finchum for the radio handset, my weapon at the ready.

Haillston had sent us a guide, or at least a trail guard. The shadow was a Marine. He sat, spread-legged in the brush, his back against the slope of the hill, his weapon across his knees. The telltale whip antenna extending over his shoulder told me something else—I could talk to him. Finchum slid the handset into my outstretched palm, holding his breath. I grasped it, keyed the mike button two times, watching the shadowy form ahead of us. He plucked a handset from inside a pocket of his camouflage jacket. My man! "Coffee Time, this is Turf Club. We have your man in sight. We are at his ten o'clock, ten meters. If you copy, stand up, over."

The Marine stood slowly, peering in our direction, the transmission otherwise unacknowledged. I rose slowly to my feet, making eye contact across the distance. We closed upon our guide silently, relieved to have effected a dangerous maneuver without incident. He led us across a deadfall of brush and tree trunks and into a jumble of rocks some twenty meters from where we had sighted him. Haillston had backtracked to his harbor site, encouraging would-be trackers to walk past him before realizing their error. We would have done the same. The harbor site was well situated for defense and expeditious withdrawal—down an intermittent streambed, a natural high-speed trail beneath the undergrowth.

First Lieutenant Earl Haillston turned out to be a man of medium height, lean as we all were, and laconic. He stood to greet me with a handshake. "Welcome to our humble abode," he whispered. "I'm Earl Haillston."

We shook hands, while Turf Club filtered into the deadfall, finding crash sites among the rocks.

"Mike Hodgins. Thanks for waiting."

"Got time for chow, Mike, then we should be moving. There's a high-speed trail above us, maybe two hundred meters from here. We checked it out this morning. It's being used. Now that we're together, the way I see it, we're too big to hide and too small to fight. I think we should hump on up here [he showed me a spot marked on his map, a "tit"—one hill of a saddle]. Get across the trail in daylight. We can set in there for the night, big ambush on the trail, then split up in the mornin'. You go south [uphill]. I'll go east. That should keep the fig leafs* happy."

*Majors, lieutenant colonels, and colonels, from the leaf that is the insignia of rank for majors and lieutenant colonels.

Haillston had done his homework while we were humping. It was a good plan, better than mine, since I had none. We would still be a klick out of our haven—a full day's hump. But, now that we were colocated with Coffee Time, our fire-support coordination problem was solved. We had lots of firepower and, once in place, a defendable piece of terrain at a known location. It was the best anyone could do. "Suits me, Earl."

Haillston was going out of his way to help get us safely out of his RAO (recon area of operation). We passed the word, shared a can of pears, and went about our business. Coffee Time led the way uphill, with Turf Club following. As we climbed, the vegetation changed, from elephant grass to broader-leafed plants and trees. By early afternoon, we were in the canopy. The undergrowth thinned, and the jungle floor became speckled with sunlight. Here and there a sunbeam fell on a tree trunk, pollen suspended in it. Unseen birds and animals screeched overhead and scurried through the underbrush. It was an eerie, dangerous place—even for sixteen Marines and a pair of ARVN Rangers. Without conscious thought, we changed our formation, spreading out into more of a wedge. Haillston's point man alerted us to the trail with a sudden raised fist.

He posted flank security from his team, a well-rehearsed maneuver, then motioned for me to move Turf Club across the danger area. I stared at Couture, willing him to following Coffee Time's example on the far side. We crossed the trail in two-man rushes without incident and found cover behind trees that must have been over a hundred feet high. Couture had taken my hint, posting a man to each flank and Sergeant Thi at the rear. Haillston's team folded into our new position without incident. The terrain, however, was not conducive to an ambush. It was a conclusion we both reached without discussion. What now, Lieutenant? Find high ground and hide. We had crossed the trail dispersed, making it unlikely that an NVA scout would discover our route, at least not in the dark. We needed to find a harbor site far enough off the trail not to be heard by passing pedestrians. We walked east, into another draw, where we scuttled into heavier brush for the night.

Couture led Turf Club into the harbor site and positioned the men in a half circle on the downhill side of our perimeter. Coffee Time took the uphill, and Haillston and I found ourselves more or less surrounded, accompanied by our primary radio operators. It was a natural solution to the tactical situation that preserved the integrity of both units. I wished I had thought of it myself. The troops settled in, divesting themselves of web gear and preparing to sate teen appetites. They appeared to be working in pairs—one watching while the other scrambled in his pack for food. All had found positions of relative comfort on the uneven ground.

"Okay, Mike. This looks good from here. Why don't we split the watch, one of yours and one of mine on the radio— save batteries and give the guys a little extra zees?" Haillston spoke softly, asserting command in a subtle way. I fell in step (accepted his authority), relieved to know that we were of like mind in adjusting to the situation. There could only be one commander. While the teams were operating together, Haillston was the man.

"Roger that. You want to call in a posrep while I pass the word to my guys?"

"Sure."

Haillston was already working on his map. It was going to be an educated guess, based upon dead reckoning—a poor turn of phrase, given the importance of getting it right. I had kept track of our progress in my mind, but I was eager to confirm my estimate. Having begun to appreciate Sergeant Couture's bush acumen, I felt confident that he had also come to some conclusion about our position. I decided to ask.

"What about claymores?" It wouldn't do to put such a powerful weapon on the perimeter without coordination. I did not know what his SOP on such matters might be. "I like to put one on my back trail and one on the way out . . ." I let the remark fade.

Haillston looked up from the map. "Sounds good to me. Run

the hellboxes [trigger mechanisms] in here, so the watch can work them. I usually stake them down with a K-bar." He held out the map for my inspection, pointing to a spot with his grease pencil. "I make us out to be about here."

I stared at the point he identified—grid ZC 178640. I smiled to myself—we were both lost in the same place. "Looks right to me."

"Okay. If we get hit, we run down this draw 'til we get to elephant grass—find a place to get extracted." Haillston drew a line on the map, then measured the angle with his protractor, a deft gesture. "I make that to be a heading of about thirty degrees, magnetic. If we stay on that, we can't go too far wrong. We'll run into this little cliff." He pointed to a spot on the map.

It looked like a perfect place to put a base camp—close to water and major trails, in defilade from all but direct fire. Still, it was the only viable route of withdrawal in the dark. We sure didn't want to run uphill into the trees. "That's it, then?"

"That's it. We'll split up in the morning. You head on up the ridge, and I'll go east. Piece of cake."

Haillston called in our posrep and intentions to spend the night, while I rejoined Turf Club and briefed Couture on the game plan. The decisions made and implemented, we settled in for the night. I found a spot near the radios, ate a cold C rat, sipped half a canteen of water, and studied the map. Gradually, a new plan took form in my mind. The trails were a problem, and a tactical objective. Our mission required that I find a way to get into our assigned haven and monitor the trail, since we had determined that it did exist and was being used. It now remained to confirm the general direction of it and the frequency of use—we should monitor the trail, a dangerous job.

The light faded to blackness while I chewed and studied. Finally, I folded the map away and settled back to ruminate between catnaps for the rest of the night. I awoke frequently, listening for the squawking of the handset in response to the query of Take Out. We were anything but "all secure." With the dawn would come new adventures. I played the next day's possibilities over and over in my mind. What to do about the trail?

The bush lore on trails was well developed and a topic of hotly contested arguments. It was common knowledge that the enemy had developed and maintained a complex network of trails linking its base areas, and that the NVA used this complex continuously. Units and individuals traveled this trail network from camp to camp as a means of defeating Allied efforts to "fix and destroy" them. If the NVA used the trails, it followed that Recon teams using trails in the base areas were likely to meet NVA, more often than not on unfavorable terms. "Breaking brush," i.e., cutting trails, was considered safer in most cases because the team could avoid booby traps and ambushes. The NVA were not known to break brush. They were known to "prepare the battlefield," however, building extensive field fortifications in remote areas in preparation for defensive battles with offense-minded Marines. Walking into a prepared position or base camp from out of the brush was no more fun than getting there on a trail. The ideal situation was to discover the trail, approach it from concealment, monitor or ambush transients for a period, then move on without giving away the fact of the team's presence. There were many instances, however, where the terrain dictated use of a trail as the only means to move. The greatest Recon successes (ambushes) and tragedies (ambushes) had occurred on trails, including Skibbe's unfortunate demise. Gregson had been shot on a trail. Pino had ambushed his NVA on a trail. Quaid's team had been ambushed on a trail. I decided to go with the percentages—we would break brush with great stealth and bushcraft, Sergeant Thi in the lead. We would head south, uphill, parallel to the trail, until we got into our haven, then find a place to set up an ambush and await results.

Haillston was an early riser. He had his team up and about with the predawn. Turf Club was not to be outdone. We packed up, cleaned up, cammied up, and were ready to move by the time the sun broke the crest of the ridge above us.

"Pleasure to meet you, Mike." Haillston extended his hand. "We're goin' to stroll on down this draw, then cut east. Luck, leatherneck!"

I clasped his outstretched hand. "Thanks for the hospitality. We're going to hump on up this finger until we're out of your haven. See you back at the ranch!" We shook hands, joined our teams, and moved off.

With Sergeant Thi on point, Turf Club moved carefully up the ridge toward my next checkpoint, Hill 864. On the heading I selected, 185 degrees, magnetic, we kept high ground and dense foliage between us and the trail. It was highly unlikely that we would be seen or heard by a passerby. We moved slowly, climbing for ten minutes, listening for five, careful to make as little noise as possible. Once we attained the spine of the ridge, the undergrowth thinned alarmingly. The trees overhead blocked the light, smothering the undergrowth. We could see a long way under the trees. There was cover, but little in the way of concealment.

I called a halt, motioned for Couture. "Sergeant Cee, I think the crest of Hill Eight-six-four is right up there." I pointed vaguely through the trees. "The trail is supposed to be on our side. Let's head south, stay on the top of the finger, spread out a little. Okay?"

I held his gaze. He had assessed the situation, perhaps reaching a different tactical conclusion than I had. We were still five hundred meters from our haven. It was not a good place to stop, for trail monitoring or anything else.

"Aye, aye, sir." Couture moved back toward the tail of our column, whispering to each man as he went.

I grasped Sergeant Thi by the shoulder, pointing with my rifle in the direction I wanted him to go. He stared at me for a moment, as if to protest, then thought better of it. We moved on up the ridge in midmorning gloom, weapons at the ready. Suddenly, Sergeant Thi stopped in his tracks, raised his clenched fist to signal a halt. I moved cautiously to see what he could see.

We had come upon an open area, relatively flat for some two hundred meters, still sheltered by tall trees. The undergrowth had been cleared away. Sergeant Thi was pointing to different sights—a punji pit, recently under construction, holding pens for hogs or ducks, recently repaired (the new sticks of bamboo shiny between the old); a bamboo aqueduct zigzagging into the gloom. I scanned the gloom, peering into the shadows, looking for movement, light, color, straight lines, anything out of place. It was still.

"Beaucoup VC here, *Tu Uy* [Lieutenant]. We go back."

Sergeant Thi wanted no part of what lay ahead. He made as if to leave. I held him by the shoulder, pulling him toward the ground as I sank to one knee myself. What now, Lieutenant? For starters, get some security. I motioned for Couture and the corpsman to join me. Then I pulled my map from my trouser pocket. The others, sensing danger, had crouched or gone prone in the sparse undergrowth, weapons at the ready.

Couture, crouching, moved to a position nearby. He took in the situation at a glance, then moved back to pass the word to the others.

"What's the buzz, Lieutenant?" Doc Pearston had moved quietly to a position on my flank, opposite Couture.

"Ask our ARVN friend, here." I gestured toward the Vietnamese. The corpsman whispered in Vietnamese, listened to Sergeant Thi's animated response, then turned to me.

"Well, sir. He says these are holding pens for livestock, hogs and ducks. He says somebody was working here when we walked up. He says the VC are preparing this place for a big unit. He says we are in deep shit, and he wants to bug out. He won't go any farther up the ridge."

I studied the map. Back tracking into Coffee Time's haven was not a go. We had to keep moving to find an HLZ. My ruminations were interrupted.

"Coffee Time just walked into a base camp, Lieutenant!"

Finchum offered me the handset. I listened briefly. They were calling in a spot (situation, position, observation, time) report. No contact. I gave the handset back to Finchum. I looked around, searching for a view of something besides tree trunks and foliage. By dead reckoning, I knew where we were within a hundred meters—not good enough if we needed artillery. If we were in fact compromised, I wanted high ground, good cover, and clear sky overhead. We had to move on up the ridge—get to Hill 1081.

"Tell Marvin here that we are going on up the ridge. He is point." I whispered to Pearston.

"Finchum, get us an OV-ten." It was insurance. The Bronco could see everything, help us get a good location, direct artillery support fire, even honcho (coordinate) an extract if necessary.

"Roger that, Lieutenant." He commenced to whisper into his handset.

I turned to face the team, gesturing with hand signals to move out. Then I turned and pushed the ARVN in the direction of march. He balked, his eyes bugged with fear.

"Pearston, tell this ugly little motherfucker that I will shoot him right where he stands if he doesn't move out, right now." I whispered harshly, maintaining hard eye contact, the muzzle of my M-16 centered on the ARVN's chest. He didn't understand the words, but he took my meaning. Before Pearston could complete a whispered translation, Sergeant Thi shrugged in resignation and turned to move cautiously around the open area. We circled the livestock pens, taking note of the size of the enemy effort, then pressed on up the slope in a dispersed formation. I called a halt, having decided to get reoriented.

"Lieutenant, I've got Hostage Duke. He wants us to mark our position." Finchum was gesturing toward me with the handset, speaking in a loud whisper. Things were improving. "Roger that." I whispered, "Pass the word for Couture to come up. Set in [take defensive positions] for five [minutes]."

I wanted the team to establish a secure position while I dealt with the issue of how to mark our position for the aerial observer (AO). Couture moved past me, taking Nichols with him to a position forward of the point. The others went to ground, more or less in a three-sixty (perimeter) around Finchum and me.

Air panels were out, too much overhead foliage. Pencil flares and smoke were out—we didn't want to compromise our position. The strobe light was out, too easily mistaken for the muzzle flashes from an NVA 12.7mm antiaircraft machine gun in this terrain. I thought I could flash the mirror through the trees without exposing us too much. The problem was that the plane had to fly on just the right heading to see it. I plucked the radio handset from Finchum's grasp. "Hostage Duke, this is Turf Club Actual. Break. We can mark our position with a signal mirror. How copy, over?"

"Turf Club, this is Hostage Duke. Roger, understand you will use signal mirror. ETA your last known pos is two mikes [minutes]."

We should be able to hear him any minute. I sat down, my back against a boulder, intending to sort out map and mirror. My preoccupation with land navigation was shattered by a burst of automatic weapons fire—an M-16. It was followed by two more, and a curse.

"We missed the little bastard!" It was Couture. I rolled prone behind the rock, then rose cautiously to one knee, peering into the gloom. Couture and Nichols were advancing up the slope in a crouched position, their weapons at the ready. I took a quick survey of the others. Everyone was alert, covering their assigned sectors.

"Couture, what have you got?" I spoke loud enough for him to hear, just above a whisper, urgency in my voice.

"Fuckin' Slope ran away, Lieutenant. But, we got his gear and his chow." He kicked a tin on the ground. It was full of rice, just cooked. "We are about to be in a world of shit . . ." His voice trailed off.

I moved to join him, staring at the tin of spilled rice. "Did he have a weapon?"

"Yes, sir. He did. But he was at sling arms when we spotted him. He just dropped his kit [bedroll] and chow and *didi*'d [left] back the way he came," Nichols answered, joining us from his trek farther up the hill. He gestured with a thumb over his shoulder. "There's a big-mother trail right up there, Lieutenant. This guy was probably a trail guard or guide."

The NVA had gone for help. That was what we needed. I looked at my watch. Two minutes were up. It was 0930 (9:30 A.M.), with no sign of Hostage Duke.

"Okay, Couture. Let's saddle up and get the fuck off this finger. We'll head that way." I pointed toward the crest of the ridge. "We've got an OV-ten on the way. Let's find a place to hole up.

"Finchum, call in a spot report. Tell 'em we made contact with one NVA at . . ." I paused to consult the map—"Zulu Charlie one-eight-two-six-two-seven."

CHAPTER FIVE
CHARLIE RIDGE

12 APRIL 1970

When men find they must inevitably perish, they willingly resolve to die with their comrades, and with their arms in their hands.

Vegetius, *De Re Militari*

"Hostage Duke, this is Turf Club. Over." I whispered the words into the handset of our PRC-25 field radio. The handset hissed back at me. The sound rasped on my nerves. Why not stand up and shout, Mikey? I stretched my arm slowly in the direction of the camouflaged radio, turned down the squelch and waited impatiently for a reply, the handset crushed against my ear. Like a stricken animal, I probed the gloom of the forest floor with all my senses. My eyes flicked involuntarily from point to point, focusing briefly on each member of the team, then probing the shadows, seeking movement, straight lines, anomalies in the undergrowth. There were none. The only movement within view was the end-over-end progress of a leech as it made its way across the jungle floor just inches from my face. I listened, frustrated that my ears were still ringing from our recent engagement. There were sounds, my own breathing, the rustle of equipment when one of the team members shifted position, wind whispering through the foliage of ancient trees that towered overhead, and far off, the chatter of animals—rock apes or birds. I couldn't say. There were odors—sweat, bug juice, fetid mud, animal dung. Here and there an errant ray of sunlight dappled the forest floor. Otherwise, we were in perpetual twilight, inhabitants of a shadow world fraught with danger. The ground vegetation was sparse, offering little concealment. I hugged the fetid earth, striving in vain to make myself smaller, more still, invisible in the shadows. Sweat trickled down my brow, mixed with cammy paint and bug juice, made my eyes tear. I shifted my grip on the handset ever so slowly, so as to blot the irritant from my eye on the sleeve of my cammy jacket.

"Station calling Hostage, this is Hostage Duke, over!" The handset screeched to life. Not so loud, motherfucker! It was a silent curse. I realized that I had been holding my breath. I shifted my gaze from the depths of the forest to my team members again. No one looked back. Each man lay prone and motionless, weapon at the ready, intent upon his assigned sector of observation. If they had not heard, no one else had. I keyed the handset and whispered, "Hostage Duke, this is Turf Club. Break. We need a posrep. Over."

The voice on the radio belonged to another Marine, an aerial observer (AO, probably another lieutenant like me) flying in the back seat of an OV-10A Bronco light-observation aircraft orbiting somewhere overhead. The fact that we could not hear his engines meant that he was still far off, below the ridge or orbiting thousands of feet overhead. Hostage was part of our team, and he was going to save our bacon, provided his map was better than mine. After two days of humping Charlie Ridge in hundred-degree heat and hundred-percent humidity, my map was all but useless, soaked with sweat, like the rest of me. Hostage had a dry map and lots of electronic stuff to help him. Not only that, he was air-conditioned, or at least conditioned by cool air. Flying around at several thousand feet was definitely more comfortable than what we had been doing, less strenuous, if no less hazardous. In a matter of hours, he would be back in Da Nang sucking on a cold beer. In a matter of minutes, we could be dead. That's what the teamwork was all about—avoiding disaster.

"Turf Club, this is Hostage Duke. Roger, you need a posrep. Break. Can you mark your position? Over."

Gradually, I became aware of the aircraft's engines far off to my left and below me. I turned down the squelch on the radio once more, keyed the handset and whispered, "Hostage, this is Turf Club. Break. No Joy! The canopy is too thick, and we have company. Break. I need a flyby. Over."

I wanted the Bronco to help me determine my location by flying on a known course (known to him) while I gave him a vector to my position from the sound of his engines as he passed. I wanted to find out where we were without compromising our position. Our game of hide-and-seek with the NVA was becoming interesting. We were belly-down in the midst of what appeared to be a well-traveled trail complex. The point-to-point contact we had made moments before meant that an NVA patrol would be arriving on the scene in the most immediate future. If we were still in this exposed position without fire support when they arrived, we were dead. We needed to move to a defendable position, and we needed to have artillery or air support to cover our movement. For that, I needed to know where we were, hence the request for assistance from the aerial observer.

We had another problem. We were supposed to be in constant radio contact with our Operations people (S-3) in battalion headquarters over the battalion tac net (a different radio frequency). Take Out, our radio relay, was off the air. Without the radio relay, I had no lifeline—no fire support, no extract, no mommy to hold my hand! I wanted Hostage to be my mommy, at least until Take Out came back on the net.

Spread out on the ground in front of me, I had the useless map, a set of shackle sheets (pages of a codebook from hell), a whiz wheel (a gadget that was supposed to be faster than the codebook from hell), a radio-message book, a grease pencil, three frags (M-26 hand grenades), my M-16, and the hellbox for a claymore mine. The cable for the claymore snaked off down the trail we had stumbled across. It covered my sector of the team's defensive position. With hand signals, I had instructed them to set up a hasty ambush, L-shaped on the long axis of the saddle in which we had found ourselves when we came onto the top of the ridge. I was the short line of the L. The claymore covered our back door.

I held the radio handset in my left hand. I shifted my position cautiously, lurching into a sitting position with my back against a tree. I looked at Finchum, the primary RTO, belly-down behind a boulder nearby. He had his back to me, his eyes glued to the trail. I nudged his boot with mine. When he turned to look at me, I motioned with my fingers and eyes, telling him to take over observation of my sector while I was busy with the radio. He nodded and turned back to resume his vigil.

Assured of security, I focused my attention on the puzzle at hand—getting a position fix. Like sailors of old, I wanted to take a sighting on a star, in this case the OV-10. I fished the lensatic compass from the pocket of my cammy jacket by tugging on its tether with my right hand. Compass in hand, I keyed the handset and whispered, "Hostage Duke, this is Turf Club. Break. I hear your orbit at my eight o'clock. Break. Make your pass November Sierra at Angels Five Zero— stand by for my mark. Over."

I was telling him to fly across the ridge on a north-to-south heading at five thousand feet, the altitude at which I hoped to see him through the trees. If everything went according to plan, I would see or hear him as he flew across the ridge just outside the eastern edge of my haven, the coordinates for which he had already noted on his map. I intended to shoot an azimuth on him with my compass, as he would do on me, when I called out my "Mark."

"Roger, Turf Club. Doing it now. Over." The aircraft rolled and dived toward the valley floor. Waiting for Hostage to make his turn, I thought to myself, I hope Charlie isn't monitoring our transmissions. If he is, Hostage's mother is going to be really mad at me! The NVA were notoriously good at shooting down aircraft once they had determined the course a plane had to fly to engage a target. Hostage was taking a risk.

Hearing the plane's engines change pitch, I shifted my

position slightly, mentally crossing my fingers. Squinting over the eyepiece of my compass, I peered out through the canopy toward a little patch of blue sky and the valley below. The sun flashed briefly off his windshield. I keyed the handset.

"Hostage Duke, this is Turf Club. Stand by Mark! Mark! Over." I looked into the compass. Azimuth 265 degrees. I dropped the compass on its tether, picked up the grease pencil, and jotted the numbers on the map.

"Turf Club, this is Hostage Duke. Roger your mark. Wait. Out." The aircraft's engine raced again as it initiated a climbing turn to a safer orbit. In the backseat, the aerial observer had set to work determining our position relative to his. In moments, we would compare notes. I turned my attention to the map on the ground in front of me, reorienting it using the straight edge of the compass. My friend Hostage was doing the same thing in the backseat of the Bronco as it circled high above. He would be using onboard electronics to fix his own position on the map, orienting himself to terrain features he could see on the ground, and using the azimuth he had shot on my mark, determining his best guess as to where I was on the ground. I had confidence in his ability. Locating targets was his stock in trade. He was as much a part of my team as any of the men on the ground nearby. I just wished he would hurry up!

"Turf Club, this is Hostage Duke. Stand by for posrep. Over!"

Jesus, this guy is loud! I thought to myself. Aloud, I whispered, "Hostage Duke, this is Turf Club. Roger, send it. Over." I picked up the grease pencil. A leech had found it. I shook the nasty creature off, waiting for Hostage to tell me where in Vietnam I was going to die.

"Turf Club, this is Hostage Duke. Break. I set Alpha Golf, I shackle Tango, Charlie, Sierra, Delta, Oscar, Hotel. Unshackle. How copy? Over."

I jotted the letters on the map. When I finished my whizwheel magic, they would correspond to a six-digit coordinate on my map, the fountain from which all future good

things would flow. I confirmed the shackled coordinates
with Hostage then dropped the handset, picked up the whiz
wheel and set to work, sweat running in my eyes. There's
got to be a better way, I thought to myself. But there wasn't.
Grid 178624. I reoriented the map, looking at the contour
lines in the general area of the grid reference the AO had
provided me. I found myself—at least I found a place on the
map that matched the terrain features I could feel around me.
This dude is not bad for an aviator, or maybe he's an artillery
guy. He's got me too low on the ridge, but I can work with
it. I wrote the new coordinates in my message book, shackled
them using the sheets, put the grease pencil back in my
pocket, took a deep breath, picked up the handset, and whispered the coordinates aloud, my eyes darting from one member of my team to another, then out around our perimeter. So
far, so good, I thought to myself, Now for some fire support,
just in case. I studied the map. If we had to run, I wanted to
go downhill and toward a potential extract by helicopter.
From the saddle in which we crouched, that meant I had to
go east, more or less. I plotted four targets on the map, the
tops of the hills on either end of the saddle, the rim of the
draw we had just navigated, and the end of a little finger of
rock that appeared to jut into the valley about three hundred
meters below me in an easterly direction. My mission was to
scout the ridge. The area of patrol assigned by the operations
officer required me to conduct my patrolling activities within
a six-klick (six thousand meters) box on top of the ridge. Inside the box, I controlled all the fire-support assets which
might be fired into it. Outside the box, I was fair game for
friendly fire as well as enemy. The little finger I had selected
was just at the edge of my haven and could be easily located
by aircraft, especially if I could put an artillery spotting
round on it first. I picked up the handset and ordered up a fire
mission from Hostage Duke.

While I was talking, I jotted down the elements of my call
for fire on an acetate-covered form. I wanted the eight-inch
artillery battery assigned as my primary fire-support asset
(one section—two self-propelled guns) to fire a marking

round over the grid I had determined was a possible extract point. Since I could neither see the target, nor talk to the artillery fire-support coordination center (FSCC—a communication facility which processed requests for artillery fire) myself, I would use Hostage. I wanted an airburst, just above the trees. I wanted a chance to see it, perhaps shoot an azimuth on it. I wanted to be able to use the artillery to blow a hole in the trees if need be, so that the helicopter sent to pick us up could get in. I had a long list of wants.

I keyed the handset and read the elements of my fire mission over the air, using the outline on my call-for-fire card. While I waited for Hostage to come back on the air, I gathered up the tools of my trade and turned my attention to getting the team moving again. Now that I knew where we were, I needed to share that information with the other members of the team and get us all out of Dodge. The mission required us to continue up the ridge. The terrain and vegetation dictated a more open formation for movement than the Indian file we customarily used. If we were going to make contact again, I wanted maximum firepower to the front and flanks, i.e., a squad wedge with Finchum and me in the middle. I needed to tell them all where our new rally point would be. These and other thoughts were running through my mind as I turned to hiss at Finchum. Behind me and farther up the hill, an M-16 went off, three quick bursts—then an M-26 hand grenade. Shit! I thought to myself as I rolled to a prone position beside the tree, weapon in hand. Aloud, I shouted, "Couture, what the fuck is going on?"

There was an eerie silence, then Couture answered, "Gooks, Lieutenant—I think me and Ward whacked two of 'em!"

"Hold your fire! I'm moving to you!" Tossing the radio handset in Finchum's direction, I said, "Hostage Duke is on tac two. Tell him we are in contact. He has a fire mission running for us. Watch your ass!"

M-16 in the assault-fire position, I rose to a crouch and shouted "Coming in!" Just as I rose to rush forward to Couture's position, he fired again. I saw movement between the trees several meters in front of him. I fired a burst from my weapon and rolled behind a tree near him. Ward was a few meters away, facing the same direction. "Okay, Couture, what have we got?"

"Two gooks with big packs and pistols, Lieutenant. I think we got one in the body. They're both in that little pocket of rocks." He pointed to a place about twenty meters in front of us.

My mind raced. Pistols—officers—packs—prisoners— ticket for an extract and an R & R. Aloud, I said, "Ward! Cover us, but hold your fire! Come on, Doc, let's see what we got."

I stood to a crouch, my weapon at the ready. I was cotton-mouthed, my stomach sour, my body tense, expecting a blow. Nothing happened. I moved toward the rocks, one step at a time. Twenty meters was a long, long way to go. Finally, I saw them, facedown among the rocks. They were wearing khaki shorts and sandals. Their shirts were neatly strapped to the tops of oversized rucksacks, the kind favored by the U.S. Army.

"*Chieu hoi* [Give up], motherfucker!" I whispered the words without realizing I had spoken aloud. One of the NVA moved, putting his hands behind his head as he remained facedown on the ground. The other groaned and tried to roll over. I saw that he was shot through the hips. His left leg was nearly torn from his body, the hipbone shattered, his entrails oozing onto the ground. Their pistols were still holstered. I saw no other weapons.

Fuck me! I thought to myself, What am I going to do now? "Pearston!" I shouted, "They're down; bring your bag!"

"Right here, Lieutenant."

I twitched, startled by his voice close behind me. I realized that the corpsman must have accompanied me on my ten-thousand-mile (twenty-meter) sojourn from the safety of the position we had occupied moments before. He was already opening his medical kit.

"Wait!" I said. "Get the ARVN up here first, and tell these guys to lay chilly."

Pearston complied, speaking the Vietnamese he had learned in the CAPs. Waiting for the ARVN Ranger sergeant to join us, I scanned the terrain around us, looking for an easy way to get off the saddle in the direction of our planned rally point. My mind raced through countless possibilities, evaluating and discarding one idea after another. The NVA lay still and silent, their eyes focused on me. They seemed to sense that their fate rested in my hands. I would decide whether they lived or died, but that was not a thought I had wrestled with yet. I wanted to move, to get the team and the prisoners as far away from the contact point as I could, and fast.

A twig snapped close behind me. I cast my eyes in the direction of the noise, my M-16 held steady on a space midway between the two enemy soldiers. The ARVN had arrived. He was all eyes, alertly taking in the situation. He positioned himself several meters to my right, with a low boulder between him and the NVA on the ground. If something shitty happened, he had cover. Clever devil, I thought to myself, You should be giving us OJT.

"Pearston," I spoke in a low voice, the command implicit in my tone, "Tell Marvin here to cuff these assholes. Have him leave his weapon on the ground behind me."

Pearston spoke to the ARVN, whose eyes flicked from the NVA on the ground to me, back to the NVA, then rested on me as Pearston finished speaking. I could see him weighing his options, "Who is more dangerous, this American who has already threatened to shoot me, or these NVA who might have a grenade under them?" He put his rifle on the ground, his eyes locked on mine. Then he shrugged out of his pack, pulled a pair of plastic ties (handcuffs) from the leg pocket of his trousers, and approached the NVA, careful to keep them between us. He said something to them, and the able-bodied one moved his hands slowly from atop his head to behind his back. The ARVN bent quickly, put his knee in the man's back, wrapped his wrists with the ties, pulled them tight and stood up.

Just like a cowboy bulldogging a calf, I thought. Maybe I had this guy wrong!

The ARVN spoke to Pearston, his eyes on me.

"He says the other guy is hurt too bad to roll over, Lieutenant. What should he do?"

"Tell him to tie his hands in front, then cut the packs off and throw the pistol belts over here." It was clear that there would be no booby trap, no last-ditch resistance. I wanted them secured and ready to move quickly. "After he does that, Pearston, tell him to guard them while you see what you can do for the WIA. Okay?"

Pearston nodded his agreement, spoke to the ARVN, then leaned his weapon against a rock and shrugged out of his pack. The ARVN completed his task, pulling the packs and weapons away from the NVA as he stood up. He smiled at me and said something. I smiled back.

"Lieutenant!" Finchum shouted, the radio handset in his hand, "Hostage says he's bingo on fuel. We have to wait for Hostage One-Six—twenty minutes!"

I quit smiling. Everyone was staring at me. Fuck! I thought to myself, We are not having a good day! Aloud, I said, "What about the spotting round?"

Finchum mumbled into the handset, listened for a moment, then motioned for me to join him. Marvin had the NVA covered, and Pearston was working on the WIA. I moved back to Finchum's position.

"What?" I spoke the word quietly, trying to convey confidence that I didn't feel.

Finchum's eyes were wide open. He was shaking. His voice broke as he spoke. "Lieutenant, Hostage says we got no fire mission. All the arty is diverted to other teams! He says we got three other teams in contact right now! We are fucked, Lieutenant!"

"Chill out, Finchum. You have too much imagination. Give me the radio. You go check out those packs."

As I spoke, I pointed in the direction of the NVA with my M-16. I wanted to give Finchum something else to think about while I tried to talk Hostage into getting us some support. While he was shrugging out of the rucksack that held the radio (and all his gear), I scanned the area once more, my eyes alert for movement. There was none. Finchum dropped the pack, handed me the handset, and moved off in the direction of the Vietnamese. My eyes followed him.

Marvin was engaged in conversation with the able-bodied prisoner. He had assumed the squatting position characteristic of his people, his weapon across his knees, and was pulling a pack of Gaulloise cigarettes from his shirt pocket. As I watched, stunned by his audacity, he stuck one of the cigarettes in the prisoner's mouth, one in his own, replaced the pack, and removed a Zippo lighter from another pocket. He obviously had less concern for compromising our position than I did! I don't believe this motherfucker! I thought to myself. I was about to move toward him, to stop him from lighting the cigarette, when the radio came to life again.

Hostage Duke had lost none of his amplitude! I keyed the handset, my eyes locked on Marvin. He was lighting the prisoner's cigarette. Fuck me! I could already smell the acrid odor of the tobacco. At least it smells like a Viet—maybe the NVA will hesitate, to make sure, before they light us up! My mind was racing as I told Hostage to send his traffic.

I wanted the aerial observer to know that he was talking to the patrol leader, so I had identified myself (Actual). I had to listen to his message before I could break my news and beg for an emergency extract. Hostage came back on the air. He told me what Finchum had told me—he was bingo on fuel and going home. My request for a spotting round had been delayed for priority fire missions, and his replacement was wheels up (just taking off) at Da Nang. And, of course, Take Out was still off the air. Ta ta.

I asked Hostage to relay to the battalion operations officer that we had two officer POWs and needed an emergency extract. And that we would need to extract by means of a ladder. The SOP for such situations now required the battalion operations officer to pull out all the stops to get us out. Prisoners were the highest priority intelligence asset that could be obtained, and we had two—officers, at that! I was sure that we would be going home shortly. I still needed a helicopter landing zone and a place to hide until the cavalry arrived.

Hostage Duke rogered my message and added that Hostage Stud had been diverted.

The handset hissed in my hand. Mommy had put away all my toys and gone out for the evening. Like an abandoned child, I wanted to cry. Suck it up, Mikey—think of something! Aloud I spoke in a quiet imperative tone, "Kelly! Finchum! Ward! Bring in the claymores! Pearston! Tell Marvin to fix those packs [the straps had been cut to remove them from the NVA] and put them on his buddy!"

As I spoke, I looked in Pearston's direction. He and Marvin were engaged in subdued conversation. Pearston was clearly upset. At the sound of my voice, he rose from his work on the wounded NVA and turned to me. "Lieutenant, you're not going to believe this!" His voice was quiet, his eyes big in his face. "Marvin says this guy is a colonel, a fucking doctor. The WIA is a major. He's a pharmacist. Marvin says they were on their way back to the division hospital from the ville [village] down below. They went for their laundry and cigarettes. Can you believe it?"

Finchum broke in, "It's no shit, Lieutenant—these packs are full of medical stuff!" He held up a surgical kit and several packets of what appeared to be drugs in vials—all U.S. issue. Scattered on the ground were several cartons of cigarettes and bundles of clothing.

"Put that stuff away, Finchum, and get ready to move! Pearston, where's the hospital?"

Pearston turned back to Marvin. There was a brief exchange in Vietnamese, and he turned back to me. "He says we're standing on it, Lieutenant." As he spoke, Pearston was standing and shrugging into his web gear. Finchum was stuffing things back into the NVA packs, and Marvin had resumed a standing position, backing away from our colonel, who remained squatting on the ground, the cigarette dangling from his lip. He had tears in his eyes. I wondered if they were caused by the smoke or the situation. The import of Pearston's words was sinking into the consciousness of each of us. I felt as if I had been kicked in the chest. What now, Lieutenant?

Behind me, Kelly spoke, "Here's your claymore, Lieutenant." He was holding out the mine, neatly wrapped in its cable, for me to stow in my asspack. His mundane gesture galvanized me to action, and a plan materialized in my mind as I spoke. We couldn't run. We couldn't shoot. We couldn't communicate. (Drumright's tactical guidance for peckerwoods: shoot, move, communicate.) We would hide. It wasn't on Drumright's list, but then he couldn't think of everything. I spoke quietly. "Okay! Finchum, get into your gear! Pearston, tell Marvin to hang those packs on Colonel Charles, here!"

I gestured toward the NVA with my M-16. (Marvin had made the two rucksacks into one load, like a paperboy's carrier. I was beginning to appreciate Marvin.) "Ward, take point . . . we're going that way." I gestured toward the east, opposite the place where we had come up into the saddle.

"Kelly, you take my spot. Take everybody down the hill a couple hundred meters and wait for me! Couture, you cover the prisoner. Have Marvin follow you—and give the major here a smoke." I spoke in a quiet voice, command imperative in it. Everyone turned to their tasks.

"Sir!" Couture was speaking. "We can't just leave the Gooner; he'll tell 'em where we went!"

"I know that, Couture. Just do what I told you. Okay?" I held his eyes with mine until I saw him give in. As he turned to organize the team, I focused my attention on the wounded NVA. He was very alert, his eyes following the movement around him. He seemed to sense that the situation was changing. Finally, as the ARVN and the colonel moved away, I positioned myself in his line of sight, the muzzle of my M-16 trained on his body. He inhaled the acrid tobacco, his eyes watering but focused on mine, as the sounds of the team's departure diminished. He smiled up at me, the cigarette dangling from his lip. I smiled back, and squeezed the trigger.

The first round caught him just under his nose. It must have tumbled after striking bone, because the whole top of his head fragmented onto the ground. The second round took him in the throat, the third in the sternum. He was dead. I bent down, placing my rifle next to the body. In the same gesture, I pulled a frag from my web gear, stripping the duct tape from the safety pin as I knelt beside the corpse. I pulled the pin, holding the spoon of the grenade with my thumb, and rolled the NVA's body onto it. He was heavy. I pulled my hand from under him, thinking, Easy does it Mikey— don't blow yourself up. I stood up, recovered my weapon, and backed away from the corpse in the direction of my teammates. Adios, motherfucker—say Hi! to your pals for us. I turned to rush in the direction of the team and crashed head-on into Marvin. He fended me off, smiling, and I real- ized that he had remained behind. He had covered my with- drawal. He had seen everything that transpired. Fuck! I thought to myself, as we both turned and ran headlong down the side of the ridge.

The team had left a trail, a fact which both comforted and alarmed me. Linking up was going to be easy, provided they didn't blow Marvin away, but the expected NVA reaction force would have no difficulty tracking us. First things first. I grabbed Marvin's pack straps, slowing us both to a walk, then pulled him to a halt. With hand signals, I instructed him to move carefully ahead, while I took a position covering our rear. We would leapfrog one another in this fashion until one of us encountered the team's rear security. The trick would be to link up without getting blown up—but then, they were expecting us. My mind was racing ahead, evaluating pos- sible solutions to our dilemma, as I backpedaled in trace of Marvin.

"*Psst!*—Skipper! Over here!"

Marvin and I dropped and rolled in opposite directions, our weapons coming to the ready. I searched the under- growth in the direction of the sound. It was Kelly, belly- down about three meters off the trail they had made. I motioned to Marvin, we stood, moving carefully and in a crouch to where the rest of the team had gathered. Kelly had doubled back on the trail they had left, setting up another hasty ambush. It was a shrewd move, and I was impressed. The rest of the team was scattered about in the undergrowth. I spotted the NVA facedown in a small depression. He had been gagged and blindfolded. Finchum was speaking urgently into the handset of his radio. He looked up as Marvin and I rejoined the group.

Kelly spoke softly, "We still got no comm, sir. There was an Arc Light [B-52 bombing raid] down below us. Lots of craters, and the trees are knocked down every which way. We might be able to hide in there, but it will be a bitch to move." As he spoke, his eyes were scanning the undergrowth. So were mine. We expected the NVA to arrive on the scene at any moment.

"Okay. Couture!" I hissed his name. "Let's peel back to one of those craters." (Our IA drills were about to pay off.) "You take point, have Ward bring up the rear." I was thinking that the blooper might come in handy.

We moved cautiously now, careful to disturb the ground as little as possible. As we moved farther down the slope, it became steeper, and the undergrowth got thicker. We moved slowly, a step at a time, shifting our bodies around and through the tangled growth until we emerged into sunlight. It was a bomb crater, actually several. Five-hundred-pound bombs had shattered the trees, cracked boulders, and strewn the hillside with debris. It was perfect. All we had to do was crawl into the middle of the mess and pray for comm with our support. Even a large NVA force would have difficulty dislodging us from this place. And, I could see terrain features below us. With these and other thoughts in mind, I gestured to my team members to deploy farther into the broken area. They moved slowly, handing our prisoner from man to man (he was off-balance with his hands tied behind his back and the rucksacks fore and aft on his torso). Finally, Couture pushed him headlong into a deep depression (maybe the impact point of a bomb) in the hillside. Huge tree trunks, split and broken by the blasts, made a roof over our heads. The place reminded me of forts I had built as a kid. I hoped the coming engagement would come out as well as those had.

We all slid into the crater and set about different tasks—Ward, Kelly, and Pearston (taking a cue from the other two) set out claymores. I removed mine from my buttpack and tossed it toward Marvin, gesturing for him to set it back down the trail we had just followed. He nodded, still smiling, shrugged out of his web gear, picked up the claymore, and moved off in the direction from which we had just come. Finchum had dropped his pack and was busy fashioning a field-expedient antenna for the PRC-25, using comm wire he carried for the purpose. Now that we were out from under the trees, the heat was numbing. I wondered how much water we had. It would be a bitch to stroke out before the NVA could take a lick. I pulled the tattered map from the leg pocket of my fatigues and set about yet another position location exercise.

In less than a minute, I determined that the terrain features I could see were not on the map sections I had retained for this mission. We would again rely on dead reckoning from the last position. I hoped that wasn't going to be a pun. We hadn't traveled that far (as the crow flies), but everyone was fatigued, a physical letdown that followed combat as night followed day. I knew from experience that everyone would be thirsty and sleepy, including me. We needed an emotional pickup. Finchum provided it. He was gesticulating at me, the radio handset pressed to his ear. I shrugged out of my web gear and moved carefully to where he crouched in the bottom of the crater. We were almost standing on the colonel. "Skipper! I got comm! There is shit going on everywhere!" He whispered, still listening.

I took the handset from his grasp, placing it next to my own ear. Finchum was right. Within seconds, I heard call signs and traffic from four different teams, all demanding support from Take Out. I quickly determined that at least two of the teams were in contact. Their situations sounded more critical than ours. I decided not to crowd in. I handed the handset back to Finchum. "Try Tac Two and the AO freqs—see if you can get us a relay to Stone Pit [i.e., the battalion]."

I wanted to get us out, but I knew now was not the time. Things were too busy. Just then, rocks and debris rattled to our feet. Startled, I looked up to see Marvin the ARVN bellying over the rim of the crater. He was still smiling as he hooked up the hellbox for my claymore. Shit! I thought to myself, We didn't even hear him coming. I've got to keep everybody on their toes! Aloud I whispered, "Couture! You and Ward take turns over there. Find some shade and keep a watch on your flank. Pearston! You and Marvin do the same on this side!"

I slipped farther into the crater, positioning myself in the shade of a shattered tree trunk, and shrugged out of my web gear. I was certain that we could not be observed from the ridge, but I didn't want to be lit up by any overzealous friendly observers, airborne or otherwise. We settled in to wait and swelter. It was going to be a long afternoon.

As the day wore on, the heat and stress began to take their toll on all of us. We dozed over our weapons, only to be jolted alert by some real or imagined noise on the hillside above us. Even the colonel, hunkered down in the sun at the bottom of the crater, seemed drowsy. He's in shock, I thought to myself as I shifted position to relieve Finchum on the radio. Just what we need! The bastard is going to die of heat prostration before I can get us out of here.

Aloud, I whispered, "Finchum! Let me take the radio. Give the colonel some water. Keep him quiet for Christ's sake!"

Finchum lurched to his feet, extending the handset to me. "Lieutenant, I don't want to give my water to no fuckin' gook. What if they don't pick us up today?" He whispered the words with great emotion, his eyes locked on mine.

"Good point. Use one of mine." With my M-16, I gestured in the direction of my web gear, which lay on the rim of the crater. Taking the handset from his outstretched hand, I asked, "What freq are we on?" I kept my voice low and unemotional. I wanted Finchum to feel my confidence, though I felt none myself. As I grasped the handset, it came alive, answering my question before he could reply.

"Turf Club, Turf Club, this is Take Out. Sitrep, please!"

Take Out was back on the net and doing their stuff. I keyed the handset and whispered, "Take Out, this is Turf Club. Stand by to copy sitrep. Over." The handset crackled and hissed.

"Station calling Take Out. Your transmission is garbled. Say again. Over." I said it again, grinding my teeth in frustration.

"Station calling Take Out. Your transmissions are garbled. Break. If you can hear this station, key your handset two distinct times. Over!" I keyed the handset.

"Roger your last. Break. If you are Turf Club, key your handset three times. Over!" I keyed the handset.

"Roger, Turf Club. Break. If you are all secure, key your handset two distinct times. Over!" I waited.

"Roger, Turf Club. Break. Understand you are not secure. Break. Hostage Stud is inbound your last pos. Break. He will come up on Tac Two. Break. If you copy my transmission, key your handset two distinct times. Over!"

I keyed the handset, my face breaking into a grin. The cavalry was coming!

"Finchum! Change the battery in this bitch, then come up on Tac Two; Hostage Stud is looking for us."

Finchum grinned and moved to his task. Sensing our movement, the other members of the team turned inward from their positions, inquiring looks on their faces. I gave them a thumbs-up and pulled on the straps of my harness. They instantly understood that we would be off the ridge soon. The change in their emotions was palpable. We had all moved from resigned determination to optimism in a heartbeat. Take Out's news was better than a letter from home!

It had been hours since our last contact. We had done nothing but sweat and listen to tactical traffic on the radio for most of the afternoon. I had begun to believe that Stone Pit had forgotten us in the chaos of radio traffic from the other teams on the ridge. The radio traffic had slowed as each

1st Recon Battalion insignia.

1st Lt. Stephen Baker CO, Charlie Company, in command.
Photograph courtesy of Michael Curry.

Charlie Company XO 1st Lt. Larry Polster (right) and the
author in the Charlie Company offices.
Photograph courtesy of Michael Curry.

Stephen Baker (left) and Michael Curry.
Photograph courtesy of Stephen Baker.

Tom Hodge (left) and Michael Curry.
Photograph courtesy of Stephen Baker.

Charlie Company, 1st Platoon, 2d Squad, March 1970.
Left to right, standing: Pfc. Vaughn, Cpl. Brasington,
Lt. Cpl. Haines; kneeling: Lt. Cpl. Cyberowski,
Lt. Cpl. Cortez, HM3 Johnson.
*Photograph courtesy of Lt. Col. B. A. Brasington,
USMC (Ret.).*

Team Detroit Tigers, Charlie Company, 3d Platoon, 2d Squad, March 1970. Above: Left to right: Pfc. R. D. Jones, Lt. Cpl. P. Hannon, Lt. Cpl. Hicks, Lt. Cpl. Tews, Pfc. Burnsworth, Lt. Lan. Below: A pensive Detroit Tigers just before insertion. The author is last man on the right.
Photographs courtesy of Stephen Baker.

The author and associates: Charlie Company, 3d Platoon,
May 1970. Left to right: Lt. Cpl. Moreno, Sgt. Wardlow,
1st Lt. M. C. Hodgins.
Photograph courtesy of Stephen Baker.

Home from the hunt. Charlie Company, March 1970.
Photograph courtesy of Stephen Baker.

Tail End Charlie at the office.
Photograph courtesy of Lt. Col. B. A. Brasington,
USMC (Ret.).

Helicopter resupply, Hill 425, Charlie Company, March 1970.
Photograph courtesy of Lt. Col. B. A. Brasington,
USMC (Ret.).

The Phu Loc Valley from Hill 425, Charlie Company,
March 1970.
*Photograph courtesy of Lt. Col. B. A. Brasington,
USMC (Ret.).*

Spider Lake from Hill 425, Charlie Company, March 1970.
*Photograph courtesy of Lt. Col. B. A. Brasington,
USMC (Ret.).*

The flying trapeze, Charlie Ridge, April 1970.
Photograph courtesy of Lt. Gen. A. C. Blades, USMC.

Emergency extract, Sunrise Bravo, 23 May 1970.
Photograph courtesy of Lt. Gen. A. C. Blades, USMC.

team's situation evolved, but I had no idea of how those situations had been resolved.

Now, it was my turn to shit or shine. I mulled our extract options as I scanned the terrain surrounding our fort. It was clear that no helicopter could land. We would need to be lifted out on the Jacob's Ladder (an apparatus consisting of steel cables and aluminum rungs that was secured to the cargo ramp of the helicopter and used to extract teams from sites where the helicopter could not land). The trees, the slope of the hill, the wind, possible enemy troop deployments, condition of the team—these and other factors swirled in my mind as I mulled over what I would say to the aerial observer (AO). This was going to be a very tricky circus performance.

While Finchum labored to change the battery in our radio, I studied my map. I wanted to move to a safer extract site, but the map offered no clues. I pulled my handy, acetate-covered message cards from the leg pocket of my fatigues and began to jot down the key elements of an LZ brief ("Helicopter Landing Zone Briefing Form") for the aerial observer. Back in the saddle we had abandoned, my frag went off! The explosion was muffled by the distance and the trees, but it could only mean one thing: the NVA reaction forces had finally got around to us. They would find our trail, and they would be pissed off!

I looked around our perimeter. Weapons in hand, everyone was wide-eyed. The colonel was staring at me, his eyes huge in his face. Finchum had gagged him again, using a bandanna made from a 5.56mm ammunition bandolier. The NVA's face was contused where the duct tape we had used earlier had been ripped off. He had no eyebrows. Blood and sweat ran together on his forehead and into his eyes. He was pale and breathing in rapid shallow snorts through his nose. I saw the tape on the ground at his feet. I hope the water was worth the pain, motherfucker! I thought as I stood to recover the radio handset from Finchum. I wondered what Finchum had done with the loose rounds from the bandolier. I looked in his direction as I put the handset to my ear. Things were about to get hairy!

Finchum had moved up the side of the crater near my web gear, leaving the old battery, the wrapper from the new one, and loose clips of 5.56mm scattered behind him.

"Psst! Finchum! Pick up that shit and stow it!" I gestured toward the litter with my M-16, the radio handset pressed to my ear. "Put on my web gear—I'll take the radio!"

He nodded, sliding back into the crater. The others were shifting into better firing positions, fidgeting with their equipment and munitions, claymore hellboxes close at hand. We were ready to fight.

"Turf Club, Turf Club, this is Hostage Stud. How do! Over." Another megaphone talker.

I turned down the squelch on the radio and replied, "Hostage Stud, this is Turf Club Actual. Welcome aboard. How copy? Over!"

I knew we could hear, but I wasn't sure about transmitting, so I was asking Hostage to tell me about the quality of my transmitted signal. With a little luck, I was going to be able to talk our way out of trouble.

"Gotcha five-by, Turf Club! How me? Over?"

Hostage Stud was a country boy. I hope he is as aggressive as he is enthusiastic. The thought flitted through my mind as I keyed the handset and read the sitrep message off my pad, giving him our position, condition, and the time.

"Fire mission follows. Over!" I wanted to get something going before the NVA had a chance to deploy against our position. If I could get some interdicting fires on the targets I had plotted earlier in the day, the NVA would play hell finding us between splashes (impacts of artillery rounds). I studied the map, waiting for the AO to confirm my transmission.

"Turf Club, this is Hostage Stud. Break. Stone Pit says 'Well done.' Break. Package is inbound. Guns on station in five mikes. Break. Call sign for your taxi is Swift One-Four on Tac Two. Break. I'll do your guns. How copy? Over."

I smiled, relieved at the news of our pending extraction.

Somebody loved me! They had ordered the Cobra gunships, assigned to escort the CH-46 transport helicopters, to race ahead to provide fire support, and Hostage would be my controller. All I had to do now was tell him where to shoot. I keyed the handset. I told him we had suspected enemy movement from grid 623676, toward us, and asked him to mark that site with white phosphorous and "light up the ridge."

I wanted Hostage to distract the NVA troops I believed were looking for us. If I could get him to strafe the saddle we had abandoned, they would have to take cover, thus slowing their progress and giving us time to get organized for the extract. I did not want to mark our position before the gunships were on station, for fear the NVA would "bear hug" us (i.e., get in too close to us to allow our supporting fires to act against them—a favorite NVA tactic for reducing the effect of our firepower) or mortar the shit out of us. Hostage had guns, rockets, and balls. He was rolling in while we were talking.

Hostage was good. Using the posrep I had transmitted earlier, he had plotted our position relative to the target I had given him and brought his aircraft in a diving turn parallel to the ridge we had left. As the aircraft approached the ground, he cut loose a pair of Zuni rockets, each tipped with a white phosphorous ("Willy Peter") warhead, followed by a long burst from his miniguns. He swooped past us, within a hundred feet of the trees as his rockets exploded. He was right on the money! As he climbed into the twilight sun, keeping us inside his turn (his weapons would be pointed away from us), we heard the distinctive *crack, crack, crack* of AK-47s in the void left by his passing. The NVA were shooting back, not with anything heavy, but it was clear from the sounds that they occupied the high ground on three sides of our position.

I informed Hostage Stud of the ground fire. As I spoke, my eyes roamed from man to man in the crater. The team was keyed up, but disciplined, each man watching his assigned sector. Finchum sat below the lip of the crater, his M-16 trained on the prisoner. The prisoner squatted in the bottom of the crater, his eyes flicking back and forth between Finchum and me. Ward, Pearston, Kelly, and Marvin lay belly-down on the rim, their weapons at the ready. They were tense, but controlled. I felt bile rising in my throat. Choking it down, I keyed the handset again, and asked after the Cobra gunships.

The NVA would be maneuvering under the trees, trying to close on us before the OV-10 could make another pass. Hostage didn't have enough firepower to keep them off us, whether they had a mortar or not. If they had a mortar, they would have the tube up any second, their unit commander having deduced that we were inside his horseshoe. I felt sick for good reason—thinking back to my Grunt experiences. *I wonder if any of these guys have been mortared before?* The thought was irrelevant. *Maybe they can't shoot from under the trees?* More relevant, but not very comforting.

"Ward! Put a flare in the blooper! Get ready to put it up over our heads on my call!" I spoke the words urgently, but in a monotone, projecting my voice sotto voce at his back. He rolled onto his side, breaking the breech on the M-79 as he did so. I turned to look for the OV-10. Hostage was just completing his orbit, coming out of the sun, bringing his wings level for another diving pass at the ridge above us. *Sunset! Shit! We got forty minutes to get the fuck out of here!* The idea of being stuck on the ridge overnight set my bowels moving.

"Kelly!" He rolled onto his side, an inquiring look on his face. "Work out an azimuth to a new rally point, that way!" I pointed my M-16 down the hill in the direction of the little finger of rock we had first identified as a potential extract site. I tossed my map in his direction. "I marked it earlier—target four—work up a fire mission for it, so we'll know where we're going if we need it."

The words were whispered with a confidence I didn't feel. He picked up the map, pulling his compass from his shirt pocket at the same time. Hostage opened up with his miniguns, the ripping, whirring sound lagging the impact of tracers as they disappeared into the canopy on the ridge.

Hostage Stud came up to inform me that the Cobra gunships were on station. As the words cackled through the handset of the PRC-25, I turned toward Ward. He was on his back at the rim of the crater, the butt of the M-79 pushed into the gravel under his armpit. The muzzle pointed skyward. His eyes locked on mine as I keyed the handset.

"Roger, Hostage. Stand by for my mark. Over!" As I spoke, I cradled the M-16 in the crook of my left arm, the handset clutched in the same hand, and extended my right arm, fist clenched, toward Ward. He shifted slightly, his finger tightening on the trigger of the M-79. Gravel trickled into the bottom of the crater, as the others also shifted positions in preparation for—whatever. They all sensed a moment of truth: we were about to compromise our position. If things didn't go just right, people were going to get hurt. As the aircraft completed its turn out of the sun, I opened my clenched fist, pointing at Ward. I keyed the handset as the M-79 went off—*pong!* The flare rushed skyward, leaving a wispy trail of grayish smoke behind.

"Mark! Mark!"

The flare burst high overhead, a red star cluster. It scattered glowing fragments in the sky several hundred feet above our heads. It could be seen for miles. Fuckin' beautiful! I thought, waiting for the moment of truth.

"Turf Club, this is Hostage Stud. Confirm red star cluster. Over."

"Hostage, this is Turf Club. Affirmative, red star cluster. Over."

"Roger Turf Club. Break. We gotcha! Scarface is going to work 'em over for you. Break. Swift One-Four is standing by. How copy? Over."

As the transmission was completed, the air reverberated with the sound of AH-64 Cobra gunships climbing rapidly from somewhere below us. As I turned in the direction of the sound, they split apart, guns and rockets firing simultaneously into the trees on the high ground on our flanks. As quickly as they came, they disappeared over the crest of the ridge. Smoke began to drift down on us from where their rockets had impacted.

I shouted to the team, "Heads up! We are out of here! Couture! Put a harness and a snap link on the colonel! Pearston! Rig the packs so we can hang 'em on the ladder! You take one! Ward, you take the other! Kelly you go first, then Marvin, then Finchum, then Pearston, Ward, and Nichols. Couture, you hang the colonel when I tell you. If he balks, coldcock the motherfucker! I'll go last, with the radio! I want each man to throw a smoke grenade and empty his weapon as he leaves. Got it?"

The orders were issued into the void left by the departure of the gunships. No sooner had I spoken than the Cobras were back, from the opposite direction, guns and rockets blazing as they popped over the top of the ridge. Fuck you and your horseshoe too, Charlie! The thought flitted through my mind as I fumbled to unclasp my own snap link and climbing rope.

As we worked to prepare ourselves for extraction, the distinctive rotor clatter of a pair of CH-46 transport helicopters could be heard reverberating off the ridge. I scanned the team as I turned to look for the origin of the sound. Each man had bent to his task, fashioning a climber's hasty seat for himself, using the rope we carried for the purpose, and attaching a snap link at his waist inside his web gear. The idea was to climb up the Jacob's Ladder (which would be let down to us from the ramp at the rear of the CH-46), two men to a rung, while the helicopter hovered some sixty feet above the ground, attach the snap link to one of the vertical risers of the ladder, and take a ride for life. As an extraction technique, it sucked. But, it was all we had.

"Turf Club, Turf Club, this is Swift One-Four. Over!"

My climbing rope dropped into the bottom of the crater as I lurched to recover the handset dangling over my shoulder. "Fuck!" The word was expelled along with my exasperation as I keyed the handset in response, reaching for the rope with my free hand as I squatted in the bottom of the crater. I was face to face with the prisoner. His breath reeked of *nuoc mam* fish sauce and garlic. His body stank of wood smoke, sweat, and fear. The contusions on his face were beginning to congeal. Scabs were forming where his eyebrows had been. I straight-armed him in the face, knocking him backward against the side of the crater, and recovered my rope from beneath his feet. Standing, I keyed the handset.

"Swift One-Four, this is Turf Club Actual. Send your traffic. Over!" I scanned my surroundings, taking in first the team, then the high ground about us, then the aircraft. The gunships were now orbiting in opposite directions around our position, swooping occasionally to draw fire from the suspected enemy positions. None came. They had either withdrawn or were laying low, waiting for a better target. The better target would be us, hanging off the ass of one of the CH-46s now orbiting over the valley. The Bronco was higher and in the sun, doing his thing with the gunships on another frequency. I knew that he would be monitoring my conversations with Swift One Four, ready to direct suppressing fires if necessary, but he would keep this frequency clear to enable us to coordinate the extraction. This was the air-ground team in action. My confidence was rising.

Swift One-Four called for an LZ brief. I looked around, the surge of confidence fading. We didn't have much of an LZ. In fact, it looked like the ladder (only sixty feet long) might not reach. I keyed the handset. "Roger, Swift One-Four. LZ is a bomb crater, ten meters circumference. Slope is thirty degrees November-Sierra. Obstacles are rocks and tree trunks, minimum clearance ten meters. Wind is five knots from the north. We have seven packs. Last contact was small arms from high ground north, west, and south. Best approach is from the east. We will mark with smoke. How copy? Over."

I had forgotten something, but I didn't know what. Waiting for the pilot to tell me, I fumbled with my climbing rope, trying to tie a one-handed knot. I saw that the rest of the team was ready to go. Fuck it! I let the rope fall to the ground and ripped the tape from the smoke grenade hanging from the shoulder strap of Finchum's pack. The pack felt heavy all of a sudden. "Finchum, what the fuck are you carrying in this thing?"

Finchum looked at me, startled that I had spoken aloud. I smiled. He shrugged, as the others turned to look at us. I tossed the smoke grenade to Finchum. "Okay gents, get ready to move when the bird swoops in here. Finchum, when I tell you, toss this bitch that way as far as you can." I pointed down the slope. "Kelly, this one is yellow. What color have you got?"

He fumbled at his shoulder harness, pulling the grenade loose. "Purple, sir!" Everyone was staring at me.

"Okay. We are going to let the Gooners shoot at Finchum's smoke. You put that one on that stump." I gestured toward the log. "When I tell you, set it off. Okay?"

He nodded. As he did, we heard the rotors of the CH-46s change pitch for a tactical approach. We looked skyward to see one of the birds dropping rapidly toward the ridge in a plunging turn out of the sun. The radio came to life. "Turf Club, this is Swift One-Four. Pop smoke. Over!"

I gestured toward Finchum, who pulled the pin on his grenade and threw it overhand down the slope. It popped before it landed, spewing yellow smoke into the twilight sky. The wind was stronger than I had estimated, flattening the plume and spreading it rapidly into the trees below us. My heart was a lump in my throat. If the NVA zeroed in on the smoke, we would be spending the night in the woods. I keyed the handset.

"Swift One-Four, this is Turf Club. Popping smoke. Over!" I pointed at Kelly, who pulled the pin on his grenade. Purple smoke billowed up all around us.

"Turf Club, this is Swift One-Four. Say color of smoke. Over!"

"Swift One-Four, we are Purple smoke. Over!" I hoped we had bought a few extra seconds with the deception. We would still be sitting ducks getting on the ladder. As I spoke, the gunships swooped simultaneously, spraying the high ground on our flanks with machine-gun and rocket fire. The run was timed to coincide with the arrival of the CH-46.

"Tallyho, purple smoke!" The pilot made a slight adjustment in his descent, and the aircraft plunged toward the crater in which we crouched. At the last instant, the aircraft lurched into a hover and the pilot swung the tail ramp around to face the side of the ridge. The clatter of the rotors was deafening. Like a miniature tornado, the rotorwash threw debris away in all directions, flattening my beautiful, multicolored smoke screen into the brush. (In the excitement of the aircraft's arrival, everyone had popped smoke.) Through gravel splattered eyes, we saw the crew chief kick our lifeline off the loading ramp of the helicopter. It fell short by twenty feet. I could see him talking the pilot into our position. The aircraft inched closer, until the bottom rung of the ladder hung five or six feet above the shattered tree trunk that had provided most of our shade throughout the long afternoon. I saw that the tree was now our stepping stone to safety. So did the others.

Ward scrambled atop the log, dragging one of the NVA packs with him. He fastened the pack to the bottom rung of the ladder, then gestured to Pearston for the other. Pearston lunged upward from beneath the log, extending the pack as he did. It was a Herculean effort! Ward caught the pack as Pearston fell back to the ground, attached it to the ladder, and began to climb hand over hand up the swaying ladder. My plan for an orderly extraction was coming apart before my eyes. I looked for the prisoner, as Pearston lunged for the bottom rung of the ladder. The NVA was in a fetal crouch in the bottom of the crater, the rotor wash pelting him (and the rest of us) unmercifully with sand and debris. Kelly and Finchum were already taking handholds on the log, climbing into position to lunge for the ladder. So was Couture. Where was Marvin? As the thought materialized, so did he. Squatting, he had positioned himself in the lee of the log, his weapon trained on the prisoner and his eyes on me!

"Marvin, I love your ugly ass!" I shouted the words into

the din of the helicopters' rotors, gesturing with my M-16 in the direction of the NVA. Marvin smiled, and slid into the crater. With one hand, he grabbed the NVA by his khaki shorts and half dragged him up the slope of the crater to where the other team members had climbed onto the log. I scrambled to join him, only to be yanked backward to the ground—I was still connected to Finchum's antenna! I pulled my K-bar from its scabbard, slashing at the comm wire binding me to the ground as gravel and other debris pummeled my face. The helicopter was drifting away! I lunged to my feet as Marvin dragged the NVA upright on the log and, using the snap link and harness we had rigged on him earlier, fastened him to the bottom rung of the ladder. With a last look at me, Marvin climbed the ladder with the agility of a trapeze artist! It was my turn. Aghast, I watched as the helicopter drifted farther down the slope. A gap opened as the ladder swung away from the log, the weight of the captured packs and the NVA prisoner acting like a pendulum. The crew chief was shouting unintelligible words and gesticulating at me. I looked down, into the crater—and saw my climbing rope in the bottom of it! I had forgotten to prepare myself for extraction. Shit!

The helicopter drifted back overhead. As the ladder swung to, I lunged for the rungs and swung into space. I wedged my left arm between the rungs, got a foothold, then lunged upward, twisting my M-16 upright between the rungs above my head. I wrapped my right arm around the receiver and clasped my hand behind my left forearm—a human snap link! I hung on for dear life as the helicopter started to lift, staggered, then swooped off the side of the hill. I felt myself twist wildly and turned my head, only to see the colonel. His face was dead white. As our eyes met, he fainted, and I remembered the omitted portion of the LZ brief—altitude! The helicopter swooped low over the trees, dropping like a rock toward the valley floor. Above and behind us, the LZ and surrounding terrain erupted in a shower of smoke and debris from the impact of dozens of eight-inch artillery rounds. Hostage and Longrifle were saying good-bye to our NVA playmates!

After staggering off the ridge, the CH-46 slowly gained altitude and turned in the direction of Da Nang, taking a wide, sweeping course over the Arizona Territory, then out over the South China Sea. As we dangled beneath the helicopter, we had a spectacular view of the entire basin. I could see hundreds of small plumes of smoke, the same ones I had seen from the window of the 707 in my other life. To my left, and slightly below us, the other CH-46 kept formation. I could see the door gunner pointing at us, and I wondered if he would be the one to see me fall. Farther out, the AH-64s clattered along. Like greyhounds, they swooped back and forth, scissoring our formation and finally raced ahead to some other purpose. Cold beer, I imagined.

"Shit!" I screamed the curse into the wind, the pain and fear tormenting me. My left arm was numb, but the receiver of the M-16 ground on the bone of my right forearm with each twist of the ladder. The pain was excruciating! I wanted to live! Take us straight home, motherfucker! Please!

The flight lasted my whole lifetime—in reality, perhaps ten minutes. As we approached the division facilities, the aircraft lost altitude and began to reduce its airspeed. I realized that someone must be talking to the pilot about how to get us down. I looked about for the other bird. Nowhere in sight. But, the crew chief was now hanging off the end of the ramp of the helicopter. I could see that he was talking to Ward. Pass the word! I tried to will them to talk to me, to no avail. I had lost feeling in both my arms. I had lost my sense of time. If we didn't land soon, I would lose consciousness, and beat everyone to the ground! I sensed that the helicopter was losing ground speed, then hovering. I felt my boots drag the pavement. There were hands on me.

Aroused from my momentary lapse of consciousness (I had fainted with relief), I realized that we were not where I had expected to be, at the Recon helipad. We were at Marble Mountain, the POW screening compound, and there was a lot of activity around me. In addition to the corpsman shoving foul-smelling things up my nose, there were security people, an interrogation team, a public information office crew, and spectators. The arrival of the team had created quite a scene for the REMFs. They were everywhere.

I struggled to my feet, only to find that my hands and arms were cramped in the positions they had held during the flight. The pain was terrible, and I felt twice as foolish, realizing that although I had held on with a death grip during the entire flight, all I had had to do was stand up on the ladder. I was definitely not cut out for the high wire!

The CH-46 had let the team down a rung at a time, then moved off after we had uncoupled from the ladder. It now sat some distance away, the rotors idling, while we got reorganized on the ground. The crew chief and door gunners scurried off the aircraft behind us and began rolling up the ladder. A major approached me from the crowd. "Good job, Lieutenant! We'll take over your prisoner from here. I'll need one man to debrief now. We'll make sure he gets chow and a ride back to your compound. I'll need the captured packs, and those, also." As he spoke, he pointed at me.

I looked around to see what he meant, then realized that he was pointing at the Chicom pistol belts draped over my shoulder. Somehow, sometime during the preparation for extraction I had recovered the pistols. They were a prized war souvenir. No way was Major REMF going to get them!

"With due respect, sir, my orders are that all captured weapons be turned in to my unit!"

The major was becoming as much a threat to my morale and welfare as the NVA had been. I attempted a painful salute and made tracks for the team, now gathering at the tailgate of the CH-46. As I approached, the pilot revved up his turbines, and the aircraft's rotors began to turn. With arm signals, I motioned the team aboard, collaring Couture as we moved toward the ramp. "Couture, get the bird moving!"

I shouted the words into his ear over the whine of the helicopter's turbines, gesturing in the direction of the intelligence officer with my M-16. Couture grasped the situation and dashed aboard the helicopter, shouting at the other team

members to join him as he passed. The REMF major stared
from me to the rear of the helicopter, noting the sudden departure of my troops. Realization of my intent registered in
his eyes. As he raised his arm in my direction, his mouth
open to shout, I rushed up the ramp, pulling the crew chief
with me, and turned to look out the back of the aircraft as the
bird lifted off. Major REMF was shaking his fist in the air. I
grinned at the thought of his frustration, then slumped on the
nylon seat, exhausted. Staring out through the yawning hole
of the cargo bay as the aircraft gained altitude, I realized that
the sun was nearly down. I watched the compound become
smaller and details of the landscape fade away as the aircraft
gained altitude. I was shaking, chills running through my
body. I looked around me. The others sat slumped against
the bulkheads of the helicopter, their eyes closed, their faces
slack beneath sweat-streaked camouflage paint. All but Marvin. As my eyes rested on him, he grinned.

CHAPTER SIX
VALHALLA

12 APRIL–10 MAY 1970

*The courage we desire and prize is not the courage to
die decently, but to live manfully.*

Thomas Carlyle (1795–1881)

We made the short flight back to HLZ 401 without further incident, too spent to take notice of our surroundings. Fatigue set in, an involuntary response to stress which overcame us once the threat had passed. Eyes closed, we sagged against the nylon webbing of our seats while the aircraft rattled through the sky toward Camp Reasoner. When the CH-46 finally flared onto the Recon helipad, the hard landing jolted us all from our reveries. Turf Club scrambled erect. Momentarily confused and disoriented, we grappled with our gear like zombies, struggling to fit the cumbersome loads to our bodies once more. The helicopter crew chief let down the tail ramp of his aircraft, and we stumbled, single file, onto the tarmac, home safe.

The sun was low in the sky, casting shadows across the asphalt. Shielding my eyes against the glare, I searched for Baker in the throng. He was not there. Another group of Marines separated themselves from the gaggle in the shade and jogged toward our helicopter. I recognized the gangling form of Charlie Kershaw in the group, as well as several other members of the Mission Impossible team. They lunged aboard the aircraft while we straggled toward the debriefing hootch. Once inside, we dropped our war gear on the deck and slouched into makeshift chairs. Couture made straight for the refrigerator and returned with cold beer, underhanding them in turn to each of the team members, Sergeant Thi included. We opened them with John Waynes, spraying cold brew across our brows with élan. Outside, we heard helicopters winding up for yet another flight. Something was amiss, but I was too tired to speculate. Inured to the perils of "tag-team warfare," Turf Club paid no attention. They had done their bit. It was someone else's turn in the ring.

"Lieutenant!" Couture spoke in a commanding voice, attracting the attention of everyone in the hootch. He raised his beer, gesturing in my direction. "Semper fi, sir!"

He grinned and tossed off a huge gulp. I matched his gesture, saying nothing, as did the others. We sat down to commence our debriefing, the moment of truth. A gunnery sergeant (E-7) emerged from a group of clerks gaggled around the situation map. He was the most senior individual in the room, aside from myself. There was no sign of the Stump, or anyone else from Charlie Company. Our escapade appeared to have gone unnoticed, even by our closest associates. I noted the fact, and an accompanying observation that the gunny appeared intent upon debriefing Couture, not me. The others sat slack in their chairs, enjoying their beer and the attention of their peers. Firefights and ladder extracts were the stuff of legends. No one really wanted to do it, but everyone wanted to say they had. Turf Club had. They were made men in the eyes of their peers, "Warriors."

"Say, Couture. You guys ready to spill your guts?" He laughed and sat down at a field desk. I saw that he had a clipboard full of message sheets (yellow pads used to record radio messages). "Says here you got two prisoners, officers. Only one turned in to the interrogation center. What happened to the other one?"

Couture looked the staff NCO in the eye. "He died of wounds, Gunny. But, we got his gear. See here."

Couture held up one of the NVA packs and dumped the contents on the deck. It was full of medical instruments and drugs, these neatly marked and labeled in French. One by one, the other team members contributed their share of the booty to a jumbled heap on the floor in front of the gunny's desk. Finally, I added the two pistol belts and pistols to the pile. A crowd of REMFs gathered around us, picking through the blood-spattered belongings of the NVA. They were envious. The capture of individual weapons, especially pistols, was a coveted experience, like counting coup. The gunnery sergeant busied himself with an inventory, while the rest of us set down brief descriptions of what had occurred. Somehow there were no words to describe the past three days, no place on the form to disclose what actually occurred. In the calm and relative safety of the compound, it was as if the whole episode had been a dream, a very bad dream. I was alone with my thoughts, the only officer in the hootch. The troops, like warriors of old, recounted their tale of gruesome glory, complete with pantomimes reliving the contacts and extract, to a group of enthralled wannabes. While they were thus engrossed, I drew up an overlay of the route we had actually walked, identified the grids where our contacts occurred, plotted our route from insert to extract. Maybe two miles as the crow flies, it didn't look like the hump it had become. I appended it to my terse summary of the patrol and handed it to the gunnery sergeant. He gave it a cursory look, then returned his attention to his inventory of the captured equipment. I turned to face the troops in the throng.

"Okay, gents, show and tell is over. Give me back both pistols, the rounds, and the web gear that went with them."

They handed them over, reluctantly. Here was some more officer chickenshit in the making. I holstered the pistols, replaced the magazines, and slung pistol belts over my shoulder. "Couture, muster the rest of the team outside." I turned and left. There was a rustle of equipment and a scraping of chairs behind me as the troops gathered up their war gear and made to follow my example. I waited outside, smoking, while the team assembled.

"Okay, Lieutenant, we are ready to secure. Have you got any word to pass?" Couture had regained his salty reserve. His voice was tinged with scorn.

"Yeah." I fieldstripped my cigarette, putting the butt in my pocket, then faced the team. "Sergeant Couture, here's a little souvenir for you." I handed him the pistol belt.

"Doc, this one's for you. You two keep the pistols and split up the rest of the web gear among the team. You'll need permits to take these things home." Couture still couldn't play poker. His eyes told the tale of his thoughts. He had expected me to keep the weapons, depriving the men of their trophies. Now, he had to rethink the whole issue. I paused to collect my thoughts. They were thoughts I could not share, at least not with these men.

"Gents, you did a great job. We are all here, alive and unhurt, because we worked together as a team. Remember that, each and every time you go to the field." I paused for effect. "Sergeant Cee, make sure everyone cleans their weapons and web gear before you go to chow. Turn in your ammo before you leave the HLZ. That's the new SOP, Sergeant Cee. Be seeing you." I made to leave.

"Detail, atten*hut!*" Couture was forceful. The team stood tall in a ragged formation. "Good day, sir!" He rendered a hand salute, which I returned with difficulty. With that I turned, struggled into my own web gear and began the slow ascent to my own hootch.

Behind me Doc Pearston spoke, "Say, Lieutenant—you better get to the BAS about that arm. You need to see a real doctor."

"Roger that."

Turf Club gave a hearty *"Oorah!"* and made for the trail back to Charlie Company. They were glad to be alive. I watched their departure for a moment, before collecting myself for the trek back to my hootch. With a sigh, I shrugged into my war gear and trudged toward the stairs. Sheer willpower got me up the hill. At the hootch, I kicked the door open, lunged inside, and dropped my war gear on the deck in my cubicle. With difficulty, I cleared and safed my weapon and hung it on its peg, then began a one-handed striptease, shouting for a mamma-san in the process. One appeared, as if by magic, just as I succeeded in wrapping myself in a towel. She gathered up my filthy clothes and web gear with a black-toothed grin and was gone, leaving the screen slightly ajar. Where was Shitbird? And my mail?

With the thoughts came the realization that the hootch was barren. Baker, Polster, Hodge, and Curry had moved out. Duda and Pino were still in the field. Their gear was untouched. Something was afoot. Vaguely perplexed, I wandered out to the shower to scrub away, one-handed, three days of grime and war paint. My arm was really beginning to hurt. Pain shot through my fingers and radiated up into my shoulder. The battalion aid station was definitely next on the list. I finished cleaning up, donned a fresh uniform and mamma-san-buffed boots, then made my way to the aid station. Sick-call hours had long since expired, but when I explained my complaint to the corpsman on duty, he thought my injury serious enough to summon the battalion surgeon, Lt. Charles "Doc" Andras, USN (U.S. Navy). I failed the grip test and a few other things. The physician determined that I had damaged the nerve in my elbow.

"Mike, this is one of those things that is going to heal itself or not. Let's give it a couple of days and see what happens. You should ice it down three times a day. Stop by here, and we'll fix you up with the ice packs. Try not to do any push-ups." He laughed, making notes on a sheet in my health record. I grimaced.

"Is it serious?" Watching him write, I was thinking about the career consequences of an entry in my health record.

"Could be, probably not. It'll hurt like hell, and keep you out of the bush for a few days. Long enough to get old Wild Bill on your ass—no Purple Heart, if that's what you're thinking." He kept writing.

"Oh?" It was a question, more than a comment, but Andras took it in his own context.

"Yeah. Drumright gave me 'guidance' on that—no blood, no iron, no Purple Heart, by God! Hell, I think you deserve something for the aggravation, but not this time."

He closed the file, standing up. I followed his example.

"Keep the sling for a day or two. See the chief if the pain gets too bad. We'll give you a magic pill or two. Buy you a beer?" He was moving toward the door.

"Yes, sir.* Later. I should check in with the company first."

We went out together, trudging up the hill in tandem. Andras dropped off at the club, while I continued across the bridge to the company area. Doc Andras had got me thinking about beer, and food. The odor of the grill followed me into the company area, setting my stomach to growling. I realized that I had last eaten more than thirteen hours before—canned peaches and lukewarm water. The thing to do was to check in with the Stump, then get some chow—and a cold beer. I went into the company office in search of my commander.

The outer office was vacant. Troops are at chow, I thought to myself. I continued to the inner sanctum. Polster was there, head bent over documents on his desk. I knocked and went in. "Where's Baker?"

Polster looked up from the desk, his horn-rims askew. "On leave. Tokyo." He took in the sling, and my bedraggled condition in a glance. "You hurt?"

"Pinched nerve in my elbow. Doc says it'll probably get better in a few days. He put me on light duty for a week. Why did you move out of our hootch?"

I wanted to change the subject. Baker on leave explained a lot. Polster focused his attention on the service record books again. "Lucky for you. It'll keep you out of the bush. What did you want with Stump? I'm acting [CO]. Maybe I can take care of it?"

I stared at the back of Polster's head for a moment, thinking . . . "Nothin'. Just wanted to give him my after-action report, in case it comes up. When will he be back?" I was not about to confide in Polster.

"Around the fifteenth [April]. What shape is the team in?"

"Nobody hurt. I gave them the night off. We got a prisoner,

---

*A Navy lieutenant is the same pay grade (0-3) as a Marine captain, i.e., one grade higher than First Lieutenant (0-2) Hodgins.

Larry. Those guys rate [earned] an R & R. What do we have to do to get them out of here?"

I made eye contact with him. He shrugged, closing the cover of the service record book he had been working on. "Don't rightly know, Mike. But they're my guys and my responsibility now. You're officially a platoon commander—Third Herd. Tom Hodge has been transferred to the Three Shop. We all have to move—Drumright's orders. He wants closer supervision of the troops. We had a couple incidents last week. Your platoon has already been fragged [tasked] with three patrols—Jim Duda is taking one, Chet Pino is taking one, and Sergeant Domnoske is taking the rest of the platoon to Ba Na to run the radio relay. No offense, but we didn't expect you back so soon, prisoner or no prisoner. Curry is out on Four twenty-five [the observation post], and my platoon is on mess and maintenance."

Polster paused for breath. He was taking his role seriously, too seriously. I decided to get out of sight before he tried to give me something to do. I sat down at Baker's desk, jotted the names of the Turf Club patrol members on a piece of paper, planning my "getaway" in the process. "Well, looks like you got a cheap Purple Heart, anyway. For a lifer like you, that's a good day's work." He laughed.

I winced. "No way. No blood, no iron, no Purple Heart. Drumright's rules. Heard it from Doc Andras himself. I may be crippled for life, but I wasn't bleeding—breaks of the naval service." I took a step toward his desk. "It's beginning to hurt like hell, so I'll probably be okay in a few days. Where's my mail?"

Polster looked up, his face stern, and shrugged. "No fuckin' idea. Check with Anderson [the admin chief]. It's a good thing for you, you're hurt. Otherwise, fuckin' Wild Bill would have you back in the bush. That bastard is crazy. He's the only motherfucker in this place who doesn't know the war is over!"

I leaned over the corner of the desk, placing my note in the center of the service record book he had been reviewing.

"These are the guys from Turf Club. Let's make sure they get the next R & R quotas, okay? I'm goin' to chow."

I went out without waiting for his response. Nothing could be settled until the Stump returned. I followed my nose to the club, found myself in line for cheeseburgers and beer. Platoon commander—gimp platoon commander. And your command has already been dispatched to war without you, Mikey. Why not Polster's platoon? After Turf Club, that would have been an easier gig. Or maybe not. What did I know about Third Platoon—nothing. Domnoske had seemed a good troop, and Tom Hodge had been running them for a couple of months. He was, by reputation, a highly respected guy. I thought I'd look him up. Ruminating, I found myself with a plate full of food in my lame hand and a beer in my good one. I could barely grip the plate, so I switched hands and carried my booty to a seat at a corner table, away from the crowded bar and went to work. I was famished. The room was noisy with AFVN radio and bullshit.

There were things going on back in the World. AFVN was carrying updates on the Apollo 13 saga, and bad music.

"We got another cluster fuck—looks like Hank Rathmell has been killed."

I overheard one of the lieutenants at the bar, talking as he ordered. It was Pete Gray, one of the Operations Alphas, a personable man, popular with the other lieutenants.

"What happened?" someone asked.

"We're not for sure on the details. Jim [Duda] called an air strike. One of the A-4s [Skyhawk close air-support aircraft] crashed, started a fire. Duda called it in. The air wing asked us to send the Mission Impossible team out to the crash site to get the pilot. Hank, Charlie Kershaw, Gunny Moore, and some other guys from the Three Shop volunteered to go."

A crowd had gathered. The noise abated. Everyone focused on the story being told. I listened, unobtrusively, from my seat.

"I guess they got out there and couldn't find an LZ. Rathmell rappelled down to the crash site, found the pilot's body. Then, the aircrew thought they were taking fire. Before the rest of the team could get on the ground, they tried to *didi* [leave]. Gunny Moore made 'em go back—threatened the pilot with his Swedish K [submachine gun]. He's going to catch some shit. Anyway, they decided to get Rathmell back with the jungle penetrator—"

"I thought we weren't supposed to use that piece of shit anymore," someone interrupted him.

"True. It broke again. Rathmell fell a hundred feet. Broke him up like a rag doll. They're still out there."

The group jostled one another at the bar, grumbling and morose. Though I had not known Rathmell, his death disturbed me, as it did the others. He had done his best to help us (Turf Club) with our insert. I felt depressed by the irony and waste in his misfortune. It was one thing to die as the result of enemy action, quite another to die as the result of an equipment failure. That three good men died this way made me angry, and fatalistic. Maybe the NVA was less dangerous than our own air wing? I resolved never to get myself in a position where we had to resort to using the jungle penetrator. With the thought foremost in my mind, I rose from my table and made my way toward the door, once more acutely aware of the abuse my body had taken in the past twenty hours. It was late, long past time to hit the rack.

Just as I reached the door, Drumright burst through, followed by the sergeant major. He was in a rage, and I was in the way. "What now, Lieutenant?" I backed up to the bar, trying to get out of his way, too late. He crashed into me, smelling of scotch and sweat, his eyes ablaze. Polster's right. He is crazy! The thought flitted through my mind as he fended me off. Glaring, he took in my battered appearance, the sling. I saw him process the encounter in his mind. His eyes focused on me. "You're Hodgins! Ain't that right, peckerwood!" I would have answered to any name to avoid the pending confrontation, but he rushed on. "Charlie Company! Turf Club! You kicked some ass out there today, boy! I'll see you get a dingleberry [personal decoration] for it! You hurt bad?"

He spun me toward the bar by my good arm. I said nothing, still shocked by the force of his personality. The rumors about his keeping mug shots of us must be true, I thought; there is no other way he could know who I am.

"Bartender, get this peckerwood a beer—get all these peckerwoods a round!" He gestured wildly in the general direction of the crowd. Court was in session.

"Drink! To Valhalla [warrior heaven]! I'll see all you bastards in Valhalla!"

Drumright's impact on the group was immediate and profound. Within seconds, he had become the center of attention. He was clearly angry, even hurt, over the tragedy of the afternoon. The others, to greater or lesser degrees, became caught up in the ritual. I waited for my moment, then slipped away. I made my way back to the hootch in the dark, stumbling down the slope in solitary. Out over the rice paddies, a flare burst in the night sky. It was followed by a siren and the rumble of an M-60 machine gun. "Water bo [buffalo] in the wire, I bet." I lurched up the step into the hootch and fell on my rack fully clothed. I was asleep in seconds.

The morning of the thirteenth (April 1970) came and went without me. I slept until the midday heat brought me to tortured consciousness. I awoke in pain, sopping wet with sweat. Groggy, I stumbled out to the showers and stood naked for ten minutes, cooling off. It was moving day, a good trick for a one-armed sick-bay commando. I decided to scout the route and my new digs before making any decisions. The new hootch was just behind the pool, selected for its proximity to our trouble spot, no doubt. I rankled at the thought of moving into such close proximity to a troop facility. Maybe the troops needed less supervision and more leadership. I had not observed my peers to be much removed from the troops in terms of their capacity to raise hell. Drumright, himself, had set an example in that regard. Still, an order was an order. It remained to get my gear and furnishings from the old hootch to the new hootch—mamma-san and a cart!

The inspiration came, and I acted upon it immediately. A few notes of MPC, and my problem was solved. I negotiated the move, recovered my weapons and war gear from the

hootch, and went to chow. My arm hurt like hell, but I had
regained limited use of my fingers, and my grip was getting
stronger. I kept the sling. The mess hall was nearly deserted,
another by-product of Drumright's crackdown. No one wanted
to loiter within eyesight of their commander; officers and
SNCOs who might have lingered in the mess found other
places to be. I ate alone, flexing my arm and contemplating
my future. Hanging around Camp Reasoner was a bad idea.
Better to get back in the bush. With the thought came the
sound of our helicopter package overhead. Duda and Pino,
no doubt. I finished my meal and strolled back to the company area. By the time I arrived, the mamma-sans had
moved me into the new hootch. Even my fan was plugged in.
Some things about being an officer were really sweet. Reflecting thus, I went in search of my peers and my mail at the
company office.

"Say, Sergeant Anderson," I addressed my remarks to the
back of his head as I stepped through the hatch into the company office, "Got any mail for me?"

He looked up. "Yes, sir. Be right with you." He spoke and
continued with his typing.

"And one of those little green notebooks, the kind you can
put in your pocket."

My new assignment required that I have a Platoon Commander's Notebook, a list of each man's name, rank, service
(ZAP) number, date of birth, hometown, marital status, MOS,
and other personal data. I intended to peruse the service-
record books for this information at the first opportunity. The
more I could learn about my troops before I confronted them,
the better. "When can I look at the service-record books for
Third Platoon?"

Anderson finished his report with a flourish. "How about
tomorrow, Lieutenant? Today is about shot, and I'm not real
organized."

"That works for me. Where's Lieutenant Polster?"

Anderson retrieved my mail from a drawer in his desk,
and handed me a brand-new notebook and two government-
issue ballpoint pens from a stash of supplies he kept in an

ammo box. "Couldn't say, sir. I think I'm the only one around right now."

"Okay, thanks." I returned to the hootch to read my mail and listen to a tape from Joyce. It was still a new technology, and listening to the voices of loved ones was becoming very popular with us. I was thus engrossed when Jim Duda and Chet Pino stormed into the hootch, burdened with personal belongings and bad attitudes.

"Say, Mike. Ain't this some shit? Where the fuck is Baker, anyway?" Duda spoke as he dumped his gear on the deck with a crash. He was sopping wet, breathing hard, and angry. Pino followed his example in silence.

I stood up to greet them. "Yeah. Shit flows downhill. You guys planning to move all your stuff by yourselves?"

"What the fuck else would we do?" Duda sat down on his pack, exasperated. He stared up at me, noticing my sling for the first time. "What happened to you?"

"Pinched nerve. I had the mamma-sans move my stuff—five bucks MPC."

Pino grinned. Duda leaped to his feet. "Well, no shit. Why didn't we think of that?"

They went out as they had come, crashing through the screen door in a rush. Shitbird darted into the hootch between their legs and jumped onto my rack, his curly tail awag. I resumed the maudlin recital, moved by the loneliness that permeated Joyce's voice. The tape covered several days. She had edited parts of it, adding a bit here and there and included several songs, my favorites. The tape-deck speaker could not do her justice, but I became homesick nonetheless. Dreaming of happier times, I dozed under my fan, the dog at my feet. The mamma-sans came and went, moving my cohorts into the hootch. In the late afternoon, they reappeared in better spirits. They had been to Freedom Hill.

"Say Mike! We bought a refrigerator. And beers!"

Garrison life had its rewards: hot chow, cold beer, running water, electricity, movies, and comradery. It was also boring as hell. Baker returned from Tokyo in rare form. He was short and glad of it. He made one trip to Wild Bill's morning coffee and spent the next two days on the OP (Hill 425). He said he was supervising, but we all thought he was hiding from the colonel. The daily grind of the Breakfast Club rubbed him the wrong way. Captain Sterling (the personnel officer) or some other REMF was always setting traps for the company commanders—another guerrilla war. Seemingly, the only lieutenant who weathered Drumright's tirades with élan was "Dog" Jones, our eccentric and incredibly competent supply officer. Baker regaled us with "Dog stories," his favorite being Jones's retort to the colonel's dressing him down about his personal appearance. "Suh! I view it as my solemn duty to set a minimum standard fo' mah troops, suh! This is the minimum standard, suh!" That Jones escaped where lesser lights had fallen was testimony to his professional competence. I reckoned that I would not fare as well. Third Platoon came and went without me. Duda, Pino, and Domnoske picked off the frag orders from Polster without so much as a by-your-leave. There was no need, as I had nothing to offer them prior to their leaving. Each patrol leader prepared a team according to his personal style, and off they went. As a sick-bay commando, I was irrelevant. Tom Hodge was helpful, though a bit distracted, when it came to our change of command. He was packing, for the second time in as many days. His words to me were, "I had it, you got it. Don't fuck it up. Domnoske is a good troop, although he is still pissed off at me for getting his ear blown off."

With those comments to work with, I decided that the best way to get acquainted with my new responsibility, in absentia, was to get on with my review of the service-record books of the Marines who had now been entrusted to my care. It was tedious work. Over the course of the next few days, I kept myself busy updating promotion scores, creating a Platoon Leader's Notebook and other mundane administrative tasks, while my arm got better, and the strength returned to most of my fingers. Four out of five wasn't bad. I discovered that Third Herd was a motley crew, most of whom were overdue for promotion. It seemed like a good way to get things off on the right foot, so I took it up with Polster. "Say Larry, how come these guys haven't been promoted? We've got guys in here who are still privates."

"Beats me. Are they eligible?"

"Everybody in this motherfucker deserves at least one stripe, Larry. Even you." I laughed, but there was an edge to my voice. Having been victimized myself as a troop, I felt a strong sense of injustice at the thought of "my" Marines being underpaid or shortchanged. "What do we have to do to get these guys promoted?"

"Well, if you're so gung ho about it, write 'em up. Sergeant Anderson does most of it, the Diary entries and all. We write up a special order, and the CO signs it."

"Swell." The project gave me something to do for the balance of the day, but after eight days in the compound, I had seen all of service-record books, Freedom Hill, and Wild Bill that I could stand. I determined that it was time to return to the bush, light-duty chit or not. I resolved to make the fact known to Baker at the first opportunity.

"Stump, I'm ready to go." We were in the company office. Baker had just returned from another commanders' conference.

"That's great, Mike. I need you for this inning. Jim Duda is going to Hill Four twenty-five. That leaves Mike Curry, the Chief, and you to take the patrols. You'll have two days to get ready, once Curry gets in. He is due back from Four twenty-five this afternoon. Your call sign is Delicatessen. You're going way out west."

Baker had moved to the situation map, a grease pencil in his grasp. He spoke over his shoulder, like the school teacher he intended to be, while he wrote on the wall. I saw that he was drawing havens on the map. He wasn't kidding about "way out west." His little box labeled Delicatessen was perilously close to the Laotian border, and outside the artillery fan. I felt a twinge of anxiety. Maybe I wasn't as ready as I wanted to be. "Can I pick my guys this time?"

"Sure. After what you went through last time, I'm sure

Curry won't mind." Baker was distracted, finishing his notations, his back to me. "Who have you got in mind?"

"Brasington. I've been out with his team once before. If
we're going way out there, it would be nice to be with familiar faces."

Picking the team was a psychological lift. Brasington was
a stand-up guy. Thinking of our last outing together, I wasn't
so sure about his team, nor they of me. I moved to a position
beside Baker, took the frag order from his grasp, and stared at
the map. My mind was already engaged in planning.

Corporal Brasington knew the drill, second time around.
In fact, it appeared that his team had incorporated some of
my "squirrelly SOP," a development for which I was certain
I would receive no credit. I took a low-key approach to the
preliminary activities, leaving most of the work to the NCO.
There was no point in breaking hard on them again. We made
the trip (to Nong Song) without incident, unless we could
call Mother Nature an enemy. After our insert, we humped
into a rubber plantation, acres and acres of ancient rubber
trees planted in neat rows across rolling hills at the base of
the mountains. It was an eerie, dangerous place, but so far as
we could tell, then uninhabited. We harbored for the night on
a low finger, surrounded by hundred-foot trees. During the
night, the weather got ugly. A monsoon storm struck with a
fury. The wind howled through the trees, driving sheets of
rain parallel to the ground. Thunder and lightning crashed
across the night sky. We huddled on the ground, wrapped in
ponchos and poncho liners, shivering like the stranded
animals we were. Around us, the forest collapsed. By morning, the storm had passed, but the ground was covered by
eighteen-inch tree trunks and foliage for as far as the eye
could see. The storm had flattened the rubber trees. It was as
if a giant hand had swept the plantation flat. We had to crawl
on hands and knees, often on our bellies, for half a klick (five
hundred meters) to get out from under the chaos. It took half
the day, and exhausted us. We were without comm and
somewhat disoriented. Remaining undiscovered, therefore,

became a priority. The second day, we harbored under the tree trunks, then moved across a stream and into the foothills. Once on high ground, we established contact with our radio relay and went on our merry way. We made a two-day fishhook out of our patrol route and were extracted from a sandbar in a streambed on the morning of April 30, 1970. Delicatessen was a piece of cake—we saw no evil, heard no evil, spoke no evil, and did no evil.

Back in the compound, we discovered that our peers had been less fortunate. One of our teams had been ambushed, and a popular Marine known as "Hoss" (because of his size) had been shot in the chest. The news took the edge off our return to camp. I left the team in Brasington's able hands and went in search of my platoon.

Domnoske and the Third Herd had been in the compound for a week, having returned while I was wandering around with Delicatessen. They had been on guard duty, mess duty, and in training. They had also been harassed to the point of rebellion. And there had been a brawl in the hootch the night before I returned from patrol. Curry was in the process of undertaking disciplinary action when I arrived back in the compound.

"Man, you missed it!" We were in the company office. Curry was in the process of organizing himself as the company executive officer (acting). I felt a twinge of envy—he would not be going to the field anymore. I let my gaze drift around the interior of the office, waiting for him to continue. Polster had transferred to division. Baker had a flight date. His replacement, 1st Lt. A. J. Pack was expected to report any day. Drumright was raising hell in the compound. Lieutenants were passing through the battalion as if the S-1 Shop were a turnstile. There were new troops in abundance. Things (rocks) were being painted. We had a new monument (for Skibbe and McVey).

"We had a USO show last night. I was OD [Officer of the Day]. What a cluster fuck! Your platoon got in a ruckus in their hootch. They've blown out the screens, broke the doors. Man, the colonel is really pissed. I've got to hold an investigation. There'll be office hours [nonjudicial punishment] for somebody—"

I broke in on his tirade, "Why don't you let me take care of it? It's time for me to get in there anyway."

Curry looked up from his desk. Relief flashed across his eyes. He had no stomach for being a disciplinarian in these circumstances. "What are you going to do?" He gave me a quizzical look.

"Don't know. Where can I find Domnoske?"

Curry shrugged. "In the hootch? They're supposed to be writing statements—"

"Okay. See ya later." I went in search of the platoon sergeant with no particular plan in mind. The first step must be to hear the facts, their facts, before rushing to judgment. Domnoske was probably the key. I found him, and the rest of the platoon, in the hootch. Curry was correct—they had trashed the place. I took in the scene as I stepped across the threshold of the door. The screen was askew, and the interior was littered with broken cots and equipment. There were beer cans and 782 gear everywhere. The troops, Domnoske included, sat astride footlockers, pencils and paper in hand. I noticed that no one had written anything. They looked up in sullen unison upon my entry.

"As you were, gents. Sergeant Domnoske, can I have a word with you outside?"

I turned my back immediately, leading the way outside and down to the pool. Behind me, I heard Domnoske scramble over the mess to follow me. There were muttered epithets, "Lifer motherfucker . . ."

I found a seat under the awning and lit up a Marlboro, waiting. Domnoske arrived, positioned himself at attention in front of me. He clearly expected to take the heat for his troops.

"Relax, Ski. This is not exactly the school solution for assumption of command, but you and I are going to be working together with these guys until we get shot or go home. So why don't we start by sorting out this situation together?" I made eye contact to reinforce my point, then continued, "I know what happened. I want to know who and why. If you tell me, it won't go any farther. If you don't, it will."

I paused, smoking, while Domnoske made up his mind.

"Sir, it wasn't their fault, sir. Things just got out of hand, you know?" I held my silence. Domnoske continued, "It just built up, sir. People were fuckin' with us. Then they had the USO show, and after the show, the girls went to the Staff and Officers' Club. Grant and some of the other guys just lost it, sir."

What now, Lieutenant? I pitched the butt of my cigarette into space. It was a moral dilemma. "Fuckin' beautiful," I swore, then turned on Domnoske. "Okay, Sergeant. This is what we are going to do. You are going to clean up the hootch, fix everything that's broken, and make it better than new—paint it. That is a platoon-size job, if it takes all night. Tomorrow morning I am going to have a look at the hootch and the platoon. This is how it works—you take care of me, I take care of you. I was a troop once, myself. Got it?"

"What about the statements, sir?"

"I'll take care of that."

We parted company to pursue our separate missions. I found Curry as I had left him, buried in paperwork. I decided he liked the XO job. "Third Platoon is under control, Mike. I think we should let the whole thing drop."

"What about punishment? We have to maintain discipline here."

"Mike, it's a hundred degrees in the shade. We're in fuckin' Vietnam. Fixing what they broke is punishment enough. They had a good reason, after all. Besides, who wants to do all the paperwork?"

"Yeah, I see what you mean. What do I tell the CO?"

"Tell him it's taken care of. That's all he wants to know anyway. These guys still have to do some war fighting. We don't have time for chickenshit. Okay?"

Curry stared at me in silence, assessing the situation. Finally, he relaxed, turning his attention back to the stack of papers on his desk. "Speaking of war fighting, here are your

frags. You've got three gigs, two radio relays and a hump in
Happy Valley. Everybody flips [simultaneous insert and ex-
tract] on the fourth [May 4, 1970]."

I took the documents from his grasp and moved to the
situation map. After two months as a warrior at large, I
was finally going to make a patrol with my own platoon, call
sign Detroit Tigers. I would finally pick my own lineup from
amongst Marines who knew that they were accountable to
me for an extended period of time. With a little luck and determination, I would be able to train and mold this group in
my own image. I was pleased, present dilemma aside. I felt I
knew a little about the platoon from scanning the men's service records. Based upon the previous night's activities, I
also knew they could fight, at least with each other. I certainly had an appreciation for Domnoske, having made the
one patrol with him and observing his impact from afar over
the past sixty days. If he could carry off his present assignment, we would be in clover. Looking at the situation map, I
discovered that Happy Valley was atop Charlie Ridge, to the
west. Maybe it wasn't clover after all.

Domnoske and the Third Herd were good for it. By the
look of it, they had been up all night. The hootch was im-
maculate, fresh paint in evidence everywhere. It was 0700,
time for chow. I made a cursory tour and sent them off, holding Domnoske back.

"Ski, when they get back from chow, put up a warning order. You and Wardlow will take the radio relays. I will take
the hump. I want your recommendations on a primary RTO,
an assistant patrol leader [APL], a corpsman, and a point
man. I'll take two new guys. Let's plan to talk this over at
sixteen hundred [4:00 P.M.]."

"Aye, aye, sir!" Domnoske rendered a crisp salute and
made tracks for the mess hall.

I followed him, at a slower pace, lost in thought. The patrol preparation cycle had a rhythm. I found myself carried
along almost subconsciously. The troops were organized.
They knew what to do, and had done it. By the time I caught
up with the platoon in the late afternoon, they had prepared

themselves for the field with the exception of my inspection and the immediate-action drills. All three of Third Platoon's teams were assembled on the HLZ, prepared to take turns on our piece of trail. Domnoske was holding class on the proper techniques for breaking contact. I decided to watch and learn.

Dawn brought the helicopters and another opportunity to distinguish myself in combat. The thought was tinged with irony; the single best way to distinguish myself was not to get in a situation that required combat. Drumright was busy giving medals to fools. It was a bitter thought that stuck with me as I made my shadowy trek to the HLZ. The troops had gathered, Third Platoon and several others. It was going to be a big lift.

Baker was there, camera in hand. "Say, Mike. Let me get some shots of you guys. I got Duda and Pino already."

I looked around. Half the teams on the HLZ were from Charlie Company, five in all. I gestured to Domnoske, Wardlow, and Hicks. They formed up, and we had a photo op for the Stump. It was bad luck.

"Well, Mike. I guess this is it. I'll be back in the World by the time you dudes get back. Anybody you want me to look up? I could call your folks, your wife?"

Baker stood awkwardly on the tarmac, his camera dangling from one hand. It was a moment he had looked forward to with dread and anticipation. He was next, going home. His war was over. Charlie Company would carry on, under a new commander—1st Lt. A. J. Pack, who had yet to make an appearance. I looked at Baker, then back at the Detroit Tigers gathered at the tail ramp of our helicopter. Duty called. I grasped Baker's outstretched hand, pulled him close, and shouted into his ear over the din of the helicopter's engines. "Naw, man. It's better they don't know what I'm doin'. See you back in the World! Maybe you should write!"

The bird was winding up. With a last shake, I turned my back on Baker and rushed to join my team. My last glimpse of the Stump was of a lonely man. I felt a twinge of remorse. Steve Baker had been more than a commander. In the brief time we had spent together, he had become a friend. Peering over the tail gunner's shoulder at the receding helipad, I realized that I would miss him.

Detroit Tigers was a ninety-four-hour nonevent. We were inserted into a blown-out area at the far west end of our haven, and humped a klick a day east to our extraction point, another streambed sandbar. The trails in the area were overgrown, showing no signs of recent activity.

Our major difficulty, aside from the heat and vegetation, was communications. I discovered that my RTO, Lance Corporal Paul Hannon, was a wizard with field-expedient antennae. Even so, we still couldn't talk to anyone until the evening of the fourth day. Even the Broncos had been grounded because of overcast on the ridge. The valley was a spooky place. Once prosperous, it was abandoned. From the concealment of the undergrowth, we saw cornfields, abandoned houses, and other evidence of happier times. We dared not explore in the open. Because of the overcast and dampness, we spent most of our time in movement. There was nothing to observe and no way to report. By the morning of our extract, we were filthy, hungry, and exhausted. From the air, Camp Reasoner looked like a resort, or a penal colony. Upon closer inspection, I concluded that the latter was more the case.

The only constant in life is change. Upon our return from the bush, I discovered that things had changed again. Mike Curry had become official executive officer. Tony Pack had taken up residence in the commander's hootch, but was nowhere evident. I had yet to meet the man who had replaced the Stump. Curry gave me the word on coming events. Third Platoon was to clean up, pack up, and go to Hill 425 in the normal rotation, in no case later than 0900 the following morning, May 10, 1970.

CHAPTER SEVEN
THE FORT

10–11 MAY 1970

The superior man is firm in the right way, and not merely firm.

Confucius, 551–478 B.C., *Analects*

From the air, Hill 425 didn't look like much, a barren sliver of rock, splattered with sandbags and radio antennae, amid countless others. I had seen at least a thousand such hills myself in the past six months. Some tactical genius had decided to occupy this one because of the view. Peering out the door of the helicopter, I could see that the hill overlooked a picturesque valley, which ran southwest to northeast out of the mountains of Thong Duc into the Arizona. There were two lakes and a heavily wooded watercourse in the valley. Spider Lake, the smaller one, at the west end, was man-made, created by a dam that was clearly visible from the air. The larger lake resembled an alligator, hence its name. The valley was speckled with abandoned structures, suggesting that it had once been a prosperous area. The layout reminded me of the French-inspired villages I had seen farther north. The terrain to the south and west of our destination resort was forbidding, steep and rugged, sparsely vegetated, cut up with ravines and rock falls—the Que Sons Mountains. Just south of the ridge, the Que Sons Valley stretched from the mountains to the shore of the South China Sea. The responsibility of the 7th Marines, it was the scene of recent bloody engagements with NVA Main Force units, including my own. I leaned farther out of the hatch, peering south—somewhere down there were the remains of two good men from Charlie Company, Skibbe and McVey. I thought to myself, They should have built the monument out here.

As the helicopter circled for its approach to the HLZ, I stumbled over troops and gear aft to the tailgate. The bird was heavily loaded. Besides our war gear, we each had a case of Cs, and assorted personal comfort items. We were, in fact, festooned with pogie bait and paraphernalia. Beneath the aircraft, a cargo net dangled, burdened with a pallet of ten-gallon water cans, C rations, crates of assorted munitions, cases of spare batteries for the radios, and ten thousand sandbags. Domnoske had assembled most of the gear from a checklist he developed on prior excursions. The sandbags had been added by the battalion supply officer (S-4), apparently in response to a request from the hill. It was a wonder to me that the aircraft was flying. I scrambled over knees and cargo to the door, grabbed a cargo strap near the crew chief, and leaned out to get a better look at the terrain around my new home.

The place was haphazardly fortified, with three strands of concertina barbed wire meandering around the perimeter. A shallow trench connected what appeared to be ten or twelve bunker/hootches in an oblong arrangement near the military crest* of the hill. Atop the whole conglomeration was a sandbagged observation tower, constructed of plywood and tin. Several two-niner-twos (radio antennae) stuck up from its immediate environs. Below the main position, red smoke billowed from a grenade burning in the middle of a flat spot on the razorback—our destination HLZ. It was barely wide enough to accommodate the CH-46, tailfirst.

As we completed our final sinking turn onto the HLZ, troops materialized from within the bunkers, stripped to the waist, and hustled down the trench line to meet us. They were carrying empty water cans, two apiece, which they stashed behind the sandbag berm while they waited for the helicopter to flare and hover over the LZ. I felt a jolt, like an ele-

---

*Highest point from which all lower elevations may be observed.

vator jammed between floors, and realized that the pilot had let go of the cargo net. The bird lifted somewhat, then lunged abruptly to the left and dropped into the valley before regaining altitude to circle above the hill. I moved back to the gunner's door and saw that the troops behind the berm had rushed out to unpack the cargo net. The HLZ was a beehive as they struggled with the contents. Within minutes, all our gear was staged at the edge of the HLZ and the empty water cans were secured in the cargo net. Another smoke grenade blossomed in the dirt, and our ride sank toward the ground. The troops rustled and shrugged into their equipment, so I followed suit. They knew the routine.

The CH-46 made another stomach-tumbling descent and set its rear wheels on the dirt. I stood behind the crew chief, waiting for the signal to leave the bird. He let down the tailgate and stepped out onto the ground, moving to one side so that his cargo could pass unimpeded. I followed him, and counted my troops off the aircraft. Hunched against the rotor wash, they rushed down the ramp toward the wire, equipment slapping haphazardly against their bodies, each with a case of C rats in one hand, holding his cover atop his head with the other. Domnoske was the last man. He checked the bay of the helicopter as he left. He was nothing if not thorough. I gave the crew chief a thumbs-up, signaling that we were all off, and moved off after the platoon. The helicopter lifted off immediately, blowing gravel and debris everywhere. I was pelted head to toe with Vietnam. I trudged off the HLZ in trace of my troops, spitting grit from between my teeth and cursing.

Jim Duda separated himself from his group of filthy teens and met me halfway to the wire. Taking my case of C rats, he turned to guide me up the hill, talking as we climbed. "Say, Mike! Sure glad to see you, be it ever so short a visit!" He laughed. "We haven't had much action up here, but it's hot wet, hot dusty, or just plain hot, take your pick. Me and my guys have to make our bird in about five mikes. Your FO [forward observer for artillery support] is a guy named Bob Wood. He is supposed to go on R & R tomorrow, so you best get with him on the IOD and our SOPs first thing. No telling what the next guy will be like. Your CP is at the end of this trench." He gestured with a hitchhiker's thumb over his shoulder. "You got any questions?"

I dropped my pack on the berm, next to his. Troops were filing past us as we stood in the parapet. Mine were seeking their favorite bunkers, or being assigned to one by Domnoske. Duda's, festooned with creature comforts, were moving down to the HLZ. I decided that I would depend on Domnoske and my own evaluation of the position. We were not going to have time to conduct the ritual "Relief in the Lines" I had learned in the Basic School. In fact, this was a situation with which I had become too familiar in the Grunts—changing defensive positions with another unit on short notice with no provision for overlap briefings on defensive positions, security routines, placement of weapons, enemy activity, or anything else. It was SOP for Vietnam. You came, you went, you suffered. Every man/lieutenant for himself. At least I would have the companionship of a friend for the evening.

Bob Wood was a Basic School classmate. He and his wife were among a group of couples with whom Joyce and I had spent some comfortable evenings while in training at Quantico. What I wouldn't give for another "country meal" at one of those restaurants! I let my gaze wander over the position while the troops trudged past. The crew-served weapons were poorly placed. Most of the bunkers were in disrepair, and too high above ground—troop engineering! (It is easier to fill sandbags than to dig trenches. That one could come from the other was a method lost on teenagers.) The wire was too close to the fighting positions. These and other thoughts flitted through my mind as I lit a Marlboro and leaned back against the sandbag berm. "So Jim, what do we do up here?" I offered him the pack of cigarettes. He took one, lit up, then answered.

"Well, mostly you eat, sleep, shit, and read fuck books. I left some good Westerns in the bunker for you. Your RTOs stand radio watch. Sometimes we are the relay for teams farther south. The IOD—integrated observation device—team watches the valley and calls fire missions on the Gooners when they can. It's hard to get clearances to fire. The biggest problem you got is water. There is never enough. If you work the troops too hard, they get stroked out. And you got to pay attention to the shitter—burn it every morning, or suffer the stink all day. It's upwind of your bunker! Other than that, enjoy your stay!"

Duda flicked the still burning butt into space and turned to shrug into his pack. The CH-46 was rushing in its characteristic spiral toward a plume of purple smoke on the HLZ. He hustled through the wire and down the slope to rejoin his platoon as the men stumbled one after another onto the tailgate of the helicopter. Last man. The bird lifted laboriously to hover thirty feet above the HLZ while two Marines on the ground (under Domnoske's supervision, I noticed) hooked the cargo net onto a cable under the aircraft fuselage. The two Marines dashed clear of the hovering bird, and Domnoske waved it away. The aircraft staggered aloft, the cargo net swinging perilously near the barbed-wire perimeter of the HLZ as the pilot banked away from the ridge, letting the helicopter fall toward the valley floor to gain airspeed. That accomplished, the helicopter gradually gained altitude and fled toward the ocean. The clatter of its rotors drifted back on the wind, then left us in silence.

Domnoske and his stevedores made their way back up the slope and through the wire, heads drooping. It had been an exhausting ten minutes. He sent them in search of shade and water, then joined me in the trench. "Got any word to pass, Lieutenant?" His eyes searched mine as he spoke. This was going to be another FNG test.

I returned his gaze, equally direct, accepting the challenge. "Not just this instant, Ski. But I want to meet with you and the team leaders in my hootch at eighteen hundred [6:00 P.M.]. You've been up here lots of times, so I'm sure you've got ways of doing things and reasons for doing them. Why don't we just go with that, for now?"

"Aye, aye, sir!" He turned away in the direction of the

nearest bunker. I watched him until he disappeared into the
hootch. Then, I shouldered my rucksack, grasped my M-16
in one hand, my case of Cs in the other, and struggled down
the trench to the command-post bunker Duda had pointed
out. Crammed into a jumble of granite boulders at the bitter
end of a "fighting trench," it was more a lean-to than a
bunker. The trench was only two feet deep and about a foot
wide, with a double row of sandbags stacked along the out-
board edge. Over the berm, I had a spectacular view of the
Arizona, all the way to Charlie Ridge and the South China
Sea. There was a rifle pit just outside the entrance to the
bunker. As I stumbled closer, I saw that it had been converted into a cooking and washing area. There was an ammo
box, 106mm, sandbagged into the berm to make a shelf, and
remnants of numerous C-rat stoves, utensils, and other paraphernalia laying about. I dropped the case of Cs in the opening, shrugged out of the rucksack, and lunged through the
opening to the bunker.

Inside, it was dark. Like the trench, the bunker floor was a
shallow excavation, just enough to level the ground. Sandbag walls had been built up on two sides, incorporating a
large boulder in the front corner. Former tenants had dug
into the hillside to make room for three cots and a makeshift
table. The overhead was plywood, topped with plastic and
sandbags, and supported by two 8x12 timbers. A kerosene
lamp and assorted candles were on a shelf at the back. All
the comforts of home, I thought to myself, but no back door.
I dropped the rucksack on the ground and went back outside,
rifle in hand.

Atop the bunker, a hootch had been constructed using engineer stakes, comm wire, plastic, and ponchos. I scurried up
the sandbags onto the roof of the bunker and peered inside.
There was another cot and assorted personal gear, including
web gear and a .45-caliber pistol—the FO's quarters, no doubt.
He had a folding camp stool and an ammo box desk festooned with candles and pictures of family—and a footlocker. Bob was a family man. His wife had been expecting

when we graduated from TBS. I took a closer look at the pictures. Sure enough! He was a daddy.

I made my way across the top of the bunker and jumped into the trench on the other side. I saw that my new quarters formed the terminal of the perimeter on the north slope of the hill. A massive, rain-smoothed granite slab jutted out into the valley just below where I stood. One of my predecessors, with great foresight and a sense of self-preservation, had caused concertina barbed wire to be draped off the end of it. The stuff festooned the brush below the rock escarpment. It was no comfort to me. I made a mental note and continued my tour of the position.

There was a crew-served weapons position immediately behind my CP. I saw that the M-60 machine gun was probably intended to cover a trail that led up to the position from the foot of the easternmost finger of the ridge. The trail zigzagged through three rows of concertina and down the hill for perhaps fifty yards before disappearing over the military crest of the hill. The gun rested in the bottom of the pit, wrapped in a poncho, the barrel flaked with rust. There were several cans of 7.62mm linked ammunition covered with dust in the bottom of the hole. I saw no sign of the spare-barrel bag, the traverse and elevation (T & E) mechanism, or the tripod. I moved on.

The trench gave way to a parapet, sandbags stacked haphazardly to chest height, reinforced with engineer stakes, which had been pounded into the hard ground. There were two more above-ground sandbag bunker/hootches abutting the rocks opposite the parapet. Clearly, they had been constructed more for protection from the elements than from enemy fire. The evidence of a continuing unsuccessful battle against the rain was everywhere. Half culverts, no doubt scavenged from some air force supply facility, had been used to create rifle pits along the sandbag parapet. An ingenious solution to an age-old problem. Each had been converted into a barby (as our Aussy friends were fond of calling outdoor cooking facilities). In some of the ammo boxes, I saw loose

grenades—smoke, gas, and fragmentation—as well as ban-
doliers of 5.56mm ammo.

As I made my way down the trench, I encountered soldiers
(i.e., members of the U.S. Army), distinguishable by their
sideburns and shoulder patches. They were the sensor team,
no doubt. The odor of onions wafted on the air from their
cooking. I resolved to ensure that we the Few, the Proud, got
onions and Tabasco on the first resupply. Maybe Domnoske
had thought of that. He thought of everything else. I continued round the bend to another crew-served weapons pit, two
more bunkers, and finally the passage down to the HLZ. A
huge boulder encroached on the trench at this end, and
masked the HLZ from direct fire from any of our fighting positions. If the enemy got in behind this rock he could frag us
forever. Not good. From there, I turned to survey the interior
of the position.

There was a mortar pit, sans mortar. There were two more
large sandbag constructions between the boulders, and atop the
whole, a plywood tower, sandbagged around its lower ex-
tremes. Inside the tower, several Marines in various modes of
attire, manned what resembled a command center. There were
several PRC-25 radios and a large electronic device on a tripod—the integrated observation device (IOD) Jim had men-
tioned. I climbed out of the trench and approached the larger of
the two interior bunkers. With my flashlight, I peered inside,
and found my mortar, along with a two-year supply of ammunition. There were cases of M-26 hand grenades; pyrotechnics;
claymore antipersonnel mines; 5.56mm ammunition, ball and
tracer; 7.62mm linked for the M-60 machine guns, and the
spare-barrel bags, T & Es, and tripods. The light picked up
markings identifying several engineer's demolition kits, crates
of mortar munitions, HE (high explosive), and ILLUM
(flares), all "protected" by two layers of sandbags over a 2x6
roof. One RPG or a mortar hit on this bunker would light up the
whole position for hours—and probably kill us all. I flicked the
light around one more time and noticed CS gas launchers—
four of them. If we didn't blow up, we could gag to death.

I flicked off the light and went out. Domnoske was nowhere in sight. I had seen enough to know that there would be plenty to keep us busy for the next two weeks. BAMCIS!* The Troop Leading Steps were already ticking off in my subconscious. I found my way back to my bunker, went inside, and slumped on the nearest cot. It was dark. I fumbled for a smoke, lit up, and found a candle with the flickering light of my Zippo. I set the paraffin wonder ablaze, dripped some wax on the overhead beam, and stuck the candle in it, just above my head. Stowing the lighter in my pocket, I turned to slump back on the rack. Outside, my troops were settling into their tempo of life on the hill. I smoked, content to wait and see what that would turn out to be.

Twilight was social hour on the hill, like a country barbecue. The troops concocted wild combinations of our twelve basic meals, liberally doused with Tabasco sauce, and lied to each other about what they had put in them. Some used the waning light to reread tattered letters from home, or to add a line or two to an Iliad of their own composition. Others fiddled with weapons and equipment in preparation for our night acts. Cooking odors, mixed with those of sweat, dust, human excrement, and kerosene drifted on the evening breeze, accompanied by whiffs of conversation and an occasional laugh. The troops were relaxing.

Finished with my smoke, I roused myself to make another circuit of the perimeter. It was time to see what Domnoske had accomplished and to catch up with my friend Bob. I decided to walk the trench all the way around the position again. That way, I could check everyone out without getting in the way of their activities. Five years as an enlisted Marine and six months in the Grunts had taught me valuable lessons about leadership. One was that troops, like children, had distinctly different behaviors when in the presence of authority than when not. I wanted to be as unobtrusive as possible. I donned my bush hat, picked up my M-16, and went out, snuffing the candle between thumb and forefinger as I turned toward the entrance to the bunker, thinking, I really want a back door to this bitch.

---

*BAMCIS: Begin Planning, Arrange for Reconnaissance, Make Reconnaissance, Complete the Plan, Issue the Order, Supervise

Outside, I climbed over the top of the bunker, catching snatches of conversation from the tower as I ducked past, and dropped into the trench on the other side. I moved unobtrusively down the trench, taking in the sights and sounds of twilight on the perimeter. As I approached our detachment of "soldiers," I heard music from the Doggie bunker—Jimi Hendrix. I climbed onto the roof of their bunker and stuck my head over the berm of the IOD tower.

Bob Wood and his crew were inside, along with Hannon, who was engrossed in developing a new watch-standers list for the RTOs. Like a submariner from the old World War II movies, Bob was draped over the handles of the IOD, scanning the valley floor for evidence of enemy activity. He looked up from the binoculars at the sound of my scrambling into the tower. "Say, Mike!" Wood moved away from the IOD to shake my hand as he spoke. I grasped his outstretched hand and shoulder in the firm clasp of friends who have known one another in happier times.

"You've lost weight." He had appraised me in a single glance, taking in the emaciating effects of my bout with Fever of Unknown Origin.

"True. Bad water, but I'm getting stronger. You, on the other hand, are uglier than I remember and too old to outgrow it!"

We laughed aloud, each of us pleased to be in the company of a familiar person, a peer, someone in whom we could confide. He, too, was lean to the point of being gaunt. His eyes were sunk back in his head, a sign of fatigue and stress. War was hard on the mind and the body.

"So, to business. How do you operate up here?"

As I spoke I moved over to the IOD, staring over the shoulder of a long-haired sergeant E-5 who was scanning the valley floor through the binoculars.

"Well, this is an 'integrated observation device.' It has a ship's binocular, which is great for both day and night observation. It has a ship's compass, sort of a bezel in the mount, which enables us to get a bearing on a target right off the sight. It has a laser range finder, which shoots an invisible beam of light at the target. The beam bounces back and the device tells us the exact range to the target from this position, within ten meters. Then, we got a 'night observation device,' a starlight scope, so we can see when it's really dark. The NOD isn't as good as the binos, in my opinion, because it blossoms out when you get shell flashes or flares. Then we got a load of radios, secure voice, etcetera, hooked in to the Regimental Fire-Support Coordination center. We locate a target, call it in to them. They clear it with whoever, then we shoot. We have a priority claim on all long-range artillery assets, and one direct support battery at An Hoa . . ."

His voice trailed off while he gazed through the binoculars. Then he turned to face me again, and continued, "We can get rounds on target faster than anybody around, but we still have problems because of NFZs [no fire zones], and limitations on adjusting fires—the Gooners can literally run out from under my adjustments. We can only adjust five hundred meters in any direction from the splash of the first round we fire during a mission—then we have to call for a new clearance."

"Do you get much activity?" I was searching for clues about our tactical situation.

"You bet. We see people—NVA—moving around all the time, day and night. They act like they own the fucking valley. Sometimes we can hose them using aerial observers, or gunships. We can direct any kind of air asset from here."

The sun was setting. It would be dark in another thirty minutes. I realized that I still had Grunt work to do, though I was fascinated with the prospects of using the IOD. I moved to the berm, and with a leg over, made a backward wave to Wood. "Bob, I need to get my troops set for the night. I'll come back after I do that, and we can talk some more. Okay?"

Wood gave a nod of assent, and I climbed down in search of my platoon sergeant. I found Domnoske near the mortar pit. He was engrossed in conversation with Sergeant Wardlow, the next senior NCO in the platoon. Nearby, Wardlow's team had assembled. They were in the process of last-minute equipment checks prior to departing for listening post (LP) duty outside the perimeter. From the look of them, it was a chore none relished, nor took seriously. They appeared to be better equipped for a picnic in the rain than for providing early warning to the rest of us. They had already donned night shirts under their utility jackets. They had shed most of the weight from their war gear and were bedecked with poncho liners, ponchos, and socks full of C rats. There was not a smudge of cammy paint among them, just sweat-shiny multi-racial faces. All this and more I gleaned from a casual glance at them as I approached.

Domnoske and Wardlow were head to head over a map, engrossed in conversation. Wardlow, flashlight in hand, was pointing to a spot on the map with a grease pencil. As I neared their position, I posed the question, "Evening, gents! What are we doing?"

They turned in unison to face me. Wardlow flicked off the flashlight. Domnoske answered up. "Well, sir, we were try-ing to decide where to have the LPs, exactly . . ."

"And what do you suggest, Sergeant?"

"Well, sir, there aren't that many good spots. We usually put one on each end of the finger, like below the LZ and about fifty meters down the finger on the north side. We were talking about whether they should be on top or off to one side, sir. On account of the wind. If we're on top, you can't hear shit, sir . . ." He fell silent. I waited.

Wardlow spoke. "Ski and I were just trying to figure out the grids for the places I had in mind when you walked up, sir!"

"Show me."

They stepped apart, expecting me to join them over the map. Instead, I turned and jumped up on the roof of the bunker, then climbed toward the tower. They scrambled to catch up. Beside the sandbagged berm of the IOD tower, I turned to face south, more or less in the direction of the high ground that dominated our position. From this vantage point, the position looked much different. I concluded that I had made a serious mistake in not doing my homework more thoroughly before we came up. I had not prepared any defensive scheme for the hill, no duty rosters, no SOPs, no nothing. If we survived the night, I resolved to make amends for all these omissions. For now, I had to cut and paste a troop-proof tactical solution to the immediate problem. I did not want to send a third of my effective strength outside the wire without any significant benefit. Better to keep them in tonight and fix everything in the morning. A violation of doctrine and division SOP, but then, what are commanders for?

Domnoske and Wardlow scrambled erect next to me, quizzical looks on their faces.

"Gents, this is called terrain appreciation." As I spoke, I made a sweeping gesture with my arm, taking in the expanse of the draw and the hillside beyond, still backlit from the sunset. "What do you see out there?"

They followed my gesture with their eyes.

"Nothin'." Wardlow was first to speak. He was clearly puzzled, even resentful.

"Ski?" I posed the question and waited for his response.

"Well, sir, I don't rightly know. It's just our pos, and the draw, and the hillside, and the top of our finger, and Hill Four ninety-three. I guess we could put some guys up there, but it would be a helluva hump, in the dark and all . . ." His voice trailed off, but he was thinking.

"Okay. Here's what I see." As I spoke, I pointed to each terrain feature. "I see high ground, dominant terrain up there [Hill 493] and all around here [the face of the slope]. I do not see that as much of a threat, because we can cover it by fire—if we don't have friendlies in the way. Down there," I pointed into the draw, "I see an avenue of approach, and a great place for an ambush. Over there," I pointed into the saddle below the HLZ, "I see another avenue of approach that needs to be covered. Let's move around to the other side."

As I spoke, I moved. They followed, stepping gingerly over antenna cables, C-rat cans, and broken sandbags.

We scrambled atop a granite boulder on the north side of the IOD tower and stood erect. "Here, I see lots of problems. The terrain supports good approaches to our position from one-hundred eighty degrees of the compass." I swept my arms in an encompassing gesture. "Especially coming up the finger and just off to the west side, where it looks steep." I pointed to the place. Their eyes followed my gesture. Their faces gave away thoughts. Domnoske was thinking. So was Wardlow. Neither was happy.

"So, gents. At this instant in time, I think we would be better served by a good fire plan and some observation from inside the pos, not LPs on exposed terrain. Have a seat. Let's develop a new game plan for tonight." I sat down. They followed suit, relaxed by the thought that I was not going to make their men take a long walk in the dark.

"Ski, how many pairs of seven-by-fifty binoculars have we got?" I leaned back against the sandbag wall of the tower, recovered my smokes from my shirt pocket, uncapped the plastic case, and offered one to each NCO.

Ski answered while waving off the proffered cigarette. "I don't know, sir. I think maybe five or six, counting yours. Why?"

I lit the smoke, shielding the flare of the match against the sandbags with my body, then turned back to face them. I took a long drag, then spoke.

"Sergeant Wardlow, I want you to get two sets of binoculars. I want you to split your team into two groups, three men in each, with a pair of binoculars for each group. Put one down there in the trench." I pointed to a position below us. "Make sure they stay in the trench while they are on watch—two guys awake at all times. They are to use the binoculars to observe the forward slope and the whole back side of this hill. I want them to move around from time to time to look and listen on both sides. I want them to scan the slope from top to bottom and back out again. If they see or hear anything, they are to tell you, quietly. You will check it out. If more is needed, wake me up. I want you to put the other group in the mortar pit. Have them do the same thing, one eighty for the south, including the finger and the draw we talked about. Any questions?"

He stood up, grinning. "No, sir. I like that idea."

"Okay, go do it." I turned to Domnoske as Wardlow scrambled down off the rock, and made eye contact. Comfort and survival were often at odds in the bush. These men, judging from what I had observed in the brief time we had been on the hill, had little appreciation for the tactical situation. To them, Hill 425 was a welcome respite, not as comfortable as life at Camp Reasoner, but neither was it as threatening as patrolling. To me, the reverse was true. I felt safer and more in control of my destiny on patrol than I did on this godforsaken little hill in the middle of Indian country. If we were to thrive and survive, I had to tighten these guys up. Domnoske was the key. He could help me win the moral authority to lead these men. Without his support, I was fucked. The situation presented what had been termed in the Basic School a "leadership challenge." It was time to get Domnoske's attention.

"Ski, how about a cup of coffee?" I smiled but my expression was cold. I moved around the tower and jumped down into the trench. Domnoske caught up with me as I ducked into the CP bunker. He followed me into the hootch, and I motioned him to a seat on one of the cots, taking the other for myself. It was dark in the bunker, so I lit a candle with the trusty Zippo, then set about heating some water for coffee mocha. Making field-expedient hot drinks was a twilight ritual that I had learned to look forward to in the Grunts, a momentary stand-down from the day's hump, the calm before the night fear, and an opportunity to get to know people. In the Grunts, I had used the occasion for various things—assessing troop morale and physical condition, listening to squad leaders report on their men, critiquing movement, developing the next day's game plan. The ritual had served me well then, and I reasoned that the same technique for informal communication would work again. (Maybe the Japanese had something with their tea ceremony after all . . .)

Dropping a match on the heat tab in the bottom of my C-rat stove, I let my mind idle, busy with the meaningless ritual, while Domnoske sat expectantly on the other cot. These troops had thought me "squirrelly" back at Reasoner, and obeyed only grudgingly. There had been no time to get acquainted before our hasty departure for the OP. Now, that lack of confidence had turned dangerous—to them and to me. If I could not win them over with discipline and compassion, people were going to get hurt, Watash first among them. There was work to be done, but cleverly.

"Ski, have you got a secret recipe for how you like your coffee, or do you want to try mine?" I made eye contact as I spoke.

Domnoske shrugged. "Why don't we try yours, sir?"

I put a canteen cup full of water on the stove and leaned back away from the fumes. "Ski, how many times have you been up here?"

"I don't rightly know, Lieutenant, maybe four or five times—five, I think. This is the fifth and the last, sir. I'm getting short. Last time I was up here, I got my fuckin' ear blown off burning stuff out of the wire. Every time I come up here I got a new lieutenant and some gung-ho bullshit or other to deal with—no offense intended, sir!"

I kept my eyes on my work, stirring packets of coffee, cocoa mix, and creamers into the canteen cup while Domnoske vented his resentment. My invitation to communicate appeared timely. "So tell me about your ear, Ski." I looked up while I spoke, taking note of the angry scar that outlined his left ear. The wound had healed well, but clearly it had been a painful insult. The more so for having occurred on a police detail rather than during a skirmish.

"It don't mean nothin', Lieutenant. Happened back in March when I was up here with Lieutenant Hodge. He had us burn the brush off the backside of the hill so we could lay concertina. Some ordnance cooked off in the fire, and a piece of it cut the top off my ear. Guess I was lucky, uh?"

I poured half of my steaming concoction into a second canteen cup and handed it to Domnoske without comment. Domnoske sipped, burned his lip, cursed. "I hate this fuckin' hill!" He said it with vehemence, and was immediately embarrassed by his outburst.

I blew on my share of the steaming brew, took a sip and

continued to probe the young sergeant. "Well, Ski, what did you learn from that episode?"

"Not a fuckin' thing, Lieutenant, not a fuckin' thing!"

"How many patrols have you done since you have been out here, Ski?"

I kept sipping, waiting for his response. Outside a commotion encroached on our conversation. The IOD team had spotted movement in the valley. "Come on, Ski, let's go watch them shoot."

I rose, cup in hand, snagged my 7x50 binoculars, and ducked through the doorway into twilight. Bob Wood was excited, in the process of calling in a fire mission. It took ten minutes to get clearance to fire a battery-three. Domnoske and I watched silently, sipping our chocolate, until the excitement abated. The artillery had "shot the shit" out of a rice paddy, in the dark, with no discernible effect on the enemy although Wood swore he saw a secondary explosion. In my own mind, I was convinced that the NVA had *didi*'d (run away) long before the first round had impacted the target area. Still, it was instructive. Where there's gooks, there's opportunity . . .

"So, Ski, you were saying?" I made eye contact with him, willing him to answer in the dark.

"Eighteen or nineteen, I guess, not counting coming up here."

"Ever do any time in the Grunts?"

"No, sir, unless you count the reaction force back in division."

"So how many times have you made contact with the enemy, been ambushed, run an ambush, run a fire mission?"

"What's the point, Lieutenant? I've been here sixteen months, if that's what you are getting at, longer than anybody else in this platoon."

I let the remark pass and asked another question. "Ski, where do you feel safer, here, in the rear, or on patrol?"

"Well, I never thought of it that way, Lieutenant. I guess in the rear, then here, then in the bush."

"This is the bush, Ski! That's my point. I haven't been

here all that long myself, but I spent one-hundred thirty-four days of my first six months in this motherfucker humping up and down these fuckin' mountains. I medevacked over a third of my troops. I've been sniped at, mortared, ambushed, and fucked with for most of my tour."

I was surprised at the level of emotion that had crept into what I had intended to be a "commander's monologue." I paused to collect myself, then continued in more measured tones. "Ski, I volunteered for this job, for payback. My goal is to finish my tour, in the bush. I intend to stay in the bush 'til it's time to go home, with no fuckups, no friendlies getting hurt. And I intend to kill a few gooks to pass the time. I need your help to do that, Ski. But I don't believe you will help me until you're convinced that I know what I'm doing. So, for tonight we'll do things your way."

I looked at my Mickey Mouse watch, the dial glowing in the dark. "Tomorrow morning, I want you to turn out the entire platoon at their fighting positions at, say, oh-seven-hundred. We'll start doing things my way at that time. Any questions?"

He stood to leave, moving toward the blackout curtain over the door to the bunker, then paused. "Sir, is it true that you wasted a gook officer on Charlie Ridge last month?"

He set the canteen cup on an ammo crate near the door, his eyes on mine. The candlelight flickered, casting shadows across the sandbag walls. Outside, an artillery flare burst over the valley. My friend Bob was still trying to improve his body count. I held Domnoske's gaze. "Who told you that, Ski?"

"Sergeant Couture, sir. He showed me the pistol and holster you gave him. I took him to catch his Freedom Bird last week. We were pretty tight."

"What else did he tell you, Ski?"

"He said you were a cold motherfucker, sir—no offense intended. And that, if not for you, they never would have got off the ridge . . ." His voice trailed off, awaiting my reply.

"Sergeant Couture is a good Marine, Ski. He did his job on that patrol. So did I. I'll catch up with you at oh-seven-hundred."

I stood up, closing the space between us, and he turned to duck through the curtain into the tepid night air. I followed, intending to get reacquainted with Bob Wood. I climbed to the tower and found him stooped over the IOD, the handset of a PRC-25 gripped in his left hand. His face was bathed in the greenish glow of the starlight scope. He was scanning the valley floor through the night observation device.

"Yo, Bob! Getting any?" I announced my presence as I climbed over the berm and dropped inside the tower. The desk was cluttered with C-rat cans, and loose 782 gear and cigarette butts. Wood had an acetate-covered map tacked to a sheet of plywood leaned up against the interior wall of the tower. He was using a flashlight with a red lens to illuminate the map. Slurping peaches and pound cake into his face from a canteen cup, his radio operator sat on the deck at the foot of the IOD tripod. He made no effort to accommodate me as I approached the IOD.

"Say, Mike. We can see 'em, but we can't hit 'em. The Gooners seem to know just how far I can adjust off my spotting rounds. They can run farther, faster, than I can shift fire. Some of these little fuckers could win medals in the four-hundred-meter hurdles at the Olympics—swear to God!"

"Is that a fact?" I moved over to the map and laid it down on the deck below the berm. Using the flashlight, I examined the map, taking note of the various markings and annotations Wood had made. "Say Bob, what kind of defensive fires have we got plotted for this place?" I was looking at the map. Wood turned away from the IOD and joined me, putting his head over my shoulder.

"Gee, Mike, I don't know. None that I know of."

"Will they let you register fires?"

"Sure, I guess. What do you want to do?"

"I want to register some defensive fires. Put one right here, on top of Hill Four ninety-three; put one down here at grid nine-nine-nine-four-six-five; put one at the base of the hill over here at nine-nine-four-four-six-six; and put one in this draw zero-zero-two-four-six-two."

"Mike, I can do three out of four."

"Oh? Why is that?"

"We can't put anything in that draw, zero-zero-two-four-six-two, because we are on the gun–target line from An Hoa, and the only way we could hit it from Baldy is with eight-inch on a high-angle trajectory. I don't think we want to register an eight-inch target in there. Do you?"

"Interesting! Okay, let's do north, south, and west. Make the draw a target, anyway. We'll think of something else for that. Why don't you call them in now and register them over the next hour or two? We've got no friendlies outside the wire tonight."

"Roger that!"

Wood returned to his little work table and began to write out fire commands in a pad. I watched in silence for a moment, curiosity getting the best of me. Then the greenish glow of the starlight scope beckoned me. I moved over and took a position behind the apparatus and put my eye to the scope. The valley floor loomed into view in an eerie greenish-yellow glow. The starlight scope was an image intensifier, amplifying the ambient light to help the viewer see in the dark. It required skill to interpret the images. I decided I would need practice, and to count on the people who were trained to use it. Behind me, Wood was calling in our first defensive target to Nigeria.

I scanned the valley floor from the lake to the ville, traversing slowly along the major trail complex, which appeared in the scope as a pale yellow-green line in a hazy green background. This equipment had real potential. Questions were forming in my mind as I practiced traversing the assembly up and down the breadth of the valley floor.

Wood was studying the map in the red beam of a flashlight while he spoke into the handset. I turned to face him, and noticed immediately that my night vision had been ruined by the starlight scope.

"Say, Bob, how about turning on the speaker so I can hear the other side?" I wanted to listen to the progress of the fire mission while I continued to familiarize myself with the fire-support-coordination equipment. Wood turned on the speaker and continued to study the map.

"Sunrise, this is Nigeria. Shot. Over." The disembodied voice from the speaker told us that the battery had fired the first round. I turned away from the IOD device and focused my attention on the dark shadow on the hillside behind us, expecting to see an illumination round burst in the air over the summit of Hill 493.

"Sunrise, Sunrise, this is Nigeria. Splash. Over."

The round was about to impact. Wood, the RTO, and I watched expectantly as the artillery round whistled through the air, high overhead and burst somewhere beyond the ridge. There was a glow as the flare burst and backlit the crest of the hill. In artilleryman's vernacular, the shot was "over." To my mind, it was pathetic. "Good shooting, Bob!"

"Fuck you, Mike. Nigeria, this is Sunrise. Drop two-hundred right one-hundred. Repeat. Over."

Wood spoke into the handset while maintaining eye contact with me. He was an intensely competitive man, and I knew he wanted to look good. The battery fire-support-coordination center (FSCC) was not helping his cause, nor was it helping my confidence very much. If we were going to use his artillery to lend dignity to our little corner of the battlefield, they would have to be faster and more accurate with the first rounds.

"Sunrise, this is Nigeria. Shot. Over." Wood acknowledged the transmission, and we watched for the second round.

"Splash. Out."

The cannister burst in the air perhaps a hundred feet over the top of the hill. Wood turned with a self-satisfied grin and spoke into the handset, "Nigeria, Nigeria, this is Sunrise. Drop one-hundred, HE, one round, registration. Over."

The radio operator at the FSCC repeated Wood's request. Within seconds, a high explosive round impacted just below the crest of Hill 493. I watched and listened while Wood went through the rest of our target list. That done, we took time to catch up on life after the Basic School. Bob had gone to Fort Sill, had a new baby—a son, born in December. He was going to Hawaii for R & R in a week, due for rotation in the morning. He quizzed me about Hawaii, as I had been stationed there. I gave him some tips about scenic spots to visit and what I had experienced on R & R with Joyce. His would be different, with a baby. Our conversation seemed out of place, as if we were transported to another world. I felt suddenly tired. My watch said 2230—time flew when you were having fun. It was clear that we would have artillery fire support on short notice. I had people watching the wire and the dark spots. There was little else to be accomplished this night. It was time to catch some zees.

"Okay, Bob. I'm going to hit the rack. If your guys see anything really special, wake me up. Otherwise, I'll catch up with you in the morning." I turned to climb over the berm, intent on making my way back to my bunker.

"Roger that!" Wood spoke to my back, engrossed in developing his next fire mission.

I made my way unobtrusively around the perimeter one last time, taking note of the positions occupied by the troops on duty. Laughter and conversation and the sound of Armed Forces Radio Vietnam drifted from the bunkers on the evening breeze. Here and there a Marine sat apart, lost in his own thoughts of home and future. It was a deceptively peaceful setting. Absent the weapons and the occasional pyrotechnic in the air over our valley, we could have been at summer camp, or spring break back in the World.

I realized that I was homesick and that I had three letters from Joyce unopened in my jacket pocket. I made my way back to the bunker, ducked inside, and by the light of my trusty Zippo, located one of my candles. I lit it, dripped the paraffin atop a sandbag, and stuck the candle in it. By its flickering light, I rummaged around in my buttpack 'til I found a can of peaches and pound cake, and sat down on my rack to enjoy an evening snack and read letters from home. When I opened her first letter, the sight of the tear-stained script was more than I could cope with. I felt my throat tighten with emotion, a life-threatening weakness. I had learned harsh lessons in the Grunts—one was that giving in to the distraction of homesickness could kill you, or someone else. I set the letter aside without reading it, finished my peaches, snuffed the candle, and lay back to sleep. The faint scent of her perfume filled the bunker, displacing the odors of war.

Dawn arrived in my consciousness like fog lifting. I had slept fitfully in unfamiliar surroundings, startled awake by the rustling of rats around the perimeter of the bunker and the anecdotal chatter of the Marines on duty in the IOD tower. The occasional pop of an illumination round bursting in the air over the valley and the distant sounds of small-arms fire had invaded my consciousness from time to time. Each time I woke, I went out to assess the perimeter, a task that was easily accomplished by strolling down the trench. Just another night in the Republic. With the sun came different sounds, troops moving around, laughter, the rustle of equipment and utensils as teenage warriors prepared the morning meal. Radio chatter from the tower overrode the other sounds in my subconscious, and I came fully awake to the realization that somebody in the tower had turned the war on again. They were in the midst of directing an OV-10 to engage a target on the valley floor.

I roused myself to the edge of the cot, splashed some water from one of the ten-gallon cans into my helmet, and took the helmet and toothbrush out through the hatch into daylight. I set the helmet in the ammo-crate shelf overlooking the valley. The OV-10 was making a pass on a tree line some three klicks (three thousand meters) northeast of our position. As I watched, he fired a long burst from his minigun and pulled up to disappear northward. That IOD must be some piece of gear, I thought as I turned and went back inside to hunt up my razor, signal mirror, and shaving cream. Back outside, I brushed my teeth, rinsing the brush in the cold water, and spitting the rest over the berm. Then I used the same water to shave. While I was thus engaged, I became aware of the rustling of equipment and voices of my troops as they took up positions around the perimeter trench. Sergeant

Domnoske appeared as I wiped the last of the shaving cream from my face. "Good morning, sir. We're all set."

"Okay, Ski. Pass the word to the team leaders to have every man who can put his hand on a claymore hellbox to do that. Be prepared to fire on my command."

Domnoske departed, a quizzical look on his face. As he disappeared down the trench, passing my instructions from position to position, I returned to morning hygiene. Finished with the dirty water, I emptied the helmet over the berm, grasped my shaving kit, and ducked back into the bunker. Within minutes, Domnoske was back, calling to me from outside the bunker. I responded by joining him in the trench. "Ski, how many of these things do you think are going to go off when you say 'shoot'?"

"Couldn't say, sir."

"Where do you think these puppies are pointed?"

"Couldn't say, sir." Domnoske was showing some stress.

"Well, Ski, let's find out." In a louder voice, I hollered up to the tower, "Yo, Bob! Get your people under cover. We're going to blow some claymores."

"Roger that!" Wood shouted back from inside his hootch atop my bunker.

I watched as the heads of his radio operators disappeared below the sandbagged berm. "Okay, Ski. Pass the word. All hands take cover in the trench."

Domnoske hollered, "All hands take cover in the trench. Prepare to fire claymores."

He repeated the command, shouting toward the ends of the trench, then looked at me. I gave a go-ahead nod of my head.

"Fire the claymores!" With the last shout he ducked into the trench, covering his ears with his hands.

The silence that followed grew in intensity with each passing second. After an interminable moment, I made eye contact with Domnoske and watched his freckled face turn beet red as he realized there had not been a single detonation. "Do it again, Ski."

He repeated the commands, "Prepare to fire. Fire!"

Again, there was a resounding silence. Domnoske was agitated.

"Ski!" I kept my face stern, not wanting to give away my amusement at his obvious consternation. "Do you think our guys might be cooking with the C-four* out of our claymores?"

"Couldn't say, sir." He avoided my gaze.

"Okay. I want you to collect all the hellboxes and put them over there. When you are sure you have all the hellboxes disconnected, bring the team leaders back here with you. Then we'll go to the next thing."

He disappeared to carry out my order. I hollered up to Wood, "Yo, Bob! We are all secure." I ducked back into the bunker to make my morning brew. I was just stirring the cocoa into boiling water when Domnoske knocked at the entrance to the bunker and announced his presence in his best Sea School voice, "Sir, Sergeant Domnoske requests permission to enter, sir!" I responded by going outside, cup in hand. The three team leaders were aligned, sheep-faced, in the trench behind him. I motioned the whole crew into the bunker, holding the blackout drape aside for each of them to pass in front of me, then followed them inside.

"Take seats, gentlemen. Anybody want coffee?" They shook their heads in unison—no takers.

"That was an inspiring demonstration of firepower this morning, gents. Just think how comforting it might have been with gooks in the wire." I let my eyes lock on one man at a time, forcing each to look away before I moved on. This was a leadership challenge, a test of will which I could not afford to lose, for their sake. "Do you suppose we could have a similar experience with our crew-served weapons?"

I leaned back against the wall of the bunker, lifting a foot up on the edge of my cot as I spoke. My body language was relaxed, my voice low and firm, my eyes cold and direct. I stared at Corporal Hicks until he answered.

"No, sir . . ." He was not convinced.

*From "Composition-4," the powerful plastic explosive that fueled the claymore.

"Well, gentlemen, when should we find out—now or later?"

Domnoske spoke up, "Now, sir." He was becoming angry. I had challenged his competence.

"Okay, Ski. Let's make a bet. Loser fieldstrips and cleans all three guns. The bet is you cannot fire a hundred rounds from any gun without a jam."

Wardlow jumped up. "That's a bet, sir!" The others nodded. They were going to get even.

"Okay, Ski. We'll start with the gun at the LZ, then work our way around. Leave the troops out of this for now."

I stood up and went out, cup in hand. They followed as I worked my way down the trench to the M-60 position at the foot of the hill. Arriving at the position, I saw that the gun was as I had observed the prior evening—wrapped in a poncho, it sat on its bipod in the bottom of the fighting hole. A ready box of linked 7.62mm sat next to it, the belt snaked out of the metal box and under the poncho. The poncho was dusty, and speckled where rain had made mud of the dust on it. Flares, frags, and other ordnance scattered round the position, all showing signs of the weather. I had a good bet. "Okay, gents! Who's going to be my gunner?"

"I am, sir!" Wardlow jumped into the hole, pulled the poncho from the gun and lifted it over the berm. The belt twisted and snaked out of the box as he lifted the gun. He bent to lift the ammo box onto the parapet, then knelt down in the hole and hefted the machine gun to his shoulder. He was ready.

"Sergeant Wardlow, how about picking a target for me before you fire. Call out a range and description, maybe?"

"Sir?" Wardlow was puzzled, his face screwed up in a squint as he looked up at me over the breech of the M-60.

"Tell us what you are going to shoot at." I took a pull on my mocha.

"Oh. Yes, sir!" He settled behind the gun again, sighting. "Troops in the open, two o'clock, three hundred meters!" As he shouted his target identification, he pulled the trigger. A single round caromed off the rocks in the draw. Gun number one was jammed. Domnoske's face was the picture of exasperation. He kicked the dirt at his feet. Hicks stared off into space. Brown watched Wardlow as he pulled the charging handle futilely.

"Why don't we try our luck on gun number two, Sergeant?" I lurched to my feet, intending to move in the direction of the next machine-gun position.

"We don't need to do that, sir. You've made your point." Domnoske spoke quietly, and I saw that he was sincere.

I pushed a little harder, "And what point is that, Sergeant?"

"That we're fucked up, sir!"

"No, Ski. That is not my point at all. You are not fucked up. The position is fucked up. The weapons are fucked up. The gear is fucked up. The fire plan is fucked up. But you are not fucked up. I just wanted to get your attention, is all. Shall we fix it?" I held his gaze.

"Yes, sir." They were all watching, listening, expecting the worst.

"Okay. Get everyone in their assigned fighting positions. Then I want you to spend the rest of the morning shooting up the ordnance that is on the fighting positions, every round, every flare, every frag goes into the brush. When you're done with that, clean the place up. Then clean all the weapons. I will be around to check on all that at fourteen hundred [2:00 P.M.]. And Ski, run it like the rifle range, with fire commands and all. Got it?"

"Aye, aye, sir!" He was animated. They were going to have some fun in lieu of an ass chewing. I swallowed the dregs of my coffee, then moved off in the direction of my bunker. Behind me, Domnoske and the other NCOs set about organizing their "mad moment." I smiled to myself, pleased with what I believed was a stroke of genius. As a troop, I had hated the idea of cleaning weapons I didn't get to fire. I had spent miserable hours as a snuffy on the armory detail, cleaning machine guns, M-14s, pistols, even .50-calibers, without ever firing a round. (Cleaning machine guns, mortars, and the 106mm recoilless rifle was a major pain in the ass—shooting them was "tits.") Cleaning a weapon you had used was different. If this worked well, I resolved that we would be fam-firing everything on the hill for the next two weeks, provided nobody got stupid or careless. I regret that I have but one career to give for my country!—that thought flitted through my mind as I stooped to enter the bunker.

I viewed my job as more of a teacher/coach than a commander. Troops followed the laws of physics, inertia being their favorite. Left to their own devices, they would lay about reading fuck books and telling pussy lies like the teenagers they were (dangerous teenagers, but teenagers none the less), or worse yet, think up things to do to amuse themselves. Over the brief time that we would spend together on the hill, I believed that I could gain the respect and confidence of these pimple-faced warriors only by setting a strong and consistent example. I intended to do everything they did, from fieldstripping weapons, to humping water cans to the LZ. I would police up my own trash, improve my own fighting position, wait my turn for Cs (a pet bitch I had heard in the Grunts was about officers rifling the C-ration cases before the troops got theirs), clean my own weapons, and help with the crew-served weapons. I intended to set a personal standard for the NCOs to live up to, thereby influencing the troops as well. This was the first day of school, and like a coach at the first team practice, I wanted to establish credibility, earn their respect, and set a standard for future performance. It was going to be a long day, and I had my own homework to do.

I was just about to reenter the bunker when Wood hollered down to me from the IOD tower, "Hey Mike, we're about to get some! Come check this out!"

I scrambled up into the IOD tower as Wood was completing his radio transmission. The clatter of helicopter rotors overhead distracted me momentarily. In the same instant, Hannon hollered out that there was a bird inbound for two packs. My friend Bob and his RTO were headed for hot showers and cold beer.

"Hostage Stud, this is Sunrise. Roger that!" Wood turned from the IOD, motioning me to take his place at the eyepiece. "We spotted a couple Gooners on a trail down by the lake. This AO must be real gung ho, 'cause he's running fixed-wing on 'em! Can you believe that shit?"

I peered over the top of the IOD to get an idea of the target area from the OV-10's position. As I watched, he swooped to mark the target. A pair of Zunis left white streamers as they streaked to earth. Overhead, the distinctive roar of jet engines announced the arrival of a flight of F-4 Phantoms. They had been circling high over the valley to the southwest. Now they swooped to close at the speed of sound on our pair of hapless Gooners—or the place where they had last been seen. The whole scene unfolded before us in slow motion, the sounds damped by distance and heavy, humid air. As the aircraft pulled up below us, the concussions of 250-pound bombs reverberated down the valley. Smoke and dust billowed from the point of impact. It was a magnificent display of earthmoving, but we could see no evidence of our targets. Neither could Hostage Stud.

The OV-10 motored over the horizon, leaving only a gray-brown cloud of dust and debris to mark its visit. Wood was excited, whether about the prospect of leaving the hill or to be using his training, I couldn't tell. He rushed to his hootch, shrugged into his flak jacket, sidearm, and rucksack, a man possessed. I shouldered his WP bag and some other gear, and we struggled down the trench to the HLZ. The CH-46 was just wallowing onto the hill as we arrived. We rushed out to the crew chief, and I handed Bob's gear into the belly of the aircraft as two men rushed off. In the clatter of the helicopter's engines, we shouted "Good-bye," and I backed away as the aircraft lifted off.

I spent the rest of the morning with BAMSIS, drafting up the daily routine, warning orders, SOPs, and other items that I should have done before making the trip. Guilt and fear helped me concentrate on my lesson plans. While the troops engaged in their "ordnance disposal" and police call under the supervision of Sergeant Ski and his fusiliers, I focused on the platoon in the defense. The first priority was a daily routine, a plan for maintaining and improving the position, training and motivating the troops, and providing local security for the position. There were thirty-three men on the hill, twenty-four Recon Marines, the forward observer (FO) team, five U.S. Army soldiers (the sensor-monitoring detachment), and our navy corpsman. I resolved that everyone would participate in the daily routine, realizing that there would be trouble with the soldiers, and, judging by the men's salty attitude, the FO team as well. I reasoned that I could count on the FO, a Marine, to keep his troops on the team. The soldiers were a different matter. I decided to stick with my TO (table of organization). We would rotate the daylight security patrol, the night acts, and the position reconstruction among the three teams on a daily basis. There would be daily police calls, training in the use of our weapons, and emergency drills. We would take turns (the NCOs and I) with the arty FO team on watch.

With a view toward improving the bunkers' value as fortifications, I made a list of the work priority for rebuilding them. After several hours of scholarly effort, I had a good plan and a schedule to go with it. It was now a matter of "winning the hearts and minds" of my troops—no mean feat. The place to start, once again, was with the NCOs. I could tell, by the absence of explosions and grumbling, that the troops had completed their task. No sooner had the realization come upon me, than Domnoske appeared at the bunker entrance to report the fact.

"Sir, we're done. The guys are having chow. What are we doing next?"

"What do you suggest, Sergeant?" I wanted to pull his chain a little harder, but Domnoske took me literally.

"Well, sir, I think we should clean weapons, put out a new issue of ordnance, and get ready for our night acts."

"Well spoken, Ski. But I'd like to have a talk with you and the team leaders while that is going on. So, why don't you get the guys started cleaning the M-60s—one gun per team? Have we got any school-trained machine gunners in this outfit?" The thought had come unbidden into my mind. I knew that our Recon Replacement School took volunteers from all

MOSs, but only luck would have put an 0331 or two on the hill with me. Having a well-intentioned private first class fieldstrip one of these weapons without proper supervision was inviting trouble I didn't need. The M-60 was a notoriously temperamental weapon. On the other hand . . .

"Belay that, Ski. Find me one machine gunner to show a man from each team how to clean the gun at the HLZ. When they're done, I want to inspect that gun and test-fire it. Then we'll do another. Okay? Have the rest of the guys clean their M-16s while we have our meeting. Pass the word on this and bring the team leaders back here in ten minutes. Okay?"

"Aye, aye, sir!" Domnoske turned on his heel and went back down the trench.

I focused my attention on the notes I had made throughout the afternoon, formulating a presentation in my mind while I awaited the arrival of my NCOs. If I could win their unqualified support for my game plan, it would work. There was no way to keep them from undermining me if they chose to do so, but with their cooperation, everything was possible. I wanted to choose my words carefully.

"Sir! Permission to enter?" Domnoske was back. I called them in, assessing each man's attitude as he found a seat within the confines of the bunker. There was no overt resistance. A good sign.

"Gents, let's make this quick and dirty. I think we can agree that there is room for improvement in our defenses and living conditions, among other things." I made eye contact with each man in turn. Their heads bobbed in agreement. There was not going to be serious resistance. It was time to get them involved in the solutions.

"Okay. While you guys were out blowing up stuff, I worked up a list of things to do. Before I share it with you, though, I want you to understand two things—first, I do not believe in busy work or harassment; I will not ask you to do anything that isn't necessary to our comfort or survival. Second, I was a sergeant once myself; I understand how hard your job is. I want to help you. I am open to suggestions on how to improve on the plan I have developed." I cast my gaze from man to man, my eyes resting briefly on each. They sat expectantly.

"Okay, for openers, this is a dangerous position. It is exposed, surrounded by the enemy, and cannot be reinforced. There is no way to withdraw from it if we are attacked. So, we need to have good defensive positions, and we need to improve them a little every day. That is part one of our mission. Part two is to observe and interdict enemy troop movements. Does anyone doubt that the enemy is moving around here, day and night?" I looked from man to man again.

"Yes, sir. There are definitely gooks around here, sir, but they generally don't fuck with us. They know we're bad!" Wardlow was convinced, the others less so. Domnoske held his own counsel.

"Wardlow, that is because we haven't been doing them any damage. I intend to change that. Then, we can expect them to fuck with us. It just makes sense to be ready. Don't you agree?" I was making a speech focused on Wardlow, but for the benefit of all of them. If they saw the merit of it, they would do the work.

"Yes, sir. That makes sense."

"Okay. So here is what we do. First, we are going to have a daily routine and SOPs for certain activities. There will be a day-long security patrol each day. There will be at least two night acts each night. There will be weapons training and maintenance for all hands each day. There will be police calls of the entire position twice per day, after chow in the morning and just before sundown. There will be a stand-to at dusk every day. There will be immediate-action drills now and again. There will be working parties every day. The working parties will be doing different things each day, but one of those things will be rebuilding the bunkers. We will do these things on a rotation, either port/starboard or a three-way split between the teams. I think the team approach is probably best. Any questions so far?"

There were only blank stares, so I continued, "Sergeant Domnoske, you will work out the details of our daily routine, including the working-party assignments. I want every weapon on the hill cleaned and test-fired every day. I want to expend all the old ordnance we have up here. We need to burn the crapper every morning. Have the doc supervise that, but make sure you don't have the same guys on that detail two days in a row. In fact, get a soldier and one of the FOs for that once in a while. They shit as much as the rest of us." There was a dim smile at that comment.

"Sergeant Wardlow, you are now the platoon guide/logistics NCO. You will be responsible for making sure we have chow, water, bullets, batteries, and tools. You will also monitor our water consumption on a daily basis and report the status to me. You will make sure that the RTOs maintain their equipment and keep us in batteries. Team leaders will turn in their supply requests to you.

"Corporal Hicks, you are now our demolitions expert. You will find some engineer demolition kits in the ammo bunker. I want you to get one and see what's in it. One of the things you will find is bars of C-4. You may distribute the C-4 in one kit to the teams for cooking. You will use the other one to blow some rocks for me tomorrow. Got it?" Hicks was grinning at the thought of blowing things up.

"Corporal Crawford, you are now our crew-served-weapons expert. You will find a mortar tube in the ammo bunker, along with the tripods and T & E mechanisms for our M-60s. I want you to clean up that tube and have it operational before sundown today. And, I want each team to clean and service one of the M-60 tripods.

"Gents, we have a lot to do, so I don't want to keep this chat going too long. Let's get the troops moving on these things. Ski, get back to me when you've got us organized, and we'll talk about night acts. Okay?"

I cast my gaze from man to man, making eye contact. There were no questions, nor could I detect any animosity. It was going to be all right. I stood up and moved to the entrance to the bunker. They followed me into daylight.

While the NCOs set off to implement the new game plan, I made another circuit of the position, taking particular note of the crew-served-weapons positions. Finally, I found a seat atop the ammo bunker and studied the terrain in the valley. What we needed to do was to find a way to get our organic weapons into action against the enemy. If we could engage them, keep them pinned down while we got clearance to fire or, better still, herd them into preplanned fires, our results would improve. Whoever had placed the 106mm recoilless rifle and the .50-caliber machine gun had done so with local-area defense in mind, or perhaps they had only been added haphazardly. And the 60mm mortar had not been in service for some time, probably because no one knew how to operate it. The more I thought about it, the more convinced I became: these weapons had offensive potential. Properly emplaced, they had the range to cover a large percentage of the trail complex in the valley. I was thus engrossed in thought when Domnoske joined me atop the bunker.

"About the night acts, sir?" Domnoske was in the frame of reference I had left him, while I had moved on to new ideas. It took me a moment to reshape my thoughts. To fill the space, I asked a question. "Ski, have you ever fired that mortar?"

"Only for illumination, sir. We got no aiming stakes or anything up here, and the baseplate is busted. You have to reset the tube every time you shoot."

"How about the fifty-cal.?"

"Yes, sir, we have. It kicks ass, but the headspace is fucked up. Sometimes you can only get off one or two rounds at a time. We need special tools to fix that, or maybe even an armorer."

"Have we got a T & E for it?"

"No, sir, we don't. But we got lots of ammo."

"Ski, when we get done here, I want you to have Sergeant Wardlow add those things to his requisition list. And ask them to send an armorer up here on the next resupply to fix the fifty. Now about night acts . . ."

Domnoske was making a note in his notebook. I waited for him to finish, then continued. "Night acts are patrols. They are dual purpose, to provide security for the main force, and to kill gooks. From now on, we will prepare for night acts just like you would for a patrol to the Que Sons or

Thong Duc—because that is where we are! Each and every man will make himself invisible and silent before he leaves the wire. They will carry a standard load of ammo. They will take no food, and only enough water to get through the night. They will test-fire their weapons and get a comm check before they leave the wire. They will go to prearranged positions, and they will be fuckin' sneaky. Am I clear, so far?"

I stared him down, then continued. "We are going to use the night acts as ambushes, to cover the most likely avenues of approach to this position. There will be no more sitting on hilltops. I want them in the draws, on the forward slopes of the hill, or up the fingers—a different place every night. And no fuckin' hootches! They're only going to be out a few hours at a time. When they get in, they get extra zees. Fair enough?" It was starting to rain.

"Aye, aye, sir." Domnoske was thinking about what I had said.

"Okay, enough of that. Get me three guys and meet me at the fifty-cal. in ten minutes. You can have your team-leader meeting after that."

I lurched to my feet and strode off in the direction of the .50-cal., leaving him no opportunity for an argument. The rain was coming down harder. The gun had been placed to cover the HLZ and the ridge behind it. In order to use it in the valley, we would need to rebuild the emplacement, a major project. I looked around the immediate area and selected a relatively flat spot at the rim of the hill. By moving the gun from its sandbagged emplacement to that spot, I believed we could fire into the valley with good effect, especially if we had a T & E. As I stood contemplating the situation, Domnoske appeared with three disgruntled Marines in tow. The rain was pouring down, and we were all soaked to the bone. I paid no attention, leaving them no room to grumble.

"Gents, we are going to move this gun from that position to a new one where I am standing. But, before we do a lot of work for nothing, I want to try it out. So, let's move it over here and bag it down. Ski, while they're moving the gun, why don't you get us the ship's binoculars I saw in the IOD tower, and break out some ammo."

The thought of firing the gun motivated my morose working party. Within minutes, they had the machine gun relocated and sandbagged into a new firing position. Domnoske reappeared, lugging two cans of linked .50-caliber ammunition. It was a heavy load, and he dropped the sealed metal cans in the mud beside the gun, gasping for breath. I pulled a sandbag off the berm and dropped it behind the gun to serve as a makeshift stool, then took a seat. Hicks appeared with the binos and their tripod as I broke open the breech of the machine gun. Domnoske pitched in, feeding the ammo belt to the gun. I closed the breech and, with an awkward lunge, I pulled the charging handle to the rear. We were ready to rock and roll.

"Okay Hicks, since you brought the binos you're to be our spotter. I'm going to zero this bitch on that trail junction at ten o'clock. Do you see it?" I intended to fire the gun at the trail junction to see whether we could in fact shoot that far. With the aid of the tracers and a spotter, I believed we could shoot accurately, at least in daylight. I took a deep breath and pressed the trigger levers down. The gun jumped as the heavy projectiles arced into the valley. They seemed to fall in slow motion. I fired two three-round bursts before ending up on my butt in the mud. The gun followed me, its recoil tremendous.

"Gents, we need to bag it down better. Get me some more sandbags on the legs."

The troops hustled off to pull sandbags from the berm, two apiece. Behind us a crowd had formed. I settled back behind the gun to try again. Three rounds, watch the arc. Three rounds, watch the arc. Hicks called the impact, and within a few bursts, I was hitting the trail consistently. I turned the gun over to Domnoske.

"Okay, Ski. You try it. Then let these guys have a go, thirty rounds apiece. Be sure to police up the brass when you're done. I'm going to get some chow."

They had forgotten the rain and my squirrelly ideas. The prospect of firing the big-mother machine gun took precedence over their discomfort. Building a gun pit was not going to be a problem. But first things first. I made my way back down the trench to my bunker while Domnoske worked out with the .50-cal. Inside the bunker, I stripped off my wet uniform and put on my sleeping shirt and a dry pair of trousers, then rummaged through my stock of C rations and selected beef with spice sauce and set about cooking lunch. While I was thus occupied, my ruminations about the condition of the hill continued, while outside the tempo of heavy-machine-gun fire clattered on the rain-laden air. I could tell by the sound that some of the would-be gunners had more talent than others. Finally, there was silence. Finished with my snack, I roused myself, put on a poncho and a bush hat, and went back out into the weather and Troop Leading 101.

Domnoske and his detail were just finishing up the police of the brass as I approached. I saw that he had covered the gun, using the cardboard from a C-ration box to prevent water from getting inside the action. Most of the troops had dispersed to their hootches.

"So, Ski, what do you say to peace through fire superiority?" He looked up from his handiwork at the sound of my voice.

"Shit hot, sir. With a little practice on our spotting, we can work out on those trails."

"Too true. And with a T & E, we can do it in the dark. So make sure we get one of those on the next resupply. For now, we'll have to make do with sandbags. After chow, get us a field-fortifications technician from each team to dig me a U-shaped hole for this bitch." As I spoke, I pulled an engineer stake from the berm with some difficulty.

"What's a field-fortifications technician, Lieutenant? I don't think we got anybody like that up here." Domnoske leaped to my assistance, and we pushed and pulled until we had it loose.

I used it to draw the outline of the fighting hole in the

mud. "A private with an entrenching tool [shovel], Ski. Have them fill sandbags with the dirt from the hole. Make a berm, three bags wide, around the edges. Okay?" I stood up from my labors, grinning and making eye contact with him to insure that he understood.

"Aye, aye, sir!" was all he said.

"Fine. That is project number one for the afternoon. Don't wear anybody out on it, and tell them that whoever digs the most, shoots the most when it's time to use the gun. Got it?"

Domnoske smiled. I had made his task a little easier.

"Project number two is a little harder. I want you to get the sixty millimeter mortar out of that bunker and get it set up. Have Corporal Crawford supervise that. I want a real mortar pit, Ski, with ammo staged for the night, HE and Illum, just like you learned in Infantry Training School. Okay?"

We made eye contact.

"Yes, sir, but the base plate is cracked, sir. And we got no aiming stakes."

He stared at me, waiting for a response.

"Make do, Ski. That's why the commandant made you a sergeant." I smiled, but kept hard eye contact. I wanted him to know that I meant it.

"Last thing—I want you to get a case of claymores out of that bunker, have the team leaders bring one to each man and a couple of sleeves from the C-rat boxes down to the HLZ. I'm going to show you something else. Give it ten minutes."

"Aye, aye, sir."

Domnoske departed giving a holler for the team leaders on his way. I turned, climbed into the IOD tower, where the IOD crew lounged in the relative comfort of dry surroundings. The rain had stopped but the sky was still heavily overcast, with dark clouds building over the mountains to the west. To the east over the ocean, the weather was breaking up, and sunlight radiated down through the slate-gray surface of the ocean. It was a spectacular sight. I fumbled open the plastic pack protecting my Marlboros, dried my hands on the underside of my shirt, and lit a cigarette. Smoking, I leaned back against the parapet to enjoy the view. Below me, my troops were milling about in various stages of meal preparation, grumbling about the "squirrelly lieutenant." Domnoske was clearly in charge, however. Within a few minutes, the work details materialized at their assigned tasks, soggy cigarettes dangling from their lips.

Domnoske hollered from the trench, "Yo, Lieutenant, we're ready."

I stood up, fieldstripped the cigarette butt and flicked the filter into space, then hollered back at him. "Okay, Ski, leave the claymores by that big rock. Take those C-rat sleeves down to the other end of the LZ and set them up in the wire for targets. I'll be with you in a moment." I jumped down into the trench and ducked inside the bunker, recovered my M-16, and slogged my way down the trench to join Domnoske at the rock.

"Kind of crummy weather for target practice, isn't it, Lieutenant?" Domnoske was soaked to the bone and starting to shiver.

"Life's a bitch, Ski, and so is the weather. This is kinda like being in the Grunts, isn't it?"

"If you say so, sir. What are we going to do now?"

"We are going to show everybody how a claymore is supposed to work. Then we are going to have that righteous experience, so we know what it feels like, then we are going to get our wet asses out of the weather."

The team leaders and their hapless assistants were making their way back through the wire, bedraggled and morose. I stooped to break open the box holding our claymores and pulled one of the mines in its olive drab cloth bag from the box. "Take seats, gentlemen, up there behind the berm."

I moved down the trail closer to the HLZ and placed the mine on its little bipod feet at the base of the trail. Its half-moon face pointed more or less perpendicular to the LZ and parallel to the surface. I put the hellbox in the leg pocket of my trousers and carefully unscrewed the green plastic tops atop the mine, inserted the fuse, and screwed the caps back in place. Then taking care not to disturb the mine, I played out the cable back up the hill to the sandbag berm, where my NCOs sat smoking and grumbling. Without a word I sat down on the sandbag berm and hooked the tails of the wire to the hellbox and laid the whole assembly in the sandbag at my feet. I hefted the M-16 under my arm and turned to face my entourage. "Gentlemen, this is an M-16. In the right hands, it is a lethal weapon." As I spoke the words, I turned casually to face the targets on the HLZ and fired three quick bursts from my rifle putting rounds left to right in each of the first three targets in the wire. The tracers told the tale of my marksmanship. I turned back to face the troops, leaned the now empty rifle against the sandbags, and casually recovered the hellbox from its resting place atop the berm, flicking the safety ring off its trigger with my thumb.

"And this, gentlemen, is a claymore mine." As I spoke the words, I compressed the handles of the hellbox. There was a thunderous roar as the mine went off. The concussion hit us like a blow, mud and debris splattered the hillside below us. In the barbed wire, all of our C-ration-box targets were shredded. Tattered remnants gave mute testimony to the effectiveness of the weapon. The troops sat in stunned silence, their eyes moving first to me, then to the wire, back to me.

"Gents, I like claymores. You will too after you get better acquainted with them. Sergeant Domnoske, I want each man in this group to set, arm, and fire a claymore under your supervision. You will use the procedure which I have just demonstrated. That is, you will remove the mine from its bag, you will put the hellbox in your pocket, you will take the mine and the wire to the bottom of the hill, you will set the mine against the rock or a flat surface, you will aim the mine parallel to the ground in the direction you want it to fire, you will install the fuse and run the wire back up here, take cover behind the berm, connect the wire to the hellbox, give a warning shout, fire the mine. In the event of a misfire, you will wait two minutes and try to fire it again. If it doesn't fire the second time, come and get me. Any questions?"

There were none. With one last look into each man's eyes, I picked up my M-16 and made my way back to my bunker. They were believers. Of that, I had no doubt.

Over the course of the next two hours, my waterlogged NCOs

familiarized themselves with the "pucker factor" attributable to using high explosives. With each concussion I breathed a sigh of relief, my career having navigated yet another of Bullwinkle's potholes in the road to success. At the rate we were going, we would set some kind of record for expending ordnance.

The weather cleared somewhat, and my machine-gun and mortar positions began to take shape. I catnapped between explosions, getting up periodically to peer through the hatch at my working parties. Finally, Domnoske reappeared at the bunker entrance.

"Sir, permission to enter?"

I sat up on my bunk and answered, "Come."

Domnoske lurched into the bunker, sopping wet, and took a seat on the cot opposite the one I occupied. Without preamble, he spoke. "Hell of a day, Lieutenant. I bet my ears will be ringing for a month. The troops are smokin' and jokin' right now. We flipped a coin for who starts the duty cycle. Wardlow has the night acts. You made believers out of everybody today. Haven't had this much fun since the mad moment at ITS [Infantry Training School]." He paused to compose his thoughts then continued, "We've got a good start on the new fifty-cal. position. It will make a good spot for sentry duty, too. The mortar is set up, and we got ammo staged like you said, sir— no telling where the rounds will land, but we can shoot the bitch. So, what about the night acts, sir?"

"Put one in the draw on the southeast side of the LZ and one out back here about one-hundred to one-hundred-fifty meters outside the wire of the finger. North is Alpha and south is Bravo. Have them take two claymores apiece and set up like an ambush. They should be ready to go by eighteen thirty. I want to check them out before they leave the wire. They report same as on patrol. And while I'm thinking about it, have Hannon run a couple of remotes in here so I can listen to the radio traffic while we are in here. Okay?"

"Yes, sir." He rose to leave.

"And Ski, we set a watch inside the perimeter also, like we did last night. Make up a crew for the fifty-cal. and another for the mortar. Make sure they know what to do."

"Roger that, Lieutenant."

He went out. I settled back on the cot to make another attempt at reading my mail by the fading light deflecting through the apertures of the bunker. After three tear-stained letters I gave up and went out to catch up with the troops. I found Domnoske and Wardlow atop the ammo bunker, head to head over a map.

"What are we doing, gents?" As I spoke, I let my eyes roam over the position. Most of the troops were occupied with eating, smoking, and shit shooting. Down on the HLZ end of the position, two men were erecting a poncho shelter over the .50-cal. in preparation for standing watch in the rain. The mortar was laid in, with the tube pointing in the general direction of Spider Lake, a tarpaulin over the muzzle. Domnoske and company had put in a full day's work.

Wardlow answered up, "We're just figuring out the grids where we want the LPs, Lieutenant."

"Night acts, Wardlow! Night acts. Not listening posts. You now have an offensive mission. And what do you suggest?"

Wardlow was not the best map reader, but he knew the ground around 425 from walking it on prior missions. There were not many comfortable sites, and he knew them all. I had thrown a wrench in the works by insisting that they not use the same site more than once a week and that they move into the actual LP after dark.

"Well, sir, up on the ridge it's real windy. We couldn't see or hear shit up there. Down below the saddle, on the forward slope would be better, sir. Ski and I were just trying to figure out the grid for the place I had in mind when you walked up, sir." He looked at me expectantly. "And for the other end, I thought maybe down in front of that big rock that sticks up next to the trail. We haven't used that for a while, and it covers the trail pretty good, 'specially if we use the claymores the way you showed us."

"Ski?" I made eye contact with him, soliciting his participation.

"Sounds good to me, sir."

"Okay, that's what we'll do. But I want two favors, Ward-low." He looked at me quizically.

"One, when you move out of here you sit at least a hundred meters from where you intend to stay until after dark. Two, you will not set out any booby traps. And I want two guys awake at all times. Okay?"

"Aye, aye, sir!" He folded the map and turned to his team. "Okay, guys, saddle up. The lieutenant wants to check us out."

As one, they shrugged into their web gear and grasped their weapons. I moved down the ragged line, examining their equipment and camouflage. They were tight.

"Okay, Sergeant. Test-fire your weapons. Everybody better put a magazine into the fifty-meter rock this time!"

Wardlow grinned and gave the shout, "Test-firing weapons! With a magazine and twenty rounds, load and lock! Prepare to fire! Fire!"

The whole team opened up with their M-16s on auto. The cacophony reverberated off the hillside. Stray rounds caromed off rocks with shrill echos.

"Cease fire! Cease fire! Clear and lock all weapons! Is the line clear? The line is clear! Reload and safe your weapons!"

Wardlow was enjoying himself. I resolved to recommend him for duty as a primary marksmanship instructor when he rotated back to the World. Test-firing weapons before each night act was a routine I had used in the Grunts, more for morale building purposes than anything else. Night acts were nerve-racking, and letting off a magazine into the rocks before leaving the wire was a great stress reducer for the troops. I intended to make a marksmanship contest out of it, challenging them to improve their shooting each day by firing on known targets at random around the perimeter. I reasoned that, if we ever did need to "fire the FPF"* for real, the guys would have a better chance if they had been shooting at things all along. If we made it a point to fire every weapon every day, it just might make a difference.

I turned toward the CP bunker while Wardlow rejoined

---

*"Final Protective Fire," i.e., if we were ever about to be overrun.

his team. He split them into two three-man groups, and they moved off to their respective staging areas, inserting fresh magazines in their weapons as they went. As I walked away, I heard them jumping up and down in the trench, one at a time. They made a game of it, but none had a rattle of unsecured dog tags, loose rounds, or paraphernalia to give him away in movement. Nor did I detect the slosh of half-full canteens. Each man had cammy paint made up as dark as the night he would hide in. They were taking my tactical tips to heart, squirrelly or not. The rumors of Turf Club had metamorphosized me in their minds. I had become Iron Mike, the last guy in the world anyone would want to fuck with. It made me sad, but it served a purpose.

CHAPTER EIGHT
THE GAUNTLET

11–21 MAY 1970

Artillery lends dignity to what would otherwise be a mindless brawl.

Unknown

My new forward observer, who dashed off the CH-46 unrecognized, turned out to be another TBS classmate—Bill Henry. Bill was an energetic, redheaded, freckle-faced jock. I remembered him as earnest and impulsive. An FNG, having just completed the integrated observation device (IOD) familiarization course at Fire Support Base Ryder, he was gung ho! While I was occupied with my homework on the platoon in the defense, Bill had moved into the bunker, then gone off to get acquainted with his detachment and equipment. Now that I had my ambushes in place, it was time to get reacquainted with Henry. Bob Wood had been a friend in Basic School, Henry only an acquaintance and a competitor. Since Henry was going to be with us for awhile, it was imperative that we establish a good working relationship. I decided to get started. With this thought in mind, I turned from the wire to climb up onto the tower.

"Yo, Mike, check this out. We got four Gooners in a tree line. I think they are NVA. I'm going to call a fire mission." Henry was hard at work on his first fire mission when I joined him in the IOD tower. He had rounds on the way within a few minutes, first a spotting round, then two adjustments, then a three-round fire-for-effect. In the Grunts, I would have waited hours for this kind of support. It was an intriguing process. Clearly, OP Sunrise rated attention from the higher powers. But, our Gooners had *didi*'d before the second adjusting round had left An Hoa. We had firepower available. What we lacked was a good scheme for employing it.

"Bill, that was very entertaining. But, I think maybe we should talk about our tactics, first chance we get. It might be a good idea to watch the two and threes, see where they go. What do you say?"

Henry was already engrossed in his search for more hapless targets of opportunity. His response was a grunt, his back turned to me. I stared at him for a moment, struggling to get a grip on my temper. It was clear, in this brief exchange, that Henry was going to present a different kind of leadership challenge. There could only be one quarterback on the team. I resolved to have the conversation again when we had fewer distractions. I climbed down from the tower and went in search of a good meal. Inside my bunker, I no sooner settled in to eat and cogitate when Henry's expletives drifted down from the tower. He had discovered another group of NVA soldiers moving through the valley. Chow in hand, I scrambled outside to see what the commotion was all about. Most of the troops had gathered in the trench to watch the show, oblivious to the potential dangers close at hand.

I gave a shout at the tower, "Say, Bill, what have you got?"

"Son of a bitch! There must be fifty of 'em! They act like they own the place!"

"Where?" I set my beef and crackers atop the bunker and scrambled up to the side of the tower. It was going to be Henry's show for the time being. I wanted to see what he could do. Domnoske materialized out of the gloom, weapon in hand. He must have been reading my mind.

Henry answered, "Down by the dam. They're just milling around. I can't shoot in there. It's a no-fire zone[NFZ]." He was animated, frustrated. The dam was a USAID* project, intended to help win the allegiance of the people farming the valley. Blowing it up was not part of the game plan. It occurred to me that the NVA probably knew that. Were they using the no-fire zone as a staging area? I recovered my supper and leaned up against one side of the tower, thinking. The rules of engagement did not prevent me from using organic weapons in no-fire zones, but the weapons on the hill would not shoot that far. The NVA were more than a mile from our position and fifteen hundred feet below us—another planet, unless they moved. I took another bite of beef and crackers.

"What are they doing now?" I asked the question around a mouthful of beef and crackers. Domnoske joined me atop the bunker.

Henry answered, "Looks like they're splitting up into three groups—yeah—they're moving along the canal—coming this way—I'm going to call a fire mission." As he spoke, he peered through the IOD, gesturing with his arm for the RTO to give him a handset.

I looked at Domnoske. He stood expectantly, anticipating my thoughts. "Want to try out your new toys, Ski?"

"Yes, sir!"

"Okay. Man the crew-served weapons. See if you can spot these guys with the ship's binoculars. We'll wait to see what the arty can do. Don't fire until I tell you."

Domnoske was all smiles. He jumped off the bunker and scrambled down the trench, shouting for his team leaders. Munching on beef with spice sauce all the while, I returned to watching Henry. Below me my troops dispersed to the crew-served weapons positions, excited about the prospect of action. It was like an old war movie, pirates preparing their ship for battle against a distant foe. We had all the advantages, including the element of surprise. The NVA did not know that we could see them in the dark.

"Vesper Bells, Vesper Bells, this is Nigeria. Fire mission.

*U.S. Agency for International Development

Over!" Henry was on the job. The irony of the call sign struck me. One of the graffiti missives from the wall of my bunker popped into my head—"Kill a Commie for Christ!"

"Hannon!" I hollered into the void, summoning the RTO.

"Sir!" He was in the trench at my feet. I was startled by his response.

"Take a radio down to Domnoske at the fifty-cal. Set it to Tac Two [alternate frequency] and tell him to give us a jingle."

"Aye, aye, sir!" He went off, while I finished my meal.

Below me, the mortar crew was busy. They had uncovered the tube, traversed it to lay in the general direction of Spider Lake, and prepared several rounds of HE (high explosive). In the gloom, I could just make out their silhouettes against the backdrop of the valley. The moon was now high in the sky, and the overcast that had plagued us for most of the day was clearing. Clouds were moving across the night sky, providing intermittent glimpses of stars. Far off, over the Arizona, an occasional flare burst in the dark—Grunts illuminating their night defensive positions. Meanwhile, our own little life-and-death struggle was taking shape.

"Corporal Crawford!" I shouted in the general direction of the silhouettes at the mortar pit. One of them answered up.

"Sir!"

"Stand by to fire the mortar. One round, Willie Pete [white phosphorous, WP], max charge!" I was telling him to use a munition that would burst on the ground, producing a fire, and to use the maximum number of propellant charges on the round, since we had no idea where the first round would land. I wanted to be able to adjust the subsequent shots from this first one—in the dark.

"Roger that, Lieutenant!" There was a bustle of activity, accompanied by muttering and curses. A disembodied form separated from the group and went into the ammo bunker—apparently, they had no WP on the position.

"Nigeria, this is Vesper Bells. Send your fire mission. Over."

Henry passed the grid coordinate, concluding with, "Troops in open. One round. Whiskey Papa [white phosphorous]. Adjust fire. Over!"

Henry was doing it again. I spat in exasperation just as Hannon scrambled atop the bunker to join me. He brought a PRC-25 radio with him, and handed me the handset.

"Domnoske is Sunrise Charlie, sir." Hannon sat down to catch his breath. "We got a team in contact on the tac net, sir! Turf Club. They got a man down. Calling for an emergency extract."

Domnoske was on the hook. I took the handset and spoke into it quietly, thinking about Turf Club. Who was the patrol leader? Who was hurt? Where were they? The situation was beyond our capacity to help. All we could do was listen, hope for the best, and continue with our own mission. In this case, maybe we could get a little payback. "Sunrise Charlie, this is Sunrise Actual. Over."

"Actual, this is Charlie. Go."

"Do you have them in sight? Over."

"That's affirmative. It's like daylight down there. Over."

"Stand by. Actual out." I tossed the handset to Hannon and turned to watch the fireworks.

"Nigeria, this is Vesper Bells. Shot. Over."

We watched the valley floor expectantly. Seconds passed before the round burst—more than three hundred meters from the grid Henry had called in. I heard him mutter an expletive, then call for another adjusting round. My radio came to life. "Sunrise Actual, this is Charlie. The enemy is dispersing to the southeast. Over!" They were moving in our direction. Luck!

"Roger, Charlie. Stand by. Actual out." Let them run out from under Henry's stuff. With a little luck we would get a crack at them ourselves.

"Nigeria, this is Vesper Bells. Check fire. Over."

Henry swore. The artillery had been placed on hold for some reason. In the valley, the NVA were making tracks across dry rice paddies toward the trail complex at the base of our hill. They had evidently concluded that the first artillery round had been an H & I (harassment and interdiction—shooting in the dark to "deny the enemy use of the battlefield"). The reason for the check-fire droned into our consciousness—another aerial observer.

"Nigeria, this is Hostage Turtle, inbound. Can you mark your target? Over."

"Hostage Turtle, this is Nigeria. Negative. Over!" Henry wasn't thinking. I reached over the plywood wall of the tower, asking for his handset in silence. He handed it over.

"Hostage Turtle, this is Sunrise Actual. Break. We can mark the target with our fifty-cal. Break. Target is five-oh troops in open, five hundred meters northeast of the dam. Over."

Hannon had joined me with the other radio. I extended my hand for the handset, waiting for the aerial observer to respond. I looked at Hannon. "Why don't you go down and see what's happening with Turf Club?" It was an order, the one he had been waiting for. He bounded off the bunker without a word.

"Sunrise, this is Hostage Turtle. Roger. Understand fifty-cal. on your pos. Break. Fire when ready. Over."

The aircraft was orbiting over the lake. I took a deep breath and keyed the handset on Domnoske's circuit. "Charlie, this is Actual. Fire! Over."

"Actual, this is Charlie. Roger that. Out!"

The .50-cal. opened up immediately, the first orange tracers floating into the valley before the sound pulverized our ears. *Chunk-chunk-chunk,* Domnoske lofted perfect three-round bursts in the general direction of the NVA formation. Over the lake, the Bronco's engines raced and the plane pulled a wingover, plunging toward the ground on a course that intersected the spot where Domnoske was directing his fire. "Sunrise, this is Hostage Turtle. Check fire, please. We are engaging your target. Over."

"Charlie, this is Actual. Cease fire. Over."

Domnoske had already concluded that the handoff was a go. The gun fell silent. "Actual, this is Charlie. Roger. Out."

Hostage Turtle closed on the now expectant NVA from an

altitude of several thousand feet to just treetop level, unleashing rockets and machine-gun fire as he came. As the aircraft pulled up, a stream of green tracers followed him, arcing into the sky from a tree line near the base of our hill. The NVA had a big machine gun, too. Theirs was 12.7mm and made for shooting at airplanes. We watched the drama unfold from afar. Hostage Turtle made several passes over the area where we had last seen the NVA. The NVA gunner was as green as his tracer; he did not get a lead on the Bronco, and his rounds fell harmlessly to earth. After the Bronco's second pass, his lieutenant must have shut him down, for there were no more bursts to give away their position. Hostage Turtle expended all of his ordnance and packed up for the night. Due to darkness, the engagement was inconclusive. At least, that's what we would have to put in the spot report. Upon the departure of the Bronco, our artillery came out of check-fire. Henry worked out in the area where we had last seen the enemy, firing several "battery threes" (six tubes, three rounds each) into the target area before another Bronco reported on station. It must have been a slow night because he, too, worked over the area until he ran out of bullets. Not an NVA was to be seen.

The troops on the hill had lost interest, myself included. The clouds had begun to obscure our vision, and it was clear that the NVA had either gone to ground or left the area. It was, however, a good learning experience. I was about to secure from battle stations and set the watch when Domnoske spoke from the shadows near the mortar pit. "Say, Lieutenant! Corporal Crawford [at the mortar] hasn't fired a round . . ."

The point was made, and not lost on me. They had done a lot of work, and stood patiently ready all this time. I lit up a Country, took a long drag, made my decision. We had to shoot. "Roger that! Let's see what that bitch can do. Try not to blow up the tower."

I shouted the order in the general direction of the mortar pit, while scrambling down the sandbags into the trench. A cheerful "Aye, aye, sir!" was followed by "Fire in the hole!" and an earsplitting *thoomp* as the mortar crew dropped the first round into the tube. It turned out to be white phosphorous, and it landed in a rice paddy just short of one of the trail junctions we had been watching. I raised an eyebrow in speculation. WP was heavier than HE. Charge four was all we could do for propellant. It meant that we could shoot at a fairly large area near the base of the hill, but we would need to find a way to get the NVA into our kill zone. And we needed aiming stakes and a proper sighting mechanism. Still, the experiment was enlightening. I decided to find out one more thing. Still smoking, I called into the darkness again. "Mortar! Fire mission. Direction two hundred ninety degrees. Deflection sixty-eight degrees. Three rounds. HE. Charge four. Fire for effect!"

I shouted the command with no idea what they would do. What they did was good. Crawford repeated the order. His crew busied themselves trying to lay the tube on the azimuth. There was no way to get the deflection. They dropped three rounds into the valley in less than a minute, with no hangfires. My career was still intact. "Okay, Ski! Let's secure all this shit!"

Hannon materialized out of the gloom. "Turf Club is out, Lieutenant. Two WIA, one KIA. Somebody fell off the ladder . . ." He spoke in a whisper, emotion contorting his voice.

I pitched the still glowing butt into space with a flick of my fingers, absorbing the news and what I had learned. The enemy had got three of ours, but our exercise in fire-support coordination was concluded inconclusively. It was a waste. At best, we had caused the NVA to break a sweat on their way into the ville for aid and comfort. We had also tipped our hand. Anyone who had not known that we could see in the dark now had at least a clue. Still, I had learned a great deal about our capabilities and limitations. It remained to find a way to pull it together. With a little leadership and teamwork, I was convinced that we could make the Phu Loc Valley into a lethal gauntlet for the NVA troops moving into the Arizona. It was time to have a serious talk with Henry about tactics.

He was in the hootch, absorbed in beans with franks. I went straight to it, still angry. "Bill, your firepower is great, but your shooting sucks! We need to get a handle on this damn quick. Why do you waste so much time adjusting on targets?"

It was the wrong way to go. Henry was instantly aggressive, defending his tactics. He had, after all, followed the book.

"Mike, I don't work for you! I work for Colonel—"

Henry was half right. He did not work for me; I was responsible for providing food, shelter, and security for his team and equipment, but I did not have OpCon (operational control). He reported directly to 11th Marines, the artillery regiment. It was a peculiar arrangement about which I had only a rudimentary knowledge. I knew that our tactical disposition was the result of careful planning by higher (even lofty) authority. I knew that it was, essentially, a defensive posture. We were going home, packing it in (Operation KEY-STONE ROBIN, the phased withdrawal from Vietnam). I knew that the Infantry regiments' tactical areas of responsibility were realigned and their maneuver elements reassigned from search-and-clear operations in the clearing zone to security patrols in the pacification zone. That was the reason that I had been reassigned from BLT 2/26. My unit had been withdrawn from the field and reassembled with short-timers for redeployment out of the theater.

So had Henry's 11th Marines. The artillery regiment, in keeping with the Infantry scheme of maneuver, redeployed the forward observation teams (FOs), its eyes and ears, which were normally attached to infantry companies, to observation posts (OPs) located on the perimeter of the division's area of responsibility. The observation posts became cornerstones of the fire-support plan for the division's area. The firing batteries were concentrated in fire-support-base cantonments so that the artillery fan (maximum range for the guns) could cover maneuver elements and installations inside the division's area of responsibility and into the recon zone. In some areas (the Arizona, Charlie Ridge, the Que

Sons) the artillery fans overlapped, enabling commanders to mass fires from several batteries on a single target. The priority of fires was also changed. The observation posts and Recon had first call. Lucky Bill Henry was assigned to OP Sunrise (Hill 425), instead of a rifle company in 7th Marines, where he would have spent his days trolling for booby traps.

As tactical commander of the hill, I was responsible for all the bad things that might happen. I wanted to influence the action, while Henry thought that he was supposed to carry out his activities independently, reporting directly to 11th Marines' fire-support-coordination center. It wasn't going to work. I interrupted him, emotion coloring my words. "Bill, this is not about who works for whom. This is about getting the job done. Do you want to smoke Slopes, or not?"

"Sure I do, but we got an SOP. We got rules of engagement—"

"We also have brains, Bill. We are paid to use our brains. Look, just listen to my idea. If you think it makes sense, we try it. I think it's pretty clear that what we have been doing doesn't work." I paused for effect, making eye contact with him in the flickering light of our candle, waiting. Henry munched on his C rat, thinking about the day's activity. I knew that he had been at least as frustrated as I was. Gradually, he relaxed. He was beginning to open up to my offer.

I continued. "Look Bill, the NVA use tactics, just like we do. They have orders, a mission. Someone has told them to move into this valley. They have been told when to move, where to move. They have scouts, flank security, even guides. That's what we've been shooting at. I am sure of it! We can really fuck 'em up, Bill! All we have to do is watch them for a while, wait for them to get together, see how fast they move from known points in the valley. Then, we register targets on landmarks we can see in the dark and shoot for TOTs [time on target, a technique for massing artillery fire]. Give 'em a lead, like shooting ducks! That way, we'll hit them with a load. They will run right into a grid square full of shrapnel."

I watched him, looking for a reaction. He was thinking.

"What if we miss? My Six [commanding officer] would be all over my ass if I fired a TOT and had no body count. Besides, we'll never get clearances for that, anyway."

"Are you kidding? You cannon cockers shoot the shit out of rice paddies all night long!" I was referring to the nightly H & I (harassing and interdicting) fires conducted by the artillery regiment. I was frustrated, but Henry had a point. Fire support coordination was a thorny issue. Because supporting (firing) and supported (calling for fire) units were often in close proximity to the indigenous population, there was a perceived requirement for tighter control of supporting arms, particularly artillery, to prevent friendly casualties. Control measures, therefore, tended to compartmentalize the battlefield. A multitude of jurisdictions, military and civilian, evolved through which "clearance" had to pass in order for a target to be engaged. Target clearance became a complicated and frustrating process except in "specified strike zones" where artillery and other supporting arms could fire unrestricted. Calls for fire, even by units actually engaged with the enemy, had to be cleared with a multitude of U.S. and ARVN military and political authorities before a fire mission could be executed. The procedure required that all fire missions be cleared through the 11th Marines' fire support coordination center (FSCC). The system was further complicated by the requirements to coordinate fires through the division air-support-coordination center (DASC), which operated the "Save a Plane" system intended to prevent aircraft from flying into artillery trajectories of fire. Calls for fire from IOD observation posts created special clearance and coordination difficulties because the artillery and infantry command and communication channels were not fully integrated. The system and rules of engagement looked good on paper, but in practice they inhibited timely attack on enemy troop movements. In fact, the NVA and VC became adroit at maneuvering their units to avoid interdiction efforts. The system was the problem. Only by skillful manipulation of the system could we achieve the desired result. I went after Henry once more.

"Look, Bill. Give it a try. At least, this way, we've got a chance. We can tighten it up by using the crew-served weapons up here to herd them into your TOT. Who knows, maybe we can pin them down long enough to get a real air strike in here. We can set that up through my S-3 [Operations] shop. We have an air liaison officer. In fact, I'll lay on the whole scheme if you want, take the heat. All you have to do is work the IOD and communications. What do you say?"

I believed in the IOD. It was a righteous piece of gear. We could see up to thirty thousand meters in daylight, and had greatly improved night vision capabilities as well. The laser enabled us to get a good range, day or night, and since we knew exactly where we were, map reading for target location was a snap. An experienced forward observer could get first-round hits on targets. The problem was that the targets moved. As soon as a round landed, the NVA would do a five-hundred-meter sprint (the direction didn't matter) to get out of the target area. The NVA knew what our rules of engagement were, that we would have to get a new clearance if we adjusted outside that initial five-hundred-meter radius. Henry would get better with experience, but he was cautious, too concerned about wasting ammunition. And, he wanted to pop everything that moved. I wanted to waste NVA, not ammo. That meant getting Henry to go for broke on larger targets. I was convinced that our sightings of twos, threes, and fives were dispersed elements of a larger unit. I was also convinced, based upon the patterns that were developing, that the enemy was using the valley as a staging area. The fact that we had observed and fired upon one larger force implied that there was a significant enemy deployment in process. Shooting at the small units was probably just warning them to use different routes and to remain dispersed, at least during daylight. The possibility of engaging larger targets intrigued me. What I needed to do was win Henry's heart and mind with a better idea. It was back to TBS leadership.

"I don't know, Mike. Let me think about it for awhile." Henry was making a career decision. If he went with my program and it worked, he was in clover. If it didn't, he was in deep shit. I decided to go around him—back to the Lieutenants' Protective Association. The thing to do was to get

Wild Bill involved. He worked directly for the commanding general. Working the problem in my mind, I came to the conclusion reluctantly. Somebody had to talk to my Six—it would have to be Gregson. I went out, looking for Hannon.

He was on watch. He looked up from a morose slump when I approached.

"Say, Lance Corporal Hannon. How about hooking me up on the secure net?"

"Sure thing, Skipper." Hannon had promoted me.* "Will you stand by on the net while I go get the gear, sir? And take a whiz?"

"Sure."

Because it used power at an intolerable rate, the KY-38 system was used sparingly to communicate with higher authority on complicated subjects only. I believed I had one.

Hannon scrambled down to his hootch, came back with his KY-38, and a battery. After a few minutes of fumbling in the dark, penlight in his mouth, he had the gear hooked up and secure communication with Stone Pit at Camp Reasoner. But Gregson was off duty until 0600 the next morning, so I left him a message to call me.

I wanted to know the lay of the land before getting too far into a hassle with Henry and the artillery. Gregson would know how to go about getting support for the plan that was forming in my mind. Morning would be soon enough.

"Hannon, set this up on the berm outside my hootch. Use the barby [fighting/cooking/shaving position]." I wanted to have my conversation in private, away from unfriendly ears, foreign and domestic. "Have the watch wake me up at oh-five-thirty. Okay?" I intended to prowl the perimeter once or twice before then, but it wouldn't do to oversleep the call.

"Roger that, Lieutenant." Hannon set off in the dark to comply.

I took a slow tour of the perimeter trench. Troops were asleep atop some of the bunkers. Others stood watch, draped in ponchos—protection against the night mist and cold. Night

*"Skipper" is usually applied to a unit's commanding officer, a captain.

sounds drifted on the breeze, bodies shifting on hard ground, the occasional metallic click of equipment being jostled, snoring, mumbling, and comm checks. Out over the Arizona, a flare burst. Haloed by the mist, the light drifted on the horizon. The sound of small-arms fire drifted on the night wind from far off. I decided to get some sleep. Inside the hootch, I smoked a Country, then pulled the canvas away from the aperture of the bunker. I had a fantastic view, all the way to the harbor. The Grunts were still putting on a light show in the Arizona. I lay back on the cot, where I slept fitfully, disturbed by dreams and subconscious thoughts. I walked the perimeter twice, checking unobtrusively to see what there was to see. Domnoske had done the same.

Sunrise was all secure. The valley below us yawned as an abyss of darker dark, the floor layered in ground fog. Staring into the gloom, I became convinced—we could seal both ends of the valley with artillery fire, light up the center with air (bombs). With a little prior prudent planning, it was the perfect terrain for a combined-arms ambush. I fell asleep, thinking . . .

Dawn. Sunlight streamed into my bunker, pierced the veil of exhaustion, and brought me to consciousness. It was hot, already. I looked at my watch. It was 0530, 12 May, 1970. Plenty of time for coffee and pound cake from a B-3, maybe with pears, before taking my call. I did the deed, burning my lip on the canteen cup in the process, and stood looking out over the valley when the radio came to life on secure voice.

"Say, Mike. This is Chip. What's the buzz? Over."

Secure voice wasn't the telephone, but he was clearly comfortable with a more relaxed communication. I went with it.

"Mornin', Chip. Did you know there's lots of NVA out here? Over."

"No shit?"

"No shit! I want to light 'em up. I'm having a little trouble with Nigeria, the forward observer team. Can you help? Over."

"What do you want? Over."

"I want to set up an ambush. Air and arty. Blocking fires at both ends of the valley, and be able to shift fire to the north and south."

"Mike, I'm looking at your spot reports. Do you see a pattern here that we don't see? Over."

"That's affirmative. Chip, I'm willing to bet my bars they'll be back tonight!"

"Okay. I'll look into it. But we need more—a pattern. We can't go to the Six with this without better intel. Over."

I signed off, disappointed. Gregson was skeptical, but I knew I was right. We had work to do! I finished my coffee, thinking.

Domnoske appeared. "Mornin', Lieutenant. The night acts are in. Everybody's havin' chow. Any word to pass, sir?"

"Yeah, Ski. I've got a list. Have Wardlow's team hit the rack, after police call. I want all the trash off the pos after chow. Get Crawford to take a patrol, five guys, up the ridge, check out Hill Four ninety-three, see what there is to see. From now on, that hill," I pointed to it, "is Checkpoint Alpha. I want every man up here to know that. I want the patrol back by fifteen thirty [3:30 P.M.]. They'll have the night acts, too. Hicks gets to blow the rock today. Have his team and the strays [unassigned men] work on that and finish the machine-gun position. When you get these guys going, come back to see me. I want to talk about the valley, and our SOPs."

Domnoske had been here more than once, and he was astute. I wanted to pick his brain. He set off to get the troops organized while I returned to my daily routine. After a shave and a smoke, I settled down atop the bunker with map, compass, and 7x50 binoculars to do my Napoleon thing—terrain appreciation. Henry was sound asleep in the bunker, snoring. In his absence, the FO team maintained a slack watch of the valley. Around me, the troops went about police call, grousing about this and that chickenshit. Crawford's team meandered across the HLZ and out through a zigzag path in the concertina. I heard them pull a comm check with Hannon. Should have checked them out before they left. The thought flitted through my mind, one of many, while I studied the map.

By the time Domnoske reappeared, the troops were in motion. A police detail was circumnavigating the position, collecting trash. Water cans were being recycled to a staging area at the helicopter landing zone (HLZ). Two groups of three were filling sandbags, and another chipping away at the new machine-gun position. The FO team was making a lazy sweep of the valley floor with the periscope, and the shitter was on fire. Life was good.

"Okay, Lieutenant. What's on your mind?" Domnoske sat down in the shade of the tower, committed to endure whatever squirrelly process might ensue.

I smiled to myself. "Ski, how much patrolling have you done off this hill?" I made eye contact, watching for attitude.

"Too much, Lieutenant. I'm short. When we get down from here, I should have a flight date."

"That's not what I'm getting at. How well do you know the terrain?"

"Pretty well, sir. I mean, I know where the trails are, the best OPs, that sort of thing. But, all the guys that have been hurt up here, except for one asshole getting bit by a scout dog and when Lieutenant Hodge got my ear blown off, were hurt on security patrols. Booby traps. That happened last time we were up here, with Lieutenant Hodge. He was big on security patrols and shit. Just like you . . . sir."

We were in emotionally heavy seas. Even the best troop had a limit. Domnoske was reaching his. They felt safe on the hill. Lots of firepower, familiar terrain, creature comforts, fortifications. They had no appreciation for their tactical vulnerability, did not understand the need for continual and aggressive patrolling to prevent the NVA from attacking the position without warning. In their eyes, I was still a fuckin' new guy, just another boot lieutenant. I decided to change the subject.

"Ski, Lieutenant Hodge is doing his second tour. He was here in sixty-five doing what you are doing. Security patrols are a necessary evil, for the safety of all of us. So is improving the defenses. But that is not what I want to talk about."

I paused, a disengagement, then continued, "I think we

can agree that there are lots of NVA around here. What I want to do is work with you to develop a daily routine to get the work done, teach the guys how to use the weapons, keep the NVA off our backs. They are a lot less likely to screw with us if they know we're ready."

Domnoske kept silent, his gaze speculative. I went on.

"We can use our time up here to train the guys in map reading, radio procedures, calls for fire, marksmanship, tactics. The more we do, the better chance they have of making their flight dates." I was picking on him a little. "But it can't just come from me. It has to come from you, and the team leaders. What do you say?" I waited, smoking, while he made up his mind.

"So, what's next, Lieutenant?" It was as close as we were going to get.

"Get with the team leaders and the FO sergeant. Work out a schedule for the IOD. We should fam-fire weapons once a day. Take turns with the M-60s so people get good at it. Same thing with the fifty. You guys get back to me with what you think will work best."

Hicks gave a shout, "Fire in the hole!" There was an ear-splitting blast. Pebbles and dust rained down on us. Then a raucous cheer. The offending boulder was cracked. Domnoske made to leave. "Anything you want on the resupply request, sir?" It was a concession.

"Some pussy?"

We laughed. Domnoske went off to do his thing, while I went back to lieutenant shit. It would have been nice to make a friend, but the mission came first. I thought about Staff Sergeant Diaz and the others from Hotel Three (3d Plt, Co. H, 2d Bn., 26th Marines). They were out there somewhere, humping the bush without me.

The afternoon and early evening passed uneventfully. After blowing up our boulder, Hicks and his crew cleared the trench in preparation for another gun pit. We ate and napped through the heat of the day and emerged from the bunkers like hibernating animals when the sun broke into its slide to darkness. Sunrise Alpha returned, bedraggled but otherwise none the worse for wear. Third Herd was settling into my routine. It was beginning to look like they would "follow the bars." It was time to get Bill Henry to do the same.

Henry was up and about, having spent most of the day in his rack reading fuck books. He was intent upon a meal concocted of beans, franks, cream cheese, and dirt. The bunker reeked of heat-tab fumes. This boy had a lot to learn about cooking.

"Want some Tabasco?" As I spoke, I pulled the canvas away from the bunker aperture, fanning the fumes away.

"Sure." His eyes watered.

"C-4 works better. No fumes. I like to do my cooking outside, on the parapet. It helps to make a hole in that crap." I gestured at the mess spilling out of the can on the dirt floor. "Put the cheese in it. That way, it won't boil over so much. Got onion?" I was trying to make friends. Henry was not making it easy.

"I'm okay." He sat back on the cot, spooning the mess into his face.

I stared at him, assessing his mood, then continued, "Look, Bill, a few months back, my platoon ambushed an NVA sapper squad coming out of a village just like Phu Loc. Intel told us that they were using certain trails out of the mountains. I think that is what is going on in the valley. I think they hustle down to the lake at dusk, hump into the ville in the dark, hustle back at dawn—make it into the mountains before sunrise. It's a pattern. It has a timetable, a route, and a known destination. We can fuck them up. All we have to do is make the nine-eight-four-seven grid square [on the map sheet] into an artillery trap."

"What do you know about artillery traps? You're not an FO." He was sullen, offended that I was telling him how to do his job.

"Three weeks of school, Bill. Air, artillery, and naval gunfire. I can call 'em all. We did it for ten hours a day. Probably as many hours as you got at Fort Sill. Only the navy uses sandtables, like model railroads—it's cool."

"Well, the Phu Loc [valley] ain't no model railroad." Henry

stood up, tossed his half-eaten ration out the aperture, into space. Disgust tainted his features. "This place sucks. I got to go on watch, Mike. Thanks for the Tabasco." He went out.

I dropped the canvas over the opening and settled in to do my own culinary miracle, with beans and franks.

"Say, Lieutenant! We got five Slopes at high port, running for the ville!" The FO sergeant shouted over the top of the IOD. He knew that they would be inside the no-fire zone before we could fire. Henry scrambled into the tower. I looked at my watch. The luminous dial said 1955 (7:55 P.M.), just like I thought. I stuck to my task, listening to the banter of the FOs.

"Here's six more of the little bastards!" It was Henry. "They're already inside the NFZ. Call in a spot report. Fuck!"

I ate, thinking, I wonder if they come back the same way? After chow, I went outside and took a position atop the ammo bunker. Like the sea captains of old, I commanded my tiny warship from the deck. I could see, hear, and otherwise sense the activity of the crew as they went about preparing for the night. Domnoske and company had bought my act. I watched the night acts leave the wire, listening to the comm checks on the speaker. Hannon had taken to his role as comm chief. The whole process was smooth.

Domnoske found me. We agreed to split the watch. I would take the last half, he the first. I made a tour of the perimeter and hit the rack. Henry crashed into the bunker before I could fully relax. He dropped onto his cot with a loud sigh. Apparently, he had concluded that the best thing he could do with his tour in Vietnam was to sleep through it. I spoke into the darkness.

"Say, Bill?"

Henry gave a grunt, his back to me.

"Do you think those guys you saw going into the ville might come back the way they went in?"

"You never give up, do you?" Henry rolled to a sitting position as he spoke.

I stayed where I was, smoking. "Not my nature. 'Betcha a can of pears and a candy bar they do."

He sighed, "How about apricots? I got no pears."

"So, it's a deal."

"Yeah."

I smiled in the dark. Now, if the fog didn't keep us from seeing them . . . Henry was coming around.

The morning of the thirteenth came in with a bang. And, I won my bet. Henry caught ten NVA on the trail, headed south two klicks west of Spider Lake. They had got through the valley in the fog. He did his typical thing, and the NVA were out of his target area before the first rounds hit—all but one. He went to ground on the first round, then did a world-class mile into the trees before Henry could make an adjustment. Henry stomped back to our hootch in a mood. I followed, to collect my bet.

"Nice shooting, Bill. Next time, we should throw rocks." I said it with a grin, but Henry took it badly.

"Fuck you, Hodgins. If you can do better, be my guest!" He slumped back on his cot, picked up a tattered paperback, as if to read. Then he put the book down, rummaged in his pack, and threw a can at me—apricots. "I'll give you the candy later, motherfucker." He slumped back on his cot, arm over his freckled face.

I laughed, "Cheer up, Bill. You've got another ten months to get it right. I, on the other hand, am getting short. So, I'd like to get it right, now." I took the can of fruit and went out to do some troop leading. Henry lay where he had fallen, abjectly contemplating the greater meaning of life. His mission, "to create peace through fire superiority" appeared doomed to failure. All he had been able to do so far was plow rice paddies and do lumberjack work. His artillery had lent no dignity to the battlefield, whatsoever.

Domnoske had done my troop leading for me. The teams were busy at their assigned tasks. I finished my fruit, tossed the can over the side of the hill and joined the crew filling sandbags for the new .50-cal. position. Nothing like a little exercise to freshen the brain. The troops were surprised at my participation—another good sign. By 1100 (11:00 A.M.), we had a good start, and it was too hot to work. The air had become still, and stiflingly hot. Overhead, the sun beat down, but the horizon was darkening—a storm. Rain. Perhaps welcome relief, if it didn't last too long.

"Let's secure this shit." I said it to the group, wiping sweat from my own brow. "It's time for chow and a nap." I followed my own example, making my way down the trench to my hootch. Inside, I dowsed myself with water from one of the cans staged there. I was almost out. So must the rest be.

"Anything you want on the resupply, Lieutenant?" Domnoske's words—fuckin'-A: better tools; a couple of engineer kits; and a water bo' (a water-tank trailer). Refreshed, I went out to find Domnoske and put in my request. The hill looked deserted. There was not a man in sight, anywhere. I found Hannon instead, crashed in the shade of the tower, and had him call in my request as a priority resupply. Without more water, very little work was going to get done. Troops, like jungle animals, knew when to sleep—the heat of the day was a good time. I went back to the bunker, intending to follow their example.

Henry was awake. "Say Mike, did you hear about Bob [Wood]?" Henry was eating, slurping peaches from a can.

"What's to hear?"

"He got killed at Ryder [fire support base]. Struck by lightning yesterday, while he was talking on the radio."

I was stunned. "How could that happen?"

"Beats me. They just called and told us to be sure all our radios are grounded. I guess the lightning hit one of the antennas, went right up the line, came out the handset."

I looked out at the darkening sky. Mother Nature was one mean, fickle bitch. I pictured Bob as I had last seen him, waving a cheerful farewell. How could he be dead? Lightning? We were in the season, thunderstorms were becoming a daily occurrence. And here we sat atop an ammo dump with lightning rods all around. Bob's death was a shock, but remote. The lesson of his fate was real, and immediate. As I had done with so many other shocks in the past eight months, I stuffed the remorse and focused on my immediate responsibility. "Have you done that, yet?"

"Nah. I think we're okay." Henry was finishing his last slice, draining the juice from the bottom of the can, his head tilted to the roof. I stared at him for a moment, thinking how different he was from Bob, from me. I thought about the gaggle of antennae, wire, and olive-green boxes (PRC-25s) scattered round the tower. I wasn't so sure. Maybe lightning didn't strike twice in the same place, but it had to hit the ground somewhere. Our antenna farm looked like a great spot to me. I ducked outside and shouted into space. "Hannon!" The RTO appeared, looking his usual bedraggled self.

"Yes, sir."

"Got a job for you. Collect the other RTOs and meet me in my hootch." It was beginning to rain again. Lightning cracked across the valley. I flinched, then shivered. Bob, if you're out there . . . The thought went incomplete. Hannon broke in.

"Sir, we got teams in the field—Turf Club, Pony Boy, Thin Man, and Flakey Snow—plus Sunrise Bravo, sir."

He meant that he could not bring all the RTOs at one time. Someone had to monitor the net.

"Tell Domnoske to have the team leaders sit in for you. Matter of fact, bring him with you."

I ducked back inside the bunker and sat down to brew a mocha. The news of Bob's death was an omen. The monsoon season was upon us. We had a ton of ammo on the hill, most of it in the bunker just below the tower. The antenna farm we had grown there had become both a tactical and a natural hazard. It was time to move them. The ammo would have to wait.

"Skipper!" It was Hannon. He sounded alarmed. I left my mocha project, lunged outside and peered up toward the tower, impervious to the drizzle.

"What?"

"Sunrise Bravo is on the hook. They got a shitpot full of gooks at the base of the hill!"

Bravo was Hicks. He was supposed to be on the pos by now. I scrambled up the sandbags to take the handset from Hannon. "Sunrise Bravo, this is Actual. Sitrep please." I kept my voice calm, but my pulse throbbed in my throat. How many? Where? What were they doing?

"Sunrise Actual, this is Bravo. We got fifty-plus bad guys moving south on the big trail due west of your pos, vicinity grid zero-zero-six-four-six-four. They are hauling ass. Over."

I looked at the arty map. The NVA were on the trail at the base of our hill, masked from view by the slope and vegetation. They were inside our NFZ, less than five hundred meters from the wire! Bless you, Bob Wood. The thought flitted through my mind as I searched his neatly annotated target list for the one on Hill 493 (Checkpoint Alpha).

"Roger, Bravo. Break. Posrep please?"

Domnoske appeared. He had monitored Bravo's transmission. I stared at him, waiting for the team's reply.

"Sunrise, this is Bravo. We are in the saddle [low point between two hills], two hundred meters due south of Checkpoint Alpha. Over."

"Roger, Bravo. Sit tight." To Domnoske, "Get the troops out. Put the M-60s on the east side, at both ends of the trench. Lay in the sixty millimeter [mortar] on ninety degrees, magnetic [an approximate compass heading in the direction of the probable enemy approach]. Nobody fires a fuckin' thing until I say so! We got friendlies outside the wire. Got it?"

"Aye, aye, sir!" He jumped into the trench and went about his work.

I made note of Bravo's position on the FO map. It was time to call the cavalry. I tapped the FO sergeant on the shoulder, gesturing for him to give up his handset. He complied, just as Henry climbed over the parapet into the tower. I made the call anyway, staring at him. "Vesper Bells, Vesper Bells, this is Nigeria. Fire mission. Over!"

"Nigeria, this is Vesper Bells. Roger, fire mission. Over."

"Vesper Bells, this is Nigeria. Troops in column. From

target Alpha Zulu Seven, Zero Four, left eight hundred, add four hundred. HE. VT. Fire for effect. Over."

"Nigeria, this is Vesper Bells. We copy. Wait. Out."

We waited. The NVA humped. My heart pumped. Henry stared at me, comprehension upon him. We could be in deep shit.

"Nigeria, this is Vesper Bells. Interrogative. Are you in contact. Over?"

I cursed. Fuck no, but the gooks could do fire-team rushes all the way onto our position by the time these guys got their act together.

"Vesper Bells, this is Sunrise Actual on your net. Break. Negative on your last. We are not in contact, but these guys can be all over us damn quick. Over."

"Nigeria, this is Vesper Bells. Roger that. Target is inside your November Foxtrot Zulu [no-fire zone]. Confirm danger close. High angle, adjust fire, on command. Over."

I cursed with frustration. The artillery fire direction center (FDC), responsible for calculating the firing solution for the guns, had changed my method of attack. The NVA were in defilade (shielded from fire from both artillery cantonments, An Hoa and Ryder). Unless I was willing to chance dropping rounds on our own position, they had free passage. It was just as Wood had said. I decided to give it a shot. "Vesper Bells, this is Sunrise Actual. Fire. Over."

"Nigeria, this is Vesper Bells. Shot. Over!"

"Vesper Bells, this is Nigeria. Roger, shot. Out." On the other radio I said, "Bravo, this is Actual. Shot. Over." Seconds passed.

"Nigeria, this is Vesper Bells. Splash. Over!"

"Vesper Bells, this is Nigeria. Roger splash. Out."

I passed the word to Bravo and waited. After interminable seconds, we heard a *crump* echo over the ridge behind us, far off. The round had landed on the east slope of the next ridge, just outside our NFZ and more than a klick from the last known enemy location. I gave the handset to Henry, concentrating on my own. "Bravo, this is Actual. Do you have the enemy in sight? Over."

"That's a negative, Sunrise. They kept on truckin'. I bet they don't even know we shot at 'em. Over."

"Bravo, this is Actual. Roger that. Come on home." I gave the handset to Hannon, making eye contact with Henry. "Hannon, call in a spot report."

"Cease fire. My security patrol is on their way in. We need to rethink all this."

Already in contact with Vesper Bells, Henry nodded his head in agreement. Vietnam had finally got his attention. I went looking for Domnoske, more concerned than ever about the vulnerability of our fort. He was on the berm, a PRC-25 at his feet.

"Say, Ski. Good work. Secure these guys. Make sure they clear and lock all weapons and post a watch. We still got Bravo outside the wire. Make sure they give us a heads-up before they come in. I don't want anybody getting shot by accident. I want two night acts on the east side tonight. Both of them will take claymores. I'll give you the grids later. Deal?"

"Yes, sir." He turned to comply.

"And Ski!"

"Sir?"

"Put in a priority request for a sight, base plate, and aiming stakes for the mortar." I now understood why the thing was up here. I leaned against the berm, staring down the slope of the hill. It was steep, covered with low brush and rocks—a tough climb. Sappers were tough climbers. The trail was a natural line of departure. The NVA could take us from there anytime. Fifty of 'em? What were they doing? Where were they going? Smoking and thinking, I studied our position. The bunkers were too high. We had no way to use the M-60s effectively, no intersecting, grazing fires as our TBS instructors had described them. What now, Lieutenant?

It was dark. I flipped the butt into space. The fag scribed an orange arc into the night.

"Sir?" It was Hannon, with the other RTOs.

"Right. Gents, tomorrow you've got a project. I want you guys to relocate all our antennae, one at a time, to a remote location up there on the east end of the hill, just inside the wire and away from all the bunkers. Got it?" It was too dark to tell. "Tonight, like right now, I want you to ground every fuckin' radio on the pos. And, Hannon, I want you to rig one of the team radios in my hootch, with a speaker. Okay?"

"Aye, aye, Skipper." They set off without comment.

"Vesper Bells, Vesper Bells, this is Nigeria. Fire mission. Over!"

I looked at my watch. It was 1920 (7:20 P.M.). The gooks were at it again, and so was Henry—"Three-zero troops in column. Grid Alpha Tango niner-eight-six-four-six-four. Direction two eight five degrees. Battery Three. HE. VT. Fire for effect. Over."

I smiled. My buddy Bill was getting his shit together. Would Vesper Bells come through?

I stared out into the Arizona. Three miles away, I saw the muzzle flashes of the 105s at An Hoa. They had sent the mail.

"Nigeria, this is Vesper Bells. Rounds complete. Over." Six guns had pumped three rounds apiece into the night. They were all in the air.

The first rounds detonated in space. Over the heads of the hapless NVA. We saw the sparkle, then heard the detonations. "Vesper Bells, this is Nigeria. Roger, rounds complete. Roger, splash. Break. Stand by for TDA [target damage assessment]. Over."

I scrambled into the tower. Henry was on the starlight scope, his sergeant standing nearby.

"The fuckin' scope blossomed!" He was livid.

"Use the ship's binos!" I was excited. He switched without a word, searching for validation.

"Well, fuck me dead!" Henry pulled away from the binoculars, grinning. He offered me a look—like the old war-movie sub skippers. I stooped to squint through the lens. There were at least nine NVA on the ground—two were moving, flopping. There was no sign of the others. I stood up. Henry was on the radio. "Vesper Bells, this is Nigeria. Confirm nine KIA. Good shooting. Nigeria, out."

Henry turned to his sergeant. "Let's keep watch for a while—see if any more try to leave the area." He was a new man—a killer.

The word spread across the hill. The troops took turns scanning the floor of the valley with 7x50s and the starlight scope. Their vigilance paid off about two hours later, when they sighted nine NVA in the same area. Henry tried again, but could not observe the results. We got our turn twenty minutes later—four NVA moving west on the trail nearest the base of the hill. They were too close for arty. I let Domnoske have a go with the .50-cal. and the mortar. It was great fun, but inconclusive.

I wondered if we had enough activity now to justify setting up the ambush. The NVA had massed and moved from the same general area, at the same time, two of the past three nights. Would they do it again? Gregson was more receptive to my second call. The spot reports were shaping up. That or they knew things that we didn't know. He said he would get back to me.

"Sunrise, this is Stone Pit. Get your Actual up on secure voice. Over." The squawk box woke me up. I waited for Hannon to answer up.

I stood up, lunged through the bunker door into daylight, and bolted up to the tower. Hannon was there with the handset.

"Stone Pit, this is Sunrise Actual on secure voice. Over."

"Roger, Sunrise. Wait, out."

I waited, staring out over the valley. A man had to be careful what he asked for in life. Sometimes, you got it.

"That you, peckerwood?"

It was Drumright. My stomach churned. "Yes, sir. Over."

"This better be good, peckerwood, or I'll have your candy ass! You tell Gregson here what you want. Target list. Air request. All that shit. I'll brief it. You'll get it. You better kill a whole lot of Communists with it. Hear me! Stone Pit Six, clear."

He was gone. Gregson came on the line. The plan was simple. The artillery would mass fires from several batteries

(eight-inch guns and 155mm howitzers) at An Hoa and FSB
Ross. The artillery would be laid in on our targets, unless firing
a priority mission, from 1900 to 2100 (7:00 P.M. to 9:00 P.M.).
They would be prepared to fire on command. A flight of
carrier-based A-6 bombers would be on station from 1900 to
1940, loaded with TPQ-10 cluster bombs. Airhose Two Eight
(an airborne forward air controller) would coordinate their attack. They would orbit above the artillery peak trajectory and
drop on our command, from altitude. It would all be a big surprise to whoever was on the ground.

"We got good intel on this, Mike. You might be shooting at
the NVA Eighty-two-B Division. Semper fi!"

The phone was dead. It remained for Henry and me to develop and call in a target list. We spent the morning doing
that, plotting the grids and bearings for the primary target
area and the places we thought they might run for cover.
With the amount of firepower that was available, we thought
there wasn't much. Domnoske and the Herd worked on the
crew-served weapons, determined not to be left out of the
action. If the enemy broke toward our pos, we would be
ready. By dusk, we were. Every man on the hill was at the
berm, passing 7x50s from face to face, making bets as to
who would spot the enemy first and on which trail. Henry
was on the IOD. I took the ship's binoculars. Domnoske had
the starlight scope down by our brand new .50-cal. position,
ammo all around. Crawford's mortar crew had rounds aplenty
laid out, including Willie Pete. We waited.

"Sunrise, Sunrise, this is Airhose Two Eight on your net.
How copy. Over?"

It was 1900 (7:00 P.M.), right on time.

"Nigeria, Nigeria, this is Vesper Bells, standing by.
Over."

It was going to be a team effort. The radios were on squawk
box. We could hear one another. I had Domnoske on Tac
Two, with Hannon manning the net, control of my "organic
weapons." USS *Third Herd* was at battle stations. All
we needed now was the enemy. Overhead, intermittent
clouds blocked the last rays of sun, deepening the shadows

in the valley. We watched, straining for the first glimpse of movement.

"Bill, I got the point—two guys, packs and rifles, on the lower trail, close to the lake, azimuth"—I looked at the beezle on the binoculars—"two seven two degrees, moving east."

"I see 'em. Vesper Bells, Vesper Bells, this is Nigeria. Fire mission. Stand by. Over."

We counted them out, holding our breath. Two, seven, thirty-five. They were moving as if on a string, two meters apart in groups of three. Fifty-five. The column split into parallel groups. Seventy. A cart—no, a 12.7mm antiaircraft machine gun on wheels. We had an NVA battalion in the open! Over a hundred and twenty strong and still coming.

"Airhose Two Eight, this is Sunrise Actual. Break. Target is one-two-zero troops in open moving east, northeast at about three miles per hour [high port]. Over."

"Sunrise, this is Airhose Two Eight. Roger that. My fast movers [jets] are making a turn now. They will drop on a heading of two-zero-zero, right down the middle. Over."

The plan called for the A-6s to drop their bombs to cover a klick (one thousand-meter square) centered on the trail junction at grid AT987478. My job was to give them a time hack, an estimate of when the enemy would be in the target area.

"Roger, Airhose. Target will reach designated area in two minutes from my mark. Stand by." I peered at the luminous dial of my watch. "Mark. Over."

"Vesper Bells, Vesper Bells, this is Nigeria. Fire mission. Target Alpha Zulu one four three. One-two-zero troops in open. Time on target. HE. VT. On my command. Over."

"Nigeria, this is Vesper Bells. Copy fire mission, target Alpha Zulu one four three. One-two-zero troops in open. Time on target. HE. VT. On command. Be advised, you are on the gun–target line. Over." The rounds from Ross would be coming right over our heads. Anything long (range error) from An Hoa would hit the forward slope of our hill. Food for thought.

"Sunrise, this is Airhose. Bombs away. Over."

"Nigeria, this is Vesper Bells. Shot. Over."

The NVA were moving fast. Some of them were already out of the target area. The rest of the column, two columns, were strung out from the lake to the trail junction—and still coming. Overhead, we heard nothing. Out at An Hoa—muzzle flashes, lots of muzzle flashes. "Vesper Bells, this is Nigeria. Roger, shot. Out."

The cluster bombs arrived, a lethal rain, in utter silence. Suddenly, the valley floor began to sparkle and pop. It turned to dust in the binoculars. The NVA disappeared!

"Nigeria, this is Vesper Bells. Splash. Over."

A freight train drowned out the radio transmission. Followed by countless more hellish rushes as round after round of 155mm artillery shells from FSB Ross passed over our heads. The valley floor blossomed in bright orange and haze. Thunder rolled up to us, as volley after volley of 8-inch and 155mm artillery rounds burst over a two-klick area. We were stunned by the violence of it. Nothing could live through that!

"Vesper Bells, this is Nigeria. Break. Shift fire. Shift fire. Target Alpha Zulu one-four-five. Fire for effect! Over." Henry was going for it! He had shifted the artillery target to the streambed, the most likely place for the NVA to hide. We hit them with another three-round salvo.

"Mike, what can you see? My fuckin' scope blossomed [i.e., is blinded by the flash]." Henry was cursing, frustrated.

"Nothin' but dust, man. Put 'em in check-fire 'til we can see what we got."

"Vesper Bells, this is Nigeria. Check-fire. Over."

"Sunrise, this is Airhose Two Eight. Can you give me a BDA [bomb damage assessment]? Over."

No, you stupid bastard. It's dark out! The thought passed. I peered through the glass, looking for movement. Aloud, I said, "Stand by, Airhose. We're counting." To Henry, "Bill. Get us some illumination."

"Roger that."

He called it in, and we soon had flares floating over the valley. Still no movement, but the dust had settled. There were, indeed, bodies on the battlefield—sixteen of them. They were dark blotches in the dry rice paddies. Everything else was torn up, cratered. The place looked like the face of the moon, with broken trees. I searched the area with the binoculars, cursing myself for being a dumb son of a bitch; we should have arranged for a reaction force. There was no way to count "body parts and drag marks" from five klicks away in the dark. I had no doubt that we had decimated the NVA formation. There had been over a hundred and fifty of them standing upright in the open when the first clusters burst in the rice paddies. The artillery had plastered the streambed—they would have run right into it. Now, the world wanted to know our results—the body count: What had we done with Uncle Sam's money?

Domnoske came up on the net, "Sunrise Actual, this is Charlie. We got movement. Four chumps at the foot of the hill. Request permission to fire. Over."

I believed him. "Get some, Charlie. Actual out." I focused back on the target area—sixteen was all I could come up with. "Bill, I count sixteen."

Domnoske opened up with the fifty. There was a *whomp-whomp-whomp,* from the mortar pit. How they could hit anything, I didn't know. Maybe it didn't matter.

"Me, too," Bill said. "We had to do better than that!" We were disappointed. The fifty kept going.

"Call it in."

"Airhose, this is Sunrise. BDA, sixteen KIA, many probable. Great target coverage. Ya'll come back, heyah!"

"Sunrise, this is Airhose. Roger, out."

He motored off. We had neither seen nor heard any of the aircraft involved in the attack. It was eerie, and awesome.

"Sunrise Actual, this is Charlie. We got three KIA at the canal. Over." I focused the binos at the foot of the hill, in the general area where Domnoske's rounds had been landing. Sure enough. It looked as if they had run right into him. Three rag dolls lay on the berm. "Charlie, this is Actual. Confirm three KIA by small arms [if you could call the .50-cal. small]. Call in a spot report. Over."

Let him take the credit he was due. I was suddenly weary, cotton mouthed. We had done something. Whether it was really good or really bad was yet to be determined. Like beauty, the glory of the deed was in the eye of the beholder. We had expended a lot of ordnance, had not a lot to show for it. In McNamara terms, we were probably fuckups. Time would tell. "Bill, let's pack it in."

I lit up a smoke, careful to cup the glow in my palm. It was hell on night vision.

"Sunrise, Sunrise, this is Hostage Six. Can we help? Over." We were drawing a crowd.

"Hostage, this is Sunrise. The party is over. Break. You can get us a TDA. Over. Talk to Nigeria on Tac Two. Out."

"Roger that, Sunrise. Hostage Six. Out."

He cruised around above the last of the flares, talking to Nigeria. I climbed down and hit the rack. The troops were up. Really up. It had been a helluva day. I closed my eyes. Outside, more illumination rounds popped. Hostage was now running the show, shooting up the shadows. I fell asleep to the sound of artillery thunder rolling through the Phu Loc— the Gauntlet.

CHAPTER NINE
THE SNATCH

21–23 MAY 1970

The Spartans do not ask how many the enemy number, but where they are.

Agis of Sparta, 415 B.C.

After our successful artillery ambush, life in the Que Sons settled into a routine. We had ours, the NVA had theirs. We kept watch night and day, searching the valley floor from Spider Lake west into the mountains, with little success. We searched the horizon, north into the Arizona, hoping to catch them moving in the open, also with little success. Our soldiers reported numerous activations of their sensor strings at the head of the valley, and our security patrols reported that the trails along the base of the hill were being used extensively, but they were masked from IOD observation by the slope of the hill. It was clear that the NVA had changed their patterns of movement in response to our increased effectiveness with supporting-arms attacks. We knew that the enemy had not given up the valley, just changed his tactics.

After discussing the situation with Domnoske, who knew the terrain around Hill 425 better than anyone else, I decided to displace a team with the ship's binoculars to a position east of our hill, where they could observe the valley floor from a different direction. With a little luck, we might be able to bring some observed fires on targets at the base of

273

the hill. It proved an entertaining decision almost immediately. The first sighting (21 May 1970) occurred inadvertently. After our scare of the thirteenth, Domnoske and I agreed to convert our easternmost night act into an observation post, leaving it in position for the day, equipped with a PRC-25 radio and the ship's binoculars, with orders to maintain a watch over the valley floor and the now infamous trail in defilade. They became an OP/FO team at daybreak. Watching Gooners in the valley was easy. Shooting at them would be hard. I told the team leaders that our chances of getting clearance to fire into the Phu Loc no-fire zone were slim to none. But, Corporal Hicks was gung ho. He wanted to run a fire mission, so he volunteered to spend the day roasting in the sun while the rest of us continued our daily routine.

I sent a team of four guys to walk a loop west and south on the ridge, with orders to scope out the valleys on either side, and to "stay off the skyline!" They were Sunrise Alpha. Hicks was Sunrise Bravo. His orders were to maintain a watch on the trail complexes at the base of the ridge, calling in a situation report every hour on the quarter hour. The rest of us slept, ate, filled sandbags, and took turns on the IOD with the arty guys. About 1500, Hicks called in a spot report. He was excited.

Hannon answered the phone in his usual taciturn fashion. As he spoke, he removed a tattered message pad from the pocket of his utility jacket and pulled a stub of pencil from behind his ear. He spoke around a plastic spoon, his mouth full of peaches and pound cake. Hearing the squawk of the PRC-25, I turned to listen.

"Sunrise, this is Bravo. Get the skipper on the hook. Over."

I recognized Hicks's voice. He did not sound alarmed, but he was clearly excited. I took the handset from Hannon. "Bravo, this is Sunrise Actual. What's the problem. Over?"

"Skipper, you're not going to believe this! We been watching the Gooners around the ville all day—they're fuckin' NVA! Over." His radio procedure had gone to hell.

I broke in, "Bravo, this is Sunrise Actual. Break. This is not, I say again, not a secure set. Use procedure and code. Over!"

He had news, but I didn't want the NVA to hear it while I did, nor did I want the division communications police on my case.

"Bravo, this is Sunrise Actual. Break. Secure your activity and return to this pos. Over." I wanted to get them back and hear the story first hand.

"Sunrise, this is Bravo. Roger that! Out." They were on their way in.

"Hannon! Get Sergeant Ski up here, would you. He's probably racked out in his bunker."

Hannon left the tower still munching his pound cake, while I pulled my tattered map flat on an ammo crate to study the terrain below Bravo's position. What could Hicks have seen? It was not news to us that the ville was full of Bad Guys. We had been telling people that all along. But the ville was also a USAID Model Pacification Village, a no-fire zone, and none of our business. It was more likely to be a problem for the Grunts to deal with. Our job was to observe and interdict movement to and from the population centers, not in them. Still, where there's Gooners there's opportunity—

My thoughts were interrupted by Hannon's return. As he clattered up the sandbag steps and fell into the tower again, I resolved to concentrate on the daily routine first. The security patrol was due back, and we needed to get the night acts sorted out, people fed, water cans staged for the resupply bird, and myriad other housekeeping chores. As Hannon climbed over the sandbag berm of the tower and took up his semireclined position on the deck in front of the radios, Domnoske stuck his head over the top. "What's up, Skipper?" He spoke the words with a quizzical expression on his face. I had summoned him a half hour before he was supposed to be awakened, and he was puffy-eyed from sleep. He was, nevertheless, his own dauntless can-do self.

I motioned him to join me at the ammo box desk where I had the map spread out. "Sorry about interrupting your zees, Ski, but we are going to have to get an early start on things for this evening. Hicks is on his way in from his OP. He's all excited about something they saw in the valley, close to the ville. The security patrol is due back any minute, and I want you to debrief them while I talk to Hicks. Get the rest of the guys up and eating, and pick your LPs. I want them on the forward slope, about here and here, tonight." I pointed to the position I had identified on the map with my grease pencil. "When you get them set, come back here and sit in on Hicks. We may have something special to do tomorrow."

He was already nodding his assent and turning to climb back down the ladder when I stopped him again.

"And Ski, I want to check those guys out before they leave the wire."

"Aye, aye, sir!" He disappeared the way he had come as the radio speaker crackled to life.

"Sunrise, this is Sunrise Alpha. Over!" The RTO was out of breath, his voice more a gasp than a statement.

Hannon responded with his usual laconic wit, "Alpha, this is Sunrise. You be huffin' and a puffin'. Send your traffic. Over." He was grinning, knowing that his partner was slogging up the ridge after a day of hauling the PRC-25 over hill and dale, something that he, personally, hated to do.

"Sunrise, this is Alpha. We are approaching your pos from the southeast. Request permission to pass the wire. Over."

I turned in the direction they were expected, picking up my 7x50s. I nodded to Hannon, scanning the hillside below us as I did.

"Alpha, this is Sunrise. Pop smoke. Over!"

Procedure was procedure, and I had drilled the Mickey Mouse ideas into their heads from the first night. I wanted no friendly-on-friendly incidents on my watch, nor did I want the team followed into the perimeter. War stories from the Basic School had made an impression on me. Better safe than sorry.

"Roger, Sunrise. Popping smoke."

Within seconds, green smoke began drifting slowly up the draw from a position some three hundred meters below. Alpha had been on one hell of a hump!

"Alpha, this is Sunrise. I see green smoke. Over." Hannon was smirking at the thought of his friends humping the last three hundred meters up the draw. In troop vernacular, it was a bitch. He gave the shout, "Patrol at the wire, two o'clock!" then slumped back on the deck.

"Sunrise, this is Alpha. Confirm green smoke. Out." The first man became visible from the cover of a large boulder in the draw. I smiled to myself. They were playing for keeps.

"Hannon!" He turned to look at me. "Get a water can, a full one, and hump it down to the LZ for those guys. Tell 'em to use the whole thing to cool off. They'll love you for it."

He glared at me, then rose to do my bidding. It wouldn't do to let him enjoy other peoples' travails too much. He was a good troop, but he tended to enjoy the perks of being the command RTO. I liked busting his balls once in a while.

"Sunrise, this is Bravo. Over!" Hicks was also back.

"Bravo, this is Sunrise. Send your traffic. Over."

I spoke the words into the handset, turning to look in the direction I was expecting his team to appear, and we went through the smoke ritual again. Then I gave the shout, "Patrol at the wire, ten o'clock!" I stood up, pulled on my web gear, climbed over the sandbag berm onto a makeshift ladder, then down to the top of the command bunker, and finally to the ground. I moved down the fighting trench to the last parapet, leaned against the sandbags and lit up a Country, waiting for Hicks's team to wend its way through the wire.

They were moving quickly for guys who had been lying in the sun all day, and I took that to be an indication of their motivation. Fatigued troops move with a slack, listless gait, their heads down, dragging dust with their boots. These guys were coming up the last stretch of the hill like racehorses, moving with confidence, purpose, and energy. I wondered if they had found the fountain of youth on their OP. Or pussy. That was something that happened a lot in the Grunts, but I thought it unlikely that boom-boom boys had the nuts to bring a girl all the way out here. Still, stranger things had happened.

The point man, O'Farrell, cleared his weapon as he came through the last strand of concertina, grinning at me as he did. He had filled a hundred sandbags two days earlier for failure to observe that little courtesy.

"How was that, Lieutenant?" He leaned his weapon against the parapet as he spoke, reaching for a canteen with his free hand. He was soaking wet with sweat, and breathing heavily from the hump.

I smiled. "Perfect, but you let your makeup run!"

His cammy paint had streaked from his exertion. I handed him one of my canteens. Before I came on watch, they had all been filled with cooler water from a can I kept in my bunker. O'Farrell's were probably ambient temperature, 104 degrees. He gulped about half of it, then poured the rest over his head. The others were arriving, clearing their weapons as they came, one at a time, through the wire. I handed each man a canteen as he came into the trench and motioned them into the shadow of one of the bunkers. Hicks was the last man. He was grinning ear to ear. I handed him the last canteen. "Okay, Hicks. Tell me about it." I tossed him the pack of Marlboros and my lighter as I spoke.

He took one, tossed the pack in the general direction of the team, lit up, then did the same with the lighter. Then he took a long drag, let the smoke out through his nose, and leaned slack against the parapet. "Skipper, we did what you said, only we couldn't see shit in the valley this morning on account of the fog. You know how it hugs the paddies in the morning. By the time it burned off, there were thirty or so Gooners working in the fields. Women from the village came out around midday with shit in baskets, food and water probably, and they gaggled up in the tree lines in threes and fours for chow. Then they went back out to working." He took another long pull on the canteen.

"So, we was getting kind of sleepy. You know how it is when you have to lay in the sun for too long. So we moved around to a shadier spot. And when we started watching again, they had all disappeared from the paddies. So, I started scoping the tree lines and sure enough, they were in there—changing clothes. Swear to God, Lieutenant! We watched them recover their weapons from the trees and shit. Then they formed up and hi-diddle-diddled up the trail at the base of the hill. It had to be the same crew we saw last week. They must have a base camp somewhere up there behind us." He gestured in the general direction of the high ground behind us.

"Did you write up a spot report?"

"Yes, sir! Got it right here in my message pad. Confirmed the grid and everything."

"Corporal Hicks, that is good shit, but we have to think about what to do with it. Take the spot report up to Hannon and have him call it in on the secure net. Make it a flash [high priority] message. Then get your guys cleaned up and fed. You, Ski, and I will have to talk about this some more later this evening. Okay?"

Hicks finished his smoke, fieldstripped the butt, and sent the filter flipping into the twilight sky. I lurched to my feet, recovered my web gear from the bottom of the trench, and gestured for the troops to return my canteens as they moved down the trench to their billets.

As the team filed past me and meandered down the trench, I turned the situation over in my mind. The powers that be would not be keen on shooting up a Model Pacification Village. We had noticed that the villagers came out early, before first light, and were working diligently in the fields until sundown. Since it was a no-fire zone, we had dedicated our efforts to areas where we could shoot. Hicks had pissed in the punch. His discovery made the significance of the NVA interest in the Phu Loc Valley clear. They were farming it! The sly bastards were cultivating USAID rice, using Red Cross tools, and UNICEF irrigation systems. Their working party strolled right by us, shielded from attack by our own safety measures. It was a well-coordinated operation, being conducted right under our noses. It explained why fifty NVA would pass within a few hundred meters of our position and not do anything about us. It was also the sort of news that the multiagency political types were not going to like.

I grabbed O'Farrell's shirt as he passed. "And the lighter, if you don't mind?"

He grinned and passed the tired Zippo back to me. The lighter was my only souvenir from Boot Camp. I remembered carrying the damned thing in my trouser pocket on the long flight from California to the Philippines. The fluid had leaked out at altitude and burned my leg. Smoking was a dirty habit. Still, it gave one something to do with shaky hands.

It had taken Hicks and his team almost an hour to get from their observation post back to the wire. He had used good bushcraft, moving carefully and by a circuitous route, back to our position. The debriefing had taken another ten minutes. By the position of the sun, confirmed by a glance at my watch, I realized that I needed to get moving with the night acts and catch up on Nigeria's plans for the evening. I decided to walk the trench all the way around to the LZ before returning to the command post bunker. That way I could check everybody without getting in the way. Moving around the perimeter, I stopped at each bunker to shoot the breeze with the men gathered around C-rat stoves.

Domnoske caught up with me as I ducked into my bunker. "So what's the scoop on Hicks, Lieutenant?" He followed me into the hootch, and I motioned him to a seat on one of the cots, taking the other for myself. It was dark in the bunker, so I lit a candle with the trusty Zippo, then set about heating some water for coffee mocha. It was the twilight ritual which I looked forward to.

Dropping a match on the heat tab in the bottom of my C-rat stove, I was about to answer, when Wardlow gave the shout, "Test-firing weapons! With a magazine and twenty rounds, load and lock! Prepare to fire! Fire!" His whole team opened up with their M-16s on auto. The cacophony reverberated off the hillside. I put a canteen cup full of water on the stove and motioned Ski outside. "Let's wait 'til Hicks gets here. I'll let him tell you himself."

We went out, into the trench to watch the sunset. Wardlow's night acts were just clearing the wire. I was pleased with their dispersion and caution in movement. If these supervised little routines instilled better bush skills, I'd have done a good job. The last men were clearing the wire when Hannon hollered down from the tower, "Skipper! The Six is on the phone!"

It had not taken long to get a reaction to my flash message. I climbed to the tower and took the radio handset from Hannon's grasp. We were on the secure-voice net. Drumright was a bear under the best of circumstances. I had no comforting thoughts about his possible responses to our message. I expected to take some flak.

"Sunrise, this is Stone Pit Six! Explain yourself, peckerwood! What am I supposed to do with this flash so-called intelligence of yours? Over!" He was pissed.

"Stone Pit, this is Sunrise. Break. No idea, sir—we thought it was important. Over!" Too late to back down.

"Listen, peckerwood! Them boys at division and III MAF will have my ass on this if'n we can't back it up, so you better come up with something."

He believed us. I stared at the handset, waiting for inspiration. None came. Domnoske and Hicks had quietly joined me on the parapet. The sun was about to drop behind the hills. Soon stars would begin to show in a rapidly darkening night sky, and the NVA would start to move into *their* night acts. We had work to do.

"Well, peckerwood!"

"Sir, understand you want corroboration. Over!" I was stalling.

"That's affirmative, Sunrise. Six out!"

I looked at Domnoske, then Hicks. They were staring at me expectantly. I gave the handset to Hannon and turned to scramble down from the bunker into the trench. "Let's go back to my hootch." I spoke the words into space, but Domnoske and Hicks followed close on my heels nonetheless.

Inside the bunker, it was full-on dark. I flipped the trusty Zippo, located another candle by its flickering light, then sat down on the cot to resume my mocha-coffee ritual. "You guys want some?"

They nodded in silence, reaching for canteen cups that were hooked on the overhead beam. While they poured water from a ten-gallon can, I cut chunks off a block of C-4 with my K-bar, dropping a piece in the bottom of each C-rat stove. (C-4 plastic explosive, which burned hotter and without the fumes of heat tabs, was our preferred fuel for heating water. Field cooking was an art form.) Gophers followed (paper matches, called "gophers" because you always had to strike one, then gofer another). With the water heating, we lay back against the rock sides of my bunker in silence, the candlelight throwing flickering shadows on the walls.

"Hey, Mike! We got some Gooners in the crosshairs! Come have a look!" Henry had fallen in love with the IOD. His career was on a fast track. He was known as the hottest forward observer in the AO, or so he had told me. Our combined-arms ambush had made him famous. Knowing more about the Corps than he did, I thought it more likely to have made his colonel famous.

"Light 'em up! I'm busy right now!" I turned to my larder for packages of coffee, cocoa, and creamer, tearing several packs open with one motion and dumping them into my cup. Hicks and Domnoske followed my example, and we sat hunched over the canteen cups, patiently stirring the lumpy mess with pilfered spoons until it resembled coffee mocha. The art was in combining the ingredients to one's taste. It was serious work. Like smoking, it gave you something to do, a distraction from stress.

"Vesper Bells, Vesper Bells, this is Nigeria. Fire mission. Over." Henry was having fun.

The hot cup in my hand, I leaned back against the wall of the bunker and made eye contact with my companions. It was time to talk about consequences. "Well?"

"Maybe we could get some pictures, Skipper. Or a prisoner. It would be a bitch to get a team down there from here, though. You can bet they got security. They watch us just like we watch them, I bet." Domnoske was a very savvy troop. Hicks said nothing. I waited.

"Nigeria, this is Vesper Bells. Send your fire mission. Over!"

I wished Henry would turn the speaker down. Maybe arty guys all went deaf while at the army's school in Fort Sill. I focused on my companions.

"It would be a helluva hump, Lieutenant. Even if we could get down there without them catching us, how would we get back? With a prisoner, I mean?"

Domnoske was thinking out loud. Hicks was just thinking. Finally, he spoke. "We should watch 'em again tomorrow—see where they go. Maybe we could catch a tail-end Charlie, or a straggler. We didn't see where they went today, or how many was in a group. If they split up in threes and fives like they do in the valley, we could snatch somebody off a trail. There is no way we could get out into the valley from here without getting wasted on the way back."

Hicks was also a savvy troop. Neither man had asked why. It was clear to me that they were only thinking about how. I wondered if the others would feel the same way. It was one thing to operate in a group, dealing with an unknown danger. It was quite another to set out deliberately to make contact far removed from support of the larger group. That was why everybody hated listening-post duty; too much imagination could make you crazy with fear. And did, from time to time. Now we were required to use our imagination to gin up a plan that would assure our survival. Like doing homework before a final exam.

"Vesper Bells, this is Nigeria. Fire mission follows. Break. Six troops in the open, HE, VT, fire for effect. Over."

Henry had learned his lessons well. He was going for the kill with the first rounds. With a little luck, the squad of NVA would still be within the five-hundred-meter square he was about to light up when the rounds burst over their heads. I smiled at the thought. "Ski, have you been off the end of this finger, down into the valley?" I was referring to our hill.

"Yes, sir. There's a good trail, but I wouldn't want to use it. The Gooners have probably booby-trapped the lower slope, just to keep us entertained. It would be safer to break brush." There was just no substitute for experience.

"Nigeria, this is Vesper Bells. Shot. Over!" The fireworks were on the way.

"Let's do this—at first light, Hicks, you and I will go out to the LP. We'll take those guys and go back to where you set in to watch yesterday. We'll scope the area and see if we can come up with a plan. Ski, while I'm out, you keep the ranch. I think what we want is a prisoner. What we don't want is to get fucked up in the attempt. Okay?"

They both tipped their heads in assent, sipping from too-hot canteen cups. C-4 could burn your lips right off. It was great for exploding beans and franks, too.

"Nigeria, this is Vesper Bells. Splash. Over!" The arty was about to land.

I snuffed the candle, stood up, cup in hand, and ducked through the poncho blackout drape on the entrance to the bunker. I emerged just as the explosions of the first rounds reverberated through the valley. I turned in the direction of the rolling thunder to enjoy the rest of the fireworks. The valley floor was already in shadows, and the air bursts sparkled momentarily, leaving little puffs of gray smoke in the air over the unfortunate NVA. Hicks and Domnoske followed me out, and we stood together watching the artillery display in the twilight sky. It didn't feel like killing.

Henry was looking for movement or other indications of the effects of the mission. It was getting too dark.

"Nigeria, this is Hostage Igor, inbound—can I be of assistance. Over?"

We heard the distant buzz of the OV-10 far off to the east, as it approached the valley from the sea. The pilot, motoring around with nothing to do, had been monitoring tactical frequencies on his radio, looking for action. He had stayed clear of Henry's fire mission until "Rounds complete." Now, he wanted to inject himself into the action. The Bronco was a speck on the horizon, backlit by the reflection of the sun on the clouds gathered over the ocean. It was Henry's gig, and I let him play it, content to sip my coffee and muse about the predicament I had got us in. Flash, my ass! I should have kept quiet.

Henry asked Hostage Igor for a target damage assessment.

The plane began a diving turn over the target area. As it crossed over the tree line marking the Phu Loc River (stream, really), blue-green tracers arced up from the ground and fell away behind him. The Gooners had some fire support, too, at least one 12.7mm antiaircraft machine gun, with a numbnuts crew. Henry got excited.

"Hostage Igor, this is Nigeria. Break. Break. You are taking ground fire! Over!"

"Roger that, Nigeria. We see 'em." The voice was laconic, as disembodied as the sounds drifting toward us in slow motion, delayed by the physics of distance. We watched as the plane completed its turn and rolled back toward the ground, miniguns streaming 7.62mm shells toward the tree line. The rounds twinkled like Fourth of July sparklers as they impacted the ground. Its firing run complete, the plane banked sharply and turned away from the target, leaving the NVA nothing to shoot at.

Out of ammunition, the aircraft then droned off toward the ocean, leaving us in silence. The aircrew had not been able to determine the results of Henry's fire mission, and the crew-served weapons teams had gone to ground for the night. I imagined that one of my NVA counterparts was slapping the shit out of a trigger-happy gunner about then. "Okay, gents, let's pack it in. Hicks, you meet me here at first light. Ski, get some zees. I'll take the first watch." As I spoke, I dumped the dregs of my mocha over the berm and turned to reenter the bunker. Hicks and Domnoske hung the canteen cups they'd been using on nails in the overhead beam, then left. I sat on my cot, pulling the makeshift map case from the leg pocket of my trousers. I took the flashlight from my web gear and wedged it under a nail in the overhead, turned it on, and studied the map in its yellow beam. How could we get down there without being seen? Or heard? Or shot to shit? The map offered a few clues, but it would take a careful eyeball recon of the terrain to be sure. There was nothing else to do for the moment. I stowed the map in my trouser pocket, broke out a fresh pack of Countrys, turned off the flashlight, and sat in the dark, waiting for my eyes to adjust. After a few moments, I rose, grasping my M-16, and went out to do my troop leader thing.

The night passed uneventfully. Domnoske relieved me just after midnight, and I slept fitfully until first light. I awoke with a start, hearing voices in the trench outside the bunker—Hicks and Domnoske. I splashed some water on my face and poured a measure into my canteen cup. Toothbrush in hand, I ducked through the passageway into slate-gray first light. "Mornin' gents." The words were shaped around the toothbrush. I spat, rinsed my mouth, spat again. "You call Bravo?"

Ski answered, "Yes, sir. They said they need water and chow for the day. Hicks and I were just talking about that."

"Okay. Let's use a couple rucksacks. One case of Cs, eight canteens. Split the load, Hicks. We'll each hump half. And two spare batteries for the Prick-twenty-five. Bring your binos. I'll be ready in ten mikes." I turned to reenter the bunker. "And Ski—tell 'em to bring in their claymores right now. Okay?" Walking up on the team was one thing, and dangerous. Walking in on the team with its claymores still armed was right foolish.

Inside the bunker, I poured a liberal dose of bug juice in the palms of my hands, mashed some cammy stick in it, and smeared the mess liberally over my face, neck, and the sides of my head, even my ears. (Troops liked to be artistic with their war paint. I just wanted to be invisible. I let nature do the streaking for me.) Then I pulled on a utility jacket, shrugged into my war gear, checked the load in my M-16, and re-emerged into the morning sun—Little Mikey Hodgins, Reluctant Warrior.

Hicks and Domnoske were at the north end of the trench, deep in conversation when I approached. "All set?"

"Yes sir, all set."

Hicks was already burdened with his own war gear and one of the rucksacks. Domnoske hefted the other onto my back. I pulled the shoulder straps tight, and we set off, Hicks in the lead. I let him clear the wire before I left the perimeter. It was a precautionary technique to which I was partial. Perimeter wire was a notoriously bad place to be caught by a sniper. That there were none in the Que Sons was a leap of faith taken only by the most foolish. Hicks acted like he expected me to join him, but I gestured him onward. I followed, never closer than fifteen meters to his broad back.

It took us ten minutes to link up with the team. They had, indeed, used up all their chow and water. The harbor site looked like a badly policed picnic area. We distributed the rations and water, and I had them police up the immediate area so as not to invite too much attention (from rats, rock apes, or the NVA).

We then moved on down the finger to spy on our farmers. It was already hot, and the fog had evaporated from the valley floor. And lo! There were farmers.

Hicks and I spent the better part of the morning engrossed in sketching a diagram of the fields, dikes, trails, and landmarks in our objective area. I took compass readings to different landmarks in the immediate area, orienting the scenery to the contour lines of the map. When we were done, we had an approach route, a possible ambush site, and an extract LZ. We just didn't know if the Slopes were going to play. I decided to leave Hicks with the team to watch the NVA withdrawal from the fields, while I went back to the pos to do some more homework. The missing ingredients would fall into place as the day progressed.

Back in my hootch, I rolled up the poncho blackout drapes on the parapet to let in what breeze there was, and made some preliminary notes. From our vantage point on the end of the finger, we could clearly see a major trail junction. It was marked by a solitary rock formation which we referred to as the "big black rock," actually a jumble of volcanic wreckage that stuck up out of the surrounding brush and elephant grass like an obelisk. On my map, it had its own contour line. While it was doubtful that it could be seen from ground level in the brush, we could certainly use it as a navigation marker and a fire-control boundary. I decided to register it as a preplanned fire later in the day.

The area north and east of the big black rock was elephant grass and low brush, fairly open and sloping toward the rice paddies we were watching. The trails leading out of the rice paddies converged on either side of the rock, merging into the single trail running up the gorge a klick east of 425. The trail was masked from our observation by higher ground. Five hundred meters or so north of the rock there were several shelled-out hootches, with dry rice paddies on their perimeter. Our farmers would have to cross the open area, probably on the dikes, to get into the mountains. Hicks had reported them doing this the day before. The tree line (a bamboo windbreak) he had scoped ran more or less east to west along the northern boundary of the dry paddies. The rice paddies under cultivation were within the no-fire zone marked on my map. In my mind, that was no accident.

The thing to do would be to set up a snatch right at the trail junction, south and east of the rock. As the crow flies, it was less than two klicks from OP 425. If we could get off the hill in the dark, get into position while the Gooners were doing their agricultural thing—I needed two teams. One to spot and one to grab. I needed fire support, and I needed an extract for the snatch team. I needed to talk to Chip Gregson in Operations! No sooner had I conjured the thought of coordinating with the battalion operations center, then the proximity of higher authority came crashing in on my reverie.

"Skipper! Chopper inbound! It's the Six!"

As Hannon shouted the news, my ears detected the familiar clatter of rotors approaching from the southwest. I was a mess, and so was the pos, in all probability. Fuck! I took a deep breath, grabbed a soft cover, and headed for the HLZ—what could he do? Send me back to the Grunts?

Domnoske joined me at the end of the trench. He must have been a mind reader.

"No sweat, Skipper. We got the place all spiffed up this morning. Everybody's working."

He had done his share of field-grade visits. The package orbited over the valley, as one CH-46 dropped out of the sky and flared to a landing over a plume of scarlet smoke on our HLZ. Drumright rushed off the ramp, CAR-15 clutched in his left fist, his right holding his cover on his head. Hunched against the rotor blast as the bird lifted off over the valley, he rushed toward the wire. At least the pilot was tactical. Leaving the bird on the LZ would have made us all nervous—too beautiful a target for NVA mortars.

"Hodge, show me whatcha got, and make it quick, boy. That bird will be back down here in ten minutes. They are picking up some dudes from An Hoa, then they'll be back for me. I want to see these NVA farmers for myself!" He bellowed his thought as he rushed past me up the trench.

I turned to follow, speaking thoughts I hadn't yet articulated to myself. "The name is Hodgins, sir—Charlie Company.

Lieutenant Hodge is with the ROKs [Republic of Korea Marine Brigade]."

Arms akimbo, Drumright glared at me. I decided maybe it would be better if he didn't remember my name. I took a deep breath, then rushed on. "Sir, we've got a team down the finger watching them, but it's four hundred meters from here. We couldn't get down there in ten minutes. I can show you the general area with the IOD, but the area in question is masked by the slope of the hill, sir. We've been working on a plan to get some proof, sir. In fact, I was about to run the idea past Lieutenant Gregson when the colonel dropped in."

He turned on me abruptly, belligerent, his jaw jutting forward in what I had come to know as his "show me" stance. "Well, peckerwood?"

I felt bile rise in my throat. "We think we can snatch a prisoner, sir." My stomach churned.

"You can do that?" He had relaxed his stance a little.

"Yes, sir. We can do that."

He had not perceived my trauma. Iron Mike, bullshitting The Man. I locked eyes with Domnoske over the colonel's shoulder. His was a quizzical look.

"Show me!" Drumright turned and rushed up the sandbag steps into the IOD tower. Ski and I followed. We gaggled around the FO's map board. A fortuitous decision, as he had all the no-fire zones, preplanned fires, etc., neatly annotated on it. I scanned the map quickly, locating the big black rock and the position of our outpost.

"Sir, this is the area where the NVA are doing their farming." I pointed to the spot with a grease pencil.

"This is the spot where Corporal Hicks is maintaining visual contact with them. He's using the ship's binoculars, so it's like watching them through a microscope. They don't know we can do that. There are several trails leading off the paddies, sir, but they all converge in the vicinity of this rock formation. There is a trail junction just south of it that can be observed from our OP. In fact, we can see everything they do from the ville to just south of the trail junction before the trail slopes up into the draw, here." I pointed to the spot on the map.

The colonel was silent. I continued. "We think we can get a team off the hill in the dark, move into position at the trail junction, and snatch a straggler or a tail-end Charlie tomorrow afternoon. With a good fire-support plan and an extract from this area [I pointed to a promising area near the ambush site], sir. It could be done, sir." I fell silent, waiting for the axe to fall.

"Sunrise, Sunrise, this is Swift Two-Two inbound your pos for one pack. How about a brief. Over!" The squawk of the PRC-25 speaker broke the silence of the colonel's musings. His ride had arrived. Hannon grabbed the handset of the auxiliary radio, answering the call as he picked up the backpack and climbed over the berm. He headed down the trench toward the HLZ. The aircraft orbited overhead. Troop talk and the steady *chuck, chuck, chuck* of shovels filling sandbags drifted on the morning air. Drumright's silence went on, seemingly interminable. He studied the map. Then he looked at Ski. Ski said nothing. He looked at the map some more. Finally, he turned on me. "Set it up. Get your plan, your air request, your fire-support request to the Three [operations officer] by fifteen hundred [3:00 P.M.]. I'll make a decision after I see your stuff."

He picked up his weapon and turned abruptly to leave the tower. Hannon had preceeded him and was talking the CH-46 down when we arrived. Without a backward glance, Drumright clutched his cover, hunched his shoulder into the rotor wash, and dashed aboard the helicopter. As the bird lifted away, I felt my stomach lurch again. What now, Lieutenant?

The silence following the departure of Drumright's helicopter was palpable. Everyone on the hill felt that something was afoot. Our lives were about to change. As some not well remembered philosopher had remarked, the fortunes of war were about to fuck with us again. I wondered if Drumright was aware of his impact, if he knew that he had goaded me into taking a risk with the lives of my Marines. I thought not, and cursed myself for letting him con me into a stupid gesture. The troops were right—"It don't mean nothin'!"

Hannon was struggling up the trench with the auxiliary radio. I stopped him at the berm, taking the handset from him. "Set the channel back to Tac Two and leave it in my hootch."

Hannon set the PRC-25 on the sandbags and twisted the dials to the proper setting without saying a word. He had already deduced that something shitty was going to happen, that I was going to do this shitty thing, that where I went, he went. Therefore, something shitty was going to happen to him. His facial expression conveyed all this, and volumes more—wordlessly.

I decided to get cleaned up and let my magnificent tactical mind do its thing. I knew the solution would come to me. I looked at Mickey Mouse. It was 1100. I ducked through the poncho blackout drape into my hootch, determined to take a nap and let the plan take shape in my subconscious. But sleep would not come. Instead, I composed the message, to be sent over the secure-voice net, which would seal my fate:

Date: 221300H May 1970

(1) Situation: Enemy has been observed farming the Phu Loc Valley. G-2 requires substantiation of report.

(2) Mission: Conduct a prisoner snatch vicinity grid BT003473.

(3) Concept of Operations: Snatch team composed of one NCO and four enlisted volunteers will depart OP Sunrise under cover of darkness, move north 800 meters to assembly area, vicinity grid BT001472, by 230400H [first light]. Support team, composed of one NCO and four enlisted, will establish an OP, vicinity grid BT001467 NLT 230430H. Support team will maintain visual contact with NVA moving in objective area, and will identify target of opportunity for snatch team. Support team will provide fire support, using organic weapons, to isolate the objective area for the snatch team. Upon execution of the snatch, snatch team will withdraw to HLZ, vicinity grid BT001475, for extraction by helicopter. Support team will provide fire support for withdrawal of snatch team and will coordinate extract.

(4) Admin/Logistics: Per SOP and verbal.

(5) Comm/Electronics: Call sign for snatch team is Sunrise Bravo. Call sign for support team is Sunrise Charlie. Radio Relay is Sunrise. Freqs per SOP.

Short and sweet, like my life. I added a fire-support request and an air request on the message pad, using the handy-dandy Platoon Leader's Notebook outlines I had pilfered from the Basic School. (Field Manuals—FMs—were sometimes good for more than toilet paper.) I went out, climbed into the tower and gave the yellow notes to the arty RTO, who had taken over from Hannon. It was "fuckin' hot out," and most of the troops had sought the shelter of the bunkers. I did as well, wishing that I had not given up thumb-sucking as a child. We were way over our heads.

"Sunrise, this is Sunrise Bravo. Over!"

The crackle of the handset jolted me into consciousness. My watch said it was 1600. I had been asleep for more than two hours. "Sunrise Bravo, this is Sunrise Actual. Over!"

I was brisk, turning to look out over the valley as I spoke. I realized, waiting for the reply, that I had subconsciously turned to gaze in the direction of the big, black rock.

"Sunrise, this is Bravo." I recognized Hicks's voice. "Skipper, they did it again! Over!" He was excited.

"Bravo, this is Sunrise Actual. Break. Secure your activity and return to this pos. Break. Clean up that area before you secure. Don't leave anything behind. Over."

I kept my voice laconic, unemotional, but inside, I was churning. The NVA had repeated their pattern leaving the rice paddies. If the snatch didn't go off, I would use the artillery again. I smiled at the thought of a battery TOT on the big black rock. It was a much more expedient solution—just kill 'em. Like the phoenix, my confidence was rising.

"Roger that! Out!"

"Lieutenant!" It was the arty RTO. "We got Stone Pit on the hook for you. They want the Actual!" It was an unusual request and the arty RTO was curious. So was everyone else. I lurched up into the tower, and took the handset from his outstretched hand. It was the secure-voice net. Serious talk. I took a deep breath and answered up.

"That you, peckerwood?" Drumright was direct and forceful in all things, and he was clearly in no mood for chitchat. "I got yer note. It's a go. The Alpha here has a target list for you. Your extract will be on ten-minute standby. You will position yourself to coordinate the entire operation. Break. You copy? Over!"

I keyed the handset, bile rising in my throat. "Aye, aye, sir. Sunrise out." I handed the handset back to the RTO. The tac net crackled to life as I turned to look out over the valley.

"Sunrise, this is Sunrise Bravo. Request permission to pass the wire. Over."

Hicks was back. The RTO did his thing, and within seconds yellow smoke was wafting in the waning light. There was work to do.

The troops were showing signs of life. That is, they were cooking and joking. I hollered for Domnoske and went back in the hootch to get my mocha going. We had plenty of time. I also had some serious leadership issues to deal with, most notably: Who was going to do the snatch? My first instinct was to do it myself. Drumright must have sensed that, because he had given me "guidance." I was not a fire-team leader. I could not coordinate the maneuver unit, the support unit, the artillery, and the aircraft from a position with the snatch team; I would be taking myself out of the movie. I wondered if the troops would see it that way. Probably not.

Domnoske broke in on my reverie. "You want me, Skipper?"

"Yeah, Ski. The snatch is a go. So when Hicks gets back, I want to talk to you and all the team leaders in here. Make sure everybody has chow before they come down. Crawford has the night acts tonight, right?"

"Yes, sir. He's getting them ready now." (Domnoske was always a step ahead of me.)

I nodded my acceptance. "Okay, let's say we have our chalk talk at eighteen thirty."

"Aye, aye, sir!" He turned to leave, the quizzical look still on his face.

The water was boiling, so I put mental energy into refining my recipe. Events would unfold in the fullness of time. I took the hot cup, my map case, and a grease pencil outside, and stood in the parapet sipping my cocoa, making notes on the acetate in the twilight. It was busy work. Around me, the troops were getting ready for another "night in the perimeter defense," to the tempo of Janis Joplin: "Daddy's goin' to buy me a diamond ring . . ." Eventually I poured the dregs of my tepid mocha mess over the berm and went back inside the hootch to await the arrival of the NCOs.

They announced their arrival in unison. They were in good spirits, crowding into the bunker as one and taking seats on the extra cots. It was a ritual we had used frequently during our time together on the hill, but this was a little different—at least in my mind. I sat up on my cot as they settled in. "Okay, gents, the smoking lamp is lit." I tossed my pack of Countrys to Hicks, who took one and passed the pack along. When it got back to me, I lit up, exhaled slowly, and resumed speaking. "The snatch is a go. We have approval to do it tomorrow."

Cigarettes forgotten, all eyes were on me. I took another drag, and continued. "The plan is to send a team down the hill tonight, off the north finger, to a harbor site at the base of the hill. In the morning, we send a support team with the ship's binoculars out to the same place we used today. They spot for the snatch team, while the snatch team moves into position at that big trail junction we scoped this afternoon. That will be after we see if the fuckin' farmers are out there. Come the afternoon, the support team will identify a suitable target, talk 'em into the ambush site, and presto! We snatch one. After the snatch, we ziggy out to an HLZ right here," I pointed to the spot on my sketch, "blow the shit out of everything behind us, and swoop. Questions?"

There was silence. I waited. Finally, Hicks spoke. "So who does what, Lieutenant?"

"Good question. The snatch team has to be volunteers. Ski, why don't you guys go talk it over, and get back to me in, say, forty mikes?"

The quizzical look remained in their faces. They stood in unison and left. I took a final drag on my cigarette, pinched it out, stripped the butt, and flicked it into a shadowy corner of the bunker. There was a rustle of movement—a rat, no doubt, eavesdropping on our plans. This lieutenant-shit sucks. The thought lingered in my mind as I reclined on my cot in the flickering candlelight, waiting to see if I was facing a mutiny or not.

They were back in less than half the allotted time.

"Sir, the thing is, everybody wants to go on the snatch. But that wouldn't be fair, sir, 'cause my team did all the shit work, and we was the ones that found the Gooners in the first place! So . . ." Hicks fell silent in frustration. I sat back on the cot. This was not the kind of problem I had foreseen. I looked at Domnoske, willing him to participate. Crawford and Wardlow were also silent.

"Well, sir, everybody thinks it would be tits to smoke some Gooners. We been doin' shit work up here for days now. But Hicks has a good point." Always the diplomat, Domnoske fell silent, short of a recommendation.

"Okay. Hicks, you've got the snatch team. Ski, you've got the support team. Corporal Crawford, you and Corporal Smedley Butler* here," I gestured at Hicks, "get together outside to coordinate getting your night act and his snatch team out on the ridge. Sergeant Wardlow, that leaves you with CP security tomorrow, and your guys stand the wire tonight. Okay?"

I stood up. They did too. "Hicks, give your guys a warning order, then come back here when you're ready to go. Ski, you stay. Gents, it's a pleasure doin' business with you!"

They went out, all but Domnoske.

"So?" I wanted a candid assessment.

"Well, sir, Hicks is gung ho, and so is his team. But, they got no trigger time. As a matter of fact, the only guys up here with firefight experience are me, Bro Jones, Moreno, and yourself, sir. I think we should save those guys for the second half, if there has to be one. They were with Lieutenant Skibbe. Wardlow has been on a lot of patrols, so has Crawford. And they've

---

*Smedley Butler, near-legendary Marine, awarded two congressional medals of honor; hence a hero.

seen people get whacked, booby traps, and what not. We lost a couple guys that way last time we were up here. But they're not real squared away, like with maps and stuff, if you get my meaning. So Hicks is the man. With him in charge, they'll go where you say go and do what you say do. I couldn't say that about everybody, Lieutenant."

He paused, as if about to add something, but remained silent.

"What else?" This was a good troop. If I got his enthusiastic support, I would have everyone else's.

"Well, sir. I was just wondering about fire support and the extract. Lot of times, the heavies say one thing and do something else. If we get these guys down there and start a firefight, the NVA will be all over them like flies on shit. I would feel better if we had some kind of backup plan for supporting them. Why couldn't we take one of the fifty-cals out there, you know, with the T & E on it like you showed us. We could bag it in and cover their flanks—keep the Gooners from coming across the open area, and we could take the right flank away, too." His eyes bore into mine in the flickering candlelight.

"That is a good idea. I put in a target request for the corners [four directions] around the snatch site, but we can't register them ahead of time. And getting a clearance to shoot that close to the ville could be a bitch. The fifty is organic weapons; we can use it. Okay, have Crawford's team hump a thousand rounds, the tripod, and the T & E out to the observation site when he goes out tonight. We'll take the gun and another two hundred rounds with us in the morning. I don't want it outside the wire at night. Anything else?"

"No, sir."

"Okay, let's go see the costumes."

He stood up, grasping his weapon, and turned toward the entrance to the bunker. I stood, shrugged into my war gear, snuffed the candles, and we went out to inspect the teams. There was extra work to do, breaking out ammo and distributing the additional load among the men going out to the LP. I stood quietly in the background, assessing attitudes while Domnoske directed the work. Finally, Hicks separated himself from the darker shadows that were the team and spoke to me in muted tones. "We're ready, sir."

"Okay. Get a comm check before you leave the wire and again when you get to the LP. Do not leave the LP until I give you a go. Got it?" I stared hard at him, but could not determine his mood under the painted face. "What's your heading off the LP?"

"Two degrees, magnetic, sir—'til we get to the bottom." He grinned.

"Good! And Hicks, take your time. Be quiet. Move *one* man at a time, cover each other, but keep your weapons safed. You've got all night to get down there, and I do not want to haul some asshole back up here with a broken ankle, or blow the whole gig with an accidental discharge. Understand?"

He laughed. "Me neither, Lieutenant!"

He turned to join the milling group in the trench, while I climbed into the IOD tower. Hannon was already there, and he handed me a steaming cup of mocha java as I dropped my war gear in a corner. I tapped the arty FO, the salty sergeant E-5, on the shoulder, then moved in front of him to swing the IOD around. It was like daylight through the image intensifier. I counted my men out through the wire, watching as they moved, single file, out of sight. Nine reluctant warriors, nearly half my force. I turned the IOD back to the arty FO and climbed over the berm to take a seat on the sandbags, my back against the tower. I settled in to wait, wishing I could smoke.

"Sunrise, this is Sunrise Alpha. Radio check. Over!" They were at the LP.

They would be getting ready to move on, dumping the extra ammo, sorting themselves out, waiting for the go. I gestured to Hannon, who passed over the handset. It weighed ten thousand pounds. "Alpha, this is Sunrise Actual. Golf. Over."

"Sunrise, this is Alpha. Roger Golf. Out." They set out.

I dozed off, only to be awakened by the staccato of M-16s on full auto, interspersed with the characteristic *crack, crack, crack* of AKs and a resounding *whump* from an M-26 hand grenade. Then silence. From the direction of the sounds, it could only be

Bravo. And they had fired first. The radio crackled to life as troops spilled out of their bunkers to take up fighting positions. From down the finger, I heard shouts.

Into the night, I shouted, "Hold your fire! Nobody shoot! We have friendlies outside the wire!"

I grabbed the radio handset from Hannon's outstretched hand. "Sunrise Alpha, this is Sunrise Actual. Sitrep, please?" I kept my voice calm, though my pulse throbbed in my ears.

"Skipper, this is Hicks! We ran into a sapper squad—at least five of 'em. With an RPG! Everybody's okay. We're back at the LP. Over!" He was gasping for breath.

If not for hearing the AKs, I would have had trouble accepting the coincidence and would have interpreted the activity as an attempt by the snatch team to get out of the mission because it had been "compromised" by the enemy. It was damned odd.

"Roger that, Alpha. Sit tight. And use proper comm procedure! Sunrise out!" The thing to do was to chill everybody out and start over. How best to do that? I turned to Henry, who had joined me unbidden on the roof of the CP bunker.

"Get me a battery-two on Charlie Zulu one sixty-three."

I wanted him to call in a fire mission on one of our pre-planned targets at the base of the hill. I reasoned that the Gooners would run downhill, probably the way they had come up. With luck, we could catch them with the arty. And it would make Hicks and company more comfortable. I was going to send them back down the hill.

Henry turned to do his thing, and I focused on reenergizing my snatch team. "Alpha, this is Sunrise Actual. Over." I peered into the darkness, willing Hicks to answer up.

Came the whispered reply, "Sunrise, this is Alpha. Over." It was Hicks. His diction was slower, and he was using procedure.

"Alpha, this is Sunrise. Break. We're going to run a Fox Mike below you. Keep your heads down. Over."

"Sunrise, this is Alpha. Roger that. Out." They are puckered assholes about now, I thought to myself, and so am I.

"Nigeria, this is Quizmaster Delta. Shot. Over!"

Henry's bunkies were hot to go tonight. He answered up, swinging the IOD in the direction of the target.

The characteristic swoosh of the rounds alerted us to their impact. The explosions first sparkled, then thundered up from the valley floor. Far off, we could see the muzzle flashes of the 105mm howitzers at An Hoa as they delivered the mail. It was eerie. But, now that the fireworks were over, I told Hicks to continue the mission.

They set out again, albeit with less enthusiasm. It was payback time.

Hicks and his team made it down the hill and into their harbor site with no further incident, although it took them until almost first light. The rest of us took turns at watch and fitful naps. As the sun broke over the horizon, Domnoske mustered his support team. A prisoner of my own thoughts, I watched them move out through the wire. It was going to be an interesting day, and hot. As the sun rose, it was already over eighty degrees.

We made the LP/OP switch without incident, although I could see that the troops were tired and apprehensive. It would be a good day to fuck off. With that thought in mind, I summoned Wardlow and gave him instructions for a skeleton perimeter watch. We would let the arty guys and the soldiers do the security work for the day. All he had to do was stage the water cans for the afternoon resupply bird. He smiled at the prospect of bearing such good news to the troops, and set off to do his duty. I relaxed in the shade of one of the bunkers, the PRC-25 close at hand, to monitor my snatch. Events would now unfold on a course unknown.

"Sunrise, this is Sunrise Charlie. Over!"

Domnoske startled me into wakefulness. He had observed the NVA following the same pattern. They were now out in the fields, and he had seen no traffic for what seemed to be a safe period of time.

It was time for Hicks to move into his ambush site. I took the handset. "Charlie, this is Sunrise. Roger your last. Break. Sunrise Alpha, this is Sunrise. Golf. Over!"

"Sunrise, this is Alpha. Roger, Golf. Break. Charlie, this is Bravo. Comm check. Over!" Hicks was moving. He wanted to be sure he could talk to his spotter. So did I.

"Alpha, this is Charlie. Gotcha five-by! How me? Over."

"Same, same. Alpha out."

Hicks and his team were moving cautiously in the direction of the ambush site we had selected the night before. What I did not know was that they had used up all their water while waiting. In the aftermath of the firefight on the hill, and the exertion of the climb down the draw in the dark, they had failed to ration their water. It was one hundred degrees, and they were down to their last canteens. What Hicks did not know was that he would make the last four hundred meters to the trail in a low crawl, through heavy brush and elephant grass.

Domnoske was watching the trails in the vicinity of our ambush site and the activity in the rice paddies to the north and east of Alpha. The plan required him to monitor the NVA activity continuously, so as to alert the team to any movement in its proximity. He was using the ship's binoculars, which made the area of the trail junction look like a zoom photo. So it was a big surprise when the outline of an NVA soldier, complete with magazine vest, pith helmet, and AK-53 assault rifle,* jumped into his close-up. A trail guard, not fifty meters from our proposed ambush! Domnoske acted immediately.

"Alpha, this is Charlie. Break. Sit down. Over!"

I was instantly alert, pulling on my war gear as I stood up. Hannon rose with my motion. I gestured him back to his pears and pound cake. "Sit tight! I'm going to stroll on down to Ski's OP." I shrugged into the rucksack housing the PRC-25, grasped my weapon and set out.

"Charlie, this is Alpha. Roger that! What's the buzz? Over."

"We spotted a guard at the trail junction. Wait. Out. Break. Sunrise, this is Charlie. Over!" Domnoske was smooth, his voice slack but confident.

"Charlie, this is Sunrise Actual. Break. Coming in. Over."

"Roger that! Charlie out."

Domnoske's detail had scattered about the forward slope of its little finger, erecting poncho-liner hootches to shelter themselves from the sun. As camouflage went, they had done a

---

*Like an AK-47 but with a folding metal stock.

good job, accidentally. They were on the lee side of most of the big rocks, tunneled under the brush like lizards. Two guys, on rear security, grinned up at me over C-rat snacks as I approached the position. Domnoske had the binos on a tripod, sandbagged and shaded by a poncho liner. They had dug a pit for the .50-cal. and had it bagged as well. Ammo boxes, the lids off, were neatly positioned near the gun.

I shrugged out of my gear and bellied in beside him. "Whatcha got, Ski?"

He moved aside for me to take a look. As I focused the binos, Gomer leaped into view. He was leaning up against a rock, in the shade, smoking. His weapon was three feet away, near what appeared to be a cooking fire. From the look of his position, it was a permanent post.

"See anybody else?" I was thinking about whether or not there was a detail, or a relief, for this dead guy. I had already decided to kill him.

"No, sir. But we've only been watching him for twenty minutes or so. From the looks of his pos, though, I'd say he was a loner for the day. They probably drop him off in the morning and pick him up on the way back."

"Where is Hicks?" It was becoming a geometry problem.

"Don't know, exactly. That's why I told him to sit down." Domnoske was staring at me, the quizzical look again.

"Okay." I recovered the handset from my radio. "Alpha, this is Sunrise Actual, posrep. Over."

Hicks answered up immediately. "No fuckin' idea, Skipper! We been crawling around in here for hours. Can't see shit! Over."

Once a civilian—"Chill out, Alpha. Break. Find a spot where you got sunlight and flash your signal mirror at the hill. How copy? Over."

"Roger that. Wait. Out." Hicks was game, just green. I hoped that was true of his companions as well. If not, they were going to die today.

I pulled the map case out of the leg pocket of my trousers as I spoke. Domnoske recovered his compass from the breast pocket of his jacket at the same time. (Great tactical minds think alike!) I handed him the map, waiting for Hicks to comply.

"Stand by, Sunrise. Over!"

"Do it!" I dropped the handset to scan with my 7x50s the area where we expected him to be, to no avail.

Ski did the same. "I got 'em, Lieutenant. They went too far north."

First rule of land navigation—make allowances for gravity. In the dark, the team had drifted farther down slope than we had planned. The good news was that they were too far from the trail to be compromised. The bad news was that they were too far from the trail.

"I think the IOD can see them." Domnoske was on the right track, and I seized the idea. Switching channels on my radio, I summoned Jesus. "Nigeria, Nigeria, Sunrise Actual. Over!"

"Sunrise, this is Nigeria." It was the salty sergeant. He sounded half-asleep.

"Get your Actual on the hook! Over."

To Domnoske, I said, "Tell Hicks what we're gonna do."

He complied, using the other radio. While I waited for Henry, I shackled up a rough grid and bearing for Bravo's position, jotting the letters on my map case with a grease pencil. Finally, Henry spoke up. "Sunrise, this is Nigeria. Send your traffic. Over." Having been awakened from a sound sleep, Henry was irritable.

I passed the grid to Henry and he read it back to me. "Now what, Sunrise?"

"Alpha will flash a mirror at you in two mikes. Get a fix on them with your toy. Over."

I gestured to Domnoske, who passed the word to Hicks.

"Roger that. Nigeria out."

Within minutes, Hicks had a solid fix on his location and realized his predicament. Domnoske gave him a vector to the ambush site. We resumed our surveillance of the valley, while Hicks and his team broke brush to make up for lost time. They were more than a klick from their objective. It was getting late in the day. Murphy's Law, with all its corollaries was working its magic on my game plan.

"Charlie, this is Alpha. Over!" It was Hicks, huffing and puffing.

I keyed the handset. "Alpha, this is Sunrise Actual. Send your traffic. Over."

Domnoske was kicking my boot to get my attention. "Skipper, check this out! The tree line, three fingers east of the big dike! (He was using hand/eye calculations to help me find the spot with my binoculars.) I see three Gooners. Two with rifles, one in jammies with a pistol belt and a handbag—maybe a map case. Looks like they're escorting him."

"Character Whiskey is a heat casualty. Break. We need to take a break. Over!"

Hicks had been moving for the better part of an hour. He was clearly stressed. With the binos to my eyes, I keyed the handset, searching for Domnoske's Gooners and answering Hicks at the same time. I found them immediately fascinating. They were moving away from the tree line at a moderate pace, taking one of the paddy-dike trails leading south across our coveted open area. These guys were going to walk right in on Hicks—with a little luck. I scanned the rice paddies. Our farmers were beginning to regroup in the tree line, leaving their labors in twos and threes. They would be starting back across the open area soon, rearmed.

"Alpha, this is Sunrise Actual. Roger that. Break. Find a clear overhead and give us another flash. Over!" I needed to know exactly where he was. "Ski, check out our trail guard."

Far off to the northeast, a pair of specks moved across the horizon. The characteristic clatter of their rotors identified them in my subconscious as CH-46s—probably headed for An Hoa, or maybe it was our resupply. The thought drifted to the back of my mind as I concentrated on locating Hicks.

The flash came from less than fifty meters off the trail we had focused on—good man! He was still in heavy elephant grass. From our vantage point, I could just make out where the trail left the paddy dike and disappeared into brush. Our Gooners were still more than three hundred meters away—plenty of time.

"Lieutenant, the trail guard is up and about. He's moved

down in front of the big black rock on the east side of the trail—looks like he's scoping the rice paddies. Probably looking for his buddies—now he's moving back to the cook fire . . ." Domnoske droned on, giving me the play-by-play.

I focused on Hicks. "Alpha, this is Sunrise Actual. Over!" I whispered, emphatically.

"Send your traffic, Sunrise," Hicks whispered back.

"You are less than fifty meters due west of your objective. We have a target in sight. ETA your pos, fifteen mikes. Break. I want you to move into position in the low crawl now. Break. Put your blooper on the right flank. Be quiet about it. How copy? Over." I wanted him to do it without thinking too much.

"Roger that. Alpha out." There was a long pause. "Sunrise, this is Alpha. We have the trail in sight, but there's no cover out there. We're ten meters off the trail. Over." Hicks was shaky.

I looked at Domnoske. "Where are our Gooners?"

"They're just coming up off the dike. He should be able to see them any minute."

"Alpha, this is Sunrise. Over." I whispered, but overhead I heard the clatter of helicopter rotors. I looked back in the direction of 425. Smoke was billowing off the HLZ. Our resupply birds were inbound.

"Sunrise, this is Alpha."

"Alpha, you got three Gooners moving north on the trail in front of you, and a trail guard near the big black rock. When you have these characters in sight, key your handset two distinct times." I waited. The birds circled behind and above us. Finally, the handset squelched.

"Roger, Alpha. When you have 'em as close as you can, shoot the escorts and grab the guy in the middle. Use the blooper on the trail guard. Over."

The handset squelched, two distinct times. Then all hell broke loose. There was a flurry of small arms, mostly M-16s, and a pair of explosions from the blooper. The CH-46s were lifting off over the valley.

"Sunrise, this is Alpha! We got 'em! We got two and cold-cocked this other motherfucker! We're taking fire from north and south. I got two guys in a bad way from heat! Over!" Hicks was doing okay.

"Alpha, this is Sunrise Actual. Break. Find a hole and sit tight. Come back on Tac One. I say again, Tac One. Over!"

Domnoske was already switching the frequency on his radio. I tossed him my handset, and took the other from his outstretched hand. He had turned away from me without a glance, taking a position behind the .50-cal. He was already chugging three-round bursts into the brush around our big black rock. The rounds seemed to hang in the air forever as they raced down into the valley. The NVA would think twice before rushing Hicks from that direction.

"Aircraft leaving Sunrise, this is Sunrise Actual. Say your call sign. Over!" Improvisation was the key to success. Drumright had said there would be an extract package on ten minute standby; I had aircraft overhead. It was no contest: a bird in the hand . . .

"Sunrise Actual, this is Swift Four-One. Break. We've been monitoring your net. How can we help. Over?"

Domnoske peered through the ship's binoculars, then shifted his fire to the open area north of Hicks. Our farmers had become light infantry. I deduced from his action that they were closing on Hicks from across the rice paddies. We had no place to run.

"Swift Four-One, this is Sunrise Actual. Break. We have a team in contact, vicinity grid zero-zero-three-four-seven-three, call sign Sunrise Alpha. Break. They have a prisoner and two heat casualties. How about a lift? Over."

The silence lasted forever. Domnoske kept up a steady *chunk, chunk, chunk* with the fifty. The helicopters were still moving off down the valley, toward Da Nang. I saw them change course, begin to orbit.

"Sunrise, this is Swift Four-One. Give us a brief. Over!" The bird was already orbiting over Hicks, high over Hicks.

"Alpha, this is Sunrise Actual. Do you copy Swift Four-One? Over." With luck, I had not lost comm with Hicks on the frequency change.

"Sunrise Actual, this is Alpha. We copy, but we can't see

shit. We're in some rocks, with elephant grass all around. I don't think the Gooners know where we are. Over!"

"Sunrise Alpha, this is Swift Four-One. Can you mark your position? Over."

"Swift Four-One, this is Alpha. We can pop smoke. Over."

"Alpha, this is Sunrise Actual. Negative, smoke. Use your mirror. Over!" If the NVA moving across the open area did not know where Hicks was at the moment, they certainly would when the smoke went up.

"Swift Four-One, this is Sunrise Actual. Break. We have the entire area under observation and fire. There are twenty-five to thirty NVA closing on Alpha's position from the north and east. We need to get them out now. Over!"

"Roger that, Sunrise. Break. Alpha, give us the mirror and get ready to hussle."

The lead bird tightened its spiral and dropped like a rock toward the valley floor. Hicks's mirror flashed as the birds approached, their door guns flickering streams of tracer into the surrounding brush. The first aircraft was on the ground, the second orbiting, guns ablaze for what seemed an eternity and might have lasted forty seconds. Then both aircraft lunged into the sky, climbing in spirals away from the melee.

"Ski! Have Nigeria hose everything in there. I'm going back to the pos. Bring all this shit back with you. Okay?" I shrugged into my war gear and moved off up the hill. Behind me, I heard Domnoske ramrodding the troops into breaking down the position. He was doing the call for fire, simultaneously. Fucker should have my job, I thought to myself as I trudged up the hill. Swift Four-One was setting down over a cloud of purple smoke as I approached the perimeter.

By the time I got inside the wire, Hicks and his team had drawn a crowd on the HLZ. The birds had departed. I moved through the position to join the throng. They had brought trophies and souvenirs. The prisoner, trussed like a Christmas goose, lay facedown in the gravel. He was bound with duct tape, gagged, and blindfolded. Next to him was the body of one of his escorts, his torso torn asunder from a tumbling round.

Scattered on the ground were paraphernalia and equipment taken from the dead NVA—a bedroll, magazine pouches, some documents, a satchel, a pistol belt, an SKS rifle. Hicks was engaged in an animated after-action report, taking slugs of water from a canteen as he held forth. The troops were passing an AK-47 from man to man. I saw that the stock was shattered. As I approached, two of the team members rolled the dead NVA onto his back, stuck a cigarette in his mouth and struck a pose for the camera Hannon was wielding.

"Secure that shit, Hannon. No more pictures, and take the butt out of Gomer's face. I want you to send a spot report on this, and an air request. Tell Stone Pit we need transport for one POW, probably VC infrastructure [VCI], and captured equipment. Wardlow, strip the prisoner and get an inventory of all his gear. Do the same to Gomer. Hicks, get your guys to the corpsman. Make sure everybody is wet down and hydrated, including your ugly ass. Then come tell me about your adventure."

I took the AK-47 from one of the troops to examine the stock. It had been split by a gunshot. I held it up to Hicks, the question unspoken.

"Three rounds, sir. Ten meters. I couldn't miss!" He grinned.

Not necessarily so, I thought to myself.

The troops broke up into twos and threes, setting about their assigned tasks while still engaged in animated discourse. They had met the enemy, and prevailed. That it was a grim, nasty job had not occurred to them yet. Nor had the fact that their elation was out of context. The aftermath of violence had its own morality. They had stalked, suffered, and killed. It felt great to be alive! So they celebrated survival while the prisoner lay mute in his own feces.

Watching them, I felt the tension drain out of me. We had done the deed. More important, everyone was back, with all their body parts. It was great for morale—payback. In two weeks' time, we had twenty-nine confirmed kills, six by small arms, two "individual weapons captured," and a prisoner with documents and equipment. We had met the enemy, and kicked his ass. Now we needed to regroup, tighten up. Third Herd would rotate back to Camp Reasoner in the morning. Within forty-eight hours, most of these guys would be back in the bush, myself included. I slumped into a supine position atop the command-post bunker and lit up a Country, vaguely aware of the concussions of artillery rounds impacting in the valley. Henry was finishing our fire mission. It would be another "TDA NFI" (target damage assessment: no fucking idea); they had waited too long for the helicopters to clear the area.

"Skipper! I got Stone Pit on the phone! They say nix, nix on the forty-six. Bring the Slope down with us in the morning."

Hannon was leaning over the berm from inside the tower. I sighed, flipped the still smoking butt of my cigarette into space, and stood up.

"Okay, Hannon. Tell 'em we copy."

EPILOGUE

10 NOVEMBER 1995

No epilogue, I pray you; for your play needs no excuse.

Shakespeare

My memory of the events chronicled in *Reluctant Warrior* was freshened by official Marine Corps documents (Patrol Reports, Command Chronologies, COC Logs, Operational Summaries, etc.), by reference to historical publications, by letters and diaries written at the time by men with whom I served, and by personal interviews with some of those men. I confess to having used "artistic license" in developing the narrative, in an effort to create for the reader the essence of the relationships which existed at the time. I also confess to having left out of this account many of the individuals with whom I served. Twenty-six years is a long time to retain names, faces, and details of each man's origins or personality, even those with whom I formed a close personal bond at the time.

Third Herd was extracted by helicopter on the morning of 25 May 1970. We were replaced by Chief Pino and the Second Platoon. We left our dead NVA on the LZ, with a note:

Dear 2d Plt: This is Gomer. We shot him. You bury him. Welcome to Indian Country! Love, 3d Herd

We brought our prisoner, our captured gear, and a new attitude home with us to Camp Reasoner. Morale was high. In a mere two weeks, the platoon had transformed itself from a motley collection of individuals into a cohesive unit. The competition and coordination that evolved between the teams during the daily routine of our deployment produced a sense of comradery among the troops. They developed confidence in one another, and to greater or lesser degrees, in me. Our results were credible: twenty-nine enemy KIA by combined arms, six by small arms; a prisoner; weapons, documents, and equipment captured.* We had planned and carried out several complex tactical engagements with the NVA and suffered no friendly casualties, an achievement of which I was particularly pleased. Our combined-arms ambush in the Phu Loc valley turned out to be a significant event, disrupting the infiltration of elements of the NVA 82B Division. At a different stage of the war, our effort might have been exploited, made into a decisive engagement by III MAF. For the time, it was enough to have interdicted the enemy movement.

Sergeant Domnoske went home. He left us all better than he found us. Third Platoon, Company C, 1st Reconnaissance Battalion carried on, with me in charge, for another seventy-six eventful days. I left them, feeling guilt and remorse at my good fortune, on August 14, 1970. I've thought about them often over the years. The bond we formed is as strong today as then. They were ordinary young Americans from all walks of life who answered their nation's call to arms, endured unimaginable hardships and accomplished extraordinary feats in a war where the outcome had already been determined. They fought and suffered for no personal gain, with no aspirations other than to survive and come home. It was a goal I shared with them. In the words of another Marine:

". . . I did not pick these men. They were delivered by fate and the U.S. Marine Corps. But I know them in a way I

*According to official Marine Corps documents, 3d Plt, Co. C, 1st Recon Bn (Rein) accounted for thirty-five (35) of the six hundred four (604) VC/NVA killed by 1st Mar Div during the month of May 1970.

know not other men. I have never since given anyone
such trust. They were willing to guard something more
precious than my life. They would have carried, by reputation, the memory of me. It was part of the bargain
we made, the reason we were so willing to die for one
another."

These Good Men, Michael Norman

Semper Fidelis!

APPENDIX ONE
I CORPS

CIRCA 1970

The Front is everywhere.

Maxim of Guerrilla War

During the war in Vietnam, military planners partitioned the country into regions to facilitate command and control of the forces operating therein. The five northernmost provinces became the I Corps Tactical Zone (ICTZ). Because the bulk of the combat forces operating there were Marines, the forces deployed in ICTZ were placed under the unified command of a Marine Corps Lieutenant General in a joint service task force known as III Marine Amphibious Force (III MAF). In the summer of 1969, III MAF was composed of two Marine Infantry Divisions (3d Mar Div and 1st Mar Div), two U.S. Army Infantry Divisions (101st Airborne and Americal) with associated support units (50,000 men), a Marine Corps Airwing (1st MAW) with over 400 aircraft and 12,000 men, a Force Logistics Command (FLC) with 7,600 Marine support personnel, and another 2,000 Marines in the Combined Action Force (CAF). Augmenting his own force, the Marine Commander of III MAF could call upon the services of an additional 28,000 support personnel from all branches of the U.S. military, a 6,000 man Republic of Korea Marine Brigade (ROK), 41,000 troops from the Army of the Republic of Vietnam (ARVNs), 65,000 Regional Forces (RFs) and People's

Self Defense Forces (PFs), and two carrier battle groups of the U.S. Navy. The mission of III MAF was to "defend" the ICTZ, which included, from north to south, the provinces of Quang Tri, Thua Thien, Quang Nam, Quang Tin, and Quang Ngai.

Upon receipt of their orders to begin redeployment (withdrawal) of U.S. Forces from Vietnam in the fall of 1969, the III MAF staff devised a plan for the defense of the ICTZ which took into account both the tactical situation then extant and the political reality back in the World. Published in December 1969, the plan was known as the III MAF/ICTZ Combined Plan for 1970. It was a voluminous piece of staff work that provided the doctrinal guidance to be used by all allied commanders in the deployment of their forces within the region. The Plan envisioned the coordinated employment of American, Korean, and ARVN regular force units within the ICTZ to "engage and destroy VC/NVA Main force units, neutralize their base areas and keep them away from populated areas." While indigenous forces and the national police concentrated on the guerrillas, Allied regulars would take the fight to the enemy. Their major task would be the "neutralization of the enemy's base areas—usually located deep in the mountain regions—which housed its headquarters, communications centers, supply dumps, training and rest camps, and hospitals."

The III MAF/ICTZ Combined Plan for 1970 stressed the concept of territorial security, the separation of the Viet Cong and NVA forces from the civilian population, as the focal objective of all allied military activity. To this end, every type of allied unit was assigned a security function in or around their cantonments, which were, or became, collocated with the indigenous population. The Plan stated that, "when not engaged in mobile operations against enemy main force units and/or base areas, allied forces are to patrol constantly to block infiltration into the fringes of cities, towns, and areas adjacent to population centers." This effort was referred to as "pacification", and became the focal activity of most maneuver units, since main force opposition was hard to find and even harder to fight once found. Pacification required Herculean coordination efforts, at least in the minds of those who dreamed it up. Thus,

ICTZ, in order to be pacified, had to be classified into one of four security categories: (1) Secure Areas, heavily populated areas where civil government functioned, commerce thrived, people were free to move about day and night, and enemy activity had been reduced to occasional acts of terrorism, rocket, and mortar assaults; (2) Consolidation Zones, where enemy main forces had been expelled, ARVN and National Police were in the process of destroying VC infrastructure, strict curfews and other population control measures were in effect, and terrorism and attacks by fire were frequent, RF, PF, PSDF, and National Police under Vietnamese politicos had responsibility for the maintenance of order; (3) Clearing Zones, "Indian Country," sparsely populated areas (the result of relocation programs, among other things), free fire zones where allied forces maneuvered to locate and destroy enemy main force elements, where the population was considered to be sympathetic to or under the influence of the enemy, where most of the farms were; (4) The Border Surveillance Zone, the mountainous hinterland, where most of the bad guys were. In each province of ICORPS, a mixture of these classifications was used to help determine the allocation of military resources. In general, support facilities were located in the Secure Areas and Consolidation Zones. These areas were mostly in the eastern piedmont and coastal plain, in proximity to, or collocated in, indigenous population centers. The Clearing Zones and Border Surveillance Zones encompassed much of the piedmont and all the mountainous hinterland that bordered the Republic.

By early 1970, the III MAF effort in ICORPS had contracted to an area concentrated around Da Nang, which became the 1st Mar Div's Tactical Area of Responsibility/Reconnaissance Zone (TAOR/RZ). It included over 1,050 square miles, encompassing all of Quang Nam Province and parts of Thua Thien and Quang Tin, from the South China Sea in the East to the Laotian Border in the West, and from the Hai Van Peninsula in the North to the Que Sons Valley in the South. Over a million indigenous Vietnamese lived in it, some 400,000 in and around the city of Da Nang and the balance in the coastal lowlands and river valleys south and southwest of the city. The Marines were flanked both north and south by U.S. Army units, the 101st Airborne and the American Division, respectively. Guided by the Plan, 1st Mar Div (Rein) planners partitioned the Division's TAOR/RZ into sectors, using natural boundaries and barriers to facilitate command, control, and coordination of military activities. Each of the Division's four Infantry Regiments was assigned a sector of responsibility within which they would conduct operations against the "evil and elusive Communist enemy." For the Grunts, these boundaries shaped the limits of their combat activities. In general, the Infantry Regiments were assigned TAORs which formed concentric circles expanding outward from what was termed the Da Nang Vital Sector (DVS), tied in at each flank with the Army Divisions assigned to III MAF. While the Army and Marine contingents operated under a unified command there were innumerable ARVN and other commands within ICTZ, both military and civilian, with which the U.S. commanders were required to coordinate operations. On paper, this deployment of forces "defended" key installations and population centers. From a theoretical point of view, it was great staff work, a textbook application of combat power.

Implementation of the Plan in central ICTZ became the task of the 1st Mar Div Commanding General, Maj. Gen. Edwin B. Wheeler. General Wheeler well understood the tactical situation facing the Marines in his command, and his mission sounded simple enough. 1st Mar Div was to "locate, interdict, and destroy enemy forces, bases, logistical installations, infiltration routes, and LOC [Lines of Communication] within the assigned TAOR/RZ." In addition, the division was to provide security for the city of Da Nang, and provide training and support for the revitalization of indigenous forces, the ARVN. All this, and prepare for the orderly withdrawal of the force on a timetable to be determined. For political reasons, this was to be done with minimal casualties and fanfare. General Wheeler soon realized that his new mission was a veritable Pandora's Box. The box had two components, ICORPS and the 1st Mar Div (Rein). One was awash in NVA. The other was showing symptoms of a serious breakdown in morale and discipline. After consultation with his staff, Wheeler mulled the issues in his mind and concluded that he would adopt what is known in the military trades as an "economy of force" game plan. A key element of the solution to his tactical dilemma would be an operational concept known as Stingray.

Maj. Gen. Ray Davis had used the concept with great success in the 3d Mar Div area of operations, saturating the enemy base areas with numerous small, highly mobile, and heavily armed patrols supported by air and artillery assets. Using heliborne insertion and clandestine patrolling techniques, these teams were able to operate deep in the enemy's territory, where they could engage enemy units with supporting arms, or ambush them, as well as provide intelligence on the enemy's facilities, activities, and whereabouts for use in large scale operations. Use of the reconnaissance assets in this way had been necessitated by the terrain in northern ICORPS, which was mountainous and heavily forested. The Recon teams were used to find, fix and/or maintain contact with main force NVA units until larger forces could be moved from staging areas near the coast to engage the enemy. Southern ICORPS presented a different tactical problem. Whereas the 3d Mar Div had an offensive mission and relatively little in the way of a population to defend, 1st Mar Div had to contend with the Da Nang Vital Sector and a large indigenous population. And, of course, the mission had changed. General Wheeler was required to deploy his Infantry Battalions in the lowlands to defend a multitude of fixed installations and to interdict efforts by the NVA and Viet Cong to infiltrate populated areas. This required that his forces be fragmented, widely dispersed and, therefore, immobile and lacking in combat power. The Marines in their cantonments were sitting ducks for enemy rocket and mortar attacks, for sappers, for snipers. Their patrolling efforts were channeled, making it easy for the enemy to inflict casualties using booby traps and ambushes. It was not the way Marines were taught to fight, and Wheeler knew that he would need to keep the enemy off balance and out of his Vital Zone if he was to have any chance to revitalize his Division. An adaptation of Stingray was just the ticket.

General Wheeler decided to adopt the concept in his 1st Mar Div Reconnaissance Battalion. Wheeler wanted a highly skilled, aggressive force, willing and able to take the fight to the bush, and a commander to lead it. He decided to get the commander and let him worry about the troops. He picked Lt. Col. William C. Drumright, known to his peers, friend and foe alike, as "Wild Bill." Drumright was a warrior, known throughout the service for his aggressive leadership style, physical courage, and charisma. Drumright had commanded an Infantry Battalion and the Reconnaissance Battalion in 2d Mar Div under Wheeler, and was currently doing an admirable job as CO of BLT 2/26 in the mountainous northern sector of the division TAOR. Drumright was a proven combat leader. He knew the turf. He was available. Wheeler summoned Drumright to the Division Command Post shortly before Christmas, 1969, told him what he wanted, then waited for Drumright's response. After a day of mulling over his options, Drumright went back to General Wheeler with a plan. It was the essence of simplicity. In Drumright's mind, the general was asking him to create a new kind of fighting force, a modern raider battalion. Drumright envisioned a highly skilled, aggressive force, willing and able to find and fight the enemy in his own backyard. But, to create such a force would require months of training and indoctrination in new tactics. There was no time for that. He had to make do with what was available, people he could count on. Like his general, Drumright's solution was to pick his leaders, the most aggressive, best-trained people available to him—Marine lieutenants with at least six months of hard Grunt (Infantry) experience.

"General, I can do what you want. I can make 'em fight. But I am goin' to need lots of fire support, and I mean dedicated assets . . . Direct Support Artillery . . . none of this 'wait your turn' bullshit. And I'm going to need dedicated air support . . . All day, everyday, twenty-four hours a day. My boys has got to know that if 'n they get in the shit, we are gonna get them out! And I need peckerwoods. I want guys who have proven themselves in fuckin' fire fights, no pussies, no staff pukes. I want authority to hire, fire and recruit—no questions asked. I want my pick from Two–twenty-six first, then wherever else we find 'em. These peckerwoods [lieutenants] are the best-trained people we got over here right now, General. You do this for me, I'll kick ever lovin' NVA ass!"

Drumright's presentation was less than smooth, but then, the situation did not call for smooth. It called for bold action. And although his leadership style was controversial, Drumright's tactical intuition was brilliant. He reasoned, correctly, that the best-trained small-unit leaders available to him were Marine lieutenants. They were extensively trained in small units tactics, scouting and patrolling, land navigation, the use of supporting arms. Those whom he could bring over from the Infantry would have endured their trials by fire. They were generally idealistic and likely to follow orders (go where they were told to go and do there what they were told to do). With proper coordination of the division's air and artillery support, these peckerwoods and the hand-picked Marines of 1st Recon Bn (Rein) could and would raise hell in the NVA base areas. Drumright liked the idea of turning these "Dogs of War" loose in the bush. So did his general.

The "Dogs" referred to were the forty odd officers and six hundred enlisted men on the rolls of 1st Recon Bn (Rein). The battalion, over strength at the time, comprised a Headquarters and Service (H&S Co.) and five operating companies, Alpha, Bravo, Charlie, Delta, and Echo (Co A, 5th Recon Bn). Each letter company was composed of a headquarters element (two officers, two Staff NCOs and a half dozen lesser ranks) and three reconnaissance platoons with one officer and twenty-one enlisted men each. Each recon platoon was made up of three teams and a headquarters element (Platoon Leader, Platoon Sergeant, and Guide). There were typically six men assigned to each team, including corpsmen. The typical recon team consisted of a Patrol Leader, an Assistant Patrol Leader, a Point Man, a Primary Radio Operator (RTO), a Secondary Radio Operator, a Corpsman and a "Tail End Charlie", another Scout/ Rifleman. The Battalion made a practice of making up an extra team in each platoon. This was done by having the Platoon Leader, the Platoon Sergeant and selected NCOs act as patrol leaders, and task organizing the teams from within the platoon according to the mission requirements. The teams were further reinforced by attachments from the ROK Marines and from the ARVN Rangers who were training with the battalion.

Maj. Gen. Wheeler tasked Drumright with keeping not less than thirty teams in the field at all times. In addition, the Battalion was required to man four fortified observation posts (OPs) located on key terrain features overlooking the major avenues of approach into the population centers of the 1st Mar Div TAOR. The OPs were to become cornerstones of the new tactical orientation of the Division. Each of these OPs required a platoon (Rein) of Marines from one of the letter companies. It was therefore not uncommon for a company to have one platoon on the OP, a platoon in training/refitting for the field and eight teams in the bush. The platoons in each company rotated through this routine on a six week cycle, spending about two weeks in each phase. Patrols were planned to span five to seven days from insert to extract, but were often impacted (shortened or extended) by tactical considerations (contact with the enemy for example), illness, accidents or weather. (Bad weather extended patrols, enemy action shortened them.) In order to meet these operational requirements, the battalion devised and published an operations schedule, a tasking of commitments for personnel and support organizations, which included a training schedule, a patrolling schedule, an OP garrison schedule and assorted special events (dog and pony shows for visiting VIPs, Emergency Reaction Force, etcetera). This was all done according to an Operations Plan which was developed in coordination with higher headquarters. The Battalion Commander, in the greater scheme of things, was a staff advisor to the Commanding General (CG), and like the Regimental Commanders, he was tasked directly with general (and sometimes specific) operational requirements.

Within the battalion, there was a substantial body of operational know-how in various techniques for deploying and supporting the teams. This trade craft had evolved and been passed down by word of mouth and example over a period of years. The team composition and equipment, the communications package, the helicopter and fixed wing air support, the artillery liaison, and the general scheme of maneuver for recon teams had been finetuned through trial and error over the years. Each Staff Section (S1, S2, S3, S4) retained enough knowledgeable people to pass on the SOP (Standard Operating Procedures) for their support function. Staff Officers and NCOs were responsible for ensuring that the requisite support activities were coordinated with the Operations Plan. Aircraft, artillery, and communications assets were available, tailored for the recon mission. But prior to Drumright's arrival the battalion, so organized, had been used as the division's "eyes and ears" in the RZ. Morale in the battalion was low, discipline lax. It did not have the "culture of the warrior."

Drumright changed all that. Within minutes of assuming command on January 27, 1970, Drumright set about changing the tenor and tempo of the battalion's operations. He made it known immediately that there was a new sheriff in town! His first order of business was to shake the place up. He began by screening the OQRs (Officer Qualification Records) of all the lieutenants assigned to the battalion, looking for those who had not been going to the field. He found ten who had been in the battalion for an extended time without going on patrol, and had them reassigned to Division the same day. He made some telephone calls to the G-1 and to friends in 26th Marines, and arranged to have some of his "talent" reassigned to 1st Recon Bn. Then he went prowling through the battalion area, "kicking over the trash cans." Everywhere he went, he raised havoc, galvanizing the troops, SNCOs and Officers into a state of anxiety. The following morning, he convened a staff conference, the first of what would become a daily trauma for attendees, to lay out the law. Within a few days, he had the battalion tightened up and focused on his game plan. His purpose was two-fold: to make the troops more afraid of him than they were of the enemy, and to make the Staff take care of the troops. He believed in leadership by example. He wanted his officers in the field to be as he himself intended to be. He wanted life in the rear to be orderly and oriented toward making the Teams' time in the rear productive and rejuvenating. He wanted the teams to be aggressive in taking the fight to the enemy. To do that they had to have faith in their support and believe some-one would get them out of any trouble they started. Drum-right's solution was to lead by example. During the ensuing eight months, he rode the emergency extract package to every fire fight he could find and terrorized the staff on a daily basis. He hired and fired like Genghis Khan, sparing no one, especially himself. His "reign of terror" masked an abiding love of his men, his country, and his Corps, and produced one of the most successful tactical efforts of the war.

APPENDIX TWO
PATROL REPORT
FOR TURF CLUB

```
OPERATION ORDER: 0381-70              1ST RECONNAISSANCE BN.
PATROL: TURF CLUB  CO. C.             DA NANG, RVN.
DEBRIEFER: GYSGT OTTINGER             121430H APRIL 1970
MAPS: VIETNAM 1:50,000 AMS L7014
      SHEET 6540 I
```

PATROL REPORT

1. SIZE, COMPOSITION AND EQUIPMENT:
   - A. COMPOSITION: 1 OFF, 5 ENL, 1 USN.
   - B. SPECIAL ATTACHMENTS: 1 ARVN ENL.
   - C. COMM AND OBSERVATION EQUIP: 2 PRC-25, 1 PRC-93, 1 7X50.
   - D. SPECIAL EQUIP: 1 M-79, 2 CLAMORES.

2. MISSION: CONDUCT RECONNAISSANCE AND SURVEILLANCE OPERATIONS WITHIN YOUR ASSIGNED HAVEN TO DETECT POSSIBLE VC/NVA TROOP MOVEMENT OR ARMS INFILTRATION AND BE PREPARED TO CALL AND ADJUST AIR/ARTILLERY ON ALL TARGETS OF OPPORTUNITY.

3. TIME OF DEPARTURE AND RETURN: 101330H/121400H

4. ROUTE: SEE ATTACHED OVERLAY.

5. SYNOPSIS: THIS PATROL COVERED A PERIOD OF 48.5 HOURS WITH 2 SIGHTINGS OF 5 VC/NVA. TEAM MADE 2 CONTACTS WITH 3 ENEMY RESULTING IN 2 ENEMY KIA AND 1 POW WITH 5 PACKS, 2 PISTOLS, 1 HOLSTER, MEDICAL SUPPLIES, DOCUMENTS AND MESS GEAR CAPTURED. NO FIRE MISSIONS WERE CALLED. TEAM WAS INSERTED BY HELICOPTERS AND EXTRACTED BY LADDER.

6. OBSERVATION OF ENEMY AND TERRAIN:

   A. ENEMY:

   120930H VIC. ZC 182627 TEAM WAS IN A CLEARING OFF A TRAIL WHEN THEY OBSERVED 1 VC/NVA WEARING GREEN SHIRT AND BROWN SHORTS CARRYING LARGE PACK MOVING EAST ON TRAIL. TEAM FIRED AT ENEMY WITH SMALL ARMS AND HE RETREATED TO THE WEST. TEAM PURSUED ENEMY FINDING MESS GEAR ALONG TRAIL BUT NO SIGN OF THE ENEMY. TEAM MOVED SOUTHWEST ON TRAIL TO VIC. ZC 182625 WHERE THEY SET UP A 360 DEGREE SECURITY SITE WHEN THEY OBSERVED 2 VC/NVA WEARING GREEN UTILITIES, SANDALS, CARRYING LARGE PACKS AND PISTOLS, MOVING NW ON TRAIL. TEAM FIRED ON ENEMY WITH SMALL ARMS RESULTING IN 2 ENEMY KIA AND 1 ENEMY CAPTURED. AFTER CAPTURING ENEMY TEAM MOVED TO VIC. ZC 180627 WHERE TEAM WAS EXTRACTED BY LADDER AT 1400H.

PAGE 1 OF 3 PAGES

2ND LT. HOLGINS
RIFLE CLUB, CO. C
PATROL LEADER

B. TERRAIN: AREA WAS GENERALLY VERY STEEP WITH 100-200'
CANOPY AND SECONDARY GROWTH, 30' CONSISTING OF VINES, SMALL
BUSHES, BAMBOO, ELEPHANT GRASS, BOULDERS, THORNS AND THICK
BUSHES. MOVEMENT WITHIN PATROL AREA WAS DIFFICULT AVERAGING
150 METERS PER HOUR. WATER WAS IN THE AREA IN THIS AREA AND
WAS NOT SEASONAL. ANIMAL LIFE CONSISTED OF ROCK-APES AND DUCKS.
GROUND SOIL CONSISTED OF HARD RED CLAY AND SAND. STREAM BEDS
CONSISTED MOSTLY OF ROCKS AND SAND.

7. OTHER INFORMATION: INSERT LZ: VIC. ZC 175649 WAS A FAIR
MULTI CH LZ MEASURING APPROXIMATELY 300X800 METERS. LZ AREA
CONSISTED OF 15' ELEPHANT GRASS. BEST APPROACH TO THIS ZONE
WAS FROM THE EAST. EXTRACT LZ: VIC. ZC 180627. LADDER ZONE
TRAILS: VIC. ZC 178 ZC. 178 ZC 1862. (1) WIDE AND RUNNING IN
ALL DIRECTIONS, WELL KEPT RECENTLY USED 10-15 APRIL. COMMUN-
ICATION WITHIN PATROL AREA WAS FAIR WITH VESPER BELLS, COFFEE
TIME, TAKE OUT AND SIERRA RELAY. MISC: TEAM OBSERVED WARNING
DEVICE VIC. ZC 181625 ON TRAIL INDICATING BAMBOO VIPER. SOME
TRAILS WERE MARKED OFF AND HAD GATES AND PUNJI STAKES WHICH
APPEARED TO BE APPROXIMATELY 2-3 WEEKS OLD AND INDICATED
MOVEMENT IN AN EASTERLY DIRECTION.

8. RESULTS OF ENCOUNTERS WITH THE ENEMY: 1 WIA/KIA AND 1
POW.

9. CONDITION OF THE PATROL: GOOD WITH 1 NBC.

10. CONCLUSIONS AND RECOMMENDATIONS: PATROL LEADER STATES
LAND NAVIGATION IS EXTREMELY DIFFICULT DUE TO CANOPY THEREFORE
IT IS IMPERATIVE THAT ARTILLERY MARK POSITIONS.

11. EFFECTIVENESS OF SUPPORTING ARMS: NO SUPPORTING ARMS WERE
UTILIZED.

12. DEBRIEFER COMMENTS: NONE

13. PATROL MEMBERS:

2ND LT.	HOLGINS	0109887	LCPL	FINCHUM	2574741
CPL	REILLY	2373855	HM2	PRESTON	B716010
SGT	COUTURE	1937233	SGT	THI (ARVN)	
LCPL	NICHOLS				
PFC	WARD	2528136			

PAGE 2 OF 3 PAGES

ENCLOSURE (5)
DOWNGRADE TO UNCLASS AFTER 6
MONTHS LAW OF NAVINST 5500.10

APPENDIX THREE
PATROL REPORT
FOR SUNRISE

Copy No. 2 of 13 Copies
1st Reconnaissance Battalion
DA NANG, REPUBLIC of VIETNAM
061435H May 1970

091370

Ref: (a) Map(s),Vietnam,Sheet(s),6640 1V
(b) DivO P03000.4
(c) 1stMarDivO P3800.1G (Intelligence SOP)
(d) 1stMarDivO P003330.2A (Rules of engagement)
(e) DivWarning Order #0518-70

Call Sign: SUNRISE C -

1. Situation (a) See current INTSUM's
(b) See current OPSUM's & PIR's
(c) Attachments: NONE

2. Mission. Conduct reconnaissance and surveillance operations within
assigned haven to detect possible VC/NVA troop movement or arms
infiltration and be prepared to call and adjust air/arty on all targets
of opportunity.

3. Execution. Depart LZ 401 on 18 May;insert haven UL(AT9947)LR(BT0145).
Extract on 24 May within same haven. Coordinating instructions are contained
in references (b) and (e).

4. Admin/Logistics. References (b) and verbal.

5. Comm/Electronics. Primary Freq: 30.5 Alt: 30.9
Artillery:ALL FM's WILL GOTHROUGH
FO TEAM NIGERIA

Tm leaders will ensure that no patrol member draws or carries more than
three days of shackle sheets. Shackle sheets will be turned into Comm
immediately after debrief.

Radio Relay: VESPER BELLS -
ZULU

W.C. GREGSON
By direction

Distribution:
CO, 11thMar   (1)
CO, 7thMar   (1)
Div FSCC   (1)
Recon S-3   (4)
CO,Co. "C"   (2)
WAGONS SIX S-2   (2)
Div G-2   (2)

A-12

CONFIDENTIAL NOFORN

OPERATION ORDER: 0518-70   1ST RECONNAISSANCE BN
PATROL: SUNRISE, CO. C   DA NANG, RVN
DEBRIEFER: GYSGT OTTINGER   241100H MAY 1970
MAPS: VIETNAM 1:50,000 AMS L7014
   SHEET 6640 IV

                    PATROL OVERLAY

1. SIZE, COMPOSITION AND EQUIPMENT:
   A. COMPOSITION: 1 OFF, 22 ENL, 1 USN
   B. SPECIAL ATTACHMENTS: NONE
   C. COMM AND OBSERVATION EQUIP: 2 PRC-25, PRC-77, KY-38
   D. SPECIAL EQUIP: 1 M-14, 3 M-79, 36 CLAYMORES

2. MISSION: CONDUCT RECONNAISSANCE AND SURVEILLANCE OPERATIONS
WITHIN YOUR ASSIGNED RIVER TO DETECT VC/NVA TROOP MOVEMENT OR
ARMS INFILTRATION AND BE PREPARED TO CALL AND ADJUST AIR/ARTY
ON ALL TARGETS OF OPPORTUNITY.

3. TIME OF DEPARTURE AND RETURN: 100930H/240930H

4. ROUTE: OP HILL 425

5. SYNOPSIS: THIS PATROL COVERED A PERIOD OF 336 HOURS WITH
2 SIGHTINGS OF 4 VC/NVA, 1 ANTI-AIRCRAFT POSITION AND 1 BUNKER
NATIVE CONTACTS WITH THE ENEMY. TEAM UTILIZED SUPPORTING ARMS OF AO
AND ARTY WITH EXCELLENT COVERAGE OF ALL TARGETS. TEAM WAS INSERTED
AND EXTRACTED BY HELICOPTER.

6. OBSERVATION OF ENEMY AND TERRAIN:

   A. ENEMY:

101830H VIC. BT026484 TEAM SIGHTED 10 VC/NVA WEARING DARK UTILITIES
WITH 4 PACKS, 5 RIFLES AND 1 POSSIBLE MORTAR TUBE STANDING AROUND
A TREE NEAR A HOOTCH. HIGHEST TEAM CALLED FIRE MISSION WITH
EXCELLENT COVERAGE OF TARGET AREA NEGATIVE OBSERVATION DUE TO
DARKNESS, BUT NOTED A POSSIBLE SECONDARY EXPLOSION.

110638H VIC. BT028482 TEAM SIGHTED 2 VC/NVA WEARING DARK UTILITIES
WITH NEGATIVE EQUIPMENT WALKING NORTH TO SOUTH ALONG TREELINE.
AO WAS CALL ON STATION FIRED 1 BURST OF MINI-GUN THEN CALLED OFF
STATION. THERE WAS NEGATIVE OBSERVATION DUE TO TERRAIN.

110910H VIC. AT978448 TEAM SIGHTED 2 VC/NVA WEARING GREEN UTILITIES
WITH NEGATIVE EQUIPMENT RUNNING NORTHEAST TO SOUTHWEST THRU PADDIES
INTO TREELINE. HOSTAGE STUD CAME ON STATION AND CALLED FIXED WING.
FIXED WING DELIVERED ON BOARD ORDNANCE ON TARGET BUT NEGATIVE
OBSERVATION DUE TO SMOKE AND HEAVY FOLIAGE.

                    ENCLOSURE (3)
PAGE 1 OF 5 PAGES   DOWNGRADE TO UNCLAS AFTER 6 MONTHS
PTL RPT # 102   IAW OPNAVINST 5500.40

LT HODGINS
SUNRISE, CO. G
PATROL LEADER

6. ENEMY CON'T:

111730H VIC. BT02284866 TEAM SIGHTED 4 VC/NVA WEARING DARK UTILITIES
AND NEGATIVE EQUIPMENT STANDING IN TREELINE. CALLED FIRE MISSION
AND RECEIVED GOOD COVERAGE OF TARGET AREA. THERE WAS NEGATIVE
OBSERVATION DUE TO DARKNESS.

111930H VIC. AT986470 TEAM SIGHTED 52 VC/NVA UNIFORMS AND EQUIPMENT
WERE UNOBSERVED, WALKING WEST TO EAST ALONG CANAL. HODGINS CALLED
FIRE MISSION BUT ROUNDS WERE NOT EFFECTIVE THEN BATTERY CHECKED
WHEN AO CAME ON STATION. TEAM PINNED ENEMY DOWN WITH 50 CAL. AND
60MM FIRE WHILE WAITING FOR ARTY. AO COVERED TARGET AREA WITH
OUTSTANDING COVERAGE OF THE AREA. AO REPORTED TAKING FIRE FROM THE
TREE LINE. ARTY CONTINUED AFTER AO HAD DELIVERED ALL ON BOARD
ORDNANCE. ARTY CHECKED WHEN AO RETURNED TO TARGET AREA. TEAM
DIRECTED AO TO INITIAL ENEMY SIGHTING. AO EXPENDED ON BOARD ORDNANCE
ON TARGET AREA. WITH NEGATIVE OBSERVATION DUE TO DARKNESS AND OVERCAST.

121955H VIC. AT986470 TEAM SIGHTED 5 VC/NVA, UNIFORMS AND EQUIPMENT
UNOBSERVED, MOVING WEST TO EAST ALONG CANAL. NEGATIVE FIRE MISSION
DUE TO ENEMY MOVING TOO FAST.

122009H VIC. BT09488 TEAM SIGHTED 6 VC/NVA, UNIFORM AND EQUIPMENT
UNOBSERVED, MOVING WEST TO EAST ON TRAIL. RECEIVED NEGATIVE CLEARANCE
FOR FIRE MISSION DUE TO CLOSE PROXIMITY OF A VILLE.

130611H VIC. AT946443 TEAM SIGHTED 10 VC/NVA MOVING NORTH TO SOUTH
ON TRAIL WEARING DARK UTILITIES AND 1 PACK WAS SEEN. CALLED FIRE
MISSION BUT 9 OF THE ENEMY WERE OUT OF THE TARGET AREA BEFORE THE
FIRST ROUNDS HIT. THE 1 ENEMY REMAINING DOVE INTO A HOLE WHEN THE
FIRE MISSION STARTED. POOR COVERAGE OF THE AREA AND NEGATIVE
OBSERVATION DUE TO TERRAIN.

131645H VIC. BT006464 TEAM SIGHTED 50 VC/NVA, UNIFORMS AND EQUIPMENT
UNOBSERVED, MOVING NORTH TO SOUTH. CALLED FIRE MISSION WITH 1ST
ROUND 1,000 METERS FROM TARGET ADJUSTED WITH POOR COVERAGE OF THE
AREA.

131920H VIC. AT981464 TEAM SIGHTED 33 VC/NVA, UNIFORMS WERE UNOBSERVED
BUT ENEMY WAS CARRYING PACKS AND RIFLES, MOVING WEST TO EAST ON TRAIL.
CALLED AO AND FIRE MISSION BUT RECEIVED NEGATIVE AO DUE TO HIGHER
PRIORITY MISSION. ARTY HAD EXCELLENT COVERAGE OF THE AREA RESULTING
IN 9 ENEMY KIA'S.

ENDORSEME (3)
DOWNGRADE TO UNCLAS AFTER 6 MONTHS
IAW OPNAVINST 5500.40

LT HODGINS
SUNRISE, CO. C
PATROL LEADER

6. ENEMY CONT:

132127 VIC. AT985475 TEAM SIGHTED 9 VC/NVA, UNIFORMS AND EQUIPMENT UNOBSERVED, MOVING WEST TO EAST ON TRAIL. NIGERIA CALLED FIRE MISSION BUT NEGATIVE OBSERVATION DUE TO DARKNESS.

132140H VIC. AT993473 TEAM SIGHTED 4 VC/NVA, UNIFORMS AND EQUIPMENT WERE UNOBSERVED, MOVING EAST TO WEST ON TRAIL. TEAM FIRED ON ENEMY WITH 50 CAL AND 60MM RESULTS WERE NEGATIVE DUE TO DARKNESS AND TERRAIN.

141929H VIC. AT981464 TEAM SIGHTED 120 VC/NVA. UNIFORMS WERE UNOBSERVED BUT ENEMY WAS CARRYING PACKS AND RIFLES, MOVING WEST TO EAST ON TRAIL. NIGERIA CALLED FIRE MISSION AT 1930H. ARTY WAS HITTING THE TARGET AREA WHEN TEAM SIGHTED 4 VC/NVA MOVING WEST AWAY FROM TARGET AREA. TEAM FIRED 50 CAL. RESULTING IN 3 ENEMY KIA'S. AT 2020H ARTY WAS CHECK FIRED BECAUSE AO CAME ON STATION. AO AND ARTY HAD EXCELLENT COVERAGE OF TARGET RESULTING IN 16 KIA'S BY ARTY A SHIFT OF TARGET AREA WAS CALLED ON SUSPECTED ENEMY REGROUPING POINTS BUT HAD NEGATIVE OBSERVATION OF THE TARGET.

150929H VIC. AT908458 AO ON ST VTOR SIGHTED 1 ANTI-AIRCRAFT POSITION CALLED FIRE MISSION BUT RECEIVED NEGATIVE FIRE MISSION DUE TO COMM PROBLEMS IN THE PLANE. TEAM FIRED SMALL ARMS (M-16) AT POSITION WITH NEGATIVE RESULTS. AT 1019H TEAM SPOTTED A POSSIBLE CAVE 200 METERS WEST OF AA POSITION. AREA WAS HEAVILY CAMOUFLAGED

151811H VIC. AT94704585 TEAM SIGHTED 30 VC/NVA, UNIFORMS AND EQUIPMENT UNOBSERVED, WALKING NORTH TO SOUTH ON TRAIL.   ATLAS 25 CALLED FIRE MISSION. TEAM HAS GOOD COVERAGE OF THE AREA BUT RESULTS WERE UNOBSERVED.

161932H VIC. AT98114640 TEAM SIGHTED 8 VC/NVA, UNIFORMS AND EQUIPMENT WERE UNOBSERVED, MOVING WEST TO EAST ON TRAIL. NIGERIA CALLED FIRE MISSION. ARTY HAD GOOD COVERAGE OF THE TARGET AREA BUT WITH NEGATIVE RESULTS DUE TO DARKNESS.

180900H VIC. BT02414849 TEAM SUNRISE "A" SIGHTED 1 REINFORCED BUNKER ALONG SIDE OF TRAIL. BUNKER WAS REINFORCED BRICKS. BUNKER MEASURED APPROXIMATELY 6'X6'X6' HIGH. THE ENTRANCE WAS 3'X3' WITH OPENING ON THE SIDE MEASURING 1'X6" HIGH. BUNKER LOOKED LIKE A DIRT MOUND FROM THE AIR. ABOUT 20 METERS AROUND THE BUNKER WERE FIGHTING HOLES. FIGHTING HOLES WERE 2' DEEP AND 3' LONG APPROXIMATELY 10 METERS APART. BARBED WIRE WAS AROUND THE BUNKER. FOUND A SIGN 15 METERS IN FRONT OF BUNKER. DID NOT CHECK THE AREA FURTHER BECAUSE THE AREA WAS POSSIBLY BOOBY-TRAPS. A WELL USED TRAIL RUNS NORTHEAST TO SOUTHWEST IN FRONT OF THE BUNKER.

ENCLOSURE (3)
DOWNGRADE TO UNCLAS AFTER 6 MONTHS
IAW OPNAVINST 5500.40

LT HODGINS
SUNRISE, O. C
PATROL LEADER

6. ENEMY CONTACT:

181145H VIC. BT031472 TEAM FOUND 1 DEAD VC/NVA WEARING DARK BLUE
SHIRT, GREEN TROUSERS AND SANDALS. ALSO FOUND A CARTRIDGE BELT
LAYING 10 METERS FROM BODY ON TRAIL. BELT WAS BOOBY TRAPPED WITH
1 CHI-COM GRENADE. GUNBIRDS MADE THREE PASSES ON AREA RESULTING
IN 3 SECONDARY EXPLOSIONS.

181942H VIC. AT98114840 TEAM SIGHTED 6 VC/NVA, UNIFORM UNOBSERVED
BUT THEY WERE CARRYING PACKS AND RIFLES, MOVING WEST TO EAST ON
TRAIL. NEGATIVE ACTION TAKEN DUE TO RVN CEASE FIRE.

191815H VIC. BT02204910 TEAM SIGHTED 4 VC/NVA MOVING NORTHWEST TO
SOUTHEAST. ENEMY WAS WEARING GREEN UTILITIES AND PACKS. ENEMY
HAD BRUSH CAMOUFLAGE ON THEIR HEADS. TEAM CALLED FIRE MISSION
WITH OUTSTANDING COVERAGE OF THE TARGET. RESULTS WERE NEGATIVE DUE
TO FOLIAGE.

211173H VIC. BT009482 TEAM SIGHTED 3 VC/NVA MOVING NORTH TO SOUTH
ON TRAIL. ENEMY WORE GREEN UTILITIES AND WERE CARRYING PACKS.
NEGATIVE FIRE MISSION DUE TO ENEMY MOVING OUT OF SIGHT.

211754H VIC. BT02244918 TEAM SIGHTED 6 VC/NVA WANDERING AROUND
A BOMBED OUT HOUSE. ENEMY WORE GREEN UTILITIES AND WERE CARRYING
PACKS. NIGERIA CALLED FIRE MISSION WITH OUTSTANDING COVERAGE OF THE
TARGET AREA. AO CAME ONSTATION AND EXPENDED HIS ORDNANCE WITH EXCELLENT
COVERAGE OF TARGET AREA. AO TOOK GROUND FIRE FROM APPROXIMATELY
400 METERS FROM THE TARGET AREA. NEGATIVE OBSERVATION OF TARGET
AREA DUE TO TERRAIN.

201000H VIC. BT03074705 TEAM SIGHTED 1 DEAD VC/NVA LYING FACE DOWN
ON THE TRAIL. ENEMY WORE BLACK PJ'S AND HAD A PACK ON HIS BACK.
TEAM DID NOT SEARCH THE BODY DUE TO TIME FACTOR AND POSSIBLE
BOOBY-TRAPS IN THE AREA. ENEMY WAS KILLED BY ARTILLERY DUE TO
THE LARGE SCRAPNEL WOUNDS. TEAM ALSO FOUND 2 PACKS, A BELT, PITH
HELMET AND 1 AK-47 RIFLE APPROXIMATELY 200METERS FROM THE BODY.
DEAD VC/NVA HAD STRANGE HAIRCUT, ALL OF HIS HAIR WAS CUT OFF EXCEPT
A SCALP LOCK ON THE BACK OF HIS HEAD. HE WAS DARK, 5'8" TALL,
ABOUT 170 POUNDS AND WAS STOCKY IN BUILD.

ENCLOSURE (3)
DOWNGRADE TO UNCLAS AFTER 6 MONTHS
IAW OPNAVINST 5500.40.

LT HODGINS
SUNRISE, CO. C
PATROL LEADER

6. ENEMY CON'T:

211500H VIC. BT015475 TEAM SIGHTED 25 VC/NVA MOVING NORTH TO SOUTH. ENEMY WORE MIXED PJ'S AND KHAKI'S AND WERE CARRYING PACKS AND SANDBAGS EXCEPT POINTMAN WHO WAS CARRYING AN AK-47 RIFLE. THEY MOVED FROM WHERE THEY WERE WORKING THE RICE PADDIES TO THE TREE LINE WERE THEY CHANGED CLOTHES AND PICKED UP THEIR PACKS AND EQUIPMENT. ENEMY THEN PUT BRANCHES ON THEIR HEADS AND STARTED MOVING ACROSS AN OPEN AREA. ENEMY WATCHED OUR POSITION AS THEY MOVED TOWARDS FOOT HILLS. TEAM ALSO OBSERVED 2 ENEMY GETTING AK-47 OUT OF A TREE. EVERYONE OF THE PEOPLE HAD BEEN WORKING IN THE VALLEY AS FARMERS IN THE FIELD. MOVEMENT MADE IT IMPOSSIBLE TO CALL FIRE MISSION.

222140H VIC. AT998463 TEAM SIGHTED 5 VC/NVA MOVING NORTHEAST CARRYING RIFLES AND 1 TUBULAR OBJECT (POSSIBLE RPG LAUNCHER) AND 1 HELMET TEAM FIRED WITH M-16 AND RECEIVED SMALL ARMS FIRE. TEAM SUNRISE "B" MOVED BACK TO SUNRISE'S POSITION THEN CALLED FIRE MISSION. RECEIVED GOOD COVERAGE OF THE AREA BUT WITH UNKNOWN RESULTS DUE TO DARKNESS.

    B. TERRAIN: OP HILL 425

7. OTHER INFORMATION: INSERT AND EXTRACT LZ: HILL 425 VIC. AT998464.

8. RESULTS OF ENCOUNTERS WITH THE ENEMY: 3 VC/NVA KIA'S

9. CONDITION OF THE PATROL: GOOD

10. CONCLUSION AND RECOMMENDATIONS: NONE

11. EFFECTIVENESS OF SUPPORTING ARMS: ARTILLERY WAS EXCELLENT WITH 26 KIA'S. 40'S AND GUNSHIPS ALSO GAVE OUSTANDING COVERAGE BUT WITH NEGATIVE RESULTS DUE TO TERRAIN AND DARKNESS.

12. DEBRIEFER'S COMMENTS: NONE

13. PATROL MEMBERS:

LT HODGINS	0109887	LCPL MORENO	2514280	PFC BUMSWORTH	2585688
SGT DOMHOSKE	2494365	CPL CRAWFORD	2478471	PFC JAMES	2559995
SGT WANDLOW	2391714	LCPL SELLS	2588944	PFC OFARRELL	2411015
LCPL GRANT	2588927	PVT JOHNSON	2523857	PFC NEWBY	2572120
LCPL STAMPER	2504570	CPL HICKS	2507734	PFC COTTRELL	2628331
PVT WALLS	2505646	LCPL TEMS	2538486	HM3 RANDLE	B537818
PVT PORTALIS	2555464	LCPL JONES	2529287		
LCPL SIMPSON	2521506	LCPL HANNEN	2546589		
LCPL JONES	2509404	PVT BATSON	2466859		

ENCLOSURE (3)
DOWNGRADE TO UNCLAS AFTER 6 MONTHS
IAW OPNAVINST 5500.40

OPERATION ORDER 0518-70   1ST RECONNAISSANCE BN.
PATROL: SUNRISE, CO. G   Da NANG, RVN
DEBRIEFER: CAPT COOK   261800H MAY 1970
MAPS: VIETNAM 1:50,000 AMS L7014
     SHEET 6640 IV

SUPPLEMENTAL PATROL REPORT

1. UNDER SUBPARAGRAPH 6a REMOVE ENTRY DATED 111930 AND INSERT
THE FOLLOWING:

111930H VIC. AT986470 TEAM SIGHTED 52 VC/NVA WALKING EAST ALONG CANAL.
NIGERIA CALLED FIRE MISSION AT 1930H WITH FIRST ROUND LANDING AT
2030H. DELAY WAS DUE TO COMM PROBLEMS WITH ARTY AND ADJUSTMENTS.
DUE TO RAPID MOVEMENT TEAM FIRED 400 ROUNDS OF .50 CAL. MACHINE GUN
FIRE AND 12 60MM MORTAR ROUNDS TO PIN DOWN ENEMY FOR ARTY. ARTY
COVERAGE WAS POOR, NELSON UNKNOWN. LO(HOSTAGE LEAR) CAME ON STATION
AND FIRED ON BOARD ORDNANCE ON ENEMY POSITION WITH OUTSTANDING
COVERAGE OF TARGET AND REFORMED TAKING FIRE FROM VIC. AT9854475
AND AT994478. NIGERIA RESUMED FIRE MISSION CALLING IN ARTY ON
LOCATION OF GROUND FIRE. STINGER 1-3 CAME ON STATION AND FIRED
HIS ON BOARD ORDNANCE ON ENEMY'S POSITION WITH OUTSTANDING COVERAGE
OF TARGET. A TOTAL OF 44 ROUNDS OF ARTY WERE FIRED ON ENEMY POSITION.
RESULTS WERE UNOBSERVED DUE TO DARKNESS AND CLOUD COVERAGE.

2. UNDER PARAGRAPH 10 REMOVE "NONE" AND INSERT THE FOLLOWING:

"IT IS RECOMMENDED THAT THE TEAM BE PROVIDED WITH A NIGHT OBSERVATION
DEVICE FOR .50 CAL MACHINE GUN, ALSO A SNIPER SCOPE FOR .50 CAL.
MACHINE GUN. STRONGLY SUGGEST SAME TYPE OF OPERATION BE CONDUCTED
VIC. GL BT0149-LR 0347, AND IT BE HELD SOME TIME AFTER FIRST LIGHT.
THE ENEMY IS WORKING (FARMING) IN THIS AREA EVERY DAY FROM FIRST
LIGHT TO APPROXIMATELY 1500H. THEY MOVE INTO RES AREA, CHANGE
CLOTHING AT FIRST LIGHT, WORK THE DAY, CHANGE CLOTHES AND RETURN TO
THE HILLS APPROXIMATELY 1900H EVERY DAY. IT IS BELIEVED THAT SOME
MAY BE LIVING IN THE AREA. THE PATROL LEADER BELIEVES THE ENEMY
HAS ESTABLISHED A BASE AREA APPROXIMATELY 2,500 METERS SOUTH OF
OP. THIS WOULD RESTRICT THE USE OF AIR UNLESS WELL COORDINATED."

PAGE 5A
PTL RPT # 102

A-45

BIBLIOGRAPHY

BOOKS

Cosmos, Graham A. and Lt. Col. Terrance P. Murray, USMC. *U.S. Marines in Vietnam: Vietnamization and Redeployment 1970–1971.* Washington, D. C.: Headquarters, U.S. Marines Corps, 1986.

Karnow, Stanley. *Vietnam, A History.* New York: Viking, 1983.

Lanning, Michael Lee and Dan Cragg. *Inside the VC and the NVA.* New York: Fawcett Columbine, 1992.

Spector, Ronald H. *After TET: The Bloodiest Year in Vietnam.* New York: The Free Press, 1993.

UNPUBLISHED GOVERNMENT AND MILITARY DOCUMENTS

Operation Order: 0264-70. Patrol: Patty Shell, Co. C, 1st Reconnaissance Battalion, Da Nang, RVN, 080650H March 1970.

Operation Order: 0346-70. Patrol: Defend, Co. C, 1st Reconnaissance Battalion, Da Nang, RVN, 2609450H March 1970.

Operation Order: 0381-70. Patrol: Turf Club, Co. C, 1st Reconnaissance Battalion, Da Nang, RVN, 121430H April 1970.

Operation Order: 0490-70. Patrol: Detroit Tigers, Co. C, 1st Reconnaissance Battalion, Da Nang, RVN, 08900H May 1970.

Operation Order: 0518-70. Patrol: Sunrise, Co. C, 1st Reconnaissance Battalion, Da Nang, RVN, 241100H May 1970.

Command Chronology, 1st Reconnaissance Battalion, 1st Marine Division, January 1970, dtd 2 February 1970.

————, February 1970, dtd 2 March 1970.

————, March 1970, dtd 2 April 1970.

————, April 1970, dtd 2 May 1970.

————, May 1970, dtd 2 June 1970.

Operational Summary, 1st Reconnaissance Battalion, 1st Marine Division, May 1970, dtd 2 June, 1970.

Journal, Combat Operations Center, 11th Marine Regiment S-1, RVN, June, 1970.

Journal, Combat Operations Center, 11th Marine Regiment S-2, RVN, June, 1970.

Journal, Combat Operations Center, 11th Marine Regiment S-3, RVN, June, 1970.

Statement, 1st Lt. J. M. Gallbaith on Emergency Extract on 23 May 1970.

Statement, 1st Lt. J. C. Owens on Emergency Extract on 23 May 1970.

Statement, 1st Lt. D. R. Mathews on Emergency Extract on 23 May 1970.

Statement, Capt. A. C. Blades on Emergency Extract on 23 May 1970.

Personal Award Recommendation, December 26, 1970, Blades, Arthur Charles.

PERSONAL DOCUMENTS AND INTERVIEWS

Baker, Stephen
Brasington, Lt. Col. B. A. (Ret.)
Drumright, Col. W. C. (Ret.)

Dyer, Edward
Curry, Michael
Gregson, W.C. B. Gen. USMC
Hodge, Sgt. Maj. Thomas (Ret.)
Jones, William P.
Kershaw, Lt. Col. C. W. (Ret.)
Norton, Maj. Bruce H. (Ret.)
Pack, Lt. Col. A. J. (Ret.)
Pino, Maj. Chester (Ret.)
Quaid, Daniel
Vaughn, Richard

MAP CREDITS

Sheet #6540 I—Series L7014 Thong Duc—Prepared by AMS
        (LU) U.S. Army, 1965. Army Map Service, Washing-
        ton, D.C.
Sheet #6540 II—Series L7014 Bach Ma—Prepared by AMS
        (LU) U.S. Army, 1965. Army Map Service, Washing-
        ton, D.C.
Sheet #6640 IV—Series L7014 Dai Loc—Prepared by AMS
        (LU) U.S. Army, 1965. Army Map Service, Washing-
        ton, D.C.

INDEX

339